PHILOSOPHY IN BRITAIN TODAY

PHILOSOPHY IN BRITAIN TODAY

Edited by S.G. Shanker

STATE UNIVERSITY OF NEW YORK PRESS

© 1986 Gordon Baker, Renford Bambrough, Antony Flew, Ernest Gellner, R.M. Hare, Rom Harré, Stephan Körner, Czeslaw Lejewski, Karl R. Popper, S.G. Shanker, Crispin Wright

First published
in USA by
State University of New York Press
Albany.

All rights reserved. No part of this publication may be reproduced or transmitted, in any form or by any means, without permission.

For information, address State University of New York Press, State University Plaza, Albany, New York 12246.

Printed in Great Britain.

CONTENTS

Preface

1. φιλοσοφία: εἰκὼν καὶ εἶδος
   Gordon Baker — 1
2. Question Time
   Renford Bambrough — 58
3. Apologia pro Philosophia Mea
   Antony Flew — 72
4. Three Contemporary Styles of Philosophy
   Ernest Gellner — 98
5. A *Reductio Ad Absurdum* of Descriptivism
   R.M. Hare — 118
6. Persons and Powers
   Rom Harré — 135
7. On Some Methods and Results of Philosophical Analysis
   Stephan Körner — 154
8. Logic, Ontology and Metaphysics
   Czeslaw Lejewski — 171
9. How I See Philosophy
   Karl R. Popper — 198
10. Computer Vision or Mechanist Myopia?
    S.G. Shanker — 213
11. Theories of Meaning and Speakers' Knowledge
    Crispin Wright — 267

Contributors — 308

Index — 312

PREFACE

At a time when so much is undergoing a radical readjustment in Britain — a euphemism for socio-economic decline — philosophy is experiencing an extraordinary growth. At the last count there were over 1,300 professional philosophers working in the nation's higher institutions, with widespread interest in the subject developing accordingly. Moreover, there are a wealth of prestigious journals, publishing houses, and societies devoted to philosophy, and a plethora of conferences graced by leading philosophers from throughout the world. Cambridge positivism, Oxford linguistic philosophy, the theory of meaning, realism/anti-realism, Fregean and Wittgensteinian studies: these are but a few of the movements inspired by British philosophers this century. How did Britain, a supposed model for insularity, become such an influential voice in modern philosophy?

The answer to this enigma most likely lies in a remark made by one of the contributors to this volume; having arrived at our final list of papers, Professor Körner pointed out that more than half of the philosophers that had been chosen were naturalised citizens of the UK. The immediate explanation for this anomaly is obvious: England and America were the main beneficiaries of the massive defoliation of European science and philosophy brought about by the Second World War. As Paris was a haven for painters and writers during the 1920s, or Göttingen for mathematicians during the first decades of this century, so post-war Britain has become a centre for philosophy. Eager to study under the auspices of these famous emigrés, the process thus set off continues to attract considerable foreign interest; three of the younger contributors to this volume, for example, come from America, Canada, and New Zealand. It seems obvious, then, that the robust health of philosophy in the UK today owes much to the enormous impetus inadvertently provided by the war. But it is not the sole explanation, for it ignores such important phenomena as the excitement that existed in Cambridge at the turn of the century: a period, let us not forget, which enticed Wittgenstein to spend his working years in a climate which, both physically and intellectually, he found enervating. And just as Wittgenstein left behind him a

Preface

legacy which has inspired and revolutionised, not just British, but all contemporary philosophy, so too, the legacy of British attitudes and thought has left behind an intellectual environment which is not just conducive to, but which positively demands a thriving state of philosophy.

It is an issue to which anyone who has studied here must have devoted a great deal of thought. On the surface England would seem to be the very antithesis of a philosophical climate: a cold, phlegmatic society, it discourages flights of fantasy and shuns metaphysics. Indeed, it is for just these traits that 'Anglo-Saxon' philosophy has often been assailed by Continental philosophers as sterile and pedantic; Dilthey's complaint that 'in the veins of the "knowing subject" constructed by Locke, Hume, and Kant runs no real blood' has found far too many sympathisers among modern Continental philosophers to be listed here. I have repeatedly encountered the complaint by European philosophers that 'Anglo-Saxon philosophy' can no longer distinguish the forest for the trees; that it has lost its sense of purpose in the dense undergrowth of logical technicalities. Perhaps in those instances where — as Renford Bambrough points out in 'Question Time', rigour has been confused with technicality — this accusation is warranted, but I cannot help but feel that such a sweeping indictment has mistaken the quest for rigour for a lack of imagination. Certainly it is in the former where I feel the secret of analytic philosophy's success lies; but it is rigour in the service of philosophical clarification, rather than as an end in itself, which constitutes its *raison d'être*.

It is important to bear in mind, when considering the significance of Britain's intellectual traditions for its present philosophical complexion, the context in which these liberal principles were first articulated. The state of nature which one encounters in the writings of the Empiricists is not at all like its Romantic counterpart. Whether or not man was an innately noble creature was completely beside the point; the liberty which British philosophers defended was one of freedom tempered by self-imposed restraint. Man might be free to do whatever he pleased — provided, of course, that it did no 'harm' (a term which with typical British tact is best left undefined) to any of his neighbours — but he also had a responsibility to himself and to the body politic; if he failed to perform his duties he would not be formally chastised, but he would suffer the even worse fate of ostracism. It is the British, after all, who developed unspoken censure into an art form; and in this sense the term 'negative freedom' can be slightly misleading. It might capture some of the British hostility towards political interference, but it totally overlooks the heavy price demanded for social acceptance, let alone public respect.

I can best bring out some of the hidden depths of the British attitude to self-development with my own experience of Oxford. Shortly before I came to study here I was given Cuthbert Bede's *The Adventures of Mr Verdant Green* to read: a gift which ensured that I came to Oxford with a picture that was almost one hundred years out of date. As it happened, this provided the perfect introduction to modern Oxford, but the real surprise came at my first tutorial. I was set the question, 'What were Descartes' reasons for doubting: were they good reasons?' Of course, the sting was in the second half of the question. It was not just a case of letting me know immediately that this was not intended as an exercise in the history of philosophical ideas; I was tacitly being encouraged to confront Descartes on an equal footing. After five minutes of my first tutorial it was clear that Descartes had won a resounding victory; but the curiosity, the feeling of independence, and most importantly, the sense of responsibility — not just to Descartes, but to the subject itself — had been planted right from the start. And the awareness of the demands that would be made by the discipline; the glazed look in a tutor's eye has surely done more to stimulate his student to further exertions than any amount of violent exhortation could hope to equal.

It was chiefly in order to convey some of this excitement which every student of contemporary British philosophy experiences that we have devised this collection. Rather than allowing this book to degenerate into a polemical treatise for any one of the major schools of thought which are currently competing for favour, we have sought to make our selection as comprehensive as possible. Thus, we invited representatives from several different fields to present either a brief intellectual autobiography and resumé of their approach to philosophy, or else a statement on what they regard as a major problem in philosophy and the manner in which it should be resolved. By balancing the approaches in this way we have sought to create not just a record of modern British philosophy in the words of some of its most authoritative spokesmen, but also an introduction to the problems and the methods which are currently the focus of their concern.

Preface

Being the editor of a volume such as this has many attractions, but perhaps chief among them is the fact that none of the contributors needs any introduction. It remains only to thank each of them here for their generous assistance and the interest which they have demonstrated. I would also like to record here the enormous intellectual debt which, as I try to make clear in my own chapter, I owe to Peter Hacker. Finally, I would like to thank Victoria College and Massey College in the University of Toronto, Magdalen College and Christ Church in Oxford, the Canadian National Chapter of the IODE, and most importantly, the Canada Council, for the opportunity they have given me to study at Oxford. I would like to dedicate my own work in what follows to my sister, Shashanna Kocinski. My greatest wish now is that others will continue to enjoy this opportunity long into the distant future; my greatest fear, that the socio-economic conditions alluded to at the outset of this preface threaten this eventuality. For the two cannot continue to proceed indefinitely in opposite directions. If the current state of philosophy in the UK owes its pre-eminence to the liberal-democratic traditions it inherited, British philosophers must now do everything in their power to ensure that those values are sustained. For, as Wittgenstein explained to Malcolm, 'What is the use of studying philosophy if all that it does for you is to enable you to talk with some plausibility about some abstruse questions of logic, etc., and if it does not improve your thinking about the important questions of everyday life?' As each of the following essays makes clear, this is a question which stands uppermost in the mind of its author.

S.G. Shanker
Christ Church, Oxford

1 φιλοσοφία: εἰκὼν καὶ εἶδος[1]

Gordon Baker

The bounds of sense should be plain, but everywhere they are in dispute. What strikes one philosopher as a truism, another calls nonsense and a third treats as an analytical hypothesis. There are parallel divisions over the question whether a proposition is profound or naïve and ridiculous, whether a conclusion rests on a solid case or hangs in the air unsupported, or whether a question requires an answer or deserves to be brushed aside. Such fundamental differences in points of view are very elusive and difficult to comprehend. Even within the mainstream of analytic philosophy, many seem unaware of the extent to which there are partings of ways long before it comes to arguments.

It has always seemed remarkable to me how little attention philosophers give to this aspect of philosophy. Has it escaped their notice? Or is it beneath their dignity to examine the rationale of their own activities? οὐ γὰρ περὶ τοῦ ἐπιτυχόντος ὁ λόγος, ἀλλὰ περὶ τοῦ ὅντινα τρόπον χρὴ θεωρεῖν.[2] I can lay claim to no special aptitude for illuminating this subject, but perhaps I do have a peculiar sensitivity to such conflicts of cultures. Brought up in the United States, I transplanted myself to Britain and put down new roots in the Old World. Trained principally in mathematics and science at Harvard, I received a second education in classics and ordinary language philosophy in Oxford, and so I came to be a practising philosopher and a lapsed mathematician. All of this helps to explain why I am left stranded on the beach by the flood tide of contemporary Anglo-American philosophy and why esteemed teachers on both sides of the Atlantic must think that they taught me far more than I learned. At the same time it also explains why I am peculiarly conscious that the world of philosophy is not identical with my world, that the world does not come to an end at the horizon, and that philosophers even in the recent past have lived in very different worlds. In my view, any philosopher is bounded in a nutshell if he cannot make sense of the

2 φιλοσοφία: εἰκὼν καὶ εἶδος

possibility of serious philosophical activity conducted along lines fundamentally different from his own. What I here address myself to is a collective weakness in imagination so impoverishing that it amounts almost to a character defect.

1. Frege's Vision

It seems that very occasionally somebody has brought about a transformation in the climate of thought in philosophy, a metamorphosis comparable to Newtonian mechanics or Einstein's theory of relativity. Frege is one of these outstanding figures. He inaugurated the modern period in the philosophy of mathematics. He swept away the logic of the syllogism with its supporting doctrine of analysing propositions into subjects and predicates; he replaced it with a system of logic incomparably more powerful and elegant, and his new creation has survived intact to the present day.

Philosophers also now credit Frege with a host of spectacular achievements in philosophical logic. He allegedly developed the idea that predicates should be analysed as function-names in the semantic analysis of declarative sentences. He is reputed to have given the first correct semantic definitions of the logical constants: truth-table definitions of the constants of the propositional calculus, and the standard semantics for quantifiers. With the distinctions of objects from concepts and of second-level concepts from first-level ones, he adumbrated the simple theory of types and thus anticipated the viable part of Russell's account of type-differences. The concept of sense was employed to solve the paradox of identity and to give the first analysis of sentence-meaning as truth-conditions. He introduced the distinction between sense and force which is indispensable for generalising truth-conditional semantics to the whole of any natural language. He first perceived the important truth that the meaning of a sentence is compounded out of the meanings of its parts according to its structure, and so he handed us the key to answering the fundamental question of how it is possible to understand a sentence never before encountered. And he furnished the correct account of the application of numbers in counting. This formidable list seems merely a minimal opening bid for a compilation of his achievements. Some commentators would argue vehemently for other claims: that he anticipated the picture theory of meaning in the *Tractatus*, that he foreshadowed Wittgenstein's later refutation of psychologism about meaning, etc. But to certify Frege's indisputable genius, there is no need to adjudicate on any claims not unanimously acknowledged even if this strategy might seem to some to understate his merits.

Closer inspection, however, makes the attribution to him of several of his putative central achievements questionable. He did not believe that the business of logic centres on the semantic analysis of sentences, and he lacked the semantic conception of validity; hence he was at two removes from the idea that the concept of sense grows out of the conception of sentence-meaning as truth-conditions. Similarly, he never formulated truth-table definitions of his primitive logical constants; these symbols have tabular explanations in *Begriffsschrift*, though they cannot coherently be construed as names of *truth*-functions, while the demand for completeness of definition in *Grundgesetze* excludes the legitimacy of truth-table explanations and undermines any rationale for distinguishing the logical primitives from any other first-level concept-words.

Whatever resists the solvent of this initial textual scrutiny manifests other defects. First, important ingredients of his thinking are seriously mistaken. He built his logical system on the presupposition that any cogent inference must have premisses asserted to be true. The very idea of function/argument analysis, in his view, presupposes that sentences are proper names of objects (originally of judgeable-contents, later of truth-values). Second, major arguments seem incredibly weak or altogether wanting. *No case is made for the notorious doctrine that the reference of a sentence in indirect speech is its customary sense. The crucial claim that predicates name functions ('concepts') lacks any defence against obvious (and devastating) counter-arguments. The thesis that the reference of a sentence is a truth-value apparently rests on a sequence of equivocations and question-begging steps of inference. Modern philosophical criticism dissolves away much of the body of this thought and leaves a heap of disconnected bones, and it shows that the catalogue of Frege's unquestioned achievements contains numerous false entries.[3]

There are three intriguing features of the contrast between Frege's reputation as the fountainhead of philosophy of language and the contents of his writings. The first is the enormous difficulty of grasping the purposes of his remarks and important differences between his framework of thought and our own. We simply assume that he compared predicates with functions in order to clarify the structure and unity of declarative sentences, whereas he apparently sought to explain the concept of a function to non-mathematicians by exploiting an analogy between the incompleteness of a predicate and the essential unsaturatedness of a function. Similarly we are wedded to the idea of a unique function/argument analysis of a sentence (or the proposition that it expresses), whereas he would have considered this to be as *absurd* as the idea that there is a unique way of presenting the number four as the value of a function for an argument. Many of the most significant aspects of his thinking are altogether invisible to us. The second point is our inveterate tendency to take the demonstration of differences between Frege's thinking and ours as a condemnation of his on the grounds that it does not measure up to modern standards of sophistication. We assume that our possession of better answers to what are taken to be his questions is the only firm basis for criticising his philosophy of logic. Hence we take it for granted that any critical analysis of his leading ideas must have the form of a comparison with our own (improved!) theories and that any radical criticism must castigate his solutions as being primitive and confused. The possibility of any different kind of philosophical criticism is neglected. This point is linked with a third one: it seems as if any critical examination of Frege's philosophy of logic can reveal nothing fundamental. All differences are treated as differences in detail within a shared framework. He offered a Platonist theory of the nature of logic whereas we are apt to prefer another explanation in terms of a general theory of meaning. He developed a logicist theory of arithmetic which we now know to be technically defective. He advocated a bizarre theory of truth which has the noteworthy demerit that it obscures the difference in the semantic roles of proper names and declarative sentences. And so on. It is allowed that we may improve on his solutions to the problems of philosophical logic, but it is not acknowledged that we might challenge the intelligibility of the problems themselves (or even differentiate his problems from our own).

The explanation of these striking forms of blindness must be that we are so fascinated by certain general contours of Frege's thought that we are unable to engage in detailed examination of his work and predisposed to dismiss differences as trivia. What is it that we find so entrancing?

One answer is that we are impressed by the elegance and technical sophistication exemplified in Frege's formal logic. We are inclined to agree with the judgement that he fashioned a new instrument, a logic, which in delicacy and range and power far surpassed anything that went by this name before, a subject revealing to this day new and unexpected depths.[4] He invented and brought to maturity the first-order predicate calculus, and he opened the road to fruitful studies in metalogic. He is the very model of a virtuoso logician, and we interpret technical ingenuity of such a high order as a symptom of depth of understanding.

A second answer is that he rejuvenated the most immediately attractive paradigm for developing theories of meaning, what Wittgenstein called 'the Augustinian picture of language'.[5] The notion that the meaning of a word is an object correlated with it had been transformed by classical empiricism into the notion that words stand for ideas, and this had come to seem problematic and confused. Syllogistic logic, incorporating the contention that every assertion expresses a relation between exactly two ideas, generated further strains and called for a sweeping application of the distinction between the grammatical form of a declarative sentence and the logical form of the proposition expressed. Frege cleared the ground of much of this scholastic clutter. He purified the Augustinian picture of the psychologism introduced by empiricism; mental entities (ideas) are replaced by Platonic ones (senses) which by themselves (that is, independently of such empirical relations as resemblance) determine what entities (concepts or objects) are their references. He discovered entities having novel logical forms (concepts and relations of different levels), and he identified a galaxy of new logical forms of thoughts, thereby licensing the possibility of a general (though not strictly universal) correspondence of thought-structures with sentence-structures. An attractive paradigm threatened with asphyxiation by masses of qualifications was granted a new lease of life,[6] and it lives on with new vigour even now.

A third source of charm is a vision of a triple isomorphism holding between three realms: language, thought, and the world. This is immediately perspicuous in a diagram that Frege devised:[7]

6   φιλοσοφία: εἰκὼν καὶ εἶδος

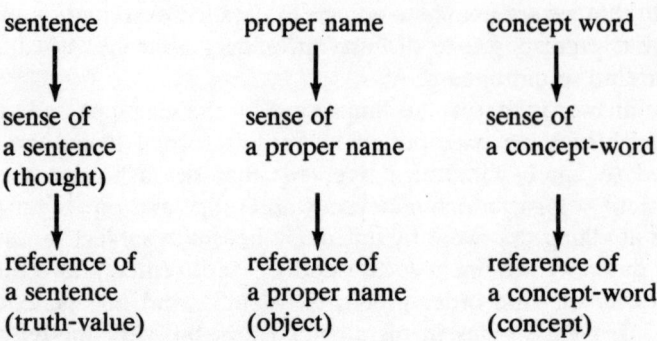

Both the sense and the reference of a proper name are completely unlike the sense and the reference of a concept-word; each of the first are 'saturated' entities, each of the second 'unsaturated'. In a logically perfect language, sentence-composition would exactly correspond to thought-composition, and hence only an unsaturated expression would count as a concept-word, only a saturated one as a proper name. Concept-script is meant to put the realisation of this ideal within practical grasp. In principle isomorphism of language with thought can be attained, and in practice even in natural languages there is a great measure of correspondence. The isomorphism of thoughts with the world takes care of itself. Frege advanced the comforting idea that this is the best of all possible worlds from a logical point of view — or at least very nearly so for someone fortunate enough to be a native speaker of German!

The combination of these ideas amounts to a revitalisation of the Pythagorean dream. Frege's logic is built on a radical generalisation of the mathematical concept of a function (the one current in his day!). His concept-script revamps statement-making discourse in the symbolism familiar from algebra and real analysis. The theses that ordinary predicates stand for concepts, that concepts are really functions, and that thoughts are isomorphic with the world, together imply that the categories of abstract function-theory are the ultimate metaphysical categories. For the very first time the vista opened of a sophisticated theoretical science of the objects of thought, even the prospect of an advanced science of language.[8] Although the world, thought, and language are not made of numbers, in both the realm of sense and the realm of reference, philosophical analysis reveals that the ultimate building-blocks are objects and functions. Frege conquered new domains

φιλοσοφία: εἰκὼν καὶ εἶδος 7

and subjected them to the sway of mathematics just as Newton had.[9] The visionary aspect of Frege's work rides on the back of an elaborate theory, the doctrines of a quasi-science. He emphasised this point. He compared the logical analysis of thoughts with the chemical decomposition of matter, and he declared that his discovery of the two logical objects the True and the False was as important as the discovery of a pair of new elements in chemistry. His novel elucidation of familiar terms ('concept', 'object', 'function', 'number') undoubtedly struck him as revelations about the real natures of what these non-technical terms had always designated. The fruits of his scientific investigations were, in his view, an axiomatisation of the general laws of logic and the rigorous demonstration that arithmetical truths are analytic, but he foresaw parallel theories dealing with other subject-matter.

The presuppositions of Frege's theory-building are important, though seldom remarked or discussed. First, it must be possible to make genuine *discoveries* in logic. In his view, no language-user had known the senses or the references of numerals or of the predicate 'number' until he revealed them. Likewise, the incorporation of syllogistic reasoning within quantification theory shows that those who had produced or followed proofs in Euclidean geometry had unbeknownst to themselves really been making use of the basic laws of logic which Frege first discovered. He also claimed to have discovered the true nature of mathematical induction. Formal definitions of words may be hidden in their patterns of use, and the genuine principles of correct reasoning may be hidden in the canons actually applied in justifying and criticising arguments.

Secondly, it must make sense to *criticise* or *reform* established patterns of word-use or acknowledged forms of reasoning. Frege often engaged in such revisionism. Negatively, he ruled that the standard form for speaking about concepts is logically incoherent because it violates his type-restrictions, and he accused us of error in conceiving of truth as a property of thoughts. Positively, he argued that mere narrow-mindedness prevents our recognising that category-restrictions among objects are logically unjustifiable, so that we should define numerical and even logical operators over all objects whatever. In his eyes, natural languages are not in good logical order, and their speakers have a duty imposed by the laws of logic to put matters right.

Finally, Frege's theorising manifests an unshakeable *commit-*

ment to the general applicability of abstract function-theory. From the beginning he worked under the conviction that *somehow* every judgement could be analysed into *function* and argument. The detailed content of his logical theory underwent a remarkable metamorphosis: in *Begriffsschrift*, concepts were taken to be functions whose arguments are objects and whose values are judgeable-contents (thoughts), whereas in *Grundgesetze*, although concepts are functions, the values of these functions are the True and the False, and function/argument decomposition is reduplicated in strict parallel at the level of sense. From his practice it is evident that he did not see his task to be to examine *whether* function/argument analysis is intelligible in clarifying inferential relations among judgements, but rather to investigate *how* logical principles can be developed within this framework.

The immense attractions of Frege's general vision together with his deep commitment to the spirit of rigorous enquiry call forth the reverence widely accorded to his work. Would it not be conclusive proof of philistinism to refuse to join the general adulation?

2. Superstition and Dogmatism

Frege evidently conceived logic and the philosophy of mathematics to be an investigation of the realm of Platonic entities conducted in conformity with the canons of scientific rigour. Logic is the science of judgements, concepts, truth-values, courses of values, etc. and its domain subsumes arithmetic as physics subsumes chemistry. His system, it seems, is to be assessed according to the criteria for the adequacy of a scientific theory: mathematical elegance, simplicity, and explanatory power. Our reluctance to dismiss any of his work as simply ridiculous stems in part from a deep commitment to the appropriateness of scientific methodology in philosophy. What seems to us truly absurd is patent departure from these norms.

This pervasive ideal can be reformulated more positively. Philosophers, like scientists, are urged to combine hard-headedness with open-mindedness. Hard-headedness demands wielding Occam's razor; speaking of theoretical or abstract entities requires justification, and it must be eschewed unless proved to be necessary. Similarly, there is the requirement of maximum explanatory power with minimum complexity of theories; a minimal set of primitive propositions should be sought to provide a theoretical

φιλοσοφία: εἰκὼν καὶ εἶδος   9

unification of 'observed' regularities (in what is perceived, in language, in the stream of consciousness, etc.). Open-mindedness demands banishing all preconceptions about the phenomena to be explained. It should include a serious attempt to exorcise all dogmatism, to scrutinise the grounds for each belief, and to call in question whatever has no more secure basis than custom or traditional authority. Methodological or Cartesian doubt is the pure form of this generalised spirit of Protestantism. What could be more worthy of admiration than a combination of hard-headedness with open-mindedness? Would any deliberate deviation from this ideal be tolerable in principle, or more likely to lead to philosophical insight in practice?

Impeccable though its credentials seem, the scientific ideal is problematic in application to philosophy. There is superstition in avoiding superstition, and so too the attempt to avoid all forms of dogmatism produces fresh dogmatism all the more insidious for being nearly imperceptible. Suspicion of theoretical or abstract entities is perhaps the most obvious case. This has ramifying roots among which two preconceptions stand out. The first is the idea that a word has meaning in virtue of standing for some entity which is its meaning. The second is the general empiricist presumption that the basis of all language consists of words directly correlated with perceptible entities (objects and properties, whether mental or physical or both). Together these contentions cast doubt on whether terms purportedly standing for imperceptible entities have any significance at all, and hence they demand some act of atonement for the sin of introducing the names of 'theoretical' or 'abstract' entities into discourse. Only if a particular 'ontological commitment' is unavoidable should it be granted absolution. The important and seldom noticed fact is that this whole conception rests on at least two dubious assumptions about the nature of meaningful language. Independently of these ideas, why would the question of whether an expression had a proper place in a scientific theory even seem to raise any issue at all about ontology? The worship of hard-headedness in its current form is far from being presupposition-free; rather, it emanates from a conception of meaning which itself stands in need of philosophical investigation.

The veneration of open-mindedness is equally dangerous in philosophy. To maintain an open mind on a particular matter is to suppose that the answers to relevant questions have yet to be discovered. The real risk of dogmatism in philosophy originates, as Wittgenstein noted, from 'the conception that there are questions the answers to which will be found at a later date. It is held that, although a result is not known, there is a way of finding it'.[10] Where does danger lurk here? What alternative strategy could conceivably be an improvement? At first sight there seems no plausible answer to either question. But reflect: to suppose that the answers to philosophical questions await discovery is to presuppose that the questions themselves make sense and stand in need of answers (not already available). Why should this not be a fit subject for philosophical scrutiny? Questions cannot be posed *in vacuo*. The formulation of a question, certainly of any that is deep and penetrating, presupposes a framework of thought which may be complex and widely ramifying. Questions, just as much as assertions, carry presuppositions. To pose a particular question is to take some things for granted, to put some things beyond question or beyond doubt, to treat some things as matters of course. Once this is acknowledged, can a philosopher reasonably turn his back on investigating the questions posed in philosophy and simply join in a co-operative search for answers, as it were, to God-given questions? The idea of open-mindedness is dangerous because it precipitates us into answering questions. We should, on the contrary, make serious efforts at raising questions about the questions commonly viewed as being genuinely philosophical. Perhaps the proper answers to such questions are often, even if not always, further *questions*![11]

Philosophers who guide themselves by the ideals of science are no more perfect than scientists in adhering to them, and no less immune than scientists to correlative illusions. They are apt to conflate mathematical sophistication with explanatory power. As if expertise in symbolic techniques were inseparable from an understanding of what is (allegedly!) symbolised. Philosophers are also exposed to the danger of sliding down the slippery slope of success. Quantification theory is an exemplary case. Frege began with a modest, perhaps instrumental conception: the representation of general judgements in his concept-script would be of utility in checking the cogency of inferences in rigorous demonstrative sciences.[12] By the end of his life he had come to think that formulae in concept-script gave an accurate picture of the structure of thought and the world.[13] He probably thought, as others do, that he had discovered *the* true logic of multiple generality.[14] His

φιλοσοφία: εἰκὼν καὶ εἶδος 11

successors have made even more sweeping claims: quantification theory belongs to the depth structure of every natural language,[15] and the whole system of classical logic delineates the essence of language, thought, and the world.[16] Modesty seems but the feeble offspring of caution, instantly killed off by the least whiff of success. Finally, philosophers are prey to the opposite danger in the face of apparent failure. They are tempted to explain away difficulties by contrasting apparent with real refutations of their theories, and they are prone to patch things up by myriad *ad hoc* modifications, pursuing the mirage that the salvation of a beleaguered theory lies in some hitherto undreamt of feat of technical ingenuity.

At the same time they pay little attention to the question what, if anything, would be achieved if a successful theory were attained. They focus, for example, on the possibility of generating Russell's paradox within Frege's system of logic, as if the *sole* defect in the analysis of arithmetic given in *Grundgesetze* were a technical one that might be surmounted by a formal modification along the lines of the theory of types in *Principia*. This neglects the possibility that there are substantial *philosophical* objections which would independently condemn as nonsensical Frege's conception of arithmetic (or the similar possibility that his *philosophy* of logic is incoherent even though his formalisation of first-order logic is isomorphic with the contemporary predicate calculus).

Frege's thought illustrates these dangers clearly. He came to a dogmatic denial that truth is a property of thoughts, asserting instead that the True is really the reference of what we misleadingly call true judgements. He invented the sense/reference distinction to salvage his function/argument analysis in the face of his need to link concepts logically with their extensions for the purpose of establishing his logicism. And he brushed off the deep incompatibility between the multiple polyadicity of ordinary predicates and the thesis that predicates stand for functions (since functions are differentiated into types by the number of their arguments). Although everything can be classified as a merely apparent deviation from a simple uniform pattern, to follow this strategy renders vacuous, and hence pointless, the assertion of genuine conformity at an allegedly deeper level.

The risk of lapsing from the standards set is not the principal problem with the application of scientific ideals to the activity of philosophising. The fundamental issue is whether these ideals are appropriate at all in philosophy. The elaboration and testing of detailed scientific theories makes sense only within the framework of ideas and assumptions that generally pass unquestioned. In the absence of consensus on a paradigm, theory-construction comes to a halt. The focus of scientific interest is on the empirical adequacy of theories, not on passing judgements on paradigms that serve as norms of representation for theories and observations alike. Philosophy should reverse this order of priority. Otherwise it would put the most crucial matters beyond question. To accept a question as making good sense and embark on building a philosophical theory to answer it is already to make the decisive step in the whole investigation.

How does the philosophical problem about mental processes and states and about behaviourism arise? — The first step is the one that altogether escapes notice. We talk of processes and states and leave their nature undecided. Sometime perhaps we shall know more about them — we think. But that is just what commits us to a particular way of looking at the matter. For we have a definite concept of what it means to learn to know a process better. (The decisive movement in the conjuring trick has been made, and it was the very one that we thought quite innocent.)[17]

This insidious dogmatism is conspicuous in Frege's thought. He replaced the traditional logical analysis of judgements into subjects and predicates by a decomposition into functions and arguments. But, at the outset, he gave no clear explanation of why the concept of a function is appropriate for this purpose, and he altogether neglected to consider whether it is *intelligible* to characterise a concept as a *function* or to take a judgeable-content as the *value* of a *function*. Later reflections did not remedy these initial defects; instead, fresh unclarities are added. It makes no sense to claim that a *concept* is logically related to its extension, and chronic vacillation between part/whole and function/argument decomposition of *thoughts* piles an inconsistency atop two incoherent ideas. Of course Frege was blind to these problems. But we too may fail to perceive that his assumptions are question-begging or incoherent for a different reason, namely that we misidentify his concept of a function. To bring his dogmatism into focus is a difficult philosophical achievement. Another's blinkers may be obvious, but sometimes they are as imperceptible as one's own, particularly if one

φιλοσοφία: εἰκὼν καὶ εἶδος 13

does not look for them in the right place. Preconceptions parallel to Frege's dominate contemporary philosophy of language. One of the most notable is preoccupation with forms of expression. Efforts to account for the various uses of sentences set out from the presumption that particular uses, or perhaps ranges of uses, are somehow determined by the forms of uttered sentences (together, of course, with their constituent terms). The search is launched for semantic mood-makers, for features that mark sentences off as metaphorical or ironic, etc. The obvious failure to find requisite characteristics merely diverts the hunt into the realm of depth structures. The underlying idea is unshakeable: somehow difference in use must be encapsulated in difference in forms (or constituents), even if we have no inkling of how this is accomplished.

What we never reconsider is the putative connection between the uses of sentences and their forms. Why must there be any rigid connection? What does it mean to claim that a particular form of sentence (a tautology) *cannot* be used to formulate a rule of inference or to state a fact? Or that an arithmetical equation *must* describe something (a relation between numbers)? Philosophy of language gives no answers to such questions.[18] The moral to be drawn from these examples of dogmatism is that no amount of open-mindedness about details in theory-construction can compensate for an *idée fixe* about the nature of the question to be answered. Negatively, this means that serious reflection, especially that of the clever, may be ruined by 'un noyeau d'erreur qui attire et assimile tout à lui-même'.[19] Positively, it means that one insight at the beginning is worth more than ever so many somewhere along the way. Wherever a philosopher states that something *must* be thus-and-so, however it may appear, and particularly when he describes things as being 'tacit', 'implicit', 'unconscious', 'below the surface', we should reach immediately for a large retort of cynical acid and apply it liberally to everything in the neighbourhood. We must scrutinise whether he offers any cogent reasons for drawing his distinction between appearance and reality — even whether it makes sense to do so.

Fascination with scientific theorising may divert philosophers' attention from their proper business. The unexamined question is not worth answering, the unexamined presupposition not worthy of adherence. Unless philosophical questions suddenly all dissipate like a mist, the task of philosophy must be literally endless. For, it should be to raise questions about every question, still more obviously to raise questions about every answer to a philosophical question. What most urgently needs questioning is the legitimacy of any general framework of thinking which gives rise to a co-ordinated set of philosophical questions and an elaborate theory giving detailed and unifying solutions to them. Far from encouraging this activity, the veneration of scientific open-mindedness in philosophy is a superstition engendering a myriad of further superstitions.

3. Hidden Depths

Suppose it were conceded that there are serious doubts in principle about the application of scientific ideals to philosophical investigations. None the less, it might be objected, we lack any viable alternative framework of concepts and assumptions (a 'conceptual scheme'). Moreover, there is urgent work to be done. It must fall to philosophy to tackle such issues as the general connections between mental states and behaviour, between thought and language, and between fact and value. Clearly much here is not perfectly understood, perhaps not understood at all. There are mysteries to be fathomed, explanations and clarifications to be given. Instead of deploring the absence of any possibility of thought unbounded by some intellectual horizon, should we not press on with the business of explaining, and hopefully coming to understand, what is opaque because of its depth and profundity?

Such a call to action is very persuasive. It draws its strength from a pervasive and deep aspect of our contemporary culture: the myth of hidden systems. This idea ramifies through our *Weltanschauung* and sprouts forth in many different places. Since only a recursion formula generates the product of *every* pair out of the infinitely many pairs of natural numbers, we are strongly inclined to accept that a child who has mastered the techniques of multiplication has accomplished something that only the technique of recursion makes intelligible. In order fully to describe the child's ability, we seemingly *must* characterise his performances as the output of this rule; and many philosophers would add that his ability must consist in his *implicit* knowledge of the recursion formula. Evidently the classroom of an elementary school is the scene of the most unexpected and profound happenings. We are readily captivated by determinism applied to the physical world:

φιλοσοφία: εἰκὼν καὶ εἶδος 15

we accept with no difficulty the contention that all events belong to a single comprehensive network of causal relations, that none stand aloof, as it were, from the rest. The picture of the physical world as a vast clockwork strikes us as interesting and worth considering, not as ridiculous. Psycho-physical parallelism evokes the same response: undergraduates and journalists chatter indifferently about the mind and the brain, and even a regimen of Socratic questioning often fails to elicit the faintest glimmer of awareness of any reasons for insisting on a distinction.

The brain is commonly held to interpret a pattern of retinal stimuli as a worm-eaten apple; or the most fundamental rules of English grammar may be held to be part of the genetically determined neurophysiology of human beings. We soon develop a capacity to take blatant nonsense in our stride as parts of explanatory theories. Few would dare to *mock* the comparison of the brain with computer hardware or of the mind with computer software. The idea that the whole of culture, or various aspects of it, are epiphenomena is widely treated as a credible and interesting suggestion. There is a widespread relish in reductionism of all forms. The contrast of appearance and reality appeals to us provided that dismissing what is familiar as merely apparent is compensated for by showing it to be the surface manifestations of some underlying system. Even crude and rebarbative features of the purported reality do not dampen enthusiasm for reductionism (for example, psychological hedonism or Freudian psychology). Claims to have discovered new systems beneath apparent chaos (for example, in history, art, or education) evoke respectful attention rather than instant rejection or contempt. We picture ourselves as afloat on a sea of limitless depth.

One focal point of this mythology is language. Thinking about language naturally starts from the assumption that a language is a system, or even a system of interrelated systems: phonology, orthography, syntax, semantics, and pragmatics. These systems are thought to be described, defined, or characterised by sets of rules, just as a game such as chess is to be analysed. Since the set of sentences recognised to be grammatical is held to be infinite, and since so too is the set of sentences understood by a competent speaker, the rules of syntax and semantics are claimed to generate recursively the sets of grammatical and intelligible sentences (respectively). Consequently, each of these sets of rules itself constitutes a structured system.[20] A philosopher may take his task to be the delineation of a general strategy for constructing a detailed description of the system of semantic rules underlying a natural language.[21] A linguist, by contrast, will probably press on with detailed theory-construction, convinced that the general principles of semantic rules are known, though the exact content of these rules is still to be discovered.[22] But all are agreed that systems of rules lie behind the workings of language, and that bringing this invisible substructure to light is an enterprise of immense importance. According to this picture of language, we come to think 'that if anyone utters a sentence and *means* or *understands* it he is operating a calculus according to definite rules'.[23] Of course, the competent speaker is not conscious of all these rules, perhaps of none of them. To suppose that he was would be manifestly absurd. Instead, he is alleged to have 'tacit' or 'implicit' knowledge of the relevant semantic rules and to have the practical ability to communicate without awareness of the theoretical principles underlying his activities.

Philosophers are particularly susceptible to the allure of the idea that language masks systems of rules. They are attracted to enlist in the ranks of those seeking a rigorous scientific theory of semantics, especially when they are allotted honourable posts in this co-operative enterprise. They march under the banner of 'constructing a theory of meaning for a natural language', and they dream of attaining to comprehensive explanations of the nature of language, mind, and the world by bringing order to the realm of semantic theories. All of this enthusiasm diverts them from scrutiny and criticism of the mythology that nurtures their vision.

What launches philosophers on the various quests of discovering hidden system beneath apparent chaos is the conviction that many important matters have not yet been understood. But what justifies that initial idea? Where does it originate from? An even more basic question is what it means to say of somebody that he lacks understanding of something. Does it make sense for a philosopher to claim that he does not already understand the nature of language, the course of his sense experience, the relation of mental states to behaviour, etc.? For if not, there is apparently no scope for explanation or clarification of these matters, *a fortiori* none for explanations revealing hidden systems!

Let us begin here. Failing to understand is correlative to understanding (and to misunderstanding). So what we evidently need is an understanding of what it is to understand something. There is

φιλοσοφία: εἰκὼν καὶ εἶδος 17

obviously a vast range or family of cases displaying many points of resemblance and many crucial differences. Consider what it is to understand algebraic topology or the homotopy lifting theorem; the principle of inertia or Newtonian mechanics; the duodecimal system; domestic electric circuits or practical electronics; the development section of the first movement of Mozart's G-minor quintet, the structure of the B-minor mass, or the classical symphony; the last couplet of Shakespeare's first sonnet, Joyce's *Ulysses*, or the Gothic novel; how to prune roses; etc. The criteria for understanding are very different in these different cases, and so too the criteria for not understanding or misunderstanding. A violinist may display his misunderstanding of the structure of a movement by misphrasing his part; a student may manifest his failing to understand a proof by his inability to produce parallel proofs of related theorems or by his incapacity to complete the proof if its structure is altered; and a gardener may demonstrate his understanding of pruning hybrid tea roses by how he wields his secateurs.

The point of reviewing these commonplaces is to raise the question of how *philosophical* understanding fits into this spectrum of cases, and how lack of *philosophical* understanding is supposed to be manifested. What shows that there are deficiencies in our understanding that philosophy might remedy? Is it the occurrence of specific puzzles and antinomies, for example, Russell's paradox or Frege's antinomy about concepts? If so, why is the construction of a general theory the appropriate treatment? Perhaps detailed probing in the immediate vicinity of the problem would prove more efficacious (for example, investigations of explanations of the term 'set' and scrutiny of how the concepts of 'intension' and 'extension' are related). And is a theory needed at all? There are many sorts of puzzlement calling for quite different approaches, for example, bewilderment about how to fit a set of parallelograms and triangles together to form a rectangle. Much theory-building in philosophy seems motivated not by specific paradoxes, but by a general diffuse sense of wonder and bafflement. We contemplate a familiar form of inference involving adverbs (for example, 'He departed quickly, so he departed'), and then, clutching our brows in anguish, we wonder how adverbs 'really work'. This bafflement itself is baffling, for the problem does not arise out of any serious uncertainty about whether specific arguments are valid. When addressed with this question, why should we not reply 'Don't you know?'? Very often, as in this case, the suspicion is that the puzzlement is the product of prior commitment to a philosophical theory. Adverbs do not fit neatly into first-order quantification theory; we have faith that this system of logic must really be sufficient to account for all valid arguments. But why elevate this recalcitrance of adverbs to fit our preconceptions about logic into the allegation that we do not *understand* the role of adverbs in language? It is predetermined by the question, what would count as understanding here. But would there be any advantage in achieving 'understanding' apart from the removal of misattributed lack of understanding? Fitting adverbs into quantification theory would further understanding only in the sense in which finding a cure for an iatrogenic disease would be a contribution to public health.

Where there is absence of understanding, there is scope for explanation, clarification, or elucidation. These concepts are correlative to understanding. If one person fails to understand something and a second person, who does understand it, explains it to him, then what is explained *is* what the first does not understand and what the second does. Explanations give understanding. (But the connection is conceptual, not causal; to understand the explanation *is* to understand what is explained.) Predictably, the variety of cases of understanding is matched by a range of interrelated cases of explanation. Consider explaining a word by giving a synonym, by translating it, by analysing it in a definition *per genus et differentiam*, or by pointing to a sample; explaining how to behave in church by giving a description of an appropriate demeanour or by setting an example; explaining how to cut dovetails by supplying a diagram or a model to follow; explaining how to construct proofs by mathematical induction; explaining why Napoleon marched on Moscow or the origins of the First World War; explaining why water expands when it freezes; etc. The criteria for giving correct explanations differ in these different cases, and so too do the criteria for completeness of explanations (where there is any such thing as completeness).

Once again the point of reviewing the variety of explanations and the variable criteria of correctness is to raise the question of how *philosophical* explanations fit into this spectrum of cases. Are they uniform in kind? Must all satisfactory ones have the structure and role of theories in the physical sciences? What are the criteria of correctness for philosophical explanations? Does it make sense to speak of their completeness, and if so, what are the criteria of completeness? Are they always clarifications of the meanings of problematic expressions? To the extent that they are, how do they relate to the practice of everyday explanation of words and phrases? If they overlap, then must their forms not be as diverse as the forms of ordinary explanations? How to fit ostensive definitions, samples, or explanations by examples into an axiomatic calculus of meaning-rules calls for considerable ingenuity and a blanket refusal to take these explanations at face value. If philosophical clarifications of meaning diverge from ordinary explanations, how are they endowed with the status and role of *rules* for the use of expressions? Whence derives their authority to pass judgements on the correctness or incorrectness of disputed applications of language? Can anything lacking the normative powers of ordinary explanations of words be intelligibly characterised as a clarification of *meaning* at all?

Correlative to these issues is the question of the criteria for *inadequacy* of philosophical explanations. Must an explanation be general? Would detailed description of the similarities and differences in verbs of perception ('see', 'smell', 'taste', etc.) be worthless if it could not be exhibited as part of a coherent general theory of meaning? Would it be refuted if the only straightforward generalisations were proved to be indefensible? A philosopher might remark that '$2 + 3 = 5$' is not what we call a statement about symbols or that it expresses a truth about numbers. Has he thereby committed himself to Platonism about arithmetic? Is his observation undermined if an alternative theory (for example, conventionalism) provides a more economical or less mysterious explanation of *a priori* knowledge? Or does dismissing a philosophical remark or point of view require a demonstration that it is nonsensical? Is the identification of nonsense itself essentially dependent on adopting an alternative theory? Does the distinction between sense and nonsense vary over time or depend on a point of view? Does the fact that some philosopher some time has argued that an apparently nonsensical statement or distinction makes sense establish that declaring it to be nonsense requires the support of a theory? Or does a philosopher's avowed suspicion that there may be no normative phenomena render defective reasoning based on distinguishing rule-governed regularities from nomological or causal regularities? Many philosophical disputes can be traced back to divergence in answers to these unexamined questions.

Diversity in the forms and roles of philosophical explanations is to be expected from the diversity of kinds of misunderstanding and lack of understanding to be rectified, and divergence in form and function from scientific explanations is also to be expected because many conceptual perplexities arise precisely from questions bypassed or suppressed in the education of scientists and mathematicians.

Both understanding and explanations are subject to assessment along a scale running from depth or profundity to superficiality or triviality. A superficial understanding of something is a close cousin to lack of understanding, and a superficial or trivial explanation is something scarcely worth possessing. Not surprisingly, then, philosophers aim at deep understanding, and to this end they search for deep explanations. But what is their ideal of depth? What is their yardstick for measuring profundity? The terms 'deep' and 'profound' carry a considerable range of connotations. Prominent among them are being recondite, recherché, unfamiliar, difficult to comprehend. But it would be naïve to suppose that we move 'beyond superficiality' and achieve profundity in explanations simply

> by a readiness to undertake perhaps far-reaching idealization and to construct abstract models that are accorded more significance than the ordinary world of sensation, and correspondingly, by readiness to tolerate unexplained phenomena or even as yet unexplained counter-evidence to theoretical constructions that have achieved a certain degree of explanatory depth in some limited domain.[24]

Pascal's *Pensees* are surely not to be condemned as superficial on the grounds that he avoided any explicit theory-construction and made no use of mathematics in expounding his arguments! Profundity must be a concept as many-faceted as the concepts of understanding and explanation.

What the appropriate criteria are for profundity in philosophy depends on a clarification of the nature of philosophical understanding and of philosophical explanation. From the outset, however, we should be on our guard against a tendency to pass the judgement that whatever does not meet the standards of depth for a scientific explanation is *ipso facto* defective in philosophy. A one-sided vision inclines us to apply a monolithic conception of profundity, to venerate technical sophistication and the reduction

φιλοσοφία: εἰκὼν καὶ εἶδος   21

of the familiar to what is mysterious, hidden, and even uncanny. As a corrective, we should bear in mind other ingredients of depth. Questions may be deep because they concern issues that move us. Perplexity about time and scepticism about the future interlock with human anxiety and insecurity. Puzzlement about the relation of mind and body links up with the importance of establishing others' beliefs, desires, emotions, etc., and with worry about one's own fate (death and immortality). Controversies about values concern matters of crucial importance to our own happiness and wellbeing. Perhaps much of the apparent depth of philosophy derives from its treatment of questions that are not purely intellectual. An explanation may also be deep because it is strikingly simple or because it makes something apparently complex utterly transparent.

Notable scientific theories share in this aspect of depth, but the purest forms occur elsewhere, especially in mathematics and logic. Frege effected a simplification and ordering of reasoning involving generalisations; by viewing expressions of generality as second-level functions, he reduced an apparent welter of forms of reasoning to variations on a single theme. Similarly, by taking truth-tables to characterise the significance of logical constants and by treating tautology as the defining characteristic of logical truth, Wittgenstein revealed something already present (but hitherto unnoticed) in Frege's explanations. In such cases the profundity of an explanation turns on its working an alteration in how we view something known and familiar. The explanation involves a shift of aspect. Sometimes lack of understanding and the need for explanation arise from the fact that 'the aspects of things that are most important for us are hidden because of their simplicity and familiarity'.[25] Reflection on the obvious varieties of depth in explanations should convince us that profundity is not a matter of the form of the explanation (whether it contains mathematical symbols or theoretical terms, whether it is simple or difficult to survey, whether it states something familiar), but rather a matter of the context in which it occurs and the use to which it is put.

These observations about understanding, explanations, and depth are not intended to settle the question of the nature of philosophy. They are meant to demonstrate that the question is not yet settled. If the ideal of science reigns over philosophers, it does not occupy the throne by divine right. It does so by the acquiescence of its subjects. And the question whence derives their duty of obedience to this monarch is a legitimate and important *philosophical* question.

4. Wittgenstein's Transformation: Rules and *Übersichten*

The combative nature of philosophers has ensured that the imperialism of the scientific ideal over analytic philosophy has met with some resistance. Among the few scattered voices of opposition, Wittgenstein's presents the most sustained negative case, and his sets of remarks on philosophy (especially in the *Investigations*) also offer a clear and positive formulation of an alternative.

These remarks reiterate earlier criticism of what Russell advocated as 'scientific method in philosophy'. According to that view, philosophy should aim at a theoretical understanding of the most general aspects of the world by pursuing the methodology of the advanced physical sciences. Covering-law explanations should be sought to unify apparently diverse data, and where several are viable, theoretical economy and degree of inductive confirmation are the criteria for selecting the fittest. The *Tractatus* retorted that philosophy does not consist of statements or theses at all: that its 'propositions' are not theories of hypotheses, but attempts simply to clarify the logical syntax of language; that Occam's razor and measures of inductive support are inapplicable to propositions plotting the bounds of sense: and that the statements of everyday language are in perfect logical order, immune to rectification or modification in the light of philosophical theorising.

Persistent antipathy to Russell's fundamental ideas is perhaps the most conspicuous point of continuity between the *Tractatus* and the *Investigations*. This continuity is an important candle to illuminate the later enigmatic epigrams about philosophy. But it is no sooner lit than it is at risk of being extinguished. Wittgenstein certainly criticised philosophers for lack of care and detail in describing the uses and explanations of symbols. He chided them for holding erroneous preconceptions, for rushing beyond description to construct spurious explanations, and for oversimplifying concepts and their interrelations. 'Look and see', he urged; 'and note the differences'. Such remarks are widely construed as laying down a blanket ban on any generalisation, as denying that a language exhibits any systematic structure at all.

φιλοσοφία: εἰκὼν καὶ εἶδος 23

According to this influential interpretation, we should constantly remind ourselves that words are extraordinarily vague and flexible in meaning, that the patterns for their correct use are always more or less indeterminate, and that there are countless ways of using words and sentences in speech. Natural languages are allegedly chaotic, and therefore Wittgenstein meant to exclude the possibility of constructing a theory of meaning for a natural language. There are only limited opportunities for giving any definite descriptions of concepts, and even then the only legitimate task for a philosopher is still destructive: 'whenever someone else wanted to say something metaphysical, to demonstrate to him that he had failed to give a meaning to certain signs in his sentences'.[26] Apart from exposing the nonsense of some philosophical pronouncements, one should apparently be content to leave *everything* as it is.

This interpretation of Wittgenstein's characterisation of philosophy is a caricature of his conception. It rightly discerns his opposition to the now fashionable idea that philosophy can be absorbed into a general science of language which marries philosophical logic with theoretical linguistics. On the other hand, it altogether misses the nature of his objection. The impossibility of a scientific theory of meaning is depicted as something ruled out by the physics of language. The phenomena are allegedly too intricate, shifting, and indeterminate to be subsumed under any workable explanatory theory. That natural languages have this character is contingent. So too is the present poverty of explanatory concepts and theories: the advance of the science of language might well throw up a satisfactory theory where we now perceive only chaos and flux. Consequently, according to this interpretation, Wittgenstein gave no definitive refutation of the possibility of a systematic theory of meaning; he merely encouraged philosophers to share his despair and to give up the quest. In fact, he thought the idea of such a philosophical theory to be incoherent, and in criticising the notion of analysis in the *Tractatus* and the conception of a language as a calculus, he advanced powerful arguments in support of this conclusion. As a philosopher, the only impossibilities that he drew attention to are conceptual ones. Hence the true grounds for his opposition to theories must be sought in his clarification of the concepts of meaning, understanding, and explanation.

There is an antithetical danger in interpreting his later remarks on philosophy. This stems from an apparent conflict between theory and practice. Although he officially eschewed explanations and encouraged detailed descriptions of differences, his later writings are peppered with important generalisations. He claimed, for example, that inner states stand in need of outward criteria, that the meaning of a word is its use in a language, that confusions about mathematics parallel those about psychological concepts, that ostensive definitions are substitution-rules for symbols, and that mathematical and geometrical propositions are rules of grammar. This might seem to be merely an extension of the practice evident in the *Tractatus*, for there his views about the descriptive task and prophylactic nature of philosophy did not prevent his constructing a complex and sophisticated theory about the essential nature of any possible language. These observations leave open a range of unflattering conclusions. Did he stigmatise others' pronouncements as theories and label his own 'descriptions' solely on the grounds that his were (true) grammatical propositions whereas theirs were not? Or did he fail to practise what he preached? Or were his remarks on philosophy disingenuous — a smokescreen to hide his own theory-building? To escape this impasse requires a more subtle elucidation of his criticism of Russell's scientific method in philosophy as well as a more perceptive account of the role of the most prominent generalisations in his own philosophical investigations.

To explore in detail Wittgenstein's later conception of philosophy would be a lengthy undertaking. My aim is at once more modest and more ambitious: simply to furnish the key to unlock the gate to this μακρότερος ὁδός. But that key itself is locked away. How can we gain access to it? Here two ideas suggest a strategy. The first is the thought that continuity in opposition to Russell between the *Tractatus* and the *Investigations* might mask a discontinuity in the rationale for the opposition. Russell's set of theses might have more than one contrary. The second idea is to question the provocative thesis that Wittgenstein's comments on philosophy in the *Investigations* have no organic connection with the contents of his substantive remarks.[27] Would we really be unable to reconstruct his views from careful study of a text from which the methodological declarations had been expurgated? Both these lines of thought indicate that we should cast around more widely to see whether his characterisation of philosophy has any intimate liaisons with what are obviously the leading themes of the *Investigations*.

φιλοσοφία: εἰκὼν καὶ εἶδος   25

Pursuing these lines of enquiry leads directly to promising results. The *Tractatus* had ruled out the possibility of any *science* of logical form because it tried to delineate the *essential* structure of any possible language (the *logical* syntax of language) and because the essential bipolarity of any significant proposition excluded the possibility of any proposition's expressing a necessary truth. The *Investigations* shared neither this ambition nor the doctrine of the bipolarity of any proposition. On the other hand, Wittgenstein now saw a different but no less fundamental difference between philosophy and science. The sole task of philosophers is to clarify the meanings of expressions which generate philosophical confusion and puzzlement. But instead of viewing meanings as something hidden which must be brought to light by logical analysis, he argued that meanings are exhausted by acknowledged explanations of meaning. Hence the job of philosophers is to make perspicuous the grammar of expressions, the rules for their correct use. But he put a particular gloss on this programme: these rules must be what we use to settle whether expressions make sense or not and whether inferences are sound or fallacious; hence they must be the explanations of meaning we actually use to teach the uses of words, to justify or criticise applications of them, etc. This gives a cutting edge to what appears to be a platitude. (The whole of modern philosophy of language is pervaded by the notion that specifying the meaning of an expression is to state the rules for its correct use.) Philosophy differs from all the sciences in that it moves within norms of representation, not among the phenomena represented. Philosophical misunderstanding betokens entanglement in these rules of grammar, whereas sound understanding is a matter of being able to find one's way about without hitches. Grammatical propositions (though no more uniform than empirical ones!) are altogether different from scientific ones. It is the acme of philosophical confusion to mistake the two. The clarification of concepts is a matter of issuing reminders about the *de jure* role of expressions in speech. It is analogous to elucidating the powers of chess pieces; it highlights sets of *rules*. Consequently there is an obvious connection between his positive conception of philosophy and his analysis of the concepts of a rule and of following a rule. This observation not only throws a flood of light on his conception of philosophy, but also manifestly integrates this conception into the mainstream of the *Philosophical Investigations*.

Gathering in this harvest presupposes two things. The first is an understanding of the nature of grammatical propositions; the second is comprehension of his controversial analysis of the concept of following a rule. The first is parasitic on the second since the focal point of all grammatical remarks is the *rules* of grammar whether or not these remarks are themselves rules of grammar. Hence we must start by making clear why Wittgenstein called explanations of meaning rules of grammar and what the implications of this terminology are. Although clouds of dust have been thrown up all around his discussion of rules and following rules, the main points are clear and simple even if they are usually lost from sight in the heat of battle.[28] First, the concept of a rule is a family resemblance concept. It is readily explained by listing paradigms, whereas all plausible analytic definitions can be shown to be defective. In addition, the relevant features of resemblance with the paradigms are principally functional or dynamic. Whether a sentence formulates a rule or not depends primarily not on its forms (whether it contains modal auxiliaries such as 'must' or 'may', whether it is declarative or imperative, whether it contains expressions of generality), but on its use; or more accurately, it depends on its standing potentiality for use in a range of distinctive normative activities. Rules are typically employed to give instructions on how things are to be done, to justify or criticise particular performances, to guide agents who intend to engage in rule-governed activities or who seek to correct errors in their own performance, etc. Anything classified as a rule must have a demonstrated potentiality to serve in these roles, typically no doubt because it is known to serve in some of them, but exceptionally because it belongs to an established genre of rules most of which have served in such roles (for example, a rule of a newly invented board-game or a legal statute whose operative conditions have never been realised). Rules may be created or abrogated. As a consequence, a sentence which once formulated a rule may now fail to do so, and *vice versa*. This dynamic and context-relative character of rule-formulations is clearest when rules are expressed concretely in charts, tables, samples, or signposts; for nothing intrinsic to such objects settles their status as rule-formulations, but only the extrinsic feature of how they relate to various human practices. The potentialities of use which are diagnostic of rules cannot be the objects of collective discovery by the agents in a rule-governed activity (just as participants in a barter economy cannot discover that some commodity has the status of money); whatever they do not acknowledge to be a rule is not a rule (though it might become one). Only an outsider may make discoveries about the rules of a practice, and he discovers not the rules, but rather what the rules are (and already were). One might epitomise these points by remarking that rules are instruments.

Second, there is a connection in grammar between a rule and acts which accord with it (and, symmetrically, a grammatical connection between a rule and acts which contravene it). The rule of chess that one cannot leave one's king *en prise* is complied with by someone's not leaving his king *en prise*. To generalise, a generic description of acts which are in accord with a rule can be generated systematically from the rule-formulation itself. In this sense, a rule and an act in accord with it make contact in language (like an expectation and the event which fulfils it). The rule and nothing but the rule determines what accords with it (and what contravenes it), that is, what counts as correct (and what as incorrect). Consequently, the question 'What makes this act accord with this rule?' will often be nonsensical (namely, whenever the description of the act is a grammatical transformation of the rule-formulation); for this form of question presupposes that the answer must be something other than 'The rule itself'. Hence, too, it will be nonsense to answer the general question 'What makes an act accord with a rule?' by saying 'An interpretation', and it will be absurd to suppose that the vista of an infinite regress of interpretations demands some alternative answer such as 'Human agreement'. The accord of an act with a rule is a relation laid down in grammar.

Third, we distinguish in many contexts between someone's following a rule and his accidentally or unwittingly acting in conformity with this rule; for example, a competent chess player follows the rules of chess, whereas an infant who shifts a knight might act in conformity with a rule of chess without following it. According to this distinction, following a rule is an intentional activity. This point does not imply that only the agent himself can know whether he is following a rule or not, and it does not imply that he cannot be mistaken about whether he has followed the rule. There are behavioural criteria for having specific intentions. In particular, there is a range of familiar criteria for someone's following a given rule, for example that he actually cites a formulation of this rule to rebut criticism of his behaviour or that he appeals to the rule in deliberating about what to do. It is part of the grammar of 'following a rule' that one ascertains that another is following a rule by reference to his satisfying these criteria. To repudiate these criteria (*a fortiori* to substitute different ones) is to modify the concept of following a rule. The truism that following a rule is an intentional action has another important facet: it guarantees the transparency of the rules of a practice to *each* agent who is a full participant in the practice (and not just to the group of participants collectively). There is no such thing as someone's following a rule hidden from his awareness or unknown to him, *a fortiori* no such thing as his following a rule never previously formulated. There is no possibility of penetrating the behaviour of an agent and discovering that he is, unbeknownst to himself, really following a hitherto unsuspected rule. At worst, he may lose sight of what rule he is trying to follow and need to be reminded of it.

The purpose of these humdrum observations is to dispel the illusion that there are hidden depths to be plumbed in the matter of rule-governed practices and the activity of following rules. There is no such thing as an undiscovered or unacknowledged rule governing any practice; there is rather the possibility of adopting new rules in place of, or in addition to, established ones. Reflection on the role of rules makes this point obvious. Rules have a distinctive 'direction of fit': if behaviour governed by a rule fails to conform with the rule, the behaviour is faulted, not the rule. Hypotheses and scientific explanations have the reverse 'direction of fit': if the phenomena fail to square with the hypothesis, it is faulted, not the descriptions of the phenomena. The motion of a hypothetical rule is therefore incoherent, as if each of two rods could on a single occasion each be used to measure the other. There is also no such thing as tacit or implicit rule-following; there is rather *conformity* with rules unknown to the agent. Measuring with rulers provides an illuminating analogy. To wield a rod in certain ways for various familiar purposes is to use the rod as a ruler to measure objects, while absence of these purposes or deviation from this practice disqualifies the activity for the description 'measuring something'. Where the agent lacks the appropriate purposes, the fact that another who had them might be properly said to measure an object in going through the same motions does not license the conclusion that the original agent was 'tacitly' or 'implicitly' measuring this object! In respect of the *rules* of a practice and the activity of *following* these rules, there is literally nothing for participants to discover.

φιλοσοφία: εἰκὼν καὶ εἶδος 29

In the context of a clarification of the concepts of meaning and understanding, these remarks have important philosophical implications. They reveal fundamental confusion in the idea of philosophical analysis which inspired the *Tractatus* and which still motivates the search for theories of meaning for natural languages. The presupposition of the intelligibility of these programmes is that, 'if anyone utters a sentence and *means* or *understands* it, he must be operating a calculus according to definite rules'. These rules must suffice to determine the meaning of any sentence from a specification of its structure and its constituents, since only the satisfaction of this constraint can account for the fact that a competent speaker can generate and understand an infinity of sentences from the finite resources acquired in his learning to speak a language. The goal of a semantic theory is to reveal the system of rules which is implicitly known by every competent speaker of a language and which is unconsciously put to use by him in speech. By tying meaning closely to what are called *explanations* of meaning and by calling explanations of meaning *rules* for the use of expressions, Wittgenstein sought to make clear an incoherence in the very idea of a calculus of rules which individually give the meaning of words and jointly determine the senses of sentences. Semantic theories are brought up against an impasse. On the one hand there is the everyday practice of giving explanations of expressions and of employing them in teaching children, in justifying or criticising particular applications of words, etc. These explanations fill the office of rules, and in speech a competent speaker may be said to follow these rules for using words. But these rules do not satisfy the demands of a semantic theory. They are not uniform in form or function. They embrace definitions *per genus et differentiam*, ostensive definitions, explanations by authoritative example, contrastive paraphrase, etc. They do not fit into a mechanical procedure for computing the meanings of complex expressions from the explanation of their constituents. Some do not fit because they are partly concrete, others because their applications are circumstance-dependent. Hence these familiar rules manifestly fail to show that the sense of any sentence can be computed from its constituents and its structure.

On the other hand, the so-called rules constituting a semantic theory typically have *none* of the roles distinctive of rules. They have no normative status in the practice of speaking a language, and a competent speaker cannot be said to follow a rule of which he is not even aware. It is an abuse of the concepts of a rule and of following a rule to claim that the hypotheses of a semantic theory are rules followed by speakers of a language. And there would be no advantage to be gained by abandoning talk of rules here; not only would that leave a lacuna to be filled with some new (and equally problematic) label, but also it would shift a conceptual muddle to a new location, for only propositions with the normative roles of explanations are relevant to giving the *meaning* of an expression. In short, there is an irresoluble tension in the notion of a *calculus* of *rules* which give the *meanings* of all the expressions of a language. What we call explanations are a *motley*, and the grammar of a language is no more systematic than it *seems*.

Although Wittgenstein's business as a philosopher is to clarify the grammar of our language in order to eliminate philosophical perplexity and confusion, he did not limit his remarks to the formulation of rules of grammar. He also made many remarks *about* grammar. These are very diverse. One prominent kind diagnoses the sources of philosophical confusion in features of grammar; for example, the misconception of meaning or understanding as a mental state is linked to the use of tensed verb forms such as 'I meant that ...' or 'Now I understand ...'. Another kind of grammatical remark calls attention to the framework-conditions surrounding the practice of laying down rules of grammar. These may indicate presuppositions of particular explanations of meaning (for example, the general coincidence of what are taken to be criteria of personal identity), or they may point out completely general presuppositions (for example, the absence of disagreement about what are to be counted as explanations of words and about what are correct applications of these rules). A third kind of remark gives a synopsis or *Übersicht* of a more or less extensive domain of rules of grammar. Philosophical confusion arises largely from losing one's way in the maze of grammar, and therefore an appropriate remedy is to provide landmarks useful for keeping one's bearings. Such a remark is meant to serve as a nucleus for condensing a cloud of philosophy into a droplet of grammar. Many apparent generalisations are meant to have this role. The claim that inner states stand in need of outward criteria offers an organising principle for detailed investigation of psychological concepts; it is intended to neutralise the inclination to suppose that introspection holds the key to clarifying these concepts. Likewise, calling geometrical propositions rules of syntax or grammar is meant to reorient philosophical reflection on geometry; it should steer one away from the conception of geometry as a science of ideal objects known to us through exercising our faculty of spatial intuition, and it should direct one towards examining the normative role of geometry in respect of descriptions of the shapes of things and their spatial relations. Though grammatical remarks all relate to rules of grammar, by no means all of them state rules of grammar.

Certain influential misinterpretations of Wittgenstein's work stem from disregarding the diversity of grammatical remarks. It is natural to assume that all of them have the same status, especially that each and every one formulates a rule of grammar. As a consequence, for example, many commentators misread his comments on the role of agreement in judgements as an attempt to define what acts are in accord with a rule in terms of the normal response of qualified participants in a practice to the demand to apply this rule. Not only is this interpretation absurd in itself, but also it conflicts with his observation that the relation of accord between an act and a rule is a grammatical relation. In a parallel way, other commentators misread his remark on the necessity for behavioural criteria for sensations, emotion, intentions, etc. as advocacy of a verificationist or anti-realist conception of meaning. But this conception of meaning would underpin the philosophical clarification of concepts only if it were part of the general *concept* of meaning. That is not Wittgenstein's contention. He did not argue that it is part of the grammar of 'meaning' that the meaning of 'pain', 'understand', 'anger', etc. must be explained by reference to behavioural criteria (or methods of verification). Rather, he suggested, everything relevant to judging whether uses of words are correct or not belongs to grammar, and therefore he noted that behavioural criteria used to support (and to deny) attributions of such 'inner states' to persons are a crucial part of the grammar of psychological concepts. This is an observation about this class of concepts, not a delineation of part of the grammar of 'meaning'.

There is yet another danger from neglecting important differences among grammatical remarks: one readily loses sight of the context-dependence of the value of philosophical *Übersichten*. These remarks are meant to counteract tendencies to become lost in following up connections among concepts, and these tendencies may vary from age to age or even from person to person under the influence of scientific or cultural changes or even because of the partial success of previous philosophical investigations. As a consequence, what is helpful to one may be a hindrance to another; analogical thinking has no intrinsic or even permanent value. Somebody educated in Frege's conception of logic as a deductive system of truths grounded in self-evident axioms may find great illumination about the nature of logical truth in the claim that the propositions of logic all say nothing; but somebody brought up to think of all logical truths as tautologies may instead find this claim the source of puzzlement. Likewise since we tend to assimilate geometrical propositions to laws of physics, there is value in Wittgenstein's noting that they discharge the characteristic functions of rules; but if we were too much impressed by this aspect of geometry, there might be value in pointing out that geometry consists of propositions (truths, theorems, objects of knowledge, etc.) and perhaps even in differentiating the autonomy of geometry from the arbitrariness of the rules of English syntax. 'Everything is what it is and not another thing' could have served as the maxim of the *Philosophical Investigations.* The role of *Übersichten* is not to urge disregard of differences, but rather to make conceptual differences visible against particular backgrounds which tend to camouflage them.

5. The Bewitchment of Philosophy by Means of Science

The connection of meaning with explanations of meaning and the characterisation of explanations of words as rules of grammar are two hawsers firmly tethering Wittgenstein's remarks on the nature of philosophy to the rest of the *Philosophical Investigations.* To see no link betrays deep misunderstanding of his writings. Conversely, to apprehend the connection makes luminous most of his most celebrated (or notorious) observations. A philosophical investigation is a grammatical one.[29] It clears away misunderstandings by clarifying the rules of grammar of our language. Consequently, it aims at revealing essence (since essence is expressed in grammar). Yet the goal is not to dig out by analysis something beneath the surface, but rather to understand something already in plain view by rearrangement of what is simple and familiar.[30] The rules of grammar are diverse and free-floating. So giving *Übersichten* of them to forestall losing one's bearings is the fundamental activity of philosophy.[31] Naturally, too, philosophy cannot give any foundations to grammar; it can make no discoveries and it cannot explain or deduce anything in the domain of grammar.[32] There is here no scope for scientific theorising; explanation must be banished, and description alone must take its place.[33] In the context of Wittgenstein's discussion of explanations of meaning and rules of grammar, the rationale of these remarks is plain. They seem outrageous only when isolated from the stream of his thinking, but there they lose their significance altogether.

Wittgenstein's conception of philosophy is manifestly opposed to Frege's theory and practice. Frege considered himself to have made important *discoveries* in logic and mathematics; he first brought to light the True and the False, the fact that concepts are a species of function, and the function-theoretic mechanism underlying all sound mathematical reasoning. He intended to put mathematics on solid *foundations*; he tried to demonstrate that mathematical induction is really a general logical law despite a contrary appearance, and that every true proposition of arithmetic can be reduced to a truth of logic. Frege did *criticise* and try to *reform* parts of grammar, notoriously interfering with patterns of speech about truth and about concepts. He did not scruple to advance dogmatic *theses*: he asserted that existence is a second-level concept, that numbers are really extensions of concepts, and that it is impossible to make inferences from false judgements. He conceived of logic as the scientific study of relations among abstract entities (concepts and judgements), and he organised its generalisations into an axiomatic system in which self-evident axioms are the guarantors of the truth of all the other propositions of logic. In Wittgenstein's view, Frege's philosophy of logic exhibits all of the confusions gathered by conflating rules of grammar with propositions of physics.

Continued opposition to Russell's scientific method in philosophy is equally clear in the *Philosophical Investigations*. Russell thought philosophy to consist of very general propositions, many of which are justified by inductive arguments and the rest of which are self-evident truths. In particular, the logical system of *Principia* is justified as the best scientific explanation of the truths of arithmetic. Since Wittgenstein held grammatical remarks to be radically unlike explanatory hypotheses in science, he thought the criteria for judging the worth of scientific theories (especially Occam's razor and degree of inductive support) to be as inapposite in assessing the clarification of the meanings of number-words as they are for judging the merits of a pianist's performance of Beethoven's 'Hammerklavier' or one of Canaletto's landscapes of London.

Although criticism of Frege's and Russell's conceptions of philosophy is no less conspicuous in the *Tractatus* than in the *Investigations*, it must not be assumed that the grounds of his objections remained constant. On the contrary, careful inspection of the details of his later criticisms of the *Tractatus* supports the initial hunch that there is a major shift in the basis for his repudiation of scientific method in philosophy.

First, the *Tractatus* is prefaced with the sweeping claim, 'I believe myself to have found, on all essential points, the final solution of the problems [of philosophy]'.[34] The central business of philosophy was finding a solution to the '*single* great problem':[35] 'My whole task consists in explaining the nature of the proposition'.[36] The correct delineation of the general form of a proposition completed this programme. It constituted a single vantage point from which everything could be seen aright. The *Investigations* repudiates not only the putative solution, but also the ambition to seek for any substitute. The aim is merely to clear away sundry misunderstandings about the uses of words. The method is to assemble reminders about the rules of grammar which are targeted on removing specific misunderstandings, like therapies for particular diseases. In this way, 'Problems are solved (difficulties eliminated), not a single problem'.[37] The therapist establishes 'an order in our knowledge of the use of language: an order with a particular end in view; one out of many possible orders; not *the* order'.[38] Clarity about this limited goal frees the philosopher from the paralysing demand that any satisfactory elucidation of the grammar of a word such as 'language' or 'sentence' must give a single formula that once and for all guarantees that all philosophical confusions about these notions shall completely disappear.[39] Different clarifications of a single expression may be useful for eliminating different confusions, and possible confusions are limitless and hence cannot be eliminated in advance. Although for every philosophical problem there is some method for removing it, Wittgenstein no longer thought that a single correct logical point of view would simultaneously remove every confusion, actual or possible.

Secondly, the *Tractatus* held that the philosopher needs to deploy formal concepts to delineate the bounds of sense. These super-concepts cannot be used to form meaningful sentences. The notorious conclusion was that the correct logical point of view is ineffable; it is shown by philosophical sentences that are literally nonsensical. As an alternative to this paradox, some might prefer the idea that philosophising is an *activity* of clarifying what makes sense and thereby indicating what does not:[40] but then this is a paradoxical activity since it has no intelligible product. The *Investigations* exposed these illusions. The so-called formal concepts are expressed by words such as 'language', 'number', 'experience', 'sentence', and 'world', which have genuine uses in our language — uses as humdrum a those of such words as 'table', 'lamp', and 'door'. Philosophically puzzling words acquire an aura of mystery of being torn out of their natural environments and used in radically different contexts without any of the necessary clarification of their novel grammatical roles. 'As if [its] sense were an atmosphere accompanying a word, which it carried with it into every kind of application.'[41] The alleged nonsensicality of all applications of formal concepts rests on a further misconception. The distinctive feature of such propositions as 'Red is a colour', '0, 1, 2, 3 ... are numbers', or 'Every proposition is true or false' is that they are formulations of rules of grammar; the difference in role between rules and descriptive statements accounts for their peculiarity without recourse to the doctrine of ineffability. Indeed, the label 'nonsense' is itself a misdescription of this difference in role. What needs to be clarified by philosophy can be said and should be said clearly.

Thirdly, the *Tractatus* aimed at delineating the *logical* syntax of language. This is not thought to concern accidental features of the syntax of natural languages which are treated in standard grammars, nor is it the syntax of a special logical notation or concept-script. Rather, it outlines the nature of any possible language, the *essence* of notation. Wittgenstein argued that all the logical constants and hence all the truth-functions are already given with the elementary propositions and that logic therefore belongs to logical syntax. 'If we know the logical syntax of any sign-language, then we have already been given all the propositions of logic.'[42] In logic, 'the nature of the natural and inevitable signs speaks for itself'.[43] Everything is grounded in alleged insights into the metaphysics of symbolism. This is held to make clear the essential validity of logical truths and to rule out the possibility of any theory of types (whether semantic or purely syntactic). It also is thought to show that logic mirrors the logical structure of the world, hence too that logic is the *hardest* thing there is.[44]

Rooted in this vision were stinging criticisms of Frege's philosophy of logic. Wittgenstein perceived a confusion of facts with objects (or sentences with names) and a corresponding conflation of operations with material functions. Neglect of the essential bipolarity of the proposition was alleged to underpin the mistaken idea that molecular propositions are constructed out of more fundamental atomic propositions, and this misconception involves viewing logical propositions as accidental truths about optional abstract entities.

Wittgenstein's later remarks on logic[45] continued to point out deep incoherence in Frege's Platonist conception of logical truths, but his arguments no longer depended on the mythology of symbolism presented in the *Tractatus*. The primary concern of logic is with rules of inference. These belong to grammar (since they regulate transformations of symbols), and hence they are arbitrarily stipulated, not discovered buried in the essential nature of language. Logical truths or tautologies reflect rules of inference; in fact, Wittgenstein remarked, the tautology p.p ⊃ q ⊃. q says nothing and would not be used to express the rule of *modus ponens*, but *that* p.p ⊃ q ⊃. q *is a tautology* can be said to express this rule. Tautologies and rules of inference are linked in grammar. Similar observations account for the insight of the *Tractatus* that logic reflects the essence of the proposition, of thought, and of inference; the laws of logic are aspects of the *concepts* of a proposition, of thinking, and of inference. To drop the principle that every proposition is either true or false is to replace our concept of a proposition by a different concept; to introduce non-Aristotelian rules of inference would be possible, but applying these rules would no longer count as thinking or drawing conclusions from premisses. There is even some sense in the *Tractatus*'s adherence to the meaning-body picture, for example to the claim that the equivalence of ~~ p with p follows from the essential nature of negation as expressed in a truth-table definition of ' ~ '. This myth about symbols too is the product of an imperfect grasp of conceptual connections (in this case, of the interlocking criteria for understanding ' ~ ' and for understanding the truth-table for ' ~ '). Wittgenstein revolved the whole of his philosophy of logic through 180°, but this did nothing towards rehabilitating Frege's conception of logic.

φιλοσοφία: εἰκὼν καὶ εἶδος 37

The picture of philosophy sketched in the *Investigations* is not by any means wholly negative. Positive suggestions grow off the same root-stock as the criticisms of scientific conceptions of philosophy, namely the autonomy of grammar. The fact that the rules of grammar are in perfect logical order, however heterogeneous and unsystematic they may seem, has the dramatic consequence that the doubts, paradoxes, perplexities, and accusations of incoherence marshalled against them by philosophers must rest on misconceptions and confusions. The kind of reflection which reaches its acme in the works of great philosophers is what generates the need for the clarificatory activity which is the proper labour of philosophers. The importance and pervasiveness of philosophical confusion gives this task its immense significance. In each case the aim is nothing less than a perfectly clear view of those parts of the network of rules of grammar in which our thinking is prone to become entangled.

One consequence of this idea is that much philosophical clarification is strictly purpose-relative and context-dependent. Since grammar is in perfect order, whenever its application proceeds without any hitches the philosopher has no employment. Clarification here would be as idle as the attempt to repair a machine that is running smoothly and efficiently. Conversely, when hitches do arise, the philosopher's business is solely to remove them, to make these particular problems disappear. A procedure which works in one case is thereby vindicated in that case, even if it has no general utility. If, for example, somebody is plunged into perplexity because he views rules as Platonic entities, it may be helpful to encourage him to think of a sentence as an instrument and of its meaning as its use and then to consider a rule to be a sentence used in a distinctive range of normative activities. Or somebody puzzled about how an ostensive definition can explain the meaning of a word may find illumination in regarding a sample as a symbol and an ostensive definition as a rule licensing the substitution of one partly concrete symbol for another verbal one. Philosophers standardly object that clarifications such as these do not cover every case or that they raise as many problems as they solve; for example, viewing a rule as a sentence with a particular use fails to account for the intelligibility of the statement that two sentences may formulate the same rule, and treating a sample as a sign does not show the nonsensicality of the request to translate a particular sample (for example, a metre-stick) into French! Such objections are inappropriate. The crucial matter is that each particular explanation does remove a particular problem, that it does serve a particular therapeutic purpose. Its failure to provide a panacea, or even the possibility that it may be used elsewhere to generate new confusions, does not detract from this concrete achievement. Conversely, the fact that an idea dissolves a wide range of problems generates no presumption that it will cure every confusion. To insist that quantification theory must provide a synopsis of all sound forms of reasoning, even those involving adverbs, modality, and tenses, is as silly as the accusation that penicillin is worthless unless it cures every disease. Relativity to specific purposes differentiates the criteria for satisfactoriness of philosophical clarifications from those for the correctness of scientific explanations. It further generates a resemblance with attempts to expose new aspects of things, say of works of art. A percipient observer may, for example, reveal an elaborate geometrical symmetry in a painting by Ucello, thus adding a new dimension to appreciation of this particular work. The value of this insight is independent of whether a similar structure can be discerned in any other Renaissance painting. Philosophical elucidations share this autonomy of aspect-seeing. Fascination with the scientific canon of generality results in unwarranted contempt for valuable achievements.

Wittgenstein diagnosed the principal sources of philosophical misunderstanding as misleading analogies in language and simplistic pictures of the world. We are inclined to presume that expressions of the same syntactic form must have identical uses; for example that numerals name Platonic entities because they are employed as nouns, that equations describe relations among numbers because they are read as declarative sentences, or that all generalisations have the same logical role because they exemplify the same sentence structure. We also unreflectively apply a host of pictures; for example the inner/outer picture of the relation of mind and behaviour, the localisation of thinking in the head, the conception of speech as the encoding of thoughts, and the notion of communication as the transfer of thoughts from one mind to another. Philosophers take these data and ruthlessly follow up their implications, undeterred by apparent absurdity. This is not simply the perpetration of blunders by the intellectually deranged. Rather, it manifests the extent to which philosophical confusion is the product of the will, not of the intellect, and hence it indicates the necessity for a kind of conversion to eliminate deep misunderstanding. Philosophical confusion often betrays desires and passions that we all share to some degree. There is a real *craving for generality*. We are dissatisfied with the variety and circumstance-dependent applicability of explanations of meaning; we demand something more homogeneous, systematic, and elegant. We do not respect a procedure of clarifying a particular domain of grammar which has no wider applicability. Similarly, we are deeply *attached* to certain fundamental pictures. We struggle to preserve them when they are threatened by recalcitrant 'data', cleaving to them as our only bulwark against the discomforts of intellectual chaos. To many it must seem that surrendering the notion of hidden depth and unity in language would make any investigation of grammar flat, stale, and unprofitable. Though we are frequently captive to pictures, this is generally in accord with our own volition. Prising somebody away from his own desires and passions is an enterprise of the utmost delicacy and one requiring infinite ingenuity and resourcefulness.

The methods for eliminating the confusions to which philosophers are prey cannot be circumscribed in advance.

Philosophy unties the knots in our thinking, which we have tangled up in an absurd way; but to do that, it must make movements which are just as complicated as the knots. Although the *result* of philosophy is simple, its methods for arriving there cannot be so.[46]

Occasionally something resembling theory-construction in science proves useful. The invention of the calculus of first-order predicate logic broke the tyranny of the traditional doctrines that all judgements had subject-predicate structure and that all genuine inferences were syllogistic: it simply presented an attractive and workable alternative. But even here such an invention threatens to foster a new set of confusions unless it is explicitly treated as a model of comparison, not as a theory portraying the ideal case to which everything really approximates.

Other methods are often efficacious. One is to expose as nonsensical the questions to which puzzle-generating theories are meant to provide the answers. An appropriate counterquestion may reveal an underlying confusion or a bizarre presupposition. It may successfully make fun of a supposedly deep problem. The question motivating semantic investigations in philosophy and linguistics alike is, 'How do we understand sentences that we have never encountered before?' The illusion that this question makes sense rests partly on a misassimilation of understanding to the category of processes or acts. If understanding is seen to be an ability, then the question becomes as absurd as the question 'How do you own a house?' or 'How do you have the ability to break a twig?' The puzzle about understanding novel sentences is often rephrased as the question 'How is it possible for a competent speaker of English to know the meanings of *infinitely many* sentences?' Should we deny that anybody does understand infinitely many sentences? Or should we clutch our heads in amazement and exclaim 'How wonderful — to learn to understand infinitely many sentences, and in so short a time! How clever we are'?[47] Such reflections manifest confusion about what it means to speak of the infinite. 'If you say "How terrific!", if your head reels — you can be sure [that you have] the wrong image.'[48] Philosophical questions are often in desperate need of clarification, and they may lose any aura of mystery upon careful inspection.

Pictures underlying theory-coinstruction in philosophy also require investigation. They often feed on one-sided diets of examples. To consider language as a system seems natural, but we readily slip from this harmless picture into the view that rules of grammar must be uniform in kind and unified within a single axiomatic structure. This conception of a system is exemplified by Euclidean geometry, but not by many structures to which we unhesitatingly apply the term 'system'[49] (for example, the Imperial system of weights and measures, the British transport system, or the system of allocating children to neighbourhood high-schools!). We forget that systems may be more or less systematic and that there is no prima facie case at all for likening the grammar of English to an axiomatised calculus! One useful method for countering such distortions is to highlight differences among what is subsumed under a given concept, to stress that apparent differences are real (for example, that explanations of meaning do exemplify a variety of patterns) and to issue reminders that in grammar all differences are big differences. Other methods include inventing intermediate or deviant cases, imagining facts of nature to be altered, and pinpointing absurd consequences of apparently straightforward applications of apparently clear pictures. The basic thrust of Wittgenstein's procedures is to show the disutility of forcing phenomena under Procrustean forms of representation and to demonstrate the baselessness of philosophical scruples arising from their resistance.

Wittgenstein's conception of philosophy is in head-on collision with the pervasive scientific conception. Philosophy consists in purpose-relative clarifications of grammar. Properly understood this excludes the legitimacy of any form of theory-construction. Attempts to render grammar uniform and systematic yield only illusory extensions of grammar, since the products lack the normative status of rules. There is no 'action at a distance' in grammar.[50] Attempts to support what cannot in principle be justified (or criticised) are as futile as erecting papier mâché columns to improve the stability of a skyscraper.[51] Justifications of language-use come to an end within the rules of grammar. The scientific conception of philosophy leads to the proliferation of nonsense. It does not tackle the confusions giving the impetus to theory-construction, and it diverts attention away from the paradigms which its theories embroider. The impulse towards simplification, schematisation, generalisation, and idealisation is powerful. In Wittgenstein's view it is as it were the original sin of the intellect. It makes the construction of scientific theories possible — and philosophy necessary!

6. Reflections of Philosophy

However relevant they may be to the conduct of philosophers, all the preceding remarks occupy the utmost heights of abstraction. Here one encounters no friction from the ether, and the visibility is always perfect. Yet in this realm there is no place to stand and nothing to be seen. Let us descend to specifics and see if we can see more clearly what previously seemed shrouded in gloom and smog. A sharpened awareness of their different conceptions of philosophy might give deeper understanding of some central remarks in the writings of Frege and Wittgenstein. Conversely, differences in the interpretation of apparently similar remarks may give some substance to the schematic and abstract description of a fundamental contrast in their philosophical goals, methods, and results.

Nothing so like, it seems, as these two remarks: 'The reference of a sentence is the True or the False' and 'An arithmetical equation is a rule of grammar'. Both appear to announce rather surprising results of philosophical investigations. Frege claimed to have discovered two new logical objects. He also boldly corrected the widespread idea that truth and falsity are properties of thoughts; the relation of a thought to a truth or falsity is not that of an object to a property, but of a sense to its reference. Wittgenstein refrained from similar pronouncements; *ex officio*, as a philosopher, he could make no discoveries in grammar and formulate no philosophical theses. None the less, his remark about equations is not something that everyone concedes; it does not seem to be a truism that merely makes explicit something familiar that we have temporarily lost from sight and need to be reminded of. On the contrary, it seems to many to be a blunder since characterising equations as *rules* apparently collides with our calling arithmetic a body of *truths* which are objects of *knowledge* established by *proofs*. To block off this damning verdict some defence will be required. This seems analogous to constructing a case in support of a thesis, and the conclusion, if vindicated, seems to have the status of a creative insight into the nature of mathematics wholly comparable to Frege's claim that arithmetical truths are propositions of pure logic. Wittgenstein even (delicately) corrected the nearly universal opinion that equations are descriptions of relations among numbers. Apart from some hair-splitting about applying such terms as 'thesis' and 'discovery', there seem to be no fundamental differences in the status of Frege's and Wittgenstein's remarks. Each calls for elucidation and defence, and discharging this task seems in principle no different in the two cases.

Frege's thesis has met a hostile reception. He had no good reason, it is thought, to extend the sense/reference distinction from proper names to sentences (and to concept-words), and he gave no cogent grounds for preferring truth-values to facts as referents of sentences. Some of his admirers declare it to be a gratuitous blunder to introduce a pair of logical *objects* as the referents of *sentences* since this obscures his alleged earlier insight into the fundamental difference in the semantic roles of sentences and proper names. Some of his critics note that his argument purporting to show that truth and falsity are not properties of thoughts, but rather the reference of thoughts, would with equal propriety prove that being analytic, *a priori*, or exaggerated are not properties of thoughts either. It is also easy to expose defects in Frege's supplementary thesis that facts are true thoughts, that is, that facts belong to the 'realm of sense' and therefore are not even

φιλοσοφία: εἰκὼν καὶ εἶδος   43

candidates for being the referents of thoughts. His explanation of 'the True' and 'the False' are scarcely pellucid; nothing corresponding to these names has swum into view in others' logical telescopes, and this lacuna threatens to undermine his mature conception of a concept (as a function whose value is always a truth-value). To cap matters, philosophers have discerned no serious motivation for the introduction of the True and the False. In the machinery of Frege's philosophy of logic, this seems to be an idling wheel, a mere ornament intended to achieve some debatable metaphysical symmetry or economy.

Wittgenstein's remark has had equally bad press notices. He is held to have given no compelling justification for calling equations rules of grammar. On the contrary, Moore and Waismann both argued that he had obviously stretched the term 'grammar' in characterising arithmetic as part of the grammar of our language; if this remark were not treated as a recommendation to extend the application of 'grammar' for the purpose of dissolving philosophical problems, it would be mere nonsense in their opinion. Many other philosophers object to his calling equations rules. It is beyond doubt that equations are not acknowledged *paradigms* of rules; although the concept of a rule is a family resemblance concept appropriately explained by examples and a similarity-rider, it would hardly accord with accepted practice to include '16 + 28 = 44' among the standard examples in an explanation of what 'rule' means. Equally, it would seem bizarre to claim that this equation if what *is called* 'a rule', even though the possibility of substituting 'is called' for 'is' is one hallmark of a rule of grammar. The only straightforward defence of Wittgenstein's use of 'rule' in this context is to argue that he characterised rules functionally (in terms of their distinctive roles in justifying and criticising performances, in teaching rule-governed practices, etc.); that he noted that arithmetical equations have the roles characteristic of rules; and that he concluded that equations are rules from the premiss that whatever has the function of a rule is a rule. This premiss might be criticised as a bit of creative legislation about the concept of a rule. Alternatively, the conclusion drawn might be treated as a *reductio*. Equations are paradigms of true propositions, of *vérités éternelles*; they are standard examples of truths known with absolute certainty; and they are established by rigorous proofs and calculations. All of these features clash with the immediate implications of calling equations rules. There is equally dramatic conflict with Wittgenstein's supplementary remarks on arithmetic. The concept of a proof seems to be distorted in the claim that a mathematical proof is the invention of a new rule of grammar rather than the discovery of a new truth. Moreover, the central idea that rules of grammar are autonomous and not answerable to any external reality seems to require the possibility of alternative arithmetics, and that in turn seems unintelligible against the background of the claim that the conclusion of any rigorous proof must already be contained in the premisses. All of these objections might be countered by further investigations into the grammar of our language. One might contend, for example, that 'true' and 'false', 'certain' or 'known', 'proof', etc. have different meanings when applied to arithmetical equations and simple empirical propositions. There is some doubt whether this defence would be successful and even whether it would carry Wittgenstein's blessing. But there is no doubt that the remark that equations are rules of grammar is philosophically contentious and that it is central to his extensive reflections on the nature of mathematics and logic. It lies at the very foundation of his analysis of mathematical proofs, his explorations of alternative forms of representation, and his conception of the autonomy of grammar. If it is mistaken, the whole of his philosophy of mathematics will collapse and little of value will be salvageable from the rubble.

In their ruminations philosophers take these two theses to be essentially similar. By respectable (and hence predictable) chains of reasoning they arrive at strikingly different conclusions in the two cases. Frege's thesis is held to be mistaken but peripheral to his philosophy of logic. We may distinguish (as he did not) between an expression's having a reference (or semantic value) and its having a referent (its standing for an entity), and then we may purge all mention of the True and the False from his writings without damaging the structure of his thinking. This charitable strategy is followed by most expositors of Frege's work. Wittgenstein's thesis is also thought to be erroneous, but it is fundamental to his philosophy of mathematics. It is the centrepiece of a revisionary conception of mathematics comparable to formalism or Intuitionism. This leaves only two stark options: *either* we accept it and then glory in (or try to explain away) its paradoxical consequences *or* we reject it and dismiss the whole of Wittgenstein's philosophy of mathematics as grounded in a basic misunderstanding. This latter uncharitable course is adopted by

φιλοσοφία: εἰκὼν καὶ εἶδος 45

most commentators. Parallel reflections thus lead to two quite dissimilar results.

Both conclusions are radically mistaken. The reasoning has gone decisively astray before it even begins. It is presupposed that the two theses are closely comparable. No attention is addressed to the question, what question each thesis is meant to answer or what purpose each is meant to serve. Did Frege arrive at the idea that the reference of a sentence is the True or the False by reflecting on the use of the words 'true' and 'false'? Or did he conclude that facts are true thoughts by careful examination of the concept of a fact? These suggestions seem laughable; viewed in such a way, Frege's reasoning would be confused, flimsy, and naïve. Did Wittgenstein employ the remark that equations are rules of grammar as a premiss for demonstrating that equations are not tautologies? Or did he base on it the claim that arithmetic has no foundations? These proposals too seem ridiculous; reasoning *more geometrico* is not a feature of Wittgenstein's philosophical investigations. It is important to clarify the motivation for formulating each of these theses and to elucidate the role each is to be understood to play in the context of wider philosophical reflection. There is no such thing as grasping the significance of such a philosophical thesis independently of understanding the architectonic of the thought of its author. Seen aright, these theses are quite unlike, and the standard verdicts passed upon them manifest basic misunderstandings. Indeed, both are inverted images of the truth.

Frege's identification of the True and the False as the references of sentences is not the product of the sort of philosophical reflections typical of attempts to construct theories of truth. To state that a thought is true if it stands for or designates the True is not a version of the correspondence theory of truth; that would have the absurd consequence that every true thought corresponds to one and the same thing, namely the True! Nor can one ascertain the truth of the thought that three is a prime number by careful scrutiny of the True; rather must one examine whether the number three falls under the concept of being a prime. Because it is not targeted on these questions, Frege's thesis does not belong to the genre of philosophical theories of truth. For this reason it is also not an optional extra stuck together with other poorly motivated and loosely integrated claims that jointly comprise Frege's philosophy of logic. On the contrary, the prose accompanying his formal system, both in *Begriffsschrift* and in *Grundgesetze*, has the status of a rigorous philosophical theory explaining the nature and articulation of his concept-script, and the thesis that the reference of a sentence is the True or the False is a vital component of his conception of logic in *Grundgesetze*. One should take seriously his commitment to the scientific conception of philosophy and therefore make it a primary task to clarify the precise role of this major thesis in his theory-construction.

From this vantage point two matters stand out. First, the True and the False are directly related to *function*/argument analysis which Frege himself pin-pointed as the key to his logical system; these two objects are the values of the functions which he called concepts and relations, and hence they are what any well-formed formula of concept-script designates (since every such formula presents something as the value of a function for an argument). It is evident that Frege did not conceive of the possibility of a *function* without *values*, and since a formula in concept-script is a *complete* expression of a judgement or thought, the values assigned to these expressions must be *objects*. Originally, in *Begriffsschrift*, he took judgeable-contents to be these objects and he treated concepts as functions which had judgeable-contents as their values; later, in *Grundgesetze*, he replaced judgeable-contents by the two truth-values in this role and therefore redefined concepts as functions whose values are always truth-values. In his view the very possibility of function/argument analysis of logical inference rests on the thesis that every formula of concept-script, indeed every declarative sentence, stands for an object. If the True and the False were expelled from this position in his mature theory, some other objects would have to take their places. So the whole logical system of *Grundgesetze* rests on the proposition that the two truth-values are the references of formulae expressing thoughts! What many philosophers now regard as peripheral (because of subsequent evolution in the concept of a function) Frege considered to be ὁ ὀμφαλὸς τοῦ ὀμφαλοῦ.

The second conspicuous point is the direct relation of the True (and the False) to Frege's logicism. He had concluded in *Grundlagen* that natural numbers must be defined as *extensions* of concepts, and therefore the formal proof that every true equation of arithmetic is a proposition of logic demanded a strengthening of the system of *Begriffsschrift* by addition of a function mapping each concept onto its extension. According to his view, this had to be a *logical* operation; by our logical faculties alone we must be able to apprehend the extension of a concept from the concept itself.[52] *Calculation* must suffice to determine the value of this function for each concept as argument. But since the extension of a first-level concept is the set of objects which fall under the concept, that is, the set of objects of which the concept is (*truly*) predicable, only by taking the values of a first-level concept (function) to be the True and the False could Frege satisfy this overriding constraint. No other objects, if taken to be the values of first-level concepts, would allow a calculation of the extension of a concept from a table correlating each argument with the value of the function for this argument. Discovery of the True and the False was a *sine qua non* of Frege's logicism, and hence in a second respect the thesis that the reference of a thought is a truth-value is a cornerstone of his philosophy. To see this as a gratuitous blunder is truly to stand Frege's thinking on its head.

Wittgenstein's observation that arithmetical equations are rules of grammar shares one important feature with Frege's thesis: it too is not the product of the sorts of reflections typical of modern philosophy of mathematics. It is not in the least parallel with Platonism, Intuitionism, formalism, logicism, finitism, or conventionalism. It is not addressed to the questions 'What is the ground of mathematical truth?' and 'What is the source of mathematical knowledge?' Therefore it is altogether misleading to pin the label 'conventionalism' on to Wittgenstein's later philosophy of mathematics in spite of his calling mathematical propositions rules of grammar or norms of representation. For conventionalism is intended to be a philosophical theory which provides the most elegant, economical, and lucid answers to these questions, whereas he argued the questions themselves to be nonsensical and therefore all the competing answers to be incoherent. Objectors to his philosophy of mathematics miss this point, and so too do defenders of his conventionalism (often dubbed 'full-blooded' or 'radical conventionalism' to distinguish it from the now unfashionable version of conventionalism associated with the Vienna Circle).

In most other respects, however, Wittgenstein's thesis is totally unlike Frege's. It does not formulate the presupposition of any formal theory. Nor does it serve as a premiss in any philosophical deduction. Wittgenstein never argued (as others often do) that since equations are rules of grammar they cannot be said to be true or that they cannot express genuine knowledge. He never proposed the view that proofs in mathematics are not discoveries because mathematical propositions are rules, not truths; on the contrary, he urged us to look and see what the role of mathematical proofs is and to avoid at all costs the dogmatic prejudice that we already know this without any investigation. His employment of the 'thesis' that equations are rules of grammar has no similarity with the role of a component proposition of a theory: *nothing* depends on it. Instead, it is used as a way of summing up a vast array of independent remarks about our use of equations, the function of arithmetical computations, the grammar of statements of counting and measuring, the use of 'true', 'false', 'believe', 'know', 'certain', etc., in connection with equations, and so on. It is always a terminus of philosophical clarification, never the starting point. Even if we do not judge it to be *das erlösende Wort*, it is certainly not an explanatory doctrine.

In fact Wittgenstein's remark can be characterised more positively. His primary aim in philosophy of mathematics, as elsewhere, was to direct attention away from the forms of expressions to their uses. He thought that we are unduly influenced by the fact that we read an equation as a declarative sentence; hence we tend, *ab initio*, to assimilate 'Two and three make five' to 'The combustion of hydrogen yields water' and to suppose that both sentences are *descriptions* differing merely in subject-matter. This leads straight to the standard questions in philosophy of mathematics about the grounds of mathematical truth and the source of mathematical knowledge. Wittgenstein thought that extricating ourselves from these conceptual snares presupposes a clarification of the distinctive *uses* of mathematical propositions, especially of the many radical differences between their employment and the employment of simple empirical propositions. The whole point of his calling equations rules of grammar is to characterise their use (and not, for example, to give a defence of empiricism). This remark is an answer to the question 'What role do equations have in our practice of speaking, especially in counting and measuring?' This is not the question addressed by *any* standard philosophy of mathematics. Moreover, in answering it by calling equations rules of grammar, he made no doubtful assumption that whatever functions as a rule is a rule or that everything labelled a rule of grammar is homogeneous with familiar rules of English syntax; nor did he commit himself to the claim that it is a truism to call equations rules or to say that they belong to grammar. On the other hand, the points encapsulated in these creative insights are not disputable theses, but familiar platitudes about the uses of equations in justifying or criticising inferences among empirical statements, in teaching children how to count and measure, etc. The role of his calling equations rules of grammar is to issue a reminder of familiar but unnoticed features of their use, features uncontroversially characteristic of the use of paradigmatic rules of grammar.

Wittgenstein's remark is not an axiom or presupposition for an elaborate philosophical theory. It has a different form of centrality in respect of his philosophy of mathematics: it epitomises a widely ramifying and barely surveyable array of observations about the use of number-words, the role of calculations and proofs, the offices of logical and metalogical calculi, etc. In fact, it is a paradigm of the formulation of an *Übersicht*, and it demonstrates the philosophical importance of this enterprise in the clarification of concepts. Such a remark is certainly a grammatical one: it makes a point about the use of symbols. But the insight embodied in it is *analogical.* It is not part of the grammar of 'rule' that equations are called rules (of grammar). Nor is it part of the grammar of 'grammar' that they belong among the rules of grammar. (By contrast it is part of the grammar of 'proposition' that 'Two plus three makes five' is what is called the expression of a proposition.) Hence to claim that equations *really are* rules of grammar would be a form of dogmatism (and it would involve an extension of the concept of a rule of grammar). Dogmatism is to be avoided by treating rules of grammar as *objects of comparison.*[53] Wittgenstein urged a strategy of comparing equations with rules of grammar in respect of their employment in order to dissolve most of the perplexities central to philosophy of mathematics. (One parallel manoeuvre is his comparing ostensive definitions with substitution-rules for the symbols to undermine philosophical misconceptions about the connection of language and reality. Another is his likening avowals of sensations with natural expressions of sensations to break the spell of the notion that each subject has privileged access to, and infallible knowledge of, his own inner states.) One deliberate analogy is introduced as an antidote to another natural one. For it is not part of the grammar of 'description' that 'Two plus three makes five' is what is called a description (or that this is a paradigm used in explanations of the concept of a description), and yet we are strongly inclined to assimilate equations to paradigmatic descriptions because of their grammatical forms. The comparison of equations with rules is meant to relieve this mental cramp. Likewise, it is not part of the grammar of 'corresponds to reality' that the proposition expressed by '2 + 3 = 5' is a paradigm of something's corresponding to reality, and yet because we call this equation true we are inclined to suppose that some reality must correspond to it. A comparison with propositions of grammar is meant to break this spell, for we have not the slightest inclination to suppose that there is some external justification ('deep in the nature of things'!) for the rule that the third-person present tense is standardly formed in English by adding an 's' to the root of a verb. (The autonomy of grammar, the arbitrariness of rules for the use of words, is transparent in the term 'grammar' itself.) The apparently problematic status of Wittgenstein's remark that equations are rules of grammar, and the correlative perception of a need to defend it against objections, is a product of failing to apprehend its role as an *Übersicht* of the role of mathematical symbols. Moreover, the analogical character of such a proposition together with its status as a grammatical remark makes clear the immense scope for *creativity* and *originality* in philosophical investigations. Not everything philosophical has the character of a truism, but that does not imply that there is scope for quasi-scientific discoveries or explanations.

Frege's thesis is integral to a vision, indeed to his whole philosophy of logic. A survey of the global structure of his thought makes sense of his stating that the reference of a sentence is the True or the False. Does it make sense of what he stated? This would now generally be judged to be unintelligible. There are serious objections to his taking judgements, truth-values, or thoughts to be the values of functions. The notion of a *logical* connection between concepts and their extensions is incoherent too (and arguably symptomatic of a deeper incoherence in conflating empirical propositions with grammatical ones). If we sweep away the defective foundations of Frege's formal logic, we are left merely with a notation and a calculus. This realisation has an important philosophical implication: even if more recent philosophy has built a coherent exposition of the predicate calculus within the framework of a general semantic theory, the calculus itself is independent of the so-called foundations since it was viable without this support. This suggests that it is absurd to seek any justification for the propositions of logic, whether justification be

φιλοσοφία: εἰκὼν καὶ εἶδος 51

sought in the depth grammar of language, the essence of human thought, or the logical structure of the world.

Wittgenstein's remark is also integral to his vision of mathematics, indeed to his whole point of view in addressing philosophical problems. A survey of his comments about philosophy and of his extensive observations about mathematics makes sense of his calling equations rules of grammar. But does it make sense of what he stated? Attempts to answer this question direct attention to the grammar of the terms 'rule' and 'grammar', and that in turn inaugurates disputation about whether there are any *facts* of grammar and about whether there are any conclusive *proofs* or *refutations* of grammatical propositions. Debate then comes to centre on epistemological issues about rules for the use of words and objective criteria for correctness. Even if sound observations about concepts are made in the course of this debate, they are uttered in the wrong register and put to misguided use; there is wilful neglect of carefully observing (without prejudice) how concepts are employed and of quietly weighing up these linguistic data. To engage in the standard debate betrays a misapprehension both of the relation of meaning to explanations of meaning and of the normative functions of explanations in speech. In order to short-circuit all of this epistemological controversy, one must return to the original question and replace it by a better one. The crucial issue is not whether Wittgenstein's statement makes sense, but rather what kind of sense it is meant to make. This might substitute fruitful investigation of concepts for fruitless general debate. If our spirit were willing and our intellects less weak, we might learn as much from comparing equations with rules of grammar as we do by organising detailed reflections on musical styles around such dicta as 'Chromatic harmony is the heart of baroque music' or 'Counterpoint did not disappear in the nineteenth century, but was transformed and broadened'. Philosophical understanding is impoverished by too narrow a conception of the possible forms that understanding may take.

Since both Frege and Wittgenstein were attentive to the nature of their own philosophical activity, there is a strong presumption in both cases that practice matches theory. We risk failing to understand all of their major ideas unless we connect their particular remarks with their general conceptions of philosophy.

52 φιλοσοφία: εἰκὼν καὶ εἶδος

7. Big Bangs and Perceptual Motion

Explanatory theories are wholly unlike synopses (*Übersichten*) of rules of 'grammar', and the methods appropriate for scientific investigations contrast with the methods productive of insight into conceptual connections. This incompatibility amounts to a clash of *Weltanschauungen*. The spirit informing his writing, Wittgenstein remarked.

> is different from the one which informs the vast stream of European and American civilization in which all of us stand. *That* spirit expresses itself in an onwards movement, in building ever larger and more complicated structures: the other in striving after clarity and perspicuity in no matter what structure ... [T]he first adds one construction to another, moving on and up, as it were, from one stage to the next, while the other remains where it is and what it tries to grasp is always the same.[54]

Philosophy so conceived sets itself the formidable task of standing firm against the flood tide of contemporary thought. It is at risk of being swept into the ocean of science. Hence in a deep sense it is now opposed to science. Its proper business is not to contribute to physics or mathematics, or even to redesign experiments or to interfere with procedures of proof. It should not meddle in the *internal affairs of the sciences*. Rather its task is to criticise the wider significance commonly claimed for scientific or mathematical findings (Cantor's diagonal proof, Russell's paradox, Gödel's incompleteness theorem, Heisenberg's uncertainty principle, etc.) and also to question the presupposition or overt declaration that the way of science is alone appropriate to any serious intellectual enquiry. The aim is merely to curb the imperialist propensities of science. This provides ground enough for bitter conflict.

Philosophy according to this specification is difficult to locate on the intellectual map. It cannot be circumscribed in the ways standard for other disciplines. It has no distinctive subject-matter: there are no indispensible philosophical concepts and no body of philosophical truths. Everything falls within its purview. Similarly, *there are no indispensable philosophical methods and none that are sacrosanct*. Any procedure may be appropriate, even questions,

φιλοσοφία: εἰκὼν καὶ εἶδος   53

jokes, metaphors, or imaginative invention. Philosophy cannot be ranked alongside the sciences, or above or below them. Being incomparable with them, it may seem anomalous and amorphous.

It is tempting to assimilate this contrast in conceptions of philosophy to some familiar distinction. We might treat it as an instance of the opposition between optimism and pessimism: the optimists believe that they confront problems which can be solved by dint of rigorous and systematic thinking, whereas the pessimists contend that the important questions are mysteries which transcend our powers to arrive at solutions.[55] Or we might view the rift in philosophy as nothing deeper than a contrast in style of expository writing: some prefer their arguments dressed in Gothic letters, logical symbolism, and algebraic computations, whereas others insist on classic English prose fully intelligible to the interested layman. Such reinterpretations of the issue are radically mistaken, tending to trivialise a profound difference. There is a continental divide within the tradition of analytic philosophy — separate watersheds of thought resting on differing insights and different forms of reasoning. A bird's-eye view of the boundary is difficult to attain. Perhaps the contrast is most illuminatingly characterised by dividing philosophers into two groups: one finds satisfaction in thinking that the world, language, and the mind are full of mysteries, perplexities, and deep antinomies, calling for almost magical solutions by reference to theories of unbelievable sophistication, and the other discerns no value in questions and answers that are not crystal clear, intelligible to any thoughtful person, and beyond dispute. The first lives for the gradual penetration of hidden depths and resents any demonstration that their problems grow out of confusion; they view the second as blind or philistine and their reflections as question-begging relative to alternative theories. The second abhors dubious assertions in reply to nonsensical questions and thirsts for perfect clarity: the first are seen as mystery-mongers who participate in worthless verbal rituals and cannot distinguish utter nonsense from profound abstract reflection. As Wittgenstein noted, no intellectual difference could cut more deeply.

Although philosophers hive themselves off from each other, some of the products of their reflections manage to cross the boundary between them. Wittgenstein's writings are sometimes argued to embody an embryonic theory of the mind or a novel theory of meaning,[56] and hence his private language argument may be incorporated into the work of some theory-builders. Conversely, something intended to be part of a theory may be accorded a different value by a philosopher seeking for a puzzle-dissolving synopsis of grammar; it may be reinterpreted as a form of representation of rules of meaning, a model for comparison with familiar rules. The use of definite descriptions may be compared (and contrasted!) with that of proper names,[57] or formulae in quantification theory may be compared (and contrasted!) with ordinary forms of generalisation.[58] What must be avoided is treating these paradigms as idealisations to which everything really conforms despite appearances to the contrary. A form of representation is legitimate and often helpful provided that its application takes care of itself. Forcing it upon phenomena produces distortion. Desire for depth induces an insouciance about obvious differences. The sanction against this activity is a choice between falsity and vacuity. If, for example, a philosopher discovers that all words are 'really' names, then what he asserts is false if he uses 'name' correctly, and otherwise it involves an apparently pointless determination to redefine 'name' as a synonym for 'word'. Provided forms of representation are not mistaken for revelations of essence or panaceas for all puzzles, they have a legitimate place in anybody's philosophy. Only the practice of total immersion is dangerous.

Most general remarks about philosophy are intended to effect a conversion to a new point of view. The reader is meant to be swept along on a wave of enthusiasm to adopt a novel outlook on a vast range of issues. Perhaps he is supposed to see that the philosophy of language holds the key to all philosophical problems, or that the principle of verifiability produces instant answers to every question. He is at least offered the prospect of immediate transport to the Promised Land, even if he is so benighted that he fails to take this up. My purpose is different: not to drive anybody out of the paradise of the scientific conception of philosophy, but rather to produce a travel brochure. There is a failure of imagination to be remedied. To somebody who has lived always in a jungle, it may be unintelligible how anybody might wish to live in a desert or even in the Garden of Eden. This essay is meant to depict the pleasures of perpetual motion in philosophising, the unceasing examination of questions. It attempts to make comprehensible the philosophical merit in cultivating the sophisticated *naïveté* of the perceptive and intelligent alien who scrutinises our pattern of life,

φιλοσοφία: εἰκών καὶ εἶδος 55

thought, and speech. Possibly a certain clarity of vision, or even nobility of mind, may reward a philosopher for the discomforts of being a perpetual exile.[59]

Notes

1. Philosophy: Simulacrum and Form. The contrasting terms εἰκών and εἶδος are prominent in Plato's theory of forms. They carry the connotations: appearance and reality. In addition, εἰκών (icon) means image, and it is used to denote analogies and metaphors.
2. Our discussion is not about something trivial, but about how one ought to carry on philosophical reflection. (An Aristotelian modulation of *Republic*, 352d.)
3. Claims dogmatically stated here are explained and defended in G.P. Baker and P.M.S. Hacker, *Frege: Logical Excavations* (Oxford University Press, New York, and Basil Blackwell, Oxford, 1984).
4. F. Waismann, *How I See Philosophy*, ed. R. Harré (Macmillan, London, 1968), p. 15.
5. L. Wittgenstein, *Philosophical Investigations* (Blackwell, Oxford, 1953), section n 1 ff. For detailed analysis and criticism see G.P. Baker and P.M.S Hacker, *Wittgenstein: Understanding and Meaning* (Blackwell, Oxford, and Chicago University Press, 1980), pp. 33 ff.
6. Partly through the direct influence of Frege's thinking, exploitation of this paradigm reached its zenith in the logical atomism of Russell and Wittgenstein.
7. Frege, *Philosophical and Mathematical Correspondence* (Blackwell, Oxford, 1980).
8. Frege did not himself pioneer the application of function theory to the syntactical analysis of sentences (*pace* P.T. Geach, 'Frege' in G.E.M. Anscombe and P.T. Geach, *Three Philosophers* (Blackwell, Oxford, 1967), pp. 142 ff.).
9. A similar concept informed Boole's earlier construction of a logical algebra. 'The laws of thought, in all its processes of conception and of reasoning, in all those operations of which language is the expression or the instrument, are the same kind as are the acknowledged processes of Mathematics ... [H]uman thought, traced to its ultimate elements, reveals itself in mathematical forms.' G. Boole, *The Laws of Thought* (Dover, New York, 1958), pp. 422 f.
10. *Ludwig Wittgenstein and the Vienna Circle: Conversations Recorded by Friedrich Waismann* (Blackwell, Oxford, 1979), p. 182.
11. L. Wittgenstein, *Remarks on the Foundations of Mathematics* (1st edn) (Blackwell, Oxford, 1964), Part II, section 5.
12. G. Frege, *Begriffsschrift*, Preface.
13. Frege, *Correspondence*, p. 63, and *Posthumous Writings* (Blackwell, Oxford, 1979), p. 266.
14. Cf. M. Dummett, *Frege: Philosophy of Language* (Duckworth, London, 1981), pp. 8 ff.
15. Cf. J. Lyons, *Semantics*, (Cambridge, 1977), vol. 1, pp. 147 f and vol. II, p. 458.
16. L. Wittgenstein, *Tractatus Logico-philosophicus* (Routledge & Kegan Paul, London, 1961), 6.12, 6.1231 ff., and 6.13.
17. Wittgenstein, *Philosophical Investigations*, section 308.
18. A critical examination of these typically unexamined questions is the chief business of G.P. Baker and P.M.S. Hacker, *Language, Sense and Nonsense* (Basil Blackwell, Oxford and New York, 1984).

19. J. Joubert, *Pensées Essais etc.* (Paris, 1850), vol. 1, p. 170.
20. Cf. Neil Smith and Deirdre Wilson, *Modern Linguistics: The Results of Chomsky's Revolution* (Penguin, Harmondsworth, 1979), pp. 13f. and 31.
21. For example, M. Dummett, *Truth and Other Enigmas* (Duckworth, London, 1978), pp. 440f. and 454f.
22. N. Chomsky, *Rules and Representations* (Blackwell, Oxford, 1980), p. 90.
23. Wittgenstein, *Philosophical Investigations*, section 81.
24. Chomsky, *Rules and Representations*, p. 96.
25. Wittgenstein, *Philosophical Investigations*, section 129.
26. Wittgenstein, *Tractatus Logico-Philosophicus*, 6.53.
27. Cf. C. Wright, *Wittgenstein on the Foundations of Mathematics* (Duckworth, London, 1980), p. 262.
28. These points are fully elaborated in G.P. Baker and P.M.S. Hacker, *Wittgenstein: Rules, Grammar and Necessity* (Basil Blackwell, Oxford and New York, 1985).
29. Wittgenstein, *Philosophical Investigations*, section 90.
30. Ibid., sections 89, 91 and 129.
31. Ibid., sections 122-3.
32. Ibid., sections 124-8.
33. Ibid., section 109.
34. Wittgenstein, *Tractatus*, Preface.
35. L. Wittgenstein, *Notebooks 1914-1916* (Blackwell, Oxford, 1961), p. 23.
36. Ibid., p. 39.
37. Wittgenstein, *Philosophical Investigations*, section 133.
38. Ibid., section 132.
39. This provides the key to resolving two conundra in interpreting the *Investigations*. It is implied that philosophers err in answering such questions as 'What is language?' or 'What is a proposition?' by supposing that 'the answer to these questions is to be given once for all; and independently of any future experience' (section 92). Wittgenstein further states, 'The real discovery is the one that makes me capable of stopping doing philosophy when I want to' (section 133). Is the point not that what may be perplexing or misunderstood cannot be foreseen, so that what is needed to answer a request for clarification cannot be determined once and for all? And conversely, that failure of a specific clarification to resolve some future confusion does not detract from or call into question its satisfactoriness in eliminating a present one? Grammar is independent of future experience, but requirements for philosophical elucidations may differ from age to age.
40. Schlick popularised this interpretation of the *Tractatus*. Cf. M. Schlick, *Gesammelte Aufsätze* (Gerold, Vienna, 1938), pp. 130ff.
41. Wittgenstein, *Philosophical Investigations*, section 117.
42. Wittgenstein, *Tractatus Logico-Philosophicus*, 6.124.
43. Ibid., 6.124.
44. Wittgenstein, *Philosophical Investigations*, section 97.
45. A synopsis of these remarks is given in Baker and Hacker, *Wittgenstein: Rules, Grammar and Necessity*, pp. 307ff.
46. L. Wittgenstein, *Philosophical Remarks* (Blackwell, Oxford, 1975), section 2.
47. Cf. L. Wittgenstein, *Wittgenstein's Lectures on the Foundations of Mathematics*, ed. C. Diamond (Harvester, Hassocks, 1976), p. 31.
48. Ibid., p. 253.
49. Cf. Wittgenstein, *Philosophical Investigations*, section 100.
50. L. Wittgenstein, *The Blue and Brown Books* (Blackwell, Oxford), p. 14; and L. Wittgenstein, *Philosophical Grammar* (Blackwell, Oxford, 1974), p. 81.
51. Cf. Wittgenstein, *Philosophical Investigations*, section 217.
52. Frege, *Posthumous Writings*, p. 181.

53. Wittgenstein, *Philosophical Investigations*, section 130f.
54. Wittgenstein, *Philosophical Remarks*, p. 7.
55. This contrast is prominent in the writings of Chomsky (for example, *Rules and Representations*).
56. For example, Dummett, *Truth and Other Enigmas*, pp. 16ff. His suggestion for interpreting Wittgenstein as an 'anti-realist' was taken up and differently developed by G.P. Baker, 'Criteria: a New Foundation for Semantics', *Ratio*, 16 (1974), pp. 156ff; P.M.S. Hacker, *Insight and Illusion* (Oxford, 1972); and Wright, *Wittgenstein on the Foundations of Mathematics*.
57. Cf. Wittgenstein, *Philosophical Investigations*, section 79.
58. Wittgenstein, *Philosophical Remarks*, 87ff., and *Philosophical Grammar*, pp. 165ff.
59. This is a completely revised and largely redrafted version of an article first written in 1980 and published under the title 'Alternative Mind-Styles' in *Philosophical Grounds of Rationality: Intentions, Categories, Ends*, eds. Grandy and Warner (Oxford University Press, 1986). Some major themes have been dropped, some transformed, and some added. Section 6 is entirely new. The original stands to Mark II as εἰκασία to ἐπιστήμη.

Many of the ideas developed here arise out of research on Frege and Wittgenstein jointly carried out with my friend and colleague Peter Hacker. My intellectual debt to him is literally incalculable. Although much of my own thinking cannot be disentangled from his, there are many points where he would dissent from my exposition at least in respect of emphasis or nuance. More substantially, he expressly rejects part of what I have here sketched as Wittgenstein's use of 'rules of grammar' and of 'grammatical propositions'. Hence for many of the thoughts expressed (and for the expression of all the thoughts) I alone should be held responsible.

2 QUESTION TIME

Renford Bambrough

For philosophy and philosophers it is always question time. Most of the questions I am trying to answer here were set by the editor of this book in his letter of invitation to the contributors. The others have been drawn from conversations recollected in tranquillity.

'What made you decide to become a philosopher?' This question struck me first and most sharply. My answer to it has led me into my answers to the other questions in the editor's list, and to some further questions that they raise. I am asked to say how I perceive the present state of the subject, and the future I would most like to see. I am invited to explain the nature of my own work, why I consider that the topics I have worked on are philosophically important, and what areas I am most interested in examining in the immediate future. It is expected and hoped that the contributors will 'contribute some autobiographical material, together with some comment on the reasons why they have chosen to become philosophers'.

It makes straightforward sense to ask a person 'Why did you decide to become a solicitor?' (or a carpenter, shopkeeper, teacher or professional musician). There is no mystery about the question 'Why did you decide to become a British citizen?' (or a member of the Liberal Party, the Roman Catholic Church or the Aristotelian Society). It may be difficult to answer any of these questions. We may not remember, or may be unable to articulate, what first led us to seek ordination, join the Army or stand for Parliament; but the questions themselves are clear, and they ask for fair comment on matters of public or private interest. There are other questions that sound like these but raise difficulties of another order.

'What made you decide to become a woman?' This question can be intelligibly asked only of a woman. It cannot be asked of any woman, or of many women. For it can be asked only of a woman who has decided to become a woman. But has there ever been a woman who has become a woman by her own decision? What the newspapers call a sex-change is understood by the new woman as the revelation and acknowledgement and confirmation of a womanhood that was there from birth, unrecognised or disguised and disfigured by shame or shock.

'What made you decide to become an Englishman?' This question could be sensibly addressed only to a man who had decided to become an Englishman, and there is no such animal. It is by birth that an Englishman is an Englishman, and by birth that a woman is a woman.

It makes sense to ask of some British citizens why they decided to become British citizens. It makes sense to ask of some British citizens why they have decided to remain British citizens. It makes sense to speak of a person's having been a British citizen and having ceased to be a British citizen, or vice versa, and accordingly it makes sense to ask of some people why they have decided to be or not to be British citizens. But the typical British citizen has never decided to be or to remain a British citizen. The question has never arisen.

Being a British citizen is a birthright that I can lose or renounce. Being an Englishman or a woman is a birthright or birth-burden that its possessor or bearer cannot lose or renounce. You cannot by taking thought become or cease to be English or female any more than you can by taking thought add a cubit to your stature.

The short answer to the question 'What made you decide to become a philosopher?' might be the question 'What made *you* decide to become a human being?'

Being a philosopher is a birthright too, but one that it is possible to renounce or lose. It is not however a right or burden that it is possible to choose to acquire. It belongs to all human beings by birth, though many afterwards lose or renounce it. Nobody can acquire it except by birth.

This is not to deny, but to put in their place, some familiar facts that I might seem to be forgetting. There is much that is connected with philosophy that may be sought and found, acquired and lost. I may seek or find recognition as a philosophical author or lecturer. I may pursue the profession of teaching or writing philosophy. Ryle boasted and confessed:

> I myself am not ashamed but, when I happen to think of it, slightly complacent to have made, as a philosophy don, my own living — and quite a good living — for half a century; and I am not ashamed but thoroughly proud, when I think of them, to

have achieved, as a philosopher, certain offices and distinctions and to have exercised a bit of influence, authority and even modest powers.

('Fifty Years of Philosophy', *Philosophy*, 1976)

Doing these things is one mode of life that may be called that of being a philosopher. But these things are peripheral and inessential. None of them was done by Socrates. Philosophy is a vocation before it is a trade or profession, whether in the life of an individual thinker or in the history of human thought. Plato in the *Meno* and Wordsworth in the 'Ode on the Intimations of Immortality from Recollections of Early Childhood' remember and celebrate this truth about the human condition. Ryle does not sufficiently remember it because he is frying other fish. Societies for the promotion of philosophy for children do remember it but misconstrue its significance. Hare in 'Philosophical Discoveries' (*Mind*, 1960) and Wittgenstein in most of his work propound and enact it, and do so without falling into sentimentality or any of the other hazards that surround it.

Wordsworth puts it romantically, Plato classically, and Hare more prosaically, but what they all remind us of is the value of keeping open our lines of communication with our earliest learning. The need for this preservation of links with childhood is not confined to philosophy. By birthright we are all not only thinkers but also singers and dancers, poets and painters, teachers and story-tellers. This means that the professional singer or painter, poet or teacher, dancer or story-teller, is a professional in a different way from the solicitor or doctor, physicist or statistician. The same is true of the professional runner or jumper, rider or speaker, gardener or interior decorator, soldier, nurse or politician.

Like the runner or the writer or the ruler the thinker may become a professional but can never become an *expert*. Even the geniuses among thinkers or writers — Shakespeare and Tolstoy, Plato and Wittgenstein — are doing to a higher power something that we all do and need to do for ourselves. This affects the light in which the thinker is regarded and the role to which he is called. The mathematician and the physicist are allowed to be technical and abstruse. The philosopher and the poet, the sculptor and the novelist, are expected to remain in touch with their roots, which are also our roots. It is they and not the statistician and the biochemist who are accused of obscurantism and mystification when they fail to communicate with the ordinary understanding of the ordinary person.

When I heard Wittgenstein at the Cambridge Moral Sciences Club in 1946 and 1947 I had already formed, even if I could not so fully articulate, some of the convictions about philosophy and its role that I am setting out in this essay. Wittgenstein's sayings, and later his writings and the sayings and writings of John Wisdom, strengthened the convictions and assisted their articulation. In particular, Wittgenstein's reminder of the importance of reminders, his insistence on the need to 'go back to the teaching', reinforced my confidence that philosophical thoughts were communicable by non-technical means, that its points of reference were landmarks familiar to human beings in general, even if I had not heard it said before that philosophy simply rearranges what we have always known, that it leaves everything as it is, that it offers no theories or explanations, brings us no news.

In those same years, as an undergraduate reading for the Classical Tripos, I was reading Plato and noticing not only the formal doctrine of *anamnesis* and the declaration in the *Phaedrus* that each of us has seen the *onta*, the eternal Forms, but also the Socratic aims and methods that were sometimes disguised by the formal and metaphysical clothes in which they were dressed by Plato. Socrates talks to one person at a time, and says that he is concerned only with what is in the mind and heart of that one person. His *elenchus* is the examination of the hitherto unexamined life and mind of Polus or Callicles, Glaucon or Adeimantos, Protagoras or Meno. The tools and materials of the examination are drawn from that mind itself, and the end in view is the modification by self-examination and self-knowledge of the same mind. The destination of a thought is as important as its origin, and Socrates sees the origin and the destination as the same.

Socrates and Wittgenstein both provide precedents for my answer to the question about my choice of topics to work on. Like them I do not see philosophy as broken up like history or biology into departmental specialisms. Even if the questions of philosophy arranged themselves into such patterns of genus and species, it would still not be a matter of choice to be interested in these topics rather than those. The philosopher is inescapably a philosopher by being inescapably, involuntarily, puzzled or perplexed. Experience suggests and theory confirms that the questions by which he is puzzled are interconnected in ways that make the task bewilderingly difficult but also make it possible to tackle it with some hope of progress. Each question raises new questions, but the other side of that coin is that when we are concerned with any one question we are likely to be able to orient ourselves for the exploration of it by remembering or being reminded of what we already understand of a matter that we can see to have a bearing on our present perplexity.

Both the puzzles and the landmarks are familiar to us from childhood. Wordsworth spoke in the Immortality Ode about those obstinate questionings 'of sense and outward things' that make the infant child into a philosopher. The questioning is at first of what is *not* seen: 'Is our house still there when I am at school?' Later what is seen is also questioned: it could *look* like that even if it were really not at all like that.

The unity of the network of questions is liable to be disguised from us because the network, though unified, is also highly ramified. The maze looks different at different points of entry, but from any point of entry or any point within the maze it is possible to travel to any other. The philosophical maze does not have edges or boundaries like the Hampton Court maze, and it has no unique solution, but its structure is otherwise similar enough to warrant Milton's use of the image in Book II of *Paradise Lost*, where devils in hell are 'in wandering mazes lost' when they debate 'fix'd fate, free will, foreknowledge absolute'.

I was in this maze from early childhood, as most children are. Besides the questioning of sense and outward things I remember being puzzled about past and future, freedom of action, causality and foreknowledge. All these, like all other interesting questions of philosophy, are central to the 'subject'. They are not chosen as topics to work on but presented as difficulties to struggle with.

This is not to deny that the presentation of the difficulties, and to some extent the form of the difficulties presented, may be influenced by events and circumstances of individual lives and particular centuries and generations. This may be the right time and place to supply, as requested, 'some autobiographical material'.

I grew up from the age of 13 to the age of 19 during the Second World War. Until 1939 my family lived in a Durham mining village, and by the end of the war I was working as a coal miner under the 'Bevin Boy' scheme. At such a time and in such an environment I soon knew the difference between being intelligent and being educated. I was surrounded by people of all ages who deserved but had not received any advanced education. Soon after the war admission to Sixth Forms and colleges and universities became more systematically 'meritocratic', but when I was an undergraduate at Cambridge from 1945 onwards there were still many who were there mainly because they could afford it, and who did not try to compete academically with the poor scholars of their generation.

Some of the miners I worked with were keen to discuss politics and philosophy. Those of my own age knew that I knew things that they had had no opportunity to learn, but they also recognised that on many of the questions we talked about there was no specialised knowledge to be had. On the rights and wrongs of socialism, communism, conservatism and liberalism, war aims and post-war planning, we were better matched than when I spoke of nineteenth-century history or Plato's *Republic* or the origin and structure of the United States of America or of the solar system. (These are all typical of the things that my fellow-workers were interested in and asked me about.)

I had already learned from school debating that people of comparable intelligence and education could disagree about important questions of ethics and politics and religion. It was through debating too that I first came to hear the word 'philosophy'. I competed in a Prize Debate on the proposition that 'The Best Things in Life are Free', and the adjudicator described the argument of my speech as philosophical. He was E.I. Johnston, the senior Classics master, and so I had opportunities of hearing much more from him, and of learning how much of what I was interested in fell under that same rubric. Later he took me through Book I of the *Republic* as a Higher Certificate set book, and in that and many other ways extended a debt which I partly discharged by dedicating a book to him. Though I stayed with the Classics not only as an undergraduate but for nearly 20 years afterwards, when I left his hands I was already convinced and confident that my main work would lie in philosophy.

At Cambridge the debating continued. Free will and determinism over coffee in the small hours. Politics in the Union Society and in the political clubs. And now in meetings and debates and lectures I could hear and assess speakers, natives or visitors, whose life work had been to think on these things: Bertrand Russell, Hugh Gaitskell, Quintin Hogg, Isaiah Berlin, John Strachey, C.D.

Broad, Herbert Butterfield, Michael Oakeshott, Karl Popper, A.J. Ayer, Gilbert Ryle, John Wisdom, Ludwig Wittgenstein.

It was not rare in those days, at least in Cambridge, to practise philosophy without reading or teaching the subject officially. Most of those who crowded into the Moral Sciences Club when Wittgenstein was chairman were students or teachers of other subjects, and all but one of the professors and lecturers of the Faculty of Moral Science had come into philosophy from other fields.

I have lived on into a generation in which the vast majority of teachers and writers of philosophy are conscious and proud of being trained professionals, and who understand the idea of a profession by analogy with that of the physicist rather than that of the writer or critic. (My colleagues were almost unanimously delighted when an empirical psychologist told them that Cambridge philosophy students, unlike recruits to psychology from other arts subjects, 'think like scientists'.)

An Oxford philosopher, asked recently by a visiting lecturer in English what the young philosophers are interested in nowadays, said: 'They are interested in rigour.' But they are not. They are interested in technicality, which is quite a different thing. Philosophy is thinking which is rigorous but not technical:

> The language of philosophy is therefore, as every careful reader of the great philosophers already knows, a literary language and not a technical. Wherever a philosopher uses a term requiring formal definition, as distinct from the kind of exposition described in the fourth chapter, the intrusion of a non-literary element into his language corresponds with the intrusion of a non-philosophical element into his thought: a fragment of science, a piece of inchoate philosophizing, or a philosophical error; three things not, in such a case, easily to be distinguished.

(R.G. Collingwood, *An Essay on Philosophical Method*, p. 206f.)

Philosophers should teach and preach that it is possible to be accurate and precise and exact without being either professional or technical. Instead they are liable to ape the external forms of mathematicians and natural scientists, or at least linguists and technical historians, in order to avoid appearing 'literary' and hence unprofessional. Their idea of philosophy is of *normal* philosophy, like T.S. Kuhn's 'normal science'. Even if they are interested in

Wittgenstein's paradigm-shifts they do not see that the whole enquiry of philosophy is a matter of paradigm-shifts — of seeing one thing as a case of another — for example, seeing a river as a fast-changing mountain and a mountain as a slow-moving river. Accordingly, the paid and trained philosophers who write about Wittgenstein turn him into one of themselves, a member of a community of ideas, a practitioner of techniques and procedures of argument or of scholarship that do not belong to the general conversation of mankind from which philosophy arises and to which it must return, as Socrates knew, from its most or least adventurous excursion.

These roots in the common understanding help to account for some familiar but sometimes forgotten facts. Philosophers take easily to questions of policy and administration. There are many philosophy graduates in the Civil Service and local government, hospital administration and similar services. Teachers of philosophy often turn to university or college administration, or combine it with their philosophical work. Members of the 'profession' are in demand as chairmen or members of government committees and commissions. What makes this natural and appropriate is that questions of policy and politics and practical ethics share their structure with those of philosophy: they are complex but *informally* complex, like the dilemmas and difficulties of ordinary life and not like problems that yield to well-disciplined formal thought or well-directed observation or experiment. Lawyers typically share an understanding of these points, since their own training is largely a training in how to understand and articulate tangles of ideas and concepts, though their institutionalised need for a yes-or-no answer for practical application sometimes makes them more rigid than rigorous in the sense of rigour that I am concerned to defend.

Graduates in philosophy are in demand by employers in the computing industry, not because they think like scientists but because they understand the need and scope for formal thinking like that of the scientist and the mathematician without forgetting the possibility and value of a logical discipline that is not so easily if at all reducible to rule. (I have found when teaching philosophy students in pairs or groups, in the Cambridge system where it is common for students to change to philosophy from other fields, that the ex-mathematician can show the ex-historian or classical or literary scholar the value of formal thinking, while learning from them in turn that not all worthwhile thinking is formal.) Philosophical training and experience are also found among graduates employed in journalism, authorship, publishing, broadcasting and television and other 'media' careers, where again there is a need for flexibility as well as force.

I have engaged in a number of the activities covered by these last remarks. Most of my broadcasting work has been philosophical, but it has usually been at points of contact with other fields and with ordinary life and the common understanding. A typical example is 'Nature and Human Nature', a series of duologues in which I interviewed eight specialists in the human and behavioural sciences — anthropology, sociology, psychology, medicine and linguistics. The participants were not much practised in philosophy, but this did not unfit them for the exercise of articulating — with a freshness that came from doing it for the first time, and in response to questions which were simple but sometimes unexpected — the assumptions on which they thought and acted in the pursuit of their professional objectives. My own role was very similar to that of a philosophy supervisor (tutor) in the Cambridge teaching system, which is best fulfilled by asking short and simple questions that may call for long and elaborately qualified answers.

That is also the Socratic role; the habit of noticing contradictions or confusions between what is said by the same person on different occasions or even on the same occasion. This is the mode of examination by which Socrates aspired to turn an unexamined life into an examined life. The same process proved appropriate to two other areas of my supposedly non-philosophical work, and especially at a juncture when the two areas were for a year or two closely similar in their needs and problems. From 1964 to 1979 I was Dean of my college. From 1964 to 1970 I was a member of the Council of the Senate, which the *Cambridge Evening News*, comically but not altogether misleadingly, always calls 'the University's "inner cabinet"'. In both capacities I saw a good deal of the 'student troubles' of the late 1960s and early 1970s, which were a question time for universities.

Most of the rebellious students were inarticulate henchpersons for a small group of leaders exercising a leadership that did not officially exist. The leaders were mainly acute and intelligent questioners, with whom it was interesting for a philosopher to discuss topics of the day and the hour. They themselves would have liked it to be topics of the minute: a rolling programme of perpetual revolution was one of the watchwords of the time. Yet even the leaders were hidebound by their little revolutionary handbooks, and acknowledged that they were disconcerted to find a college Dean, who ought by the book to have been confined to the role of 'bureaucratic formalist', asking them questions more far-reaching than those concerned with the latest demonstration or breach of rules. The College radicals solemnly considered at one of their meetings a motion of protest to the Master and the College Council that it was unfair to them that the office of Dean should be occupied by a philosopher, a person more at home than they were in arguments on matters of principle. To my disappointment, one of their number was alert and prudent enough to suggest that they were in danger of making themselves ridiculous, and the motion was withdrawn.

The discussion of these high matters could be continued in college societies concerned with philosophy or history or literature or religion. I was also a member of a university committee of senior and junior members set up to review the disciplinary regulations of the university. In all these contexts it was noticeable how much practical importance can attach to the discussion of what look like abstract theoretical issues. On the senior as well as on the junior side there were many whose grasp of the issues was implicit or insecure, and who needed and welcomed the help of spokespersons with some taste and zest for the dialectic.

I have dwelt on these relatively trivial events because I believe they illustrate in their small scale the role of a philosopher in a community large or small. What I represented to the students was not only my own idiosyncratic opinions but the unspoken sense of purpose of a college and university community. The challenge of the rebels was a demand for an explicit justification of every rule or practice that was ever questioned. When it transpired, as it inevitably did, that such a process of attempted justification came fairly abruptly to points at which it was hard to avoid the appearance of mere dogma, the rebels were encouraged and their opponents, junior as well as senior, bewildered by the experience, familiar to every victim of the Socratic gadfly, of knowing that what he is asked to agree to must be wrong, yet being unable to *say* what is wrong with it. If the structure of the issue can be more fully articulated and explained, the original challengers will be little if at all affected. They are not interested in finding the answer but in making capital out of the question. But the bystanders — who are usually in such cases the bulk of the population — will feel better armed against what they recognise to be a threat to more than their peace of mind.

Political and moral philosophy as applied to the life and work of the larger community are writ small but legibly in these parochial events. 'Society', like an individual institution or tradition of thought or teaching, is a going concern whose basis may not be capable of being rendered explicit in the way demanded by its critics. But its critics are themselves beholden to it for the sources of their criticism and of their constructive offerings if they have any to make.

What is wider and more fundamental still is that *all* reasoning is a going concern in the same sense, and subject to the same difficulties. We did not create our society by act of will or by adopting a set of conventions. We equally did not at any time adopt principles or practices of thought and speech. An act of criticism, theoretical or practical, is an act that belongs within a tradition of theory or practice. What Wittgenstein dangerously calls our 'form of life' — our whole human existence — is transmitted and inherited and modified, but it was not made by us and cannot be renounced by us.

This brings us back to my 'own work' in the only sense in which I am prepared to regard it as professional. In the first place it speaks of the *role* that belongs to a philosopher, one which invites and provokes a special attitude towards him on the part of other people. He is their critic but also their representative. He speaks against them when he exercises his talent for noticing contradictions, but he speaks for them when he invites them to resolve their contradictions by being more faithful to the coherences of the inherited human understanding. The double process prompts a double attitude, or an oscillation: the victims and beneficiaries may welcome his help or resent his interference; they may crown him with laurel or dose him with hemlock.

But there is another and more familiarly professional way in which these examples return us to my philosophical work, past, present and future. I have been concerned with Wittgenstein, and with concepts of scepticism and justification; concerned with Wittgenstein because I have been concerned with scepticism and justification. The question why I have *chosen* to be concerned with these questions is adequately dealt with — though for reasons given there, not straightforwardly answered — in my earlier remarks about choice and interest and choice of interest. But I can now answer another of the editor's questions: why do I regard the topics that I have been concerned with as important? My answer will also explain why I intend and expect to continue to be concerned with them, and this whole package can be wrapped in an account of some work in which I have long been engaged, and which has raised for me some of the questions now raised by the editor.

I am approaching the closing stages of a project launched by a paper given to the Moral Sciences Club in 1962 and published in *Philosophy* in 1964. The title, '*Principia Metaphysica*', was deliberately chosen to imply an ambitious objective. The paper was a prospectus and a manifesto for a wide-ranging view of philosophy and for the book in which it would eventually be more fully expressed.

'*Principia Metaphysica*', though designed to be a draft of the first chapter of the book, was itself in origin a sequel to 'Universals and Family Resemblances', published in the *Proceedings of the Aristotelian Society* in 1961. This earlier paper was nearly but not quite explicit about two of the purposes of the whole programme: to express the main results of Wittgenstein's thinking more clearly by setting them out more systematically than he or his disciples had thought reasonable or even possible; and to demonstrate the continuity between his work and that of his predecessors.

It is again becoming fashionable to question the unity and continuity of philosophy from its Greek origins to the present day. In particular, it is questioned whether *epistemology* is a permanent element in the philosopher's preoccupation. Some suggest that it originated with Descartes, or died with Wittgenstein or Heidegger or Frege or the pragmatists. In its place, we are sometimes told, we must install or have installed something else, called ontology or philosophy of language or 'edifying' discourse — there is greater unanimity about the disease than about the remedy. The diagnosis and the prescriptions seem to me to be misconceived. All these physicians have allowed themselves to confuse differences of fashionable idiom with differences of philosophical substance. The use of a linguistic or logical or epistemological or psychological or ontological clothing for philosophical reflections commonly indicates a distinctive view of the nature of philosophy, but it ordinarily disguises only thinly a concern with a set of relatively permanent philosophical preoccupations. The most central are those which, when clothed in the epistemological idiom against which we are now so sternly warned, are summed up in the question 'What if anything do we know, and how do we know it?' It may be expressed in a number of other familiar idioms: What is real? What exists? What are the basic features of the world or the universe? How is language possible? What is thought or understanding?

Wittgenstein was as suspicious of the questions, in any of their traditional forms, as he was of the theories or theses in which philosophers had undertaken to supply the answers. But his repudiation of traditional forms of expression, which caused himself, his critics and his disciples to exaggerate the novelty of his work, was itself another of the changes of idiom on which philosophers base their periodical cries of revolution. There was a polemical and therapeutic point to Wittgenstein's announcement that he was engaged in 'an activity that is one of the heirs of the subject that used to be called philosophy', but every such paradox calls for redress after it has redirected our attention. Wittgenstein was a philosopher, and hence an epistemologist. This becomes clearest in his latest work, *On Certainty*, where he explicitly discusses the concepts of knowledge and belief and doubt and certainty, and the unmistakably and unashamedly epistemological work of Moore, and yet is largely faithful to the methods and results of the *Philosophical Investigations*. Like Moore, he is concerned with the common understanding, and with the demonstration that it is an *understanding*, and that it is *common* — shared by all human beings, and by all beings who could intelligibly be conceived as rational.

This recognition of the unity of humankind and hence of the human understanding again links Wittgenstein with Socrates and Plato, and also with Aristotle, for whom we are *logika zoa* (talking and thinking animals) as well as *politika zoa* (animals adapted and disposed to live in communities). Plato's picture of these unities is painted in the *Phaedrus* myth, where the gods impose an important constraint on the transmigration of souls between animal and human bodies and lives. No soul may embark upon a human life unless it is one of the privileged and enlightened souls who have seen the Forms. When this is translated into plainer prose by Wittgenstein it amounts to saying that all human beings share a background of understanding which is the source of all their questionings and all their answerings; a stock upon which we can all draw in our internal or external conflicts and perplexities. The Socratic examination is designed to determine which of the conflicting *logoi* best coheres with the fundamental knowledge that is shared by all of us. An important corollary is that to be in error is also to be confused, since it is to be in conflict with oneself as well as with the truth. The truth is in us, and when we deny it we are literally contradicting *ourselves*.

In the re-presentation of Wittgenstein's results that I am offering it first seemed to me that I should need to be not only more systematic than he had been but also more abstract. The issues, I thought when I wrote 'Universals and Family Resemblances' and '*Principia Metaphysica*', were logical and not biological — as Wittgenstein's recurrent talk of 'natural history' seemed to suggest. I have since learned from Peirce and James that it is possible to achieve great clarity and wide scope without abandoning the recognition that to describe thinking and reasoning is to describe thinkers and reasoners — 'a *very* familiar class of animals' (Wisdom, *Philosophy and Psycho-Analysis*, p. 112). I have also learned that to be as systematic and far-ranging as I wish to be is not necessarily to lose Wittgenstein's respect for the particular and his suspicion of the generalities of other philosophers, and one's own. Wittgenstein tried to guard against the ill effects of exaggeration by confining himself to remarks, instances and well directed rhetorical questions. He accordingly risked losing some of the benefits of scope and range that more systematic philosophers have purchased at the risk of simplification and distortion. In self-examination and in self-tuition, as in tutorial teaching of others, we combine both sets of advantages if we allow the dangerous exaggerations to display themselves and then correct them by the proper provision and judicious use of question time.

3 APOLOGIA PRO PHILOSOPHIA MEA

Antony Flew

> To yield to every whim of curiosity, and to allow our passion for inquiry to be restrained by nothing but the limits of our ability, this shows an eagerness of mind not unbecoming to *scholarship*. But it is *wisdom* that has the merit of selecting, from among the innumerable problems which present themselves, those whose solution is important to mankind.
>
> *Immanuel Kant*

In this respect, if in no other, like a remarkably high proportion of those whose names appear in the *Dictionary of National Biography*, I was a son of the manse. But my father was a minister of religion in the Wesleyan Methodist rather than the established church. Although his heart remained always in evangelism and in circuit or, as Anglicans would say, in parish work my own earliest memories of him date back only to the period after he had been directed to become a Tutor in New Testament Studies at what would, after Methodist union, become the Methodist theological college in Cambridge. Later he succeeded the then Head of that college, and eventually he was to retire and die in Cambridge.

In addition to the basic scholarly and teaching duties of these offices he undertook a deal of work as a Methodist representative on various inter-church organisations. In the late 1930s my mother and I — I was the only child — accompanied him to international Faith and Order conferences held in Denmark, in Switzerland, and in Scotland. He also served one-year terms as President both of the Methodist Conference and of the Free Church Federal Council. During the war years and for some time afterwards documents kept pouring through the post bearing the logo 'The World Council of Churches (In Process of Formation)'.

That said, I have in defence of my father's good name to protest that this gestating WCC was an altogether different animal from the full-grown monster which it has since become; an incongruous crossbreed perhaps best and most briefly described as UNESCO in a dog-collar.[1] I am myself quite sure that, had he been alive to see this development, he would have done his utmost to persuade his church, by withdrawing from an organisation now as much Leninist as Christian, to follow the principled lead of the Salvation Army. Father always admired the Army, both for its sacrificial devotion in all manner of good works, and for its dedication to preaching a simple Gospel message. Certainly, whenever I read or hear news items about the WCC — its frequent subventions to guerilla groups bent on establishing irremovable Marxist-Leninist despotisms, or its regular refusals to come to the aid of the Christians persecuted in socialist countries — certainly then I seem to hear my poor father turning miserably in his grave!

Reviewing these facts about him it becomes obvious that there are important continuities. Although I can only half agree with John Austin's mischievously provocative insistence that 'Importance is not important: truth is', I have never found it difficult to sympathise with the scholar's passion to get everything exactly right — regardless of all consequences; or of the lack of them. 'A Grammarian's Funeral' has for the Flews been a three-generation family favourite:

> So, with the throttling hands of Death at strife,
>   Ground he at grammar;
> Still, thro' the rattle, parts of speech were rife:
>   While he could stammer
> He settled *Hoti's* business — let it be! —
>   Properly based *oun*
> Gave us the doctrine of the enclitic *De*,
>   Dead from the waist down.

Nevertheless, notwithstanding our sympathy for 'an eagerness of mind not unbecoming to *scholarship*', father and son were both by both inclination and conviction disposed to follow what Kant indicated as the path of '*wisdom*'. My father's substantive convictions were not, of course, mine. But, once granted those Christian convictions, then there could be nothing 'more important to mankind' than the elucidation, propagation and implementation of whatever is in truth the teaching of the *New Testament.*[2]

To grow up during the 1930s and the 1940s in such a household was to be in Cambridge but not of it. (Any sociologically initiated reader will construe this as their cue to begin speaking of marginality.) For a start theology was not then and there, if it ever had been, accepted as the Queen of the Sciences. Nor was a ministerial training college, especially one belonging to what the Royal Air Force taught me to think of as one of the Other Denominations, any sort of mainstream university institution. And from 1936, when I started boarding school, I was anyway almost never in Cambridge during term-time.

So, even had I had the talents of a Gwen Raverat, there was no chance to accumulate sufficient materials for a rival to her supremely delightful *Period Piece*.[3] Yet even she might have envied us our first Cambridge house. Erected on a site formerly used by the Hobson of Hobson's choice, number 31 Jesus Lane is hard by Jesus College and the scanty ruins of the Nunnery of St Rhadegund. Also, number 31 still glories in a chimney fashioned to accommodate nesting storks.

Those enamoured of notions of persistent marginality should here note that for all but five terms of my professional life I have been employed outside the Oxbridge-London triangle; an area which houses all the present philosopher Fellows of the British Academy. One could perhaps call on these same fashionable sociological notions to help explain why my own first contacts with philosophy were made only about half way through boarding school. After all, Jack Smart — Professor J.J.C. Smart of the Australian National University — whose earliest years were spent in Cambridge, before his father was appointed to the Chair of Astronomy in Glasgow, recalls many admittedly quite unphilosophical occasions shared with the Moore family. (G.E. Moore was at that time Professor of Philosophy.) I went away to Kingswood School, a school founded by John Wesley, and still catering in the main for sons of Methodist ministers, at the end of the summer of 1936, the summer in which Spanish radio had given the code signal to start the Spanish War: 'There is a clear sky over Spain!'

In those days I claimed to be a Communist, and I remained a hotly energetic left-wing socialist until the early fifties. Kingswood I entered as a committed and conscientious yet none the less unenthusiastic Christian. I never could see the point of worship, and have always been far too unmusical to enjoy or even to participate in hymn-singing. I never have approached any religious literature with the same unrestrained eagerness with which I have consumed books on politics, history, science, or almost everything else. Going to chapel or church, saying prayers, and all other religious practices, always were for me matters only of more or less weary duty. Never have I felt the slightest desire to commune with God, or, as the Inter-Varsity Fellowship would say, 'to have Jesus for a friend'. So I was very ready to mark the sinister Tiberius a few notches up in my estimation when I learnt that, after succeeding the Emperor Augustus, he peremptorily dismissed a blasphemy charge by ruling: 'If the gods are insulted, let them see to it themselves!'

My long-standing interests in religion have never been, therefore, anything other than prudential, moral, or simply curious. Prudential, since if there is a God, or if there are gods, and gods who — unlike the deities of Epicurus — involve themselves in human affairs, then it would be madly imprudent not to take care as far as may be to keep on the right side of them. Moral, since I too should be glad to believe that I had found 'The eternal *not ourselves* that makes for righteousness.'[4] Or simply curious, since any scientifically-minded person must want to discover what, if anything, it is possible to know about these matters. All this having been said, no one should be surprised at my present reluctance to spend time and effort examining those proposed or supposed religious systems which do not even pretend to make substantial and evidenced claims about how things actually have been, are, or will be.[5]

Kingswood School was in my day an enormously lively place, presided over by a man who surely deserved to be rated one of the great Headmasters. In the year before I arrived it had won more open awards at Oxford and Cambridge than any other Headmasters' Conference school, notwithstanding that we were only a third or half the size of many of our competitors. Nor was our liveliness confined to the classroom and the laboratory. The Headmaster loved to boast of the number of his open scholars and exhibitioners who also played in the first fifteen.

No one has any business to be surprised that, placed in this stirring environment, I began to question the firm faith of my fathers; a faith to which, as has emerged already, I had never felt any strong emotional attachment. It must have been either not long before or not long after my fifteenth birthday that I reached — much too quickly, much too easily, and for what now seem to me the wrong reasons — negative conclusions. These negative conclusions I have since reconsidered at length and often. But I have never found grounds sufficient to warrant any fundamental reversal. For the sake of domestic peace and, in particular, in order to spare my father I tried for as long as I could to conceal from everyone at home my irreligious conversion. But by at latest my return to Oxford in January 1946 the truth had, as it is said that it will, outed. It had progressively become manifest to all that I was both an atheist and a mortalist, and that it was now in the last degree unlikely that there would be any going back.

Until that return from the war, and the consequent beginning in the School of Literae Humaniores, to read Philosophy as well as Ancient History, all the philosophical problems in which I had ever been seriously interested had been ones which I saw as relevant to questions of world-outlook: often these were problems which I could not then recognise as being philosophical. Mainly they referred to what Kant picked out as the three great, religiously oriented issues of metaphysics — God, Freedom and Immortality. But some seeds of other future interests were sown; interests much less closely connected with the rejection of religion.

Three merit mentions here. First, many of us at Kingswood were by the expository writings of C.E.M. Joad[6] led on to read some best-selling but, as I was later to learn, lamentably unreliable books about psychical research; or, as is now more usually said, parapsychology.[7] These books for me raised questions of the philosophy of parapsychology. For instance: 'Are the facts of psychical research, if they are indeed facts, compatible with (what I then called) materialism (but would now be more inclined to speak of as either naturalism of scientific realism)?'

Second, there were two interests aroused by consuming a lot of popular scientific writing, mainly books reprinted by the Rationalist Press Association in the old Thinkers' Library, and in Allen Lane's then new Pelican series. These many books were only part of what I tackled both as a schoolboy and after, in Oxford for the first six months of 1942, and then in the RAF. (In the RAF, after a false start in aircrew, I learnt to read Japanese, very slowly and with great difficulty, and later employed this knowledge for Intelligence purposes.)

The first of these two fresh interests was in the suggestion that evolutionary biology could provide a guarantee of inevitable progress. This suggestion was powerfully pressed in one of Julian Huxley's early *Essays of a Biologist* — a collection reprinted as one of the very first ten Pelicans. He pursued it, with increasing desperation, for the rest of his life. In *Time, the Refreshing River* and

History is on Our Side Joseph Needham tried, as I myself also then wished, to combine this suggestion with a Marxist philosophy of history; an historicism in Sir Karl Popper's sense of a doctrine asserting natural laws of inexorable historical development. It was in order to settle accounts with this literature that, when asked in the mid-1960s to contribute to a series of New Studies in Ethics, I offered to do a monograph on *Evolutionary Ethics*.[8] That work aspired to be, and has by a few been accepted as, definitive.

Third, the second of the two interests aroused by reading a mass of popular scientific literature was in attempts to draw neo-Berkeleyan conclusions from twentieth-century developments in physics. The main source books here were the works of Sir Arthur Eddington and Sir James Jeans, especially the three which were reprinted as fairly early Pelicans: *The Expanding Universe* by the latter; and *The Stars in their Courses* and *The Mysterious Universe* by the former. It was Susan Stebbing, whose *Philosophy and the Physicists* was reprinted as a Pelican in 1944, who taught me how to begin cutting my way out of this particular jungle.[9] At much the same time I read, and was exhilarated by, Lenin's *Materialism and Empirio-Criticism.* I read it again at Oxford, and then once more in the early 1960s, when I went on to write a constructive critique, eventually published, before that unacceptably freethinking and catholic journal was finally suppressed, in *Praxis* (Zagreb). This suppression was achieved through the instrumentality of the union of its printers, an early warning perhaps of the shape of things to come nearer home.[10]

So far it may have appeared that I was, from well before I went up to university, all set to pursue a career in philosophy, and all set also to produce the sort of stuff which I have produced, and intend to go on producing. In fact I only began to see this career as a possibility a few months before taking Finals. Had my fears of being placed in Class II been realised I should have proceeded to fulfil arrangements to read for a second set of Finals in the new School of Philosophy, Psychology and Physiology. Instead I went straight on to work for the then equally new-fangled B.Phil. under the supervision of Gilbert Ryle. It was, however, only in the last weeks of 1949, after being appointed to a probationary Studentship at Christ Church, that I burnt my boats by refusing an offer to join the Administrative Class of the Home Civil Service; a decision which seemed to have been vindicated generously when, a few days later, I was awarded the John Locke Scholarship.[11] I had some rather bitter second thoughts about all this when, at the end of the probationary year 1949, to my shock and surprise, the Governing Body of the college, by a massive majority, decided not to admit me to a Studentship. But these regrets ceased when, some months into 1950, the University of Aberdeen offered me a Lectureship, five steps up the increment scale, to begin with the academic year 1950/1.

That I came to be reading Philosophy as a university subject at all was a matter of constrained choice rather than direct intention. There was, before it was taken over by the Leys School, next to no science teaching at St Faith's. Nor did my father ever at any time waver from his conviction that, at least for his son, Oxford 'Greats' was the only possible climax to an education: 'The man with a First in "Greats" has the world at his feet.' So, when I arrived in Kingswood, the alternatives were to enter the Upper Vth (classical) or the IVth Form (modern).

That I found myself reading Philosophy and Ancient History on returning to Oxford after the war is to be put down to the weakness of my will to shift to 'Modern Greats'; in which, had I switched, I should certainly have begun by concentrating on either Politics or Economics. (I have always reckoned to be able to pass as a PPE man!) I only began to put more weight on the Philosophy than on the Ancient History leg after being awarded a Casberd Scholarship, on the strength of performances in internal college examinations; and after having been with gentle caution assured by my Philosophy tutors — John Mabbott and Paul Grice — that I need have no fear that this choice of emphasis would prejudice my prospects in Finals.

In Oxford — for two years as an undergraduate, for another as a postgraduate, and then for 18 months as a junior tutor — I saturated myself in the notorious New-Look philosophy, which its many almost always grotesquely misinformed enemies characterised as 'linguistic' or 'ordinary language'. I was, as has been said, supervised by Gilbert Ryle, and, after my appointment at Christ Church, I became an unfailingly faithful attender at John Austin's Saturday mornings — described once by Paul Grice as 'the class for all those whose classes have no members'.[12] Already, before leaving Oxford, I had delivered materials for the first collection of *Essays in Logic and Language* to the publisher.[13] Soon after reaching Aberdeen I found myself acting in Scotland as a sort of official spokesman. So when the Scots Philosophy Club launched the *Philosophical Quarterly* the Editor — the formidable T.M. Knox — asked me to respond to an attack marshalled by Peter Heath. 'Philosophy and Language', in a modified form, afterwards became the introductory chapter for a third collection of papers in the same genre, *Essays in Conceptual Analysis*.[14]

That Oxford philosophy of the 1940s and the 1950s provided several valuable insights, on none of which am I myself aware of having ever since relaxed my grip.[15] Perhaps the most important and wide-ranging of these insights was to become constantly and crisply conscious that and how all philosophy, in so far as philosophy is a conceptual enquiry, must be concerned with correct verbal usage. This is because we have and can have no access to concepts save through study of the usage and, hence, the use of those words through which these concepts are expressed. When, as I was once most beneficially reminded by my father, the Biblical scholar wants to become seized of some peculiar *Old Testament* concept he does not strain after an introspective revelation. Instead he collects and examines, with as much context as he can find, all available contemporary examples of the employment of the relevant Hebrew word. We should never forget that Austin was a considerable Classical scholar before he began to apply this method to ordinary modern English usage.

It should also be recognised that this New Look philosophy was neither so new nor so necessarily narrow as it sometimes appeared. Certainly, what was in those days rated a revolution in philosophy involved the rejection of a starting point first formulated by Descartes, and later accepted without question by most of his greatest successors; by Locke, for instance, and by Berkeley; by Hume and by Kant. For, once philosophers had begun to ask how the meanings of the words of the vernacular could be taught and learnt, it became clear that we could not describe an essentially incorporeal subject of perhaps only logically private experience without assuming, in a way quite inconsistent with the claims of Cartesian scepticism, that we had and had had knowledge by acquaintance of the logically public ('external') world — including that knowledge by acquaintance of other people which was always surreptitiously presupposed in loose talk (not of *my* but) of *our* cognitive predicament.[16] Nevertheless the Plato who wrote *Theaetetus* and the Aristotle of the *Nicomachean Ethics* would have been entirely at home in seminars run by Ryle or Austin; seminars which did in fact often attend directly to these and other works by Plato and by Aristotle.

While the linguistic turn was not so new, nor so sharp as to constitute an abandonment of the activity pursued by the men of old, neither was it so necessarily narrow as some dull and blinkered practitioners made it to appear. In vehement reaction against this unnecessary and unconscionable narrowness I wrote, and read to the B. Phil. Club, a paper entitled 'Matter that Matters'. I indicated several of the things which I believed needed to be done, and which I also argued could and should be done without prejudice to our standing as soundly 'with it' Linguistic Philosophers. When in the early 1970s the Radical Philosophy Group launched their journal, *Radical Philosophy*, with a manifesto listing all the areas and people allegedly neglected up till then by what they saw as the class enemy, I realised that, long before any of these new Philosophical Radicals had even begun their studies, I had myself published work on every one of these allegedly neglected topics. But of course what, as Mr Samuel Goldwin had it, would have included me out was not narrowness, not even 'bourgeois narrowness', but opposition to their less explicitly proclaimed collective commitment to revolutionary, Marxist-Leninist socialism; socialism total and hence, inevitably, totalitarian.

When I first rejected the faith of my parents, and my teachers, I was inclined to concede that the burden of proof, or rather of disproof, lay not on the believers but on me as the non-believer. But this is one of the things which I have since come to realise is not so. The rational person who, as Hume tells us, 'proportions his belief to the evidence', must, rather, insist: first, that any concept of God proposed must be explained, and shown to be coherent and capable of application; and, second, that some sort of sufficient reason must then be offered for concluding that that concept does in fact have application. This thesis I first argued at length in 'The Presumption of Atheism': urging that the earlier of the two stages must be, if anything, the more intractable; and that this first stage had traditionally been almost entirely neglected.[17] I have since tried to meet criticism in another article, 'The Burden of Proof', due to appear in 1985 in a collection sponsored by the Theology faculty of Boston University. This conscripts arguments from Parts I and II of the *Discourse on the Method* to support unCartesian conclusions: first, that the beliefs most properly to be doubted are theological beliefs; and, second, that all these ought to be put in limbo until and unless some sufficient justification can be found for holding some one particular set. The same applies, of course, to all positive beliefs about life after death.

The central argument of that first rejection was that the claim that the Universe is the creation of an all-powerful and infinitely good and loving God is flatly incompatible with all manner of undeniable and undenied gross facts. Since becoming a professional philosopher I have devoted much attention to what I suspect that I was the first to label the Freewill Defence.[18] This urges that God gives man freewill, that all or most of the obvious and scandalous evils are immediately or ultimately due to misuse of this dangerous gift, but that the end results will be the realisation of a greater sum of greater goods than would otherwise be possible: *O felix culpa quae tantum ac talem meruit habere redemptorem.*

All my earlier treatments of questions about choices and causation, both in their religious garb as questions about 'freewill and predestination', and in their secular suiting as questions about 'freewill and determinism', were — in terms of a terminology which again I may have been responsible for introducing — Compatibilist rather than Incompatibilist. Indeed I may have believed that my conclusions could only be derived from Compatibilist premisses. The Compatibilist, to squeeze the heart of the matter into a single sentence nutshell, is a person who maintains: not only that it can be consistent to say both that someone will make a free choice and that the sense of that future choice is known beforehand to some second party; but also that free choices could be both free and choices even if they were physically caused to be made in the senses in which they are made, and even when their being made in these senses was determined by some law or laws of nature.

While still accepting, indeed insisting on, the truth of the first of these two contentions I have for some time now been persuaded that the second is false.[19] For a law of nature is not a statement of a mere brute fact, that a specimen of one particular sort of ongoing will (as it happens) succeed or accompany a specimen of some other sort of ongoing. It is, rather, a claim that an occurrence of one particular sort physically necessitates the occurrence of a token of some other occurrence type; that it makes its non-occurrence physically impossible.

We also need to distinguish two radically different senses of the word 'cause', with corresponding distinctions between senses of determinism'. The causes of human actions are fundamentally, and most relevantly, different from the causes of all those events which are not human actions. Given the full cause of — say — an explosion it becomes impossible for any power within the Universe to prevent that explosion. But, if I give you sufficient cause to celebrate, then this by no means necessitates any making of whoopee on your part.

One perhaps disturbing corollary of all this is that not every movement of human organisms can be completely determined by necessitating physical causes. Ever since we first met on Bletchley station at the beginning of the academic year 1946/7, my good friend Jack Smart has been assuring me that particle physicists have — long since and rightly — abandoned all such notions of total causal determinism. But he, and many others, nevertheless remain obdurately reluctant to accept that the most complicated objects in the known Universe are, even in the slightest degree, indeterministic. As 'An epistle containing the strange medical experience of Karshish, the Arab physician' concludes: "It is strange."'

Much of the much which I have published about freewill or — better — choice, both in religious and in secular contexts, requires revision and correction in the light of this defection from full Compatibilism. Unfortunately I was not able to do the necessary on the relevant chapter of *The Presumption of Atheism* before its recent reissue as *God, Freedom and Immortality*.[20] But I do still hope to persuade some publisher to reissue a revised edition of *Crime or Disease?*[21] Certainly its message was one which the worlds both of law enforcement and of mental healing still need to take to heart — and to mind. It is a message which I am continually trying to spread by all available means: by lecturing; by writing letters to editors; and, on those rare occasions when such opportunity knocks, through the electronic media.[22] The book itself, dedicated to the memory of my Magistrate mother-in-law, was a development of an article under the same title. This was provoked by various items in *Probation* and other similar journals which I found in her home; and it was published in the *British Journal of Sociology* for 1954. Here is the place to mention also an article on 'The Justification of Punishment', quite often noticed in the subsequent literature.[23]

The main message of *Crime or Disease?* was, or is, that pleas, or diagnoses, of mental illness provide possible excuses for what would otherwise constitute criminal action or criminal negligence, and possible occasions for treatment by Hippocratic doctors, definitionally dedicated to meeting the wishes and promoting the welfare of their patients, *only and precisely in so far as mental illness is construed as being, like physical illness, incapacitating and/ or painful.* Although I can vouch for the fact that it was in 1973 forcefully put to the Butler Committee on the Mentally Abnormal Offender, this crucial point is not taken in the latest British legislation. This retains the confused definition of the 1959 Mental Health Act: 'In this Act "mental disorder" means mental illness, arrested or incomplete development of mind, psychopathic disorder, and any other disorder or disability of mind; and "mentally disordered" shall be construed accordingly.' Psychopathy, which merely describes an anti-social kind of character, is thus mistaken to be a condition excusing all actions of the sort characteristic of the people called psychopaths. So an obnoxiously disorderly disposition becomes an excuse for itself.[24]

Perhaps more surprisingly, the crux seems never to have been firmly seized by Sidney Bloch and Peter Reddaway, authors of the standard work on abuses of psychiatry by the forces of repression in the Russian Empire.[25] For, although they open with a chapter on 'The Vulnerability of Psychiatry', a chapter in which they notice that expressions such as 'mental illness' or 'mental disorder' are employed in various very different and often unfortunate ways by different psychiatrists even outside the USSR, in their subsequent review of KGB practice they allow all the cases to be discussed in terms of normality and abnormality. Yet it is, surely, perfectly obvious that the brave dissident victim patients indeed are, in both the prescriptive and the descriptive interpretation of that here inappropriate term, in the highest degree abnormal? They are, that is to say, abnormal in their defiance of the prescriptive norms of Soviet society. They are also statistically abnormal, in that they are members of a tiny minority standing out against the overwhelming oppressive power of government and of the monopoly party in the socialist state. What they are not is patients of a condition which can properly be rated an illness. For they are not in any relevant way incapacitated. It is not that they are incapable of refraining from — for example — engaging in religious devotions, or protesting against the Red Army's 'normalisation' of Czechoslovakia or 'pacification' of Afghanistan. Rather it is that they refuse to refrain. Nor do their very real sufferings arise from their own internal psychological states, as opposed to the outrageous external impositions of the Soviet authorities.

Returning now from questions about freedom to questions about God, I should perhaps say that I have come to see the contradiction or, if you like, the apparent contradiction, between Christian claims concerning God and the undeniable and undenied facts of the Universe, as one particular token of a type of incongruity afflicting many other religious belief systems also. This incongruity — and I suggest that it is, generally and essentially, only an incongruity rather than a contradiction — consists in insisting that a Creator God, upon whom the whole creation is supposed to be in every way and at all times totally dependent is, as it were, a committed partisan in certain fundamental conflicts within that creation. It would, surely, be natural to think of a God who is, or which is, in this traditional sense, a Creator as 'lying beyond good and evil' — as, I am told, certain Indian religious thinkers have thought. But, by the same token, the existence of any such God must become a matter of the most purely academic interest.

My own first publication in this area was a 1,000-word piece, commissioned as the first item in the first issue of a short-lived local Oxford journal, *University*. It was intended to start a discussion. It did. To my certain yet almost certainly incomplete knowledge 'Theology and Falsification' has since been reprinted no less than 31 times, including translations into German, Danish, Italian (two), and Welsh. (This must, surely, constitute some sort of record?) It concludes with a challenge: 'I therefore put to the succeeding symposiasts the simple central questions, "What would have to occur or to have occurred to constitute for you a disproof of the love of, or of the existence of, God?"'

It has often been asserted, most commonly perhaps in North America, that 'Theology and Falsification' expresses Flew's view of the meaning, or rather of the meaninglessness, of all religious language; while many have wanted to dismiss that view, and anyone so unfashionable as to continue to harbour it, on the grounds that verificationist accounts of meaning have long since been discredited. But I have in fact never held that all religious utterance either possesses or lacks one same single sort of meaning. That is a silly view, because so obviously false. In truth the only comprehensive thesis about meaning which I maintained there was truistic: 'Now to assert that such and such is the case is necessarily equivalent to denying that such and such is not the case'; or, as I added helpfully in a footnote, 'For those who prefer symbolism: $p \equiv \sim \sim p$.'

As the concluding challenge should have made clear, my purpose was, in the first instance, purely clarificatory. I wanted to bring out what, if anything — and in particular what, if anything, of any human interest — actually was being asserted. I was in fact well aware, if only from having previously read a similar but longer paper to the Socratic Club, that my challenging question would by different spokespersons be answered in radically different ways.[26] My own counter-responses were then, and always will be, tailored to fit the actual contents of the original utterances; as elucidated by the reactions actually provoked by my challenge. If and when I am told that there can be no conceivable occurrence or non-occurrence which could show some claim about God to be false, then I am inclined to reply: not that that claim is, in the old Logical Positivist phrase, 'without literal significance'; but that it is very likely unorthodox and, for sure, disappointingly empty and boring.

Four years later Alasdair MacIntyre and I produced a substantial collection of contributions to this sort of New Look philosophy of religion.[27] This work was at the time rather nicely, by the *Times Literary Supplement*, described as 'possessing a certain virginal freshness'. Over a long run it seems to have sold, taking hardcover and paperback together, about as well as either of the two *Logic and Language* volumes. Eleven years later I published *God and Philosophy*.[28] This was an attempt to present and to examine a systematic case for Christian theism. About this project the point of most continuing interest is that I could not find any previous presentation of the case which was widely accepted by contemporary believers as either adequate or standard. I tried asking Christian friends and colleagues for suggestions. But I found that there was little or no overlap between the resulting somewhat hesitantly offered lists. So I had myself to assemble from several sources the strongest case I could, urging anyone who was dissatisfied themselves to buckle to and produce something which they and their co-believers might find more satisfactory.

Had I been writing now rather than the mid-1960s I should, of course, have devoted a lot of space to the Christian tripos of my Keele successor, Richard Swinburne.[29] My own latest contribution in this area was Part I of *The Presumption of Atheism*. This work consisted entirely of previous papers, revised and rewritten to form chapters in a book.[30]

Certainly there are other things which I should like to do, had I but world enough and time. I should like, for instance, to try to make some sense of the great historic disputes about the structure of the Trinity and about what is going on in the Eucharist. But by the late 1960s it had become clear to me that my services were urgently needed elsewhere. I knew that for the rest of my working life I must concentrate my energies into the broad secular areas of philosophy of social science and social philosopy — 'among the innumerable problems...whose solution is important to mankind'.

But, since I have in the past had a deal to say about the philosophy of religion, I remain in academic duty bound to respond to criticism whenever occasion arises; either admitting that I had got it wrong, if I had, or else explaining that and why I am still unable to agree with my critics. But there must be no major, self-indulgent, new initiatives here.

Kant's third Great Topic does not, however, fall under this embargo. Indeed I now confess, not very shamefacedly, that even as long ago as 1952, while I was working on *A New Approach to Psychical Research*,[31] I entertained the idea that, in the unlikely event of my one day becoming a Gifford Lecturer,[32] my chosen subject would be 'The Logic of Mortality'.[33] Certainly, if I do have a claim to have made any modestly substantial and original contribution to the progress of philosophy, it must rest on what I have done to show that the question of a future life is not at the same time both perfectly straightforward and wide open. It is not, that is to say, a question not yet but eventually to be settled; either by the impersonal progress of parapsychology; or else by our individually dying and finding out, each one of us for ourselves. Bertrand Russell, therefore, was in error when he declared: 'All the questions which have what is called a human interest — such, for example, as the question of a future life — belong, at least in theory, to special sciences, and are capable, at least in theory, of being decided by empirical evidence.'[34]

My contributions on and around this supremely important topic have been fairly frequent, but scattered. Some appeared first in philosophically somewhat peripheral journals, while others took the form of perhaps not obviously relevant critiques of treatments of persons and personal identity in classical philosophers.[35] These critiques were, however, very much to the point. For most of the classical philosophers so criticised mistook persons to be essentially incorporeal and disembodiable, construed the problem of personal identity as the problem of how such elusive entities could be and are reidentified, and therefore — whether or not they recognised this — were entirely at a loss to solve a surely insoluble problem. No doubt it is the scattered and peripheral form of presentation which in large part accounts for a curiously patchy response or lack of response to my challenge to the Russellian view.

This challenge was so fresh and startling when it was first thrown down, in a BBC Third Programme broadcast in 1951 and in a subsequent piece in *University*,[36] that several of my father's Christian friends, who had had no doubts about the sincerity and seriousness of 'Theology and Falsification', told him that they considered that I was being, on the present issue, flash and disingenuous. Yet, less than 20 years later, in the Introduction to his *Death and Immortality* in a series of New Studies in the Philosophy of Religion, D.Z. Phillips was to take it as quite obvious that 'The notions of the survival of non-material bodies, disembodied spirits or new bodies, after death, all seem open to fatal objections.'[37] So he proceeded in the main text to write as if this had always been equally obvious to all the Saints and the Fathers, all the Councils and the Popes. More than ten years later still John Mackie, in the Introduction to his own mortalist and atheist book on *The Miracle of Theism*, wrote that 'there is no great difficulty in conceiving what it would be for there to be a person without a body: for example, one can imagine oneself surviving without a body, and while at present one can act and produce results by using one's limbs or one's speech organs, one can *imagine* having one's attentions fulfilled directly, without such physical means.'[38]

Mackie, it seems, felt no call to address the argument of 'Can a Man Witness his own Funeral?' That contended that what we can undoubtedly imagine is: not our witnessing our own funerals, but our own funerals. The heart of the matter is that in this kind of context almost everyone takes absolutely for granted a Platonic-Cartesian view of the nature of man, assuming that we already possess a viable concept of the person as a disembodiable incorporeal entity. On such a view members of our species are composed of two disparate elements — body and mind, or body and soul — of which only the latter is the real or essential person.

Actually to possess such a concept we should have to be in a position to identify, and to reidentify through time, specimens of the supposed species incorporeal person.

The truth, however, is that we neither are nor could be masters of any such concept. We are nevertheless inclined to believe that we could be, and are. This is partly owing to confusions over what is or is not imaginable or conceivable, but mainly because we misinterpret our ordinary and ordinarily intelligible talk about bodies and minds. When we say, for instance, that Ethiopia's win in the Marathon was a triumph of mind over body, or that Jean's performance in Finals manifested a First Class mind, we suggest that we have access to incorporeal agents; logical substances capable of serving as the hypothetical entities in some scientific theory construction. But, of course, all these picturesque idioms can, without remainder, be translated into pedestrian terms carrying no similar suggestions. And all our person-words both are and have to be defined, immediately or ultimately, by ostensive reference to specimens of our own peculiar and special sort of creatures of flesh and blood; the sort of which we are.

It was in order to attack popular misrepresentations of the putative psi-phenomena — misrepresentations mistaking these to constitute fresh and decisive evidence in favour of a Platonic-Cartesian view of the nature of man — that in 1951 I wrote and delivered a pair of broadcast talks, 'Minds and Mystifications' and 'A New Name for Guesswork'. It was these, later translated into German and published in *Merkur*, which prompted the invitation to write *A New Approach to Psychical Research*.[39] Some at least of the excruciating stylistic defects in 'that juvenile work' may be put down to the fact that the first contract was voided by publishers who claimed that what they had always wanted was a merely frivolous essay. The young would-be author was rescued from his resulting predicament only by an offer from the Secretary of the Rationalist Press Association to put out a book half as long again as the original manuscript.

The book also had several more substantial faults. On the empirical side, notwithstanding my already high threshold for positive belief, I accepted the since discredited experimental work of S.G. Soal. On the philosophical side, I had not yet grasped the full significance for parapsychology of the sort of argument sketched by Hume in Section X of his first *Inquiry*.[40] Again, it was only much later that I realised that the fact that 'telepathy' and 'clairvoyance' are not names for recherché mechanisms (but refer to results supposedly achieved without the employment or sensory or other means) carries a surprising implication. It is that bodiless beings could not conceivably know that they were either acquiring or transmitting information 'by exercising their psi-capacities'.[41] Nor was it until I was preparing for what turned out to be an unusually hard-hitting symposium on 'Can an Effect precede its Cause?' that I appreciated that the suggestion of now making something either to have happened or not to have happened is immediately incoherent. In so far, therefore, as it is defined in terms of such backwards causation, the concept of paranormal precognition cannot conceivably have application.[42]

The only further published contribution which I hope to make to the philosophy of parapsychology — a subject in which I currently teach a course at York University, Toronto — is to compile a book of readings more satisfactory than any previously available. It should be possible, either in the Introduction or in the little prefaces, to say again all those things which, though somewhere or other said before, will still bear repetition.[43]

Vice-Chancellors, members of the University Grants Committee, and spokespersons for the Association of University Teachers, often talk about the cross-fertilisation of teaching and research. I am pretty sure that what they say is not equally true, or even true at all, of the university teachers in all disciplines and indisciplines. But it certainly has applied to me, most especially in my 17 years in the University of Keele. Fully aware of how my own education had suffered from the erection of a great structural divide between the Arts Side and the Science Side — the Snow Line — I straightaway plunged into the whole Keele enterprise with an enthusiasm which never diminished. (John Mabbott had been about this, as about all similar matters of matching men to jobs, right.) It was the demands of teaching at Keele which led me into a philosophical study of Darwin and Malthus. And it was different Keele teaching demands which led me to write a book about Hume's first *Inquiry*. Up till then this book was — despite the protests of its author — usually treated as a mere miscellany of afterthought essays; a poor come-down when compared with the massive masterpiece he himself so testily dismissed as 'that juvenile work'.

Since the books are all in print, and those articles which have not been superseded by books are tolerably accessible, what I have done in these three areas can to anyone who may happen to be interested be left to speak for itself. It should be sufficient here just to say where that work is to be found, while perhaps indicating how it satisfies that motto mandate from the Sage of Kaliningrad.

In the first case there is a book *Darwinian Evolution*,[44] which supersedes various earlier pieces, starting with 'The Structure of Darwinism' in the 1959 centenary issue of the now long defunct Penguin Books occasional journal *New Biology*. That some understanding of evolutionary biology is essential to anyone labouring to shape an integrated, comprehensive and realistic world-outlook can be taken as given. But it is perhaps worth mentioning that this book both notices the influence on Darwin of Adam Smith and those other Scottish founding fathers of social science who first began to explore ways in which what looks like design may be produced as an unintended consequence of intended action; and takes time to examine, and dismiss, the oft-reiterated claim — first made by Engels in his speech at the graveside — that Marx did for sociology what Darwin did for biology. (It is in fact a claim demonstrably almost if not quite as false as the recently exploded story that Marx asked Darwin to accept the dedication of Volume I of *Capital.*)

Earlier essays on 'The Structure of Malthus' Population Theory' and the like were superseded by the Introduction to my edition of his *First Essay.*[45] It is remarkable but true that this was the first edition of that enormously influential yet widely misunderstood and misrepresented classic to supply Notes, identifying the author's allusions and quotations, and providing at least a minimum of biographical information about people mentioned.

More recently I have come to recognise how much can be made in the philosophy of the human sciences of a comparison between the fundamental conceptual schemes of Malthus and Darwin. It can and should be employed in order to bring out one absolutely crucial and all-pervasive difference: whereas the former needed to take account of the realities of choice, the latter did not.[46]

The further and chief human interest of Malthus arises, of course, from his subject. Since the spread of modern methods of death-control has so far outstripped that of any means of birth control, the population bomb must be at lowest the number two problem for all those sincerely concerned for the maintenance and relief of the estate of man. It was, in particular, the vilification and distortion of Malthus by Marx and Engels which continues to mislead those claiming the Marxist name to deny the reality and urgency of any problems of overpopulation — the Chinese Communists, most importantly, for nearly 30 worse than wasted years, until someone turned up a saving 1881 letter from Engels to Kautsky.

The idea of writing a whole book about Hume's first *Inquiry* arose from experience of a peculiar Keele institution, the Foundation Year Terminal Tutorial. In this a tutor met a group of, typically, eight students for one hour a week throughout a nine-week teaching term. The tutor's remit was to do something which would be worthwhile even for pupils who would never touch that particular subject again, yet at the same time providing a sample sufficient to enable them to make well-warranted decisions whether they should go further. Having tried various other classics, both ancient and modern, it soon became clear to me that the *Inquiry Concerning Human Understanding* was the ideal set-book for such a course. It could be made to yield the right number of immediately appealing and sharply distinguishable essay topics. Furthermore, these are topics which might be picked out for attention by responsible '*wisdom*' as opposed to feckless '*scholarship*'. It was these characteristics, combined with the existing interpretative void, which pretty well dictated the subject of *Hume's Philosophy of Belief*.[47]

Although the presumption must be that a second edition will never be possible, there is one major matter calling for extensive corrections. The three chapters on 'The Idea of Necessary Connection', 'Liberty and Necessity', and 'Miracles and Methodology' all need to be rewritten in the light of my new-found awareness that Hume was utterly wrong to maintain that we have no experience, and hence no genuine ideas, of making things happen and of preventing things happening, of physical necessity and of physical impossibility.

Generations of Humeans have in consequence been misled into offering analyses of causation and of natural law which have been far too weak; while in Part II of Section VIII 'Of Liberty and Necessity' and in Section X 'Of Miracles', Hume himself was hankering after, even when he was not actually employing, notions stronger than any which he was prepared to admit as legitimate. In Part I of Section VIII Hume was able to deploy a Compatibilist resolution of 'the most contentious question of metaphysics, the most contentious science', only because, having first presented the antinomy in stronger terms, he went on to construe natural necessitation as nothing more than regular succession.[48]

On Darwin and Malthus I believe that I have already done everything which it is in me to do. On Hume, on the other hand, I am actually under contract to produce another whole book. This is for a Blackwell series which has to emphasise connections with, and implications for, the social sciences. Although Hume was the first of the aforementioned Scottish founding fathers, this is an aspect which has generally been neglected. Yet his great insight, that for all we can know *a priori* anything may be the cause of anything, is the indispensable propaedeutic for a constant awareness that things most often happen for reasons other than that some 'they' intended that this and nothing else should be what comes about.

This work on Darwin, on Malthus and on Hume all bears on, even when it can scarcely be rated as, social philosophy and philosophy of social science. But that collected, revised and rewritten in *Sociology, Equality and Education* and in *The Politics of Procrustes* is all central to one or other of these two areas of my present and future concentration.[49] The first book polemicises against various false and anti-educational doctrines currently propagated most urgently by certain — may we be permitted to say? — moles within what Tom Lehrer would have us call Edbiz. For instance: the opening essay deals with a curious revival of philosophical idealism which, though supposedly derived from what practitioners insist on labelling sociology of knowledge rather than sociology of belief, denies the very possibility of objective knowledge. Believe it or not, this appears to be a large part of what is now taught as sociology of education in the lecture rooms of the University of London Institute of Education, as well as preached as the corresponding Gospel from the radio pulpits of the Open University.

The Politics of Procrustes was directed mainly against the nowadays almost universal assumption that justice, or at any rate social justice, requires the imposition on all of an ever greater, if never perhaps total, equality of condition. I argued that, whereas this Procrustean ideal is forward-looking, the ideal of justice is equally essentially backward-looking. It is concerned with the securing of people's antecedent, and presumably by no means invariably equal, deserts and entitlements. I also pointed out, turning a Marxist weapon against some of its usual users, that this misconception of (social) justice serves as the uniting and justifying ideology of the New Class of those who have found, or hope to find, within the ever-extending machinery for its enforcement, positions of satisfyingly unequal power and profit for themselves.

To those who know anything of that journal and its readership it will seem wryly significant that the reviewer in *New Society* first pretended not to know at whom the book was directed, and then went on to suggest that it was in any case all stale stuff long since refuted. In fact I have come across only two attempts to answer my sort of objection. Neither was even relevant. The first digressed to describe a socialist Cloud-cuckoo-land, in which everything — including, presumably, people's deserts and entitlements — will be:

> changed, changed utterly:
> A terrible beauty is born.

The second dismissed my contentions as 'merely verbal', proposing to give to the word 'justice' some new meaning more to the writer's own taste. But he still helped himself to all those previous implications of its employment which he wished to retain.[50]

It is easy to understand why Procrusteans are so resolute to retain the word 'justice' for their own very different ideal. It permits them to think of themselves as the *Shane* figures from the best sort of traditional Western, men doing the justice 'which a man has to do'. It also equips them with a ready response to dissidents daring to question their right to impose by force their own bureaucratic and repressive ideal. For are we not all agreed that one of the most fundamental functions of state power is to ensure that justice is done?

Let us conclude, however, with a Parthian shot, pointing out a further implication; and one which, to my knowledge, no other writer has ever attempted to press home against the often rather conspicuously underdeprived fuglemen of (social) justice. I can well understand that the reviewer for *New Society* wanted to protect both fellow contributors and readers from such embarrassing challenges!

For, if the maintenace of a universal equality of goods really were the supreme imperative of justice, then precisely and only one equal share would be all that anyone either deserves, or is entitled, to have and to hold. So each one of the many who are in fact enjoying more, and show no sign of surrendering this surplus, should on this assumption be seen as a person in possession of stolen property; and that necessarily property stolen from others worse off than himself. Now will all those underdeprived Procrusteans, please, forthwith display a minimal decency: by either surrendering to some of the others who have the right to it whatever they have themselves wrongfully possessed; or else by ceasing to preen themselves on their 'progressive', 'liberal', and 'compassionate' commitment to the promotion of (social) justice?

Notes

1. See, for instance, Bernard Smith *The Fraudulent Gospel: Politics and the World Council of Churches* (Foreign Affairs Publishing, Richmond, Surrey, 1977) and E.W. Lefever *Amsterdam to Nairobi* (Ethics and Public Policy Centre of Georgetown University, Washington, DC, 1979).
2. R.N. Flew's books were: *The Idea of Perfection in Christian Theology* (OUP, London, 1934); *Jesus and His Church* (Epworth, London, 1938); and *Jesus and His Way* (Epworth, London, 1963). He was also largely responsible for the text and wholly for the title of *The Catholicity of Protestantism*, edited by R.N. Flew and R.E. Davies (Butterworth, London, 1950). It was pleasing to us both that my father lived long enough to recognise that, in at least one respect, I was following in his footsteps — by devising such swinging yet faithfully informative titles as 'Is Pascal's Wager the Only Safe Bet?' and 'Can a Man Witness his own Funeral?'
3. *Period Piece: A Cambridge Childhood* by Gwen Raverat (Faber, London, 1952).
4. Matthew Arnold *Literature and Dogma*, Ch. VIII, italics original.
5. See, for instance, Schubert Ogden in the *Religious Studies Review* for July 1977 (vol. III, no. 3). He complains that a then recent work of mine 'confines its considerations to the same narrow range of alternatives with respect to questions of religious belief, to which Flew has long seen fit to restrict his attention'. That narrow range, as Ogden also notices, consists in questions about what could be said and even known to be true.
6. Little did I or any of my schoolfriends think that I should — 40 years on! — compose the replacement for his contribution to the long-running 'Teach Yourself' series; namely, *Philosophy: An Introduction* (Hodder and Stoughton, London, 1979).
7. Since the books are still available in many public libraries, and appear to be consulted frequently, perhaps I should list them here, along with some suitable antidotes. First came *The Most Haunted House in England* and *The End of Borley Rectory* by Harry Price (Longmans, London, 1940 and 1946), both decisively disposed of in *The Haunting of Borley Rectory* by E.J. Dingwall, K.M. Goldney and T.H. Hall (Duckworth, London, 1956). There follow *An Adventure* by C.A.E. Moberly and E.F. Jourdain (Macmillan, London, 1911) and *An Experiment with Time* by J.W. Dunne (Faber, London, 2nd edn, 1929). I did short hatchet jobs on both these much reprinted works in successive Appendices to *A New Approach to Psychical Research* (C.A. Watts, London, 1953). Later works by Trevor Hall, especially *Search for Harry Price* (Duckworth, London, 1978), are also strongly recommended.

8. This was originally published as a slim paperback. But it is now available only as the third item in vol. II of *New Studies in Ethics*, edited by W.D. Hudson (Macmillan, London, 1974). The Select Bibliography at pp. 282-5 contains particulars of all the relevant works by Huxley and Needham.

9. This excellent and still by no means dated book was published originally in hardcover in 1937, reprinted in 1944 as a Pelican, and since reissued yet again in a third different pagination by the Dover Corporation of New York. The Select Bibliography provides particulars of all relevant works by Eddington and Jeans.

10. The materials in this article were recycled to make Ch. X of *A Rational Animal* (Clarendon, Oxford, 1978) 'Lenin and the Cartesian Inheritance'. For a tale of a similar, but happily less drastic and less permanent, organisational constraint upon editorial freedom compare the brief account of 'the *Black Paper* which was itself once "blacked"' in my *Sociology, Equality and Education* (Macmillan, London, 1976) — Ch. I, 'Where We Are Going', p. 50.

11. 'Studentship' is the Christ Church term for 'Fellowship'. John Locke himself was just such a Student; until his ejection, by royal command, as a dangerous Whig. His namesake Scholarship is in fact the university prize by examination.

12. See G.J. Warnock's, Ch. III 'Saturday Mornings' in Isaiah Berlin and others *Essays on J.L. Austin* (Clarendon, Oxford, 1973).

13. (Oxford, Blackwell, 1951) The Second Series came out from the same publisher in 1953. I pre-empted unfriendly comment on these editorial exercises by myself describing the first as a ploy in academic lifemanship: 'How to produce a book without actually writing one.'

14. (London, Macmillan, 1956) After long runs in both hardcover and paperback with Macmillan this was in 1981 reissued as a hardcover by the Greenwood Press of Westport, Connecticut.

15. The most widely circulated and long-sustained onslaught ever directed against this revolution in philosophy is Ernest Gellner's *Words and Things* (Gollancz, London, 1959; Pelicanned in 1968). Those honestly desirous of taking the true measure of Gellner's polemic ought themselves to compare it with some of Austin's posthumously assembled remainders. The most relevant is perhaps 'A Plea for Excuses', reprinted in *Philosophical Papers*, edited by J.O. Urmson and G.J. Warnock (Clarendon, Oxford, 1961).

It is damagingly significant that, although *Words and Things* is full of complaints against the alleged methodological secretiveness of Linguistic Philosophy, it makes no attempt to come to terms with this most explicit methodological statement. Gellner is, surely, the immediate or ultimate source of innumerable slick and ignorant put-downs in the subsequent literature. See, for instance, for a very recent example, Tom Bottomore *Sociology and Socialism* (Harvester, Brighton, 1984), p. 25.

16. Compare, for instance, the first chapter cited in Note 11, above; or, for a much fuller account, Chs. VIII-X of *An Introduction to Western Philosophy* (Thames and Hudson, London, 1971).

17. This paper is revised and reprinted in *The Presumption of Atheism* (Pemberton/Elek, London, 1976), a book which was in 1984 reissued by Prometheus of Buffalo as *God, Freedom and Immortality*.

18. See, for instance, 'Divine Omnipotence and Human Freedom' in A.G.N. Flew and A.C. MacIntyre (eds.), *New Essays in Philosophical Theology* (SCM, London, 1955); also reprinted in G.I. Mavrodes and S.C. Hackett (eds.) *Perspectives in the Philosophy of Religion* (Allyn, New York, 1967) and in P. Angeles (ed.), *Critiques of God* (Prometheus, Buffalo, 1976).

19. *A Rational Animal* was my first book written in the light of this long delayed recognition. (See Note 11, above.) An insistence that there are not and

could not be natural laws determining the senses of human action is going to be a main feature of my forthcoming *Thinking about Social Thinking* (Blackwell, Oxford, 1985). This is one of several innovations which will make that very different from the usual introductions to the philosophy of social science.

20. See Note 18, above.

21. (London, Macmillan, 1973)

22. Compare, for instance: 'Mental Health, Mental Disease, Mental Illness: "the Medical Model"' in P. Bean (ed.), *Mental Illness: Changes and Trends* (Wiley, New York, 1983); 'What Cures for Religious Souls?' in *Quadrant* (Sydney, NSW) for November 1983; and 'Brainwashing, Deprogramming and Mental Health', long overdue to appear in a Psychiatry and Freedom special issue of *Metamedecine*, guest edited by Thomas Szasz.

23. First published in *Philosophy* in 1955; reprinted in H.B. Acton (ed.), *The Philosophy of Punishment* (Macmillan, London, 1967), and in J. Hospers and W. Sellers (eds.), *Readings in Ethical Theory* (Appleton-Century-Crofts, New York, 1970). Excerpts are included in R. Garber and P. MacAnany, *Contemporary Punishment* (Notre Dame UP, Notre Dame, Ind., 1972). I hope that all future readers will take note of the page in the Acton collection giving my second thoughts in response to criticism from, especially, Mabbott.

24. Compare *Crime or Disease?* (Macmillan, London, 1973), pp. 35ff and 75ff.

25. *Russia's Political Hospitals*, with a Foreword by V. Bukowsky (Futura, London, 1978).

26. On the Socratic Club see M. Diamon and Y.V. Litzenburg (eds.), *The Logic of God* (Bobbs-Merrill, Indianapolis, 1975), pp. 270 ff.

27. *New Essays in Philosophical Theology* (SCM, London, 1955).

28. (London, Hutchinson, 1966) This is in 1984 about to be reissued by Open Court of La Salle, Illinois as *God: A Philosophical Critique*. There was a Spanish translation as *Dios y la Philosophia* (El Ateneo, Buenos Aires, 1976). A contract was signed and an advance paid by an Italian publisher. But the person who undertook to do the translation disappeared without trace. So that project was abandoned.

29. *The Existence of God, The Coherence of Theism* and *Faith and Reason* (Clarendon, Oxford, 1979, 1977 and 1984).

30. See Note 19, above.

31. See Note 8, above.

32. Our friend Rex Knight, then Professor of Psychology in the University of Aberdeen, used to speak of that city 'as lying in the Gifford Belt'. My dutiful attendance at (some of) the Gifford Lectures of Paul Tillich gave me a head start over the competition in recognising that he was in fact, well before this became quite the 'in' thing among professedly Christian theologians, an atheist.

33. This is already the title of an epitome article, due to be published by Macmillan of London in 1985, in a volume of papers edited by Paul Badham.

34. *Our Knowledge of the External World* (Illinois, La Salle, Open Court, 1914), p. 28.

35. But see now Part III of the book described in Note 18, above; also the long Introduction to and the little prefaces in A. Flew (ed.), *Body, Mind and Death* (Collier-Macmillan, New York, 1964).

36. 'Death', reprinted as the final item in *New Essays in Philosophical Theology*: see Note 19, above. Unlike 'Theology and Falsification' this piece has never to my knowledge been reprinted again, although both the chapter of *A New Approach to Psychical Research* and the two other articles recommended in a footnote were all later recruited to serve in various philosophical anthologies. Indeed, one of these articles 'Can a Man Witness his own Funeral?', has since

reappeared in five such collections and been illicitly précised in another.
37. (London, Macmillan, 1970), p. xi.
38. (Oxford, Clarendon, 1982), pp. 1-2: italics original.
39. See Note 7, above.
40. It is that, in order to establish the reality of phenomena of some kind previously with good reason believed to be impossible, we must have repeatability. See my Introduction to *Hume: 'Of Miracles'* (Open Court, La Salle, Illinois, 1985).
41. See, for instance, 'Parapsychology: Science or Pseudo-Science?' in M.P. Hanen, M.J. Osler and R.G. Wayant (eds.), *Science, Pseudo-Science and Society* (Wilfred Laurier, Waterloo, Ontario UP, 1980); also reprinted in the *Pacific Philosophical Quarterly* for 1980 and in P. Grim (ed.), *The Occult, Science and Philosophy* (SUNY UP, Albany, NY, 1983).
42. See PAS Supp, vol. XXVIII; and compare the article mentioned in 43, above.
43. To be published by Prometheus Books, of Buffalo.
44. (London, Granada, 1984)
45. *Malthus: An Essay on Population* (Penguin, Harmondsworth, 1970).
46. See Chs. I and II of *A Rational Animal*, bibliographically described in Note 11, above.
47. (London, Routledge and Kegan Paul, 1961)
48. See 'Another Idea of Necessary Connection' in *Philosophy*, 1982; 'Inconsistency within a "reconciling project"' in *Hume Studies*, vol. IV; and the work described in Note 42, above.
49. The first of these two books — a one person collection of more or less philosophical *Black Papers* — is bibliographically described in Note 11, above. The second was published in 1982 by Maurice Temple Smith of London.
50. See, for a faithful dealing with such arbitrary and abject responses, 'Justice: Real or Social?' in *Social Philosophy and Policy*, vol. I, no. 1 (Autumn 1983).

4 THREE CONTEMPORARY STYLES OF PHILOSOPHY

Ernest Gellner

I have been asked to write about the present and recent state of philosophy in the United Kingdom, and in particular to relate it to my own intellectual development, and to my rejection of the erstwhile philosophic orthodoxy in *Words and Things* (1959): to explain not only my rejection of that version, but also what led me to philosophy in the first place, and to comment on developments since then. Philosophy in the UK, one should say at this point, is not nowadays separable from the rest of Anglophone philosophy.

To begin at the beginning: what had led me to philosophy. It was certainly no accident. I was led to the subject because I found philosophical questions personally unavoidable. Initially I tried to think myself out of predicaments which perhaps have no solution; in the course of this, I found that one could make a living, of a kind, out of not solving them. The propaedeutic doubt thus became a profession. The deep ambivalence I felt about doing this also made me turn to anthropology and sociology.

I was not selected for philosophy by ability. I think this differentiates me from many, though not all, who were led to academic philosophy at about the same time. The basic fact about the then upper class education in Britain, as it relates to philosophy, was this: there was a strong selection at school of the ablest minds towards the classics. The best minds, unless they had an independent bent and were willing to assert it, which at a tender age is rare, were pushed towards classics, whilst the less able went to science, modern languages or worse. At Oxford, a further selection took place within the field of classics: once again, if no strong interest intervened, philosophy had a somewhat higher ranking than classical philology and history. The consequence of this prolonged egg-sorting machine was that a number of people of high ability, but no natural orientation towards philosophical problems, ended up as specialists in philosophy and possibly professional practitioners of it, without feeling any spontaneous impulse towards philosophical problems. Prestige of the activity at each stage, rather than any attraction to its content, was liable to push or pull them towards it, if no other strong intellectual interest intervened to propel them in some other direction. This of course is enormously significant if one is to understand the post-war orthodoxy. Those recruited simply lacked a nose for sensing the absurdity which lurked at the base of that orthodoxy. Had they been spontaneously bothered by philosophical issues they could never have swallowed the view that philosophy is merely a kind of linguistic indigestion.

There most certainly was such an orthodoxy, though this is sometimes denied nowadays, and was also denied at the time. It was rooted in the then unpublished later writings of Ludwig Wittgenstein, and disseminated through samizdat versions thereof, and through the now rather unjustly forgotten and very witty writings of Professor John Wisdom of Cambridge, and also through the teaching of men such as Gilbert Ryle and J.L. Austin.

The basic idea of this orthodoxy was astonishingly simple, and its simplicity is certainly no defect whatever. It is not one of the charges that can be held against it. The idea was a naturalistic view of language: language is what people do, in concrete social contexts. What else could it be? Well, the answer is that previous philosophers had often either assumed or actually taught that it was indeed something else — either that it recorded or reflected platonic entities, or that it was, if irrelevant excretions were excluded, a careful recording of 'facts' which constituted the bricks of reality. The new linguistic naturalism repudiated these theories, and, far more contentiously, argued that what had been proposed as 'philosophical problems' were a kind of shadow, cast by these mistaken theories of language onto human thought. Once you realise the truth about language, these questions would not be solved, but *dissolved.*

The argument which claims that such 'dissolution' should be possible, was again both simple and made to seem plausible and persuasive. Briefly stated, it can be put as follows: concepts are not platonic entities, they are the rules governing various words or clusters of words. Philosophical problems, it had been widely (though certainly not universally) agreed, are about concepts. But if concepts are what we *do* with words, then find out precisely just what indeed we do with the relevant words, and there you have your answer. What other kind of answer could you possibly have or desire? What other answer could there possibly be?

Two questions now arise: was there indeed such an orthodoxy (a claim which has been challenged), and what is wrong with it?

The question of the existence of this consensus is a historical matter, and its final resolution could only be achieved by a very thorough, and somewhat tedious, survey of the surviving documentation of the period. In the meantime, some persuasive general considerations can be adduced. A major change of style indisputably occurred in academic philosophical writings in this country as between the pre-war and the post-war periods. In the second stage, it suddenly became increasingly common for people to invoke 'ordinary language' and what we ordinarily do and do not say, and so forth. At the same time, a theory came to be available in the writings of Wittgenstein, which if true would justify and warrant that change of style. If Wittgenstein's theory, which I briefly sketched, is correct, then, as of course he himself insisted, the procedural shift is entirely appropriate. At the same time, Wittgenstein and those in contact with him were treated with great deference and respect. Now if a large number of people drastically change their habits, and the change follows from a certain doctrine, and the person who has expounded that doctrine is revered, it is not unreasonable to attribute the acceptance of the doctrine to the people who have changed their style, irrespective of whether they themselves have explicitly formulated and endorsed the doctrine. All the more so if the doctrine itself teaches that it ought not to be formulated, but *practised.*

It was almost impossible, during that period, to find a dissentient voice raised against that orthodoxy. There were of course opposing voices from people discounted as 'old fogeys' (*sic*), members of the previous generation who disapproved of the new orthodoxy, without being fully privy to its logical secrets. The orthodoxy itself was represented by a few leaders drawn from the middle aged and older generation, plus the younger generation, among whom *no* audible dissent was to be heard. It is quite impossible, for the period in question, to find any significant corpus of articles which are both critical and written by younger philosophers who were occupants of professional posts in England. This is a curious fact, but it squares entirely with what I recollect of the period.

But now to the second question — why is that philosophy so wrong? First of all, I ought to say that I have no objection whatsoever to a naturalistic theory of language (or, if it comes to that, a naturalistic theory of anything). The issue is not directly relevant to any of my own concerns; the fact that I find a naturalistic theory of language acceptable does not constitute very important support for that theory, so I am not inclined to push the matter. The naturalistic attitude can live without or with my endorsement, and in any case has no need of it. The point is that it isn't *this* which one finds really unacceptable in Wittgenstein and his intellectual progeny. It is the inference *from* the naturalistic theory of language, the conclusion drawn from it, which is so totally repellent. Because speech is but custom, no questions should remain when the custom is properly observed in all its diversity, and consequently — it was argued — philosophical problems have been dissolved. They are not: but it is a curious comment on the working and life situation of those who have found the theory acceptable, that they did not find it grossly repellent.

It was and is quite obvious to me that we cannot in this way transfer sovereignty over our conceptual, moral, political and social life to our verbal custom. Yet the contrary assumption that this can be done is essential, central for this method, and not something tangential, not an exaggeration which could be sloughed off. For if there are extra-customary constraints or authorities concerning how we think, then *they*, and not verbal custom, must be investigated. What they might be is a terribly difficult problem — but that *is* philosophy, and it cannot be conjured away. The deep absurdity which the adherents failed to sense was precisely this — the idea that our verbal custom could be the foundation of the legitimacy of our ideas, in morals, science, politics, anywhere. But our custom is a problem and not a solution.

For instance, the morality of any given age may indeed be embodied in its verbal behaviour, but obviously this doesn't mean that we must uncritically accept the morality of any given age or culture. In practice, the practitioners of this philosophy were so busy with trying to *apply* it, were practising the promised dissolutions by examining our uses of words, that they never quite came to face this problem, though they faced it tangentially.

Then one of two things is liable to happen. Either they assume, with a kind of innocent expression, a certain kind of irrationalism as self-evident. They would *frequently* say things like: of course, as philosophers, trained in logic or in understanding the use of words, we cannot pontificate about issues of morality, which in the nature of the case must be left to inspired preachers, seers, etc. In other words, the aspiration of mankind to subject all allegedly inspired preachers, seers, and others to rational scrutiny was simply dismissed, as a self-evident corollary of an allegedly obvious philosophic mistake. Alternatively, (and we shall have cause to discuss this at greater length) they did expressedly embrace a kind of romantic communalism, a view that the spirit of the community (expressed in its language) is the only foundation one can ever have for the basic principles of one's activities, whether moral, aesthetic, scientific or any other. Stanley Cavell, an American Wittgenstein-enthusiast, sums it up succinctly:

> ... all [that] ...Wittgenstein calls 'forms of life'. Human speech and activity, sanity and community, rests upon nothing more, but nothing less, than this.[1]

In other words, cultures are self-legitimating, and validate the norms of conduct and sanity found within them.

The claim incidentally that there was diversity in views or method within the movement cannot be sustained. The central guiding intuition, the criteria of problems and solutions, was very homogeneous. Of course there was a great deal of diversity on detail, and some diversity even in style. For instance, what Wittgenstein and Austin had in common was that neither ever developed any serious dissolutions of any problems. Wittgenstein indicated where the dissolution could allegedly be found, but didn't actually carry it out. Austin carried out the groundwork for the alleged dissolution, but never quite got there. This distinguishes Gilbert Ryle from both of them: his *The Concept of Mind* was a very brave book in as far as it unambiguously delivered a would-be dissolution of the problem of relationships of mind to body. It was simply behaviourism with a linguistic face. It wasn't very sensible, but it was brave.

So much for the past. What has happened since then? Not everything which has happened since the gradual dissolution of the linguistic movement after 1960 has any kind of interesting relation to it, and the scene is in any case now rather variegated and eclectic, and there are some aspects of the current scene which I'll simply leave aside, and I have no complaints about them and feel much admiration for them. For instance, this is true about a great deal of philosophy of science, or the outburst of fresh activity around what has come to be called cognitive science. But there are three prominent styles or movements on the philosophic scene which do deserve some critical comment.

1. Quiddity on Wheels

> ... *Entity, Intentionality, Quiddity* and rather insignificant words of the school.
> (Thomas Hobbes, *Leviathan*, Ch. IV)

Wittgenstein had reached his communalistic-hermeneutic position by a rather curious and unusual path. He viewed language, as stated, naturalistically, and also insisted (rightly enough) on the diversity of the functions it performed and on its social involvement. This naturalistic and social vision was reached, in his case, by reaction to a strange monistic theory of language expounded in his youthful *Tractatus*, which saw language as having the same structure as the notation of modern logic. The world was atomised into 'facts', which reflected the mutually independent propositions of the calculus of propositions, and the internal structure of facts was such that all these assertions mirrored the notation of logic and set-theory. These assumptions engendered the vision contained in his own *Tractatus*, but in his view they *also* engendered (and here he was quite wrong) all the other monistic, unificatory philosophies which have pervaded the history of thought. Wittgenstein's really central mistake was the supposition that these two approaches, the monistic one inspired by logic, and the naturalistic-plural-social one, were exhaustive. (Hence if one of them was shown to be wrong, the other one remained as the sole alternative.) No other approaches were possible. No other approaches had indeed been experienced by *him*, but that is quite another matter.

Here I might as well indicate what I believe to be the truth in this very important matter. Conceptual monism, the supposition that the world can be seen in a single idiom, in which all facts can be cross-related to each other, seems to me one of the most important and positive achievements of mankind. Science is not possible without it. The attainment of a single conceptual currency, in principle, is at least as important for intellectual advance as the attainment of monetary currency is for the furtherance of trade. The achievement of this single intellectual currency is a long and complex story, which I do not think anybody has yet properly unravelled. My own belief is that a jealous and exclusive deity was what, above all else, had taught mankind, or a proportion of mankind, a respect for the Law of Excluded Middle, and that when this jealous exclusivity fused with systematised logic and geometry and astronomy, and with scholastic attempts at unifying the vision of a society, they jointly prepared mankind for the possibility of the notion of *Nature*; in other words of a unitary and orderly system which could be investigated, and which could *only* be investigated, through its isolated manifestations in observation and experiment. The fact that the jealous deity also came to be a hidden deity, spurning direct revelation or manipulation of the world, and thus obliged men to seek its purpose only through observations of permanent regularities, no doubt also helped a good deal.

Whatever the explanations of the emergence of a Single Currency idea, its importance simply cannot be overrated. Those who live under its sway sometimes underrate its importance simply because they have come to take it for granted. But historically it is eccentric and unusual, and its emergence is something which needs exploration. I have merely sketched in some possible elements of such an explanation.

What Wittgenstein in effect proposed can only be described as a reversal of this trend, as the recommendation of a collective Infantile Regression for all mankind. The unitary vision was to be abandoned, and we are to retreat to the plurality of only socially (but not logically) connected 'language games', each of which then interacts with the world only in part referentially, but in the main socially, and each of which constitutes its own automatic vindication. Pre-scientific and in effect pre-rational humanity did speak and think *precisely* in this way; but our world has been totally transformed by two odd millennia of, in the end, partially successful efforts to get away from that vision and unify the world. Wittgenstein in effect wanted to scrap all this (though he didn't quite understand what he was doing) and return to a pre-unitary world with its very low capacity for cognitive growth, and one innocent of the Single Currency principle. Treated as a source of ideas for the reconstitution of primitive thought, Wittgenstein is valuable. Treated as a solution of *our* predicament, he is not.

The real point about him is this misunderstanding of the roots of our unificatory effort. He thought that it emerged from the magic cast by the notation of logic, a magic to which he himself had indeed been powerfully subject in his own youth. But that is only one, and a relatively unimportant and late way by which people reach the unitary vision; moreover, and this of course is supremely important, the unitary vision is not a mistake. Its merits and ultimate vindication are something which may be open to debate, but that is another matter. The path by which Wittgenstein had reached both unificationism *and* its repudiation was a very curious and highly eccentric one: the logician's way to Single Currency. It deserves special comment.

There had always been a style of philosophising about nature which started from what one might call formal concepts, that is, very general terms, which seem to embrace everything. Substance, accident, relation, are very obvious terms of that kind. It looks as if everything could be fitted into them. You then examine what these concepts contain and imply, and hey presto, you have a kind of science of the world, without even needing to do any further research. The scholastics had reasoned in this way. In the seventeenth century this method, in conjunction with a compassionate unifactory impulse, had engendered the stunning, notoriously intoxicating vision of Spinoza. A little later, Leibniz had produced another philosophy, less intoxicating and indeed rather puzzling, not to say surrealist, by a sustained reapplication of a similar method, and with different and much less exhilarating results.

Thomas Hobbes and others had satirised the pointlessness of this kind of procedure in a very effective way, and one might have thought that there would be no revival of this method in modern times. But such a supposition has proved mistaken. There has been one very important revival of the scholastic deployment of formal concepts, and it took place early this century, and young Wittgenstein took part in it. There was a rather special reason for it: the emergence of modern formal logic. Now there is an enormous difference between modern mathematical logicians and medieval scholastics, but there is also something they have in common. What they have in common is that they proceed from formal concepts. What distinguishes them is that the machinery erected with the help of these formal concepts by the scholastics was, despite or because of ponderous scholastic verbiage, extremely non-rigorous. It wasn't really a genuine, operational notation of the mathematical kind. If one uses it for a long series of inferences, there is no reason whatever to suppose it to be truth-preserving. It continues to be empty, but apart from that emptiness, it isn't even true in whatever sense formal systems can be true and rigorous. As this eventually became evident, this whole style of thinking about the world was abandoned.

By contrast, modern set-theory and logic, though formal and in some sense empty, are extremely rigorous. This rigour was I suppose intoxicating, and it inspired those who developed or mastered the technique to revive what might be called philosophy in the formal mode. *Quiddity* returned, but this time it was on wheels, or perhaps one should say it was computerised. None the less, it was a mistake as a *philosophy*. Lack of rigour, the failure to be truth-preserving, of the *earlier* scholasticism, was only *one* of its two sins: the formal emptiness was another, and probably, in this context, a more relevant one.

And here we come to the really strange event in modern philosophy, and in particular in some of the developments since the apex of the Wittgensteinian fashion. The later Wittgenstein perceived the futility of trying to see the world or language through formal notation, through formal concepts, as mirroring their structure, and he repudiated it with great emphasis. In fact his passionate repudiation of it became the very centre of his later thought. He muddied the issue a bit by conflating this repudiation with a simultaneous repudiation of conceptual monism, *and* totally misdiagnosing the roots of that monism into the bargain. He thought the problem was rooted in the formalism. In fact it has other and deeper roots. Above all, he mistakenly thought that there were only two intellectual options facing mankind, either naturalistic pluralism or formalistic monism. He passionately opted for the former.

The curious feature of one contemporary style of philosophising which I am inclined to call Quiddity on Wheels (and there is an awful lot of it about) — R.G. Collingwood called it philosophy by typographical jargon — is that somehow or other it tacitly assumed that Wittgenstein's mistaken supervision of two-paths only was correct, and having then tired of his linguistic naturalism and pluralism, it turned to what then seems the only other available path — without actually giving any reasons for so doing. It was as if it knew how to do two things only, either observe linguistic custom, or project logic onto the world — and having got tired of the former, there was nothing else to do but return to the latter. Curiously enough, this means ignoring the one element in Wittgenstein which is entirely valid; the perception of the pointlessness of trying to understand the entire world by simply forcing it into formal notions. The notation of set-theory and logic is of course of supreme importance in engendering the rigorous calculi, in illuminating the foundations of formal reasoning in general, and in providing a basis for a wide range of applications, in so to speak operational formal systems, in computers and elsewhere. On the other hand, a return to the scholastic Quiddity technique, of talking about diversified and complex phenomena of the world as if they were best understood when tormented into these forms, is without value. One can only repeat, it is most curious that this should have been done in defiance of the one valid insight of the Master, and without any genuine discussion of this second *volte face*.

The new Quiddity, like the old, tends to paralyse all one's logical intuitions, and thereby fortify the authority of the teacher. Wittgenstein had offered a diagnosis of that paralysis (which he called 'cramp'): formal concepts cannot be forced into either language or our normal thinking about things. The diagnosis, valid enough for the Quiddity style though not for philosophy in general, he mistakenly applied to philosophy at large.

To be accurate, the logical paralysis which cowes the learner subjected to Quiddity-reasoning has at least three elements: (a) the one diagnosed by Wittgenstein, the forcing of all material into an inappropriate formal mould; (b) the genuine technical difficulty of modern logic; and (c) a special confusion which haunts areas where the form and content of thought resemble each other. For instance, when the written form of a proposition is said to act as the 'name' of the proposition it expresses, one has acute difficulty in keeping the various aspects separate. It is very hard to keep apart the reality to which the proposition refers, the proposition itself, and its verbal expression. Our minds slide from one to the other, not fully under our control, the way in which our vision jumps from one *Gestalt* to another when a given visual pattern allows or encourages more than one interpretation. Our minds seem to be so made as not to be able to resist this *slide*. It is difficult to sort this out and keep one's mental gaze steady. Nothing really hinges on this and no serious problem was ever advanced by steadiness here; but these slide-inducing multi-level conceptual mind-twisters are constantly deployed in modern Quiddity, and though otherwise without much relevance, serve their purpose of overawing learners. I am not sure about the proportions in which (a), (b) and (c) contribute to this effect. Perhaps someone could do some research on this. But motorised Quiddity is back again, with a vengeance.

2. Idealism with a Semantic Face

The style describable as Quiddity on Wheels continues roughly in the general idiom of Wittgenstein, takes over one of his crucial assumptions (we must indulge either in scholastic formalism or in the description of natural languages, *tertium non datur*) and disastrously ignores his one valid insight (namely, that the functioning of natural languages cannot be reduced to a small number of formal concepts, whether those of set-theory or those of anything else). But there is another important and pervasive style of philosophising which proceeds precisely from the insight which Quiddity on Wheels ignores. It is an insight which could be called (though it was never so called by the Master) *Hermeneuticism*.

The point is this: the meanings contained in our communications are not dictated to us by the nature of things or set-theory or anything else, they are artefacts or customs of linguistic communities. In terms of the famous slogan, meaning is use. If you want to know what a given expression means, don't ask what it refers to, ask what it *does*. Explore the social context in which it operates and the multiform purposes which it serves.

So far so good. This is merely a restatement of what we call the naturalistic theory of language. But this insight or way of looking at language can be credited with a certain very interesting and very important corollary: it is a way of establishing, with *apparent* conclusiveness, convincing to some of the adherents of this outlook, the autonomy, the independence of human cultures. They cannot be reduced to nature, they cannot be merely a shadow play on the surface of things, controlled by the reality underneath.

The argument can be conveyed as follows. Supposing members of a given culture respond to and act in terms of a given meaning M. Suppose also, as is not at all implausible, that the meaning M is idiosyncratic, and occurs only in the culture or language in question. Assume also, and this again is quite plausible and probably often applies, that M cannot be translated into or reduced to some entity or process or whatever definable in neutral, extra-cultural scientific terms. All this seems to show that when people are reacting to, or are inspired by, or communicate M, what they are doing simply cannot be explained, for instance, as the result of some kind of causal mechanism operating in their physical environment or in their neurophysiology or anywhere else. *Ex hypothesi*, the natural processes of the environment are of neurophysiology operate in terms other than M, and not translatable into M. They are themselves M-blind. Consequently there can be no deterministic causal generalisation which would link *physical* antecedents with *social* consequences including M. The physical antecedents, as it were, are unable to pick out M or bring it about, because they are blind to it. If human beings act and define their actions in terms of concepts, and if these concepts (or some of them) are socially constructed in an idiosyncratic way, then neither cultures nor human conduct can be causally, naturalistically explained, for the categories in terms of which nature itself operates simply will not mesh in with the ones which each culture has rolled for itself. This, in one sentence, is the argument from cultural semantics to the autonomy of men and cultures.

This informally sketched argument is meant to convey just how the stress on the autonomy and irreducibility and the human-social production of meaning, can serve as a premiss for what can only be described as a new version of Idealism. The old type of Idealism, so fashionable in Europe and especially in Germany at the turn of the eighteenth and nineteenth centuries and during the early nineteenth century, tended to operate in terms of 'concepts'. As these concepts were assumed to operate impersonally and be linked to entire cultures and historic change, there really wasn't all that much difference between that old kind of Hegelian romanticism and the contemporary hermeneutic fashion. It is true that Hegelianism had the added interest of being concerned with the actual concrete changes that had occurred in history, and striving to account for these in terms of the self-transformation of that guiding abstract concept. Consequently it could be very suggestive for historical interactions, whereas our contemporary idealism is rather static and historically insensitive. But anyway, in formal presentation, there is this much difference — the old species tended to speak of concepts or ideas, whereas the contemporary variety concentrates on *meanings*.

Idealism of this kind, whether true or false, has an enormous attraction. If only it is valid, it establishes definitively that there is no danger to human freedom from some kind of natural determinism, and if at the same time it vindicates the diversity of human cultures, and protects them from the encroachment of standardisation, scientism, mechanisation. It is of course precisely this combination of attractions which constituted the appeal of romantic idealism in the first place. In fact, if this kind of Idealism were valid, it would be very difficult to understand how that encroachment of standardisation could ever have taken place: it can only be explained as some kind of terrible mistake, and it is then difficult to see why that mistake would have such a hold not only over human minds, but actually over human institutions and entire societies. In our time, the appeal of Idealism with a semantic face is further reinforced by another consideration. Within the now vastly expanded social sciences, there is a running battle between what might be called hard-headed positivists, quantitativists, reductionist-empiricists, on the one hand, and the meaningful-humanist, culture-respecting interpretationists on the other. An alleged philosophical proof of the autonomy of meaning and its pervasiveness in human life provides a most welcome charter or vindication or ammunition for the latter school. Some like it for this reason, some because it seems to protect cultures from erosion, and some because it protects human freedom from 'reductivist' sciences.

The central ideas of Wittgenstein have been enthusiastically adopted by followers of this very widespread tendency. It is less prominent among pure philosophers, and rather more prominent among social scientists, literary scholars and others. Some of the philosophers who have adopted this viewpoint have continued to concentrate on Wittgenstein, but that is relatively rare. Usually, this particular deployment of his ideas is found fused with other trends, springing from phenomenology, Dilthey, cultural anthropology, the so-called Frankfurt school, and, curiously enough, Marxism. This is strange indeed: anyone who bothers to re-read the abuse poured by Marx and Engels on the original version of romantic idealism in *The German Ideology* would find such a fusion surprising. Nevertheless, it most emphatically exists, and indeed is very widespread. Marxist theoreticians nowadays tend to be anti-empiricist in the social sciences (they use a special term, 'positivist', to designate anyone using facts against Marxist theories), and in their eagerness to protect interpretations from mere fact (discounted as superficial) they have been entirely willing to enlist this Idealism under a new name.

I do not myself believe that the autonomy either of men or of cultures can be so easily vindicated, though of course the question of human freedom is not settled so easily one way or the other; moreover, the deployment of this approach tends to lead to a sad underrating of the regrettable, but only too blatantly real, *non-semantic* constraints in human history and society, springing from violence and poverty. The fact that it is sad that we do operate under those constraints does not mean that we can conjure them away by conceptual hocus-pocus. More specifically, by discounting the new unification of the world, organisationally and conceptually, as some kind of puzzling and wicked error, this approach makes it extremely hard to *understand* it. The phenomenon of Disenchantment has roots far deeper than mere philosophical error, and cannot be conjured away by a philosophical counter-doctrine, even if its arguments were cogent, which alas they are not. Its practitioners promise a guaranteed Re-Enchantment, but their warranties do not survive scrutiny.

3. Mayflower Casuistry

There is another very pervasive style of philosophy which has become prominent in the recent decades, and which owes little or nothing to the central ideas which were so prominent during the post-war period. If anything, it may owe a great deal to simply ignoring and bypassing certain problems which at that stage had seemed obsessional. The trend I have in mind here is the one in which philosophers, lawyers, games theorists and economists, but not quite so much other social scientists, warmly co-operate. It consists of trying to establish and explore the implications of basic social, moral and political principles, not merely in the abstract, but with a view to rapid and serious applications to current social problems, such as for instance, the issues of justice and distribution. Though this school started in America, it has many followers and practitioners in Britain.

In various ways, this style is markedly distinct from what had prevailed before. On the whole, philosophers before and after the war, when they dealt with these problems, seemed to be fascinated, and one might say paralysed, by the fundamental and initial problem of any thought in this sphere: how does one bridge the gap between facts and values, or more generally, between that which can be rationally established, and that which is evaluative, and can constitute a claim over our moral (as opposed to merely our logical) obligations. A large proportion of thinkers who contemplated the horrifying chasm, which yawns between these two shores, seemed then to be petrified into a kind of immobility. They would either expatiate at length on how that Grand Canyon had come to be there, and what it meant for us and what restraints it imposed on our intellectual aspirations, or move around it in the nervous hope that some kind of bridging might be possible after all; but they most certainly did not *ignore* the problem. On the contrary, an observer might well gather the impression that the entire subject had become a permanent lament on this problem and its insolubility, and on the implications this has for human life. Positivists tried to pretend that it was only a logical point, that it really had nothing to do with them professionally, and that there is no cause to get hot under the collar about it, whilst people such as existentialists made quite a song and dance about it, almost literally, finding it both tragic and exhilarating or indeed tragically exhilarating, or exhilaratingly tragic. There were of course some, such as G.E. Moore early in the century, or R.M. Hare after the war, who combined an acute sense of the great Chasm with a conviction that they had found a way of working on the other bank nevertheless, and though the earlier part of their argument explained the Chasm, the latter part contained substantive moral judgements and social recommendations which were somehow meant to derive from the initial philosophical insights. But I think they were untypical. The basic condition of the moral philosopher in that period in face of the Is/Ought dichotomy, was that of a rabbit paralysed by the looming snake.

All that has changed. The snake has disappeared, it seems, and the rabbit has totally recovered his mobility and is rushing about like mad. To me, it is all a bit of a mystery — just what has made the cobra disappear? Is there a secret way of exorcising it, for making it disappear? I, who from time to time was as frightened of it as anyone, would be only too glad to be told how it was done. No one has told me. As far as I can see, nobody has forced the cobra to disappear, it is just that the rabbit nowadays behaves as if it weren't there. Happy rabbits.

Let me say first of all that I have no intention whatever of criticising the rabbits for ignoring the cobra. On the contrary, I rather admire them for having the sangfroid required for simply ignoring it, and going about their business as if it weren't there. The ultimate validation of values is a mystery and a problem, and it is quite wrong to pretend either that we have solved it, *or* that the absence of a solution doesn't matter. But given the fact that indeed we have not solved it, and that it is unlikely to be solved, and given the fact that we simply must face value problems whether we have a logical permit to do so or not, I rather admire rabbits who go about it with such a verve and energy and industry.

It is interesting to note, however, that the cobra which paralysed their predecessors no longer paralyses them, though it has emphatically *not* been exorcised. It is an interesting and perhaps deeply significant feature of our intellectual scene, but this isn't meant as a criticism of the procedures of the rabbits. I think it is probably rather a good strategy to pretend for a while that the cobra isn't there. Quite frankly, moaning about it and diagnosing one's own paralysis in the face of it was getting a bit boring. That is perhaps one of the reasons, though certainly not the only one, why the change has taken place.

Another reason often given is that the moral crisis of the Vietnam war obliged American professional philosophers to attend to practical moral issues, and that philosophers elsewhere followed suit. I am not convinced by that particular explanation, simply because a very profound moral and political crisis had been about for a long time, not more so recently than before, and if that were the explanation, the phenomenon to be explained should have occurred much sooner, or perhaps should never have been absent. I think part of the explanation is that a substantial proportion of the members of the very extensive academic philosophical profession simply had no inclination for, or possibly skill at, Quiddity on Wheels, the most favoured rival style within the trade. Though some of its tools were deployed in the style now under discussion, it can also be done without technicalities, and its technicality-saturation is much smaller.

Though I do not wish to criticise members of this general school for ignoring or quietly bypassing the problem of the fact/value distinction, or if you like the general problem of the validation of normative reasoning, but on the contrary sympathise with them in this, I do wish seriously, however, to query their procedures on quite a different count. To put it simply, they are profoundly unsociological, they have no sense of the diversity of social structures and cultures, of the way in which totally different kinds of constraints operate on human beings and their decisions in different societies, or the way in which cultural assumptions and values enter the minds of men, and reappear to them as their own, spontaneous and self-evident, compulsive logical or moral intuitions. On the contrary, they seem to treat the manner in which our souls regurgitate the constitutive principles of our cultures and societies as compulsive inner revelations, entirely at face value. Where the adherents of Idealism with a semantic face rhapsodise over the cultural roots of conceptual and moral intuitions (and leave it at that), the Mayflower Casuists singly ignore it. Personally, I'd like to see a sense of culture to be treated seriously but with reserve, as a problem and not as a final solution — but not ignored either.

All this is specially highlighted by one of the most famous and influential exercises in this genre. The book in question tries to clarify the notion of justice and specify its effective and binding content. The reader is invited to take part in the following mental experiment. He is asked to imagine himself stripped of all his specific attributes and in particular his advantages, and to think of himself as completely naked, devoid of attributes, especially with respect to the kind of characteristics which normally might persuade him to support this or that social arrangement because it happened to be to his specific advantage. Having thus gone through this kind of conceptual quarantine, a moral de-lousing, he is then invited to ask himself what kind of society he would favour. Note that he is now unlikely to choose a society which would have special privileges for the rich, or special rewards for the clever or the beautiful, because he has no idea whether he is himself rich, clever or beautiful. So his choice of a social order is very likely to contain generous provisions for those who have none of these advantages. After all, they tend to outnumber those who do. It is a curious fact that in American philosophy, such 'cosmic exile' has been much denigrated and ridiculed in the theory of knowledge, but *nur mit ein bisschen anderen Worten*, is all the rage in moral and political philosophy.

I have no objections whatever to the specific values and recommendations which the author in question extracts from this *Gedankenexperiment*. They are excellent lib-lab values, allowing moderate enterprise but with ample insurance to safeguard the well-being of those who fall behind. No man who is one of nature's social democrats could possibly fail to have his heart warmed by such values, and I certainly have not the slightest objection to them. As far as I am concerned, a good society may well be defined by their implementation.

But that is not the point. What one can and I fear should object to is not the values themselves, which seem admirable to me, but the way in which they have been established, or if you like, the illusion *that* they have been established at all. Are they chosen in this imaginary situation because they are good values, or are they good values because, by definition, anything chosen in this situation is good? Do you *know* that other people, who are unlike yourself, would also choose them? Anyway, the main point is that the conceptual and moral nakedness, practised in the experiment, is entirely spurious. One can well assume oneself ignorant of what worldly advantages one possesses and lacks, but one still retains an enormous corpus of values and assumptions and expectations about the institutional environment, which remain with one when one sees oneself in this imaginary situation. But assume people from completely different types of society to pass through the same experiment — say people drawn from a caste society, or a tribal society, or what you will — and supposing that they can make sense of the experiment at all, which is not obvious, the answer with which they will come out will of course be totally different.

One might as well call all this Mayflower Casuistry or the American Illusion. Early Americans (and evidently in some cases late Americans too) were drawn towards Social Contract reasoning, and assumed that they could form a consensual, contractual society, on the basis of values and ideas which they had brought with themselves from some kind of pre-social conceptual outer space. This of course was not so. They had come from a very unusual north-west European society, and in fact were selected from certain rather more extreme tendencies within it, and even if they did arrive on the American shores without major property or rank differentiation, they still brought with them an entire, strong, distinctive and fascinating culture. It was a culture with a high valuation of conscience and individualism, which could rely on individuals retaining their convictions even when stripped of specific positions and their accoutrements. This internalisation of a self-sustaining conscience made this society particularly liable to see itself as based on a Contract of the Naked. But a philosophy which generalises this condition for all mankind fails to understand both its own society and that of others.

So it seems that the habit of supposing that it could establish society on values which it did not itself engender, but which ratified and formed *it*, has remained with this tradition. The supposition that one can possess pre-social 'self-evident' premisses absolutely pervades the experiment and the whole thought-style of which it is an example, and is of course enshrined in the American Constitution. But all this kind of experiment really does is simply lead us back to our own values, plus the illusion that they are extraneously grounded and self-evident.

One should add that this new casuistry is fairly scholastic. It goes through prolonged, abstract, often formalistic reasoning; yet it is not genuinely rigorous and truth-preserving in its inferences. Anyone in rough sympathy with the underlying moral intuitions of an argument will usually accept its conclusions, and perhaps derive some satisfaction and reinforcement of faith from the exercise. But no one, I think, will be compelled by these exercises to adopt conclusions with which he is not in sympathy in the first place. He will easily find rival arguments whose conclusions are more in line with his own values. This being so, it is not clear what purpose is served by the formal elaboration. It orchestrates themes already accepted for other reasons, but it does not establish anything.

There is an interesting contrast between styles (3) and (2), between Mayflower Casuistry and Hermeneutic Idealism. Mayflower Casuistry has no sense of society and culture at all, but assumes all men to think and act in the same kind of general space, similarly conceptualised. By contrast, Hermeneutic Idealism has a most exaggerated sense of and respect for cultural systems, their autonomy and incommensurability. In principle, it endorses and loves them all, etc. It assumes that they are somehow self-contained and authoritative, and it pays insufficient heed to the objective, earthy and material constraints to which they are subject, constraints which may well be similar for a variety of cultures, and which restrain their conceptual fantasy. It ignores the supremely important fact that they are now all involved in a global process which, for very deep and powerful reasons, has been imposing a single conceptual currency on all of us, and which plays by different rules from the historically earlier, semi-autonomous cultural cocoons. This fact is ignored by Hermeneutic Idealists, and in a curious way both ignored and naïvely exemplified by Mayflower Casuistry. Style (1), Quiddity on Wheels, on the other hand has no sense of society at all, and is exceedingly scholastic to boot.

How can these styles be assessed, and what could be the way forward? As far as the operationalised scholasticism of (1) is concerned, one can only say that these techniques unquestionably have an important part to play in the investigation of formal systems, in the foundations of mathematics, and the extremely important applied fields in which formal systems are deployed. But they probably have no significant role in the investigation of structures such as natural languages. It is unlikely to make any contribution to the illumination of philosophical problems.

As far as the other two styles are concerned, the way forward seems to me clearly to lie in avoiding the excesses of each. Philosophy should return to a more concrete concern with real societies and with historical development, but without, on the one hand, pretending that all cultures are alike (whilst in fact naïvely universalising one's own), or, on the other hand, exaggerating the autonomy and authority of all cultures. A new 'philosophical history' is required which could attempt to understand the overwhelming changes which have taken place in recent centuries, but without the intoxication and naïveté which characterised nineteenth-century philosophies of Progress. Those are no longer viable, but they have not alas yet been adequately replaced. In contrast with Mayflower Casuistry, we need a sense of the diversity and radical transformation of human societies, and we must refrain from spuriously vindicating our own by ignoring the others. Unlike the Semantic Idealists, we must not absolutise them all and ignore the unique problems and claims of our own. Unlike the Quidditists on Wheels, we must refrain from scholasticism in the name of technique. We need a sense of the absolutely fundamental nature of change and a determination to understand it, but without any of the messianism which had accompanied the earlier efforts in this direction. Vertigo without messianism might perhaps be the correct slogan.

Note

1. *Must we mean what we say?* (Cambridge University Press, 1976), p. 52.

5 A *REDUCTIO AD ABSURDUM* OF DESCRIPTIVISM

R.M. Hare

Most moral philosophers are, I suppose, descriptivists of some sort; and most of those who become so (unlike John Mackie, who was one of the few exceptions[1]) do it because of a certain motivation. They have a deep desire to establish something that can be loosely described as the objectivity of moral judgements. And this desire in turn arises from a still deeper one, the desire to do one's moral thinking in a rational way. The route from the desire for rationality via the desire for objectivity to descriptivism is a well trodden one; but it is nevertheless a primrose path; for, as we shall see, it leads those who follow it into one or another form of relativism, which is precisely what these thinkers are trying to avoid. They can only avoid it by retracing their steps.

This primrose path starts from the assumption that the only way to achieve rationality is to secure objectivity. This assumption might be acceptable, if only the word 'objectivity' had a clear and unambiguous meaning. But it notoriously has not. The primrose path is followed by those who take it as obvious that the only kind of objectivity is that provided by descriptivism. What this kind is we shall see in a moment.

Luckily we now have available a very elegant illustration of how one may proceed down the primrose path, in Professor MacIntyre's presidential address to the American Philosophical Association at its Eastern Meeting in New York in December 1984.[2] This is so well written and so larded with excellent examples that I shall be able to describe the route more briefly and clearly than if I had to take the reader through the more tortuous writings of some other primrose-fanciers.

I am sure that MacIntyre is a descriptivist, and that he has proceeded all the way down the primrose path to relativism; but I am not sure what motives have led him down it, or whether they are as I have been describing. His thesis is a quite general one. It applies not only to moral and other evaluative words, but to expressions used in science and even to proper names. He does not indeed claim that in any of these areas of discourse it affects all words; but

A Reductio Ad Absurdum *of Descriptivism* 119

he implies that it affects enough of them to establish his pessimistic conclusion. I shall in what follows largely confine myself to the bearing of his thesis on moral philosophy, partly because I am only an amateur in those other fields, and partly because, as MacIntyre rightly implies, it is in moral philosophy and in its close relation political philosophy that the thesis would, if true, have its greatest practical impact.

The thesis is this, if I may attempt a brief summary which does not do it too much injustice. A very large number of words in all languages are culture-bound in this sense, that their serious use in speech-acts to which the speaker subscribes is not available to those who are not participants in the culture. So much is familiar from other authors, and indeed from MacIntyre's own earlier writings. What is more peculiar to him is the political pessimism.

MacIntyre thinks we cannot use the words of a culture in which we are not participants, and therefore cannot by using them communicate with those who are, in order to discuss with them the moral and other disagreements between us. His reason is that the meaning of these words is tied to common beliefs and values and traditional texts, shared by the participants but not by others. For the same reason it is, he thinks, impossible for participants in one culture to use words which are tied to their own culture in order to discuss differences with members of other cultures. They will just not be understood. And so, if the differences are important ones with political consequences which the disputants think vital, their only recourse, MacIntyre implies, will be to violence and the struggle for power. MacIntyre's arguments for untranslatability are different from, and largely independent of, those of the Quine-Davidson school, so I shall not in this chapter discuss the latter.

I agree that if the thesis is accepted, these consequences are likely to follow. But unlike MacIntyre I regard this as a *reductio ad absurdum* of the thesis. For although it must be admitted that there is too much violence in the world, not all disputes between people of different cultures are settled by violence or power struggles. It would have been worth MacIntyre's while to look more closely at how they are sometimes settled even by more or less rational discussion.

The essentials of an understanding of how to bring this about were explained a long time ago in my *The Language of Morals*[3], but in terms of an example (missionary converting cannibals) which MacIntyre might not like, and which in any case introduces irrelevant factors. Perhaps there are those now who think that it is colonialistic and wrong to convert cannibals so that they no longer go scalp-hunting. And in most cases, unlike that which I described, force played a part in the suppression of cannibalism. And even where it did not, it is unlikely that rational discussion had much to do with the cannibals' conversion.

So let me take a different example; that of a discussion between, say, a Sudanese and an American of the practice of female circumcision. (I will use this familiar term, although to be accurate one should use the more specific terms 'clitoridectomy' and 'infibulation'.) While I was writing this chapter and had already chosen the example, I was lucky enough to be lent a very illuminating as well as horrifying booklet on this subject.[4] The main author is a Westerner, but several of her collaborators were from cultures which practise female circumcision. The fact that they could jointly produce the booklet casts some doubt on MacIntyre's thesis. Evidently people from different cultures *can* discuss a question like this, because the contributors *had* discussed it, and reached the rational conclusion that the practice is wrong. Their reasons are in the booklet. The discussion is mainly factual, but it does make some use of value-words. The ones that occur most commonly are words like 'harmful'. This shows that such discussions can have a utilitarian basis. 'Rights', however, are also mentioned, so that is another possibility, although it would be a mistake to suppose that utilitarians cannot also use the term 'rights'.[5]

I have read at least one article by a Western journalist highly sympathetic to this practice as an element in an indigenous culture with which it would be wrong to interfere; so it is at any rate *possible* for Westerners to respect the values of other cultures. But let us suppose that our American is not so sympathetic, and thinks the practice wrong. The Sudanese, on the other hand, thinks it is obligatory upon young Sudanese women: they would be doing wrong if they did not follow the custom.

They will naturally use the word 'wrong' in discussing their difference (let us suppose that the Sudanese speaks English). One of them will say that it is wrong to circumcise girls, and the other that it is wrong not to circumcise them. Is it MacIntyre's view that communication must inevitably break down, because the word 'wrong' will have different meanings in their two mouths? I cannot answer this question, at least until I have drawn attention to a distinction, which ought to be already familiar,[6] between two classes of evaluative words, in order to forestall an arrant piece of argument-rigging to which descriptivist philosophers often have recourse. They have repeatedly urged us to turn our attention away from the more 'general' evaluative words like 'wrong' and towards more 'specific' words like 'cruel'. Because 'general' and 'specific' have other uses, I prefer to use 'primarily evaluative words' or 'primary value-words' for the first class, whose evaluative meaning is primary, and 'secondarily evaluative words' or 'secondary value-words' for the second, whose evaluative meaning is secondary to an entrenched descriptive meaning. The object of this common descriptivist ploy is to suck the greatest possible advantage from the fact that the descriptive meaning of the second sort of words is entrenched. We *know*, they wish to argue, that to inflict pain just for fun is cruel.

I shall not now labour the obvious prescriptivist counter-argument that it is just as important to turn our attention in the opposite direction too, towards primary value-words like 'wrong', in order to get the whole picture. Secondarily evaluative words were not a new discovery, nor was their behaviour unexplored, when these writers pounced on them. My purpose in mentioning the distinction is that it plays an important part in showing why MacIntyre is too pessimistic.

The Sudanese and American, I am going to argue, *could* communicate if they had a primary value-word 'wrong' which meant the same in both their mouths. It would not make any difference if, instead of this, there were a primarily evaluative Arabic word which meant the same as the English word. In either case they could communicate about their difference, using the Arabic or the English word, once they were assured of their equivalence. The issue between MacIntyre and me concerns whether there can be this equivalence. We can readily grant him that, if they were confined to the use of secondarily evaluative words, it might well be the case that the appropriate Arabic word of this secondarily evaluative sort did *not* mean the same as its nearest American equivalent, because its use carried with it substantial evaluative commitments, necessary to the understanding of the word — commitments which the American could not accept. I do not disagree with MacIntyre about the limitations on the use of such words. The question is whether there are any words apt for use in their dispute which are not subject to these limitations.

Whether 'wrong' could be such a word, or whether it could have any serviceable Arabic equivalent, cannot be determined without some more ethical theory: it will depend on the answer to some important theoretical questions. Let us first make another concession, that *if* descriptivism were correct, and 'wrong' were a descriptive, that is, a purely descriptive,[7] word, it could not serve their purpose of communication, because, for the reasons MacIntyre gives, it could not be univocal in their two mouths.

I say it *could* not be univocal; but this may have been to overstate MacIntyre's case. There are more ways than one in which it might be univocal without ceasing to be descriptive. First of all, there might be common values which the American and the Sudanese shared, and to which they could both appeal. In that case we should expect there to be common univocal words, or equivalent words in the two languages, for invoking these values, and these words could have a common descriptive meaning. This is what happens all the time between members of the same culture, and the Sudanese and the American might to this limited extent *share* a culture. However, though MacIntyre might well agree to this, it is not unrealistic to suppose that in our imaginary case it might not be so, but that nevertheless the way to a discussion of their dispute in a common language might still be open. Later we shall be exploring this way.

It must be added that it is not necessary, and is probably wrong, to give a descriptivist interpretation of this phenomenon. Moral philosophers of the sort that used to be called 'naturalists' (people now try to make us give up this useful expression) would say that the descriptive meaning of these words is the only meaning they have, and seek to give a definition or at least explanation of the words in terms of non-moral expressions. But a non-descriptivist like myself can give a better, because less vulnerable, explanation by saying that, although the words might indeed have such a common descriptive meaning, this might not be the only element in their meaning. They might have an evaluative or prescriptive meaning too, which might also be common to the two disputants. I shall later be giving an account of this common prescriptive meaning, which, as we shall see, offers the possibility of rational discussion between them even when they do *not* initially share any common values. I shall also be saying more about how the two kinds of meaning can combine and interact.

Another possibility is that, although they shared no values which could be appealed to in this dispute, they might have a

A Reductio Ad Absurdum *of Descriptivism* 123

common stock of value-words which were the names of 'non-natural qualities' of an intuitionistic sort, of which wrongness might be one. I put the suggestion in this Moorian way, not to caricature it, but to place it in its historical context. However, this manoeuvre is not going to save the intuitionist from relativism of a different sort. For in cases where the disputants remained irreconcilable, as they might in this case, they would each be left relying on their own intuitions or convictions, and there would be no way of deciding which was right, as there should be if 'wrong' were a genuinely descriptive word. It would, indeed, be possible to say, Tarski-fashion, that the statement that the practice is wrong is true, and the person who makes it is right, if and only if the practice is wrong. But if this is all they can say, and each is left in complete liberty to go on maintaining that he is right, although both cannot be, the realist claim is empty, and no different from relativism. If there are no constraints on what we can attribute non-natural properties to, they are descriptive of nothing in particular.

However, if we grant to MacIntyre what he seems to want to say, that there are cases in which none of these expedients will serve (that is, cases in which there are no relevant common values to be appealed to, and in which their *intuitions* about the wrongness or obligatoriness of the practice of female circumcision remain irreconcilable) is there any way, in spite of what MacIntyre says, in which they might discuss their difference rationally and reach agreement (if necessary by questioning those irreconcilable intuitions)? Such a way could *ex hypothesi* not make use of intuitions. I shall argue that prescriptivism, unlike descriptivism of MacIntyre's or any other sort, does offer such a way.

Let us start with a very simple model, which, since I am not an ethical imperativist,[8] I do not think to be an example of a moral dispute at all, though it is, like moral disputes, about a prescriptive question. The example is designed to show that there can be a common *prescriptive* element in language, even when there is no agreement about the truth of any descriptive statements about values. I say to someone 'Shut the door'; and a third party says to the same person 'Do not shut the door'. It cannot be denied that all three of us might understand what was being said. However, the two people making the requests might share no values, nor any factual opinions that are relevant to our present argument. They would have, of course, to agree on what it is to shut a door, and agree that there is a door, and perhaps that the addressee is able to shut it; but these presuppositions, as they are called, are immaterial to the present argument.

The example shows that there can be a common understanding of prescriptive expressions even where there is no agreement on the *reasons* for the requests or other prescriptions that they are used to express. This is important, because the whole drift of MacIntyre's argument is the following: No shared values; therefore no serviceable common language for discussing their dispute; therefore no reasons that either can adduce why the other should change his opinion. Notice how it is the underlying descriptivism that leads to this train of argument: since meaning on this view has to be descriptive meaning (there being no other kind of meaning for it to be), if two people do not have common descriptive rules for the use of expressions, those expressions cannot have a common meaning for them, and therefore cannot be parts of a common language. And since, on this view, the descriptive rules, specifying what words one can correctly apply to what, also specify the reasons for the application (analogously to 'You can call it a triangle because it has just three straight sides'), in the absence of shared descriptive rules there will be no shared reasons.

This is a good point at which to make clear what exactly *is* the descriptivism that I am attacking, before I go on to show why the imperative example I have just given should lead us to reject it. Descriptivism (or the descriptive fallacy as Austin called it[9]) is the belief that all words get their meaning in the same way as descriptive words and statements do, by having application-conditions or truth-conditions. The importance of imperatives for ethics is not that moral judgements *are* imperatives, but that imperatives are a standing counter-example to refute this mistaken view. To explain the point more fully: descriptivists think that for any sentence to having meaning is for there to be some condition under which statements expressed by it would be true; and this in turn would depend on the conditions for the correct application of the descriptive expressions in it. It will also depend on the reference of the referring-expressions in it, and perhaps on other things too; but that need not here concern us.

Descriptivism is tailored to fit the case of descriptive statements, and perhaps works all right for these;[10] but it is mistaken to extend the doctrine to all kinds of speech act. It obviously does not work for imperatives, which cannot be true (there are no *application-rules* for the imperative verb-form). To know the meaning of 'Shut the door' is not to know under what conditions we can truly say it, nor even under what conditions we can say it at all.[11] The Latin word '*esto* (let it be so)', which we may take as a pure imperative verb-form, does not get its meaning from rules which tell us when and what we can, when using it, command or request.

That MacIntyre is a descriptivist in this sense seems evident from what he says about communication between members of different cultures, and in particular about bilinguals.[12] The problems of communication between cultures and the personal problems of the bilingual arise, in his view, because of divergence between different 'standards of truth and justification' (p. 10 and elsewhere). His idea seems to be that the different cultures use different standards of truth, and that therefore they have 'rival conceptual schemes' (ibid.), and their words are mutually untranslatable, because a word in one language will lack any equivalent in the other. His thought is, evidently, that if there are different 'standards of truth' (truth-conditions), there must be different meanings, and untranslatability is the consequence.

MacIntyre intends this to apply not only to descriptive words but to evaluative and prescriptive ones too. This is clear from the fact that he includes, among the choices that confront people in such a conflict between cultures, the choice of a 'way of life' (ibid.). As he says earlier (pp. 81f.), very different cultures may still share a common stock of expressions such as 'Snow is white'; and from this we may infer that it is, by contrast, the evaluative words in their languages that will create the trouble. And we may agree that *if*, as MacIntyre appears to think, all these evaluative words had their entire meaning determined for them by descriptive meaning-rules or truth-conditions, the trouble would indeed be unavoidable. For there would then be no evaluative words that were not culture-bound; when discussing questions of value, one could not open one's mouth without, by the use of some value-word, committing oneself to the values of one culture or the other. There would be no evaluative language available in which communication could take place *between* cultures.

But this is all on the assumption that descriptivism is correct, which our imperative example shows it not to be. The position is radically altered if, as in fact is the case, our languages contain, besides secondarily evaluative words which *are* culture-bound, primarily evaluative words which are not. The biggest contribution that moral philosophy can make to the resolution of conflicts between cultures and ways of life, and in general between adherents of conflicting values, is to explore the logic of these primarily evaluative-words, in order to show how people who disagree can reason with one another. Is it not possible that these words, like 'ought' and 'wrong', are among the 'large parts of every language that are translatable into every other' (pp. 8f.)? The 'every' may be an exaggeration; for no doubt there are languages which do not contain equivalents of these words, any more than languages in tropical countries, perhaps, contain words for snow; but it would be surprising if evaluative words of this culture-independent kind were not available to the disputants in most intercultural disagreements.

I shall come later to a possible objection that MacIntyre might make, namely that even these primarily evaluative words like 'wrong' are culture-bound too, and therefore are not apt vehicles for communication between cultures. One might think this for two reasons, one of them obviously a bad one and the other more plausible. The more plausible one is that since, as I shall be arguing, the logic of these words does constrain us to reason in accordance with certain rules, and therefore in principle will lead us to certain conclusions, it is not neutral, and therefore must be culture-bound. To this form of the objection I shall return.

The bad reason is that the *descriptive* meanings attached to all value words reflect the ways of life of different cultures (as they do) and that therefore by using even primarily evaluative words we bind ourselves to a culture. This is indeed true of secondarily evaluative words, as we have seen. But the primarily evaluative words are so classified just because their descriptive meaning is secondary, and is therefore more able to give way when attitudes change, the evaluative meaning remaining unaltered. It is possible, as we shall see, to argue in terms of these words without clinging to their existing descriptive meanings, because it is not the particular descriptive meanings that determine the logic of the argument, but the evaluative meaning. The latter, indeed, does carry with it the requirement that, because of universalisability, there has to be *some* descriptive meaning at any one time;[13] but it is not required that it remain unchanged through time.

That evaluative and descriptive meanings can thus vary independently of one another can be shown *a fortiori* by considering the case of secondarily evaluative words, of which we may take as a well-worn example 'cruel'. If people's attitude towards the treatment of animals changes, they will start to speak of 'cruelty to animals', where earlier the infliction of pain on animals for fun would not have been called cruel. The suffering inflicted in those earlier days was part of the fun, and was not condemned; so the pejorative word 'cruel' could not be used of it. But in these kinder times the descriptive meaning of 'cruel' has changed. Before, one could not call badger-baiting cruel; now one can. If I now say 'Tom is a cruel man', it will have become the case, as it was not before, that one possible confirmation of this statement is that Tom indulges in badger-baiting. But the word may not have altered its evaluative meaning at all. It may be no less, and no more, pejorative than before.

This possible independent variation of the evaluative and descriptive meanings might be denied by those, of whom MacIntyre seems to be one, who think that in principle no distinction can be made between these two elements in the meaning of value-words, or, less extremely, that the meanings cannot be detached from each other in the way I have been assuming. It seems hard to sustain this view in the light of the phenomena I have been describing. One argument used for it rests on a fact to which MacIntyre also draws attention, that we have (as indeed we have) 'a power to extrapolate from uses of expressions learned in certain types of situation to the making and understanding of new and newly illuminating uses' (p. 9). It has been argued that we could not perform this extrapolation on the basis of the descriptive meaning alone, and that therefore the evaluative meaning must be part and parcel of the whole meaning of the word.

I cannot follow this argument. In the natural sense of the words, it can be readily agreed that both kinds of meaning are part and parcel of the whole meaning. But this does not prevent our distinguishing them. We can do so by specifying each separately.[14] The suggestion is that if we had just the descriptive meaning to go on, we should not *know* how to extend it to new uses. We need the evaluative meaning to show us what new sorts of thing we can apply the word to, and thus extend the adverse or favourable evaluation to a new kind of object. But I can see no difficulty here.

The matter may become clearer if we attend to a pervasive feature of language which was noticed a long time ago by the pragmatist F.C.S. Schiller, and called by him 'the plasticity of meaning'.[15] Almost any use of any descriptive word can in principle (perhaps subtly and slightly) affect its accepted meaning. For example, whenever we use the word 'white' for some object, we do not merely rest on the basis of a convention about its use; we signify our subscription to the convention. It will be taken that we do accept that such objects can truly be called white. Often the effect is only to reinforce the convention, but sometimes, if the object in question was just outside the previous borderline, we thereby make a move towards altering it by extending the meaning of the word. If others follow us, the change will stick, and the convention will thereafter be different.

How, it may be asked, do we *know* when to extend meanings in this way? In the strict sense we do not know; we decide. Obviously, if we want to be followed in our extended use, we must not go too far beyond the existing use. We must not stretch the analogy further than other users of the word will tolerate. But subject to this constraint we are at liberty to extend our uses of words, and it is not a question of knowing what we may or may not do, but of what we can get away with.

If this is true of pure descriptive words, it is true all the more of the descriptive meanings of secondarily evaluative words. Here too we must not stretch the analogy too far. Cruelty to animals has to be *like* cruelty to people in more or less obvious ways. But how do we *know* whether to call badger-baiting cruel? As before, we do not know; we decide. We decide on the basis of a changed sensibility which has made us feel about badgers some of the sentiments we feel about humans in analogous situations. I shall come later to arguments for extending our sympathies in this way, as it is very natural to do;[16] but nothing about the descriptive meaning of the word 'cruel' compelled us to, for that is not firmly attached; it does not determine our attitudes but follows them. A quite different sort of argument is needed to justify the change in attitude, which a deeper understanding of ethical theory and of the *prescriptivity* of moral judgements would explain.[17]

What happened in the badger-baiting case was that our evaluations changed (and whether or why they *should* have changed is another matter); and so we started to use this secondarily evaluative word with an extended descriptive meaning. That this can happen does nothing to show that the two elements in the meaning cannot be distinguished, nor even that they cannot be separately specified.

In the case of primarily evaluative words what happens is even clearer. I said earlier that the two kinds of value-words are distinguished by a difference in the firmness with which the two elements in their meaning are attached to them. In the case of the primary value-words, it is likely to be the descriptive meaning that gives way; in the case of the secondary value-words, the evaluative. But this is only a matter of probability and of degree. We have just been looking at a case in which it is the descriptive meaning of a secondary value-word that yields. In the case of such words, as we saw, it cannot yield too abruptly or too far, because the analogy cannot be stretched more than other people will tolerate, or we shall be misunderstood.

But in the case of primary value-words like 'ought' and 'wrong' the position is reversed. That is one of their most useful features, because it enables us to go on using them when our values have changed, and to use them to discuss value-disputes between cultures or between individuals who disagree; these words, unlike secondary value-words, are not tied so firmly to one value-system. We might, if our sensibilities and our attitudes changed in the way I have described, say 'One ought not to treat badgers like that; it is wrong.' If we said this, we should be *understood*, even if we had said something was wrong that nobody had seen anything wrong in before, nor in anything like it. People would understand us, though they would wonder why we said it. We must not confuse being unable to understand what somebody says with being unable to understand why he says it.[18] If we could not understand what he was saying, we could not even begin to wonder why he said it, because we should not know what *it* was. We would know what words he uttered, but not what he meant by them; and we have to do the latter if we are to be perplexed at his holding such an opinion. We have, that is, to know what the opinion is before we can be perplexed.

Because the descriptive meaning of primarily evaluative words like 'wrong' and 'ought' is relatively loosely tied to them, and they therefore have the useful feature just noticed, these are the words that our American and Sudanese are likely to use in talking about female circumcision. But before I show how, I must deal with two moves, both of them inspired by Wittgenstein, which are sometimes made in this argument. The first concerns *rules* for the uses of words.[19] The model commonly used is that of extending a series in arithmetic. Suppose that somebody tells us to extend the series 2, 4, 6 ... Do we know what to do? When we get to 200, do we know that we are not at liberty to go on '200, 204, 208'? The natural answer is that we do not, if *all* we have been told is to extend the series 2, 4, 6. If that is all we have been told, we do not know whether, when we get even to 8, we are on the right lines in continuing '10, 12 ...' To know that, we should have to have been given the rule for extending the series, namely 'Add 2'.

There is a dilemma here: either we have the rule or we do not have it. If we have it, we can extend the series indefinitely. If we do not have it, we cannot extend it at all. I said, we have to have *been told* the rule. But it would do as well if we had caught on to it by ourselves,[20] provided that we were sure what it was. The important thing is that the rule should be definite in our minds. This does not, needless to say, require an ability to formulate the rule in words; we can have a rule in this sense if, as Ryle put it, we 'know how' to extend the series.[21]

The same dilemma applies to word-use. Either we know the exact meaning of a word we are going to use, or we do not. In the case of all ordinary words (exceptions being the precisely defined terms of some sciences and of mathematics) we most probably do not, since their meanings are not exact and do not need to be. To the extent that we do not, we are *at liberty* to extend the meaning in the way I have been illustrating. But, as we saw, it is not a question of *knowing* how to extend it; we can extend it in ways we can get away with, if we are so inclined. When using purely descriptive words, we may have reasons for being so inclined, though they have to be fairly obvious ones if communication is not to break down.

In the case of secondarily evaluative words, the reason will be a change in attitude or in sensibility; and here too, if we are to go on using a word *of this secondarily evaluative sort*, the change will have to be not too abrupt. There are even cases, like that of 'super apple', where we are not allowed to change the meaning at all without higher authority.[22] But with primarily evaluative words, the change can be much more abrupt. Prophets and moral reformers can preach against new sins; they may be thought crazy, but their words will be understood. Was not Pythagoras understood when he said that one ought on no account to eat beans? Or Govind Singh when he said that Sikhs ought never to cut their hair?

The other Wittgensteinian move has become very fashionable in moral philosophy, though I should be surprised if the Master himself would have used it in this area. He said 'If language is to be a means of communication there must be agreement not only in definitions but, queer as this may sound, agreement in judgements also.'[23] This may be true of descriptive words whose meanings are determined by truth-conditions. The 'paradigm case argument', which used to be more popular, even in ethics where it is clearly inapplicable, than it is now, has this much to be said for it, that if we do not agree, regarding some typically white things which are plainly visible to us, that they are white, we can hardly be said to understand the use of the word. It is a crass error to extend this argument to value-words; and the same error is committed by those who invoke this Wittgensteinian dictum in ethics. It has the highly conservative consequence, which it shares with most forms of naturalism, that we have, on penalty of failure of communication, to stick to the values which have given moral words their descriptive meanings hitherto. This will no doubt be palatable to those who do not want to have to think about whether to abandon their existing mores. It is more curious to see how at least one would-be revolutionary struggles to escape from this consequence, thereby landing herself in a kind of non-descriptivism hardly distinguishable from that which, without perhaps fully understanding it, she thought she had summarily discarded at the beginning of her book.[24] There could no better illustration of how 'realists',[25] starting from a desire to discipline their thought by attaching it to supposed moral 'facts', end up in a position which allows them to say whatever they feel like saying.

Because prescriptive words do not get their meanings from truth-conditions, neither the paradigm case argument nor this Wittgensteinian move applies to them. This is most clearly seen in the case of imperatives, which obviously can be used in communication between people who do not agree in the prescriptions they accept. But for the same reason they do not apply to the prescriptive meanings of evaluative words either. They therefore ought not to be used in ethics, and I hope will cease to be when the nature of moral words is better understood. What is extraordinary is that descriptivist philosophers should make such heavy weather of these familiar phenomena, which are easily explicable on lines quite consistent with the views of their opponents, and base arguments on them which, once the phenomena are understood, at once collapse.

Applying all this to MacIntyre's views, we see that the existence of secondarily evaluative words whose use is tied to the mores of particular cultures is no reason for pessimism about the possibility of changing these mores by rational discussion with members of other cultures. All that has to happen is for attitudes to change; and they can change *through* the rational discussion, *talking about* these culture-bound words and the mores they reflect, but *using* the more general words which the languages of the reasoners are likely to have in common. To use the example with which we began, they can discuss whether the practice of female circumcision *is wrong* and whether the mores which require it *ought* to be changed. In the course of the discussion, the descriptive meanings attached to the words by either party may change in the ways I have described, to reflect new attitudes.

The task of the moral philosopher is not (congenial as this may be) to mope about the violence and irrationality that there is in the world, but to do something as a philosopher to remedy it. There is indeed cause for pessimism, but the cause is not the inadequacies of our language, but the unreadiness of so many philosophers to explore and exploit its resources in a helpful way. This they will do, if they examine the logic of the primarily as well as the secondarily evaluative words, in order to determine what rules this logic imposes upon our reasoning in situations of moral dispute — even dispute between members of radically different cultures.

I have not much doubt that if our American and Sudanese were to consider at all deeply (perhaps with philosophical help) what they can say about the question of female circumcision, and in particular whether it is wrong, they will reach agreement on the basis of their understanding of the word 'wrong'. This is likely to have the same prescriptive or evaluative meaning in both their languages, although the descriptive meanings will be different. They will have to forget, for the purposes of their argument, these descriptive meanings. If descriptivists were right, this would leave the word with no meaning at all. But in fact it is fairly easy to throw open the descriptive meanings of such general value-words. What will guide their discussion will be the evaluative meaning and the logic determined by it. I have in my recent book discussed what this logic is,[26] and it is not my purpose here to repeat that discussion. But briefly, when they become fully cognisant of the effect of the experience of female circumcision on the victims, and ask themselves whether they can prescribe universally (for all cases including their own) that such suffering be inflicted, they will at least start to ask what advantages it may bring to the victims or others that could compensate for the suffering. The enquiry will then take a factual turn; they will explore the consequences of the practice and of its abolition. If this factual enquiry discloses no consequences of the practice which they can evaluate highly enough to make them accept a universal prescription that people be made to suffer in that way, they may come to agree that it *is* wrong. The argument is a longer one than this, but I can do no more than summarise it.

A retort that is likely to be made is that the word 'wrong', as bound by these universal-prescriptivist rules, is itself tied to particular mores and therefore not available to disputants one of whom has the mores and the other does not. Even if this were true, it would not be so bad. For though there may be languages that do not contain a universal-prescriptive word equivalent (in its evaluative meaning) to 'wrong', I think it fairly certain that the disputants in our example would have such a word. MacIntyre disguises this fact by making so much play with the divergent *descriptive* meanings.

However, even if the disputants do not have any such word in common, it is possible for either of them to *learn* the word. They can do this without as yet unlearning any of their other words or the mores that go with them. In this sense the new word, and its attached logic, is neutral. *After* they have learnt the new word, they can reason, and they may come to think that it would be wrong not to abandon some of the old words and the mores that they reflect. But this is no different from the case where somebody learns how to count above ten for the first time, and thus becomes able to say 'I have fifteen sheep, and so I have more than so and so, who has fourteen.' Some people might not want to learn to count above ten, and they might not want to learn to use the word 'wrong'; but if they wanted to be able to talk and think about things which can only be talked and thought about by those who have these means, they will have to adopt them. It is my belief that many disputes that there are in the world might be peaceably ended if more people either adopted such words or, as is probably all that is necessary in nearly all cases, understood more fully the logic of similar words already available in their languages, and in particular learnt to distinguish their evaluative from their descriptive meanings, and to utilise the resources of the former in their reasoning. And to help people to do this is a main task for moral philosophers.

Notes

1. J. Mackie, *Ethics: Inventing Right and Wrong* (Penguin, London, 1977). See also my *Moral Thinking: its Levels, Method and Point (MT)* (OUP), 1981), pp. 78-86, and 'Ontology in Ethics' in *Morality and Objectivity*, ed. T. Honderich (Routledge, London, 1985), where I give reasons for thinking the term 'descriptivism' more perspicuous and helpful than 'realism', 'cognitivism', 'objectivism' and the like.
2. *Proc. of Am. Ph. Assn.*, 59, no. 1 (September 1985), p. 5. Page references are to this paper unless otherwise specified.
3. *The Language of Morals (LM)* (OUP, 1952).
4. S. McLean, *Female Circumcision, Excision and Infibulation*, with contributions from Marie Assaad, Eddah Gachukia, Esther Ogunmodede, Awatif Osman, Isabelle Tevoedfre and Awa Thiam (Minority Rights Group, London, 1980). See also *Sister Links* (Foundation for Women's Health, Research and Development, London, 1984).
5. See my *MT*, Ch. 9, 'Rights, Utility and Universalization' in *Utility and Rights*, ed. R.G. Frey, (Blackwell, Oxford, 1984), 'Arguing about Rights', *Emory Law J*, 33, 1984, 'Liberty and Equality: How Politics Masquerades as Philosophy', *Social Philosophy and Policy*, 2, 1984, 'Utility and Rights: Comment on J. Lyons's Paper', *Nomos*, 24, 1984.
6. See my *LM*, p. 121, *Freedom and Reason (FR)* (OUP, 1963), pp. 24ff.
7. For descriptive meaning as one element in the meaning of prescriptive expressions see my *FR*, Ch. 2.
8. See my *LM*, pp. 2, 175ff., 181, *FR*, pp. 5, 36f., 202n., 'Some Confusions about Subjectivity' in *Freedom and Morality*, ed. J. Bricke, Lindley Lectures, U. of Kansas, 1976.
9. J.L. Austin, *Philosophical Papers* (OUP, 1961), p. 234, *How to Do Things with Words* (OUP, 1962), p. 3.
10. For doubts see a useful discussion by H. Lewis and A. Woodfield. 'Content and Community', *Ar. Soc.*, supp. vol. 59, 1985.
11. See my *MT*, p. 70.
12. For the predicament of bilinguals see my *LM*, p. 121.
13. See my *LM*, p. 122, *FR*, Ch. 2.
14. See my 'Descriptivism', reprinted from *Proc. of Br. Acad.*, 49, 1963 in my *Essays on the Moral Concepts* (Macmillan, London, 1972) pp. 57ff., *MT*., p. 74.
15. F.C.S. Schiller, *Logic for Use* (Bell, London 1929), pp. 56ff.
16. See P. Singer, *The Expanding Circle* (OUP, 1981), and my review in *New Republic*, February 1981.
17. See my *MT*, Chs. 5, 6.
18. See my 'Descriptivism', cited above, p. 71.
19. See J. McDowell and S. Blackburn in *Wittgenstein: to Follow a Rule*, eds. S. Holtzman and C. Leich (Routledge, London, 1981); Wittgenstein, *Remarks on the Foundation of Mathematics* (Blackwell, Oxford), pp. 3ff.
20. See the quotation from Hesiod in Aristotle, *Nicomachean Ethics* I, 1095b 10.
21. G. Ryle, *The Concept of Mind* (Hutchinson, London, 1949), pp. 29ff.
22. See J.O. Urmson, 'On Grading', *Mind*, 49 (1950), p. 152.
23. *Philosophical Investigations* (Blackwell, Oxford, 1953), section 152.
24. S. Lovibond, *Realism and Imagination in Ethics* (Blackwell, Oxford, 1983).
25. On 'realism', see note 1 above.
26. *MT*, Chs. 5, 6.

6 PERSONS AND POWERS

Rom Harré

Years of teaching applied mathematics meant that I had a strong predilection for the formal techniques which were the mark of philosophy of science in the 1950s. When I began to study philosophy seriously the legacy of Russell's attempts to create a kind of 'mathematical philosophy' was everywhere evident. First order predicate calculus was the tool of analysis. The project of philosophy of science was to display the rational nature of the scientific enterprise by rewriting scientific discourse in such a way that all content was eliminated and only the stark formal structures expressible in this kind of formal logic remained. Disparities between the way science actually 'worked', as evinced in the intuitions of the scientific community, were to be resolved by yet more elaborate exercises in formalism. The elimination of content from the structures upon which analysis was finally exercised left philosophers of science free of the necessity to struggle with metaphysical issues (all ontological problems being settled by the question-begging slogan 'to be is to be the value of a variable'). This meant too that theory could be treated positivistically as formal machinery for prediction. The apotheosis of this trend was Hempel's well-known thesis that the only difference between prediction schemata and explanations was the insignificant matter of the relative times of the events in question and the performance of the relevant logical acts of deduction. Modality too was to be studied by creating calculi rather than undertaking the painstaking exploration of the way concepts of necessity and possibility were used in scientific discourse.

I remember very well the steps by which my growing disillusionment with this programme developed. It began with the arguments of my tutor Peter Strawson, against the claims of the material implication relation to represent conditionality or implication, and his demonstration of disparities between the behaviour of the English word 'and' and the logical connective of conjunction. Many years later, in a discussion with Alonzo Church, I realised that the same kind of disparities beset quantifiers too. For instance, the universal quantifier of first order predicate calculus was insensitive to the different forms of universality expressed by the English words 'all', 'each', 'every' and 'any'. The alleged virtue of clarity, to which all doubts about the formal method were usually referred, was a myth. The formulas of quantification theory were actually intolerably vague, in contrast to the precision of ordinary English. I felt impelled to go back to real examples of scientific reasoning to look for the principles that were actually at work. Perhaps an account of scientific rationality might be extracted from them.

This impulsion led to two complementary projects. The first was indirectly inspired again by some of Strawson's observations. It involved a careful cataloguing and study of the actual evaluative terms in which the assessment of the value of a scientific hypothesis was expressed. Markedly absent from the list were terms for truth or falsity. Utilitarian and/or aesthetic notions were prominent. The second project, stimulated by a reading of Toulmin's little book *Philosophy of Science* and a prolonged study of the writings of N.R. Campbell, was aimed at elucidating the cognitive processes required to create and develop theories, with the ultimate object of setting out some kind of normative framework, which owed little or nothing to the kind of normative considerations implicit in Hempel's deductive-nomological account of theorising. This led to a long-running study of the role of models, analogies and metaphors in the process of theory-construction. At the time I was struggling with these projects I had not at all grasped the importance of a theory of meaning in all this. But one thing was clear. Ontological or metaphysical underpinnings were involved in any theory construction, and the way some system of analogies was deployed could not be understood without taking that into account. I became fascinated by the way metaphysics had controlled not only the content of Newtonian science, but also the experimental programmes that were begun under its influence. I embarked at that time on a study of the works of Gilbert and Hales, to try to follow in detail the way that method and metaphysics were interwoven. Each had produced supreme classics of the experimental way, but each too was animated by a powerful metaphysical vision of the nature of the beings and substances upon which experiment was to be exercised. About the same time I stumbled across Maclaurin's paradox, the startling demonstration of the inconsistency of Newtonian science that had so profound an effect on eighteenth- and nineteenth-century physics. Here was another example of metaphysical presuppositions, summed up in the corpuscularian philosophy, interacting with empirically ratified laws, the principles of Newtonian mechanics. But the total structure was beset by contradictions. Each way of resolving the paradox led on to a different style of physics in the nineteenth century. The extremes were represented by the field theories on the one hand and positivistic mathematicism on the other. Dynamical concepts developed in close harmony with ideas of the romantic movement led to the metaphysical/mathematical syntheses of Faraday and Maxwell. The positivistic retreat from deep explanations led to the rational mechanics of D'Alembert. The latter seems to have been one of the sources of the mathematical positivism of Duhem. Of course historians of science had already begun the study of these matters, and one found that one's way through a vast literature was made easier by the publications of such writers as Thackray, Knight, Pearce Williams, L.L. Whyte, and many others. But what of the metaphysics which animated the scientists of the period in question?

Field-thinking tended to emphasise dispositional descriptions of physical beings. Fundamental entities tended to be described in terms of the effects that they could bring about, rather than as the bearers of occurrent properties. Gilbert had sharpened up Robert Norman's field concept with his idea of the 'sphere of power', but the concept had lain fallow till reinvented by Boscovich, from whose writings it re-entered physics and was never to be lost again. But why were philosophers so keen on Hume's treatment of causality when physicists seemed to be happy with the concept of causal power? Was the active, necessitarian element in causation just a projection onto a mere regularity of a habit of thought, psychological expectation engendered by the repeated experience of correlations among types of events? I happened across an ally in my determination to upset the hegemony exercised by the Humeans over the concept of causality, in the person of E.H. Madden.

As we began to study the arguments of the opposition it became clear that at least three matters were in dispute. Part of the attraction of the Humean position was that it was the natural account of causality to go with the view that scientific theories were mere logic machines. If theories did not describe the causal mechanisms which produced effects when stimulated by causes but merely permitted prediction of like effects, the meaning of the concept of causality could be reduced to 'repetition of like patterns amongst events'. A defence of a realist reading of scientific theories, that is that substantive terms did refer to hitherto unobserved entities and processes, was an essential stage in the defeat of Humean analyses of causality. Then there was the metaphysical issue of the choice of ontology on which to base the natural sciences. Was science about things and substances or about events? Humean causal theory required an event ontology. It was the happening of impressions that constituted the world of science for Hume. Once the ontological assumption had been made it was an easy step to a kind of atomism. Events which were successive in time could not interpenetrate one another. There was no existent within this scheme which could bind causes and effects together. But if one could defend the priority of an ontology of persisting things and substances then another of the presuppositions of the Humean view would be eliminated. Finally there was the issue of meaning. If the words of a scientific discourse (and the other symbols, for instance mathematical and iconic) acquired their meaning by reference to publicly observable entities, and could acquire meaning only in this fashion, that is by ostension, then the idea that the senses of theoretical terms which seemed to be used to describe unobservable beings actually did so was an illusion. All that these terms could mean really was to be explicated by reference to the empirical basis of a science, what could be observed. The use of terms which seemed to refer to efficacious (powerful) entities which, when stimulated by a cause event produced an effect, or to other kinds of unobserved mechanisms which produced the patterned event sequences which a human observer could study empirically, were really picturesque ways of referring to nothing but the observed patterns themselves. To tackle this issue took us back again to the status of theory.

But why devote oneself to the study of such problems? Why not let the logicists have their way? This touches on what for me is a deeply felt moral issue. I was brought up in an atmosphere in which reverence for the achievements of the natural sciences was taken for granted. This attitude was based not just on the vast amount of new and interesting information about our physical surroundings that the natural sciences had accumulated but also on a sense of the moral superiority of the society of scientists. Members of that society pursued knowledge in a disinterested fashion, so I was taught to believe. They were ready to follow the rigours of experimental testing however much that involved the abandonment of pet ideas. They respected each other's achievements, depending on a broadly based trust in the honesty of their fellows. What a comfort to anti-scientists and other self-deceivers is the scepticism and relativism that are engendered by adherence to the logicist approach to understanding and evaluating the scientific achievement! Since those naïve and adolescent days I have come to have a great deal of respect for much contemporary sociology of science. The maintenance of the strict morality of the scientific community is some kind of miracle. Sociological studies have shown not only the importance of diffuse influences from the lay society but also the force of the internal social organisation of scientific institutions. The latter may exert a malign influence on the progress of a scientific speciality. The control of publication outlets and of the membership of professional scientific associations permits a good deal of informal censorship to prevent the spread of new approaches which would upset the hegemony of some well-entrenched group. I have been accumulating a file of some quite outrageous cases, but its publication will have to be posthumous, for obvious reasons. The scientific community, like any other human society, is always in danger of corruption. So much more important then is it to defend a conception of scientific activity, both practical and theoretical, that counters the slide into scepticism. Science, as human beings can practise it, cannot deliver unrevisable truth, nor could any scientific practice show conclusively that some speculation was false. Yet scientists, practising their craft, do tell us things about a world, existing independently of our wishes and our theories, that are worthy to be believed. Science is, I believe, the greatest *moral* achievement of mankind. To ask too much of it is as sure a way of undermining its pretensions as to ask too little. The defence of science then calls for an attack on logicism and the associated reductionist theories of meaning that lead to Humean conceptions of scientific knowledge, and at the same time a repudiation of those kinds of realism which enshrine unattainable epistemic ideals.

The idea that the rationality of a practice must somehow be able to be displayed in the schemata of traditional logic is deeply entrenched in contemporary philosophy of science. It is worth pausing briefly to look at two striking examples. What lies at the heart of the paradox of the ravens? Hempel, who invented the paradox, argued as follows: we could imagine a simple law of nature expressed as 'All ravens are black'. Empirical support for this law could be found by examining ravens. Suppose indeed that we find only black ones. But 'All ravens are black' is logically equivalent to 'All non-black things are non-ravens'. The contrapositive matches the positive truth for truth, falsity for falsity. Empirical support for the contrapositive, if looked for on the basis of the principle that set us searching among the raven population for support for our original hypothesis, would be looked for among those things that are non-black, for instance white. On finding a white shoe a cry of 'Eureka!' involuntarily escapes us, for a shoe is a non-raven. The white shoe lends empirical support to 'All non-black things are non-ravens', so, one is tempted to conclude, it must also lend support to all statements which are logically equivalent to that law. So a white shoe provides empirical support for 'All ravens are black'. Yet our intuitions balk at this consequence. I am indebted to J. Aronson for clarifying my own approach to this problem. It is not wholly pointless to look among white things to see if any of them are ravens. But is that likely to convince us that 'All ravens are black' has something of the standing of law of nature? Neither lots and lots of black ravens nor heaps of white shoes, that is for sure. They could be mere coincidence. Rather we turn to theory. Darwinian evolutionary theory, coupled with modern genetics, provides the backing for the belief that being the kind of bird it is, then that is the kind of plumage we would expect. To gain support for the proposition we go more deeply into ravenhood, rather than set out to scour the universe of white things, hoping that none will be a raven. But why should anyone be tempted to the latter course? The answer is immediately obvious, if we bring out the logical schema which traditionalists use to explicate the form of the proposition in question. This is 'For all x if x is a raven then x is black'. What is the range of the 'x'? Why everything! Once this mode of analysis is adopted the paradox of the ravens is inevitable. There is no formal way of confining the range of relevant entities to the beings with which ornithology and avian genetics deal. The search for a deep solution to the paradox is nothing more, nor less, than a search for an alternative apparatus for bringing out the structure of the original general sentence with which this discussion began.

A philosophy of science inspired by the writings of Sir Karl Popper has been popular among some scientists, though it has inspired a good deal of resistance among philosophers. Popper seems to have gone further than most philosophers to committing himself to a logicist account of the rationale of science. The method of conjectures and refutations for the advocacy of which he has become famous, is really a celebration of the validity of the logical form *modus tollens*. The only truth which bears on the truth or falsity of a general statement is that truth which would show it to be false. 'Every a is a b' entails 'This a is a b'. But should this a turn out not to be a b then 'Every a is a b' is surely false. It should be rejected and another conjecture proposed to be tested in its turn. We should provisionally accept only those conjectures which have so far survived rigorous test. A great many objections to this classical simplistic rendering of Popper's methodology have been raised. The most powerful, which ultimately inspired Lakatos's methodology of scientific research programmes, was the observation that belief in a theory may and frequently does override the force of counter examples to a hypothesis. The way experiments, theories and hypotheses are interwoven is not captured by the logical form we call *modus tollens*. Among other matters the rationality of scientific practice must be referred to the metaphysical basis (that which Lakatos called the 'hard core') on which a theory is ultimately based. Our assessments of beliefs about the ultimate nature of the physical universe are not based on the use of the formal schemata of logic, but the weighing up of a multitude of similarities and differences, through which trains of analogies and metaphors lead to our deepest metaphysical assumptions.

How might an interest in the metaphysics of science be pursued? I believe that it is in the science of physics that the cutting edge of metaphysical speculation is to be found. By that I mean that in physics we find both explorations of the limits of some metaphysical scheme (such as I mentioned above in the case of the breakdown of Newtonian physics) and the tentative creation of new schemes different from those embedded in our ordinary language and material practices. Physicists do seem to persist with dispositional concepts. The more deeply a physical theory penetrates into nature the more hazardous are its speculations about the ultimate groundings of the ways things behave. But the more clear do physicists become as to the clusters of powers and dispositions that characterise different kinds of beings. Philosophers have struggled with dispositional concepts through most of the modern era. Locke called them 'powers' and connected their ubiquitous role in Newtonian science with the distinction between real and nominal essences. More recently their fate has been bound up with debates about the status of modalities, necessities and possibilities. Plainly to ascribe a disposition to a being not currently behaving in the appropriate way may be quite proper. But on what is that propriety based? If we say that it is justified because the being is one of the kind of things which usually behave that way in the relevant circumstances, then not only like Locke are we obliged to give an account of kinds but we must also find a defence of inductive reasoning from past instances in which things of the kind displayed such and such behaviour to the samples we are now contemplating. But more importantly we are committed to giving possibilities a central role in our metaphysical scheme. To describe a thing or substance in terms of dispositions is not only to say what it is currently like but also what it would or could do under appropriate circumstances, that is to refer to possible as well as actual behaviour. Some philosophers have tried to defend the idea of a manifold of possible worlds which somehow exist along with the actual world. Others would have it that possibilities are conceptual, thoughts. This is not the place to tackle the problems in any definitive way, but how we answer it deeply affects the way we understand space-time, the probabilistic aspects of quantum mechanics, the meaning of the Feynman diagrams which have guided much recent research in high energy physics, and many other matters.

But there is another way in which metaphysics enters into the science of physics. Giving joint classes on the philosophy of special relativity with my colleague Ian Aitchison brought home to me how important are the criteria of co-variance, symmetry and conservation in the methodology of contemporary physics. The principle of co-variance requires that laws of nature take the same form under a group of co-ordinate transformations. But then why should these formal properties of laws have become so prominent? I believe that adherence to them ensures a kind of intelligibility to the assumptions underlying their application. It is the intelligibility that accrues to thought forms based on a traditional metaphysical notion, that of enduring substance. The associated principles of symmetry and conservation lead one to the creation of novel concepts which obey the general rules of substance concepts. And thus I believe ensure the ultimate intelligibility of physics. 'Energy' is one such concept the substantialist character of which is plain in the way that Lagrangean formulations of laws of nature have become so common in physics. Much of general philosophical interest is to be found in these areas of philosophy of science. The problem of the status of possibilities is not yet solved to the satisfaction of most philosophers, and the exploration of the metaphysical commitments of fundamental physics is scarcely begun.

Many years ago I was asked to take part in a university class, the subject of which was the use of models in the human sciences. My ignorance of such specialities as social anthropology and social psychology was profound. While the contributions of social anthropologists to our joint endeavour seemed both scientific and intelligible I was completely baffled by what I heard from social psychologists. Their empirical methods sounded more like the techniques of alchemy than of the natural sciences and their substantive theories seemed to require that human beings were unsophisticated automata. The following term I attended a graduate class in which the methods and results of several social psychological research projects were described. I must confess I found the expositions almost unintelligible. There was nothing in my reading or experience on to which they could be connected, so to say. The methods bore little more than a superficial resemblance to the empirical methods of chemistry, physics or biology (though much the same terminology was in use) and the results were so counter-intuitive that one found oneself jibbing at every turn. So I embarked on a systematic study of the social psychological literature. It became very clear that the baffling quality of much of the work reported in books and papers came from two sources, both philosophical. One was a theory about people, and the other a theory about science. Both theories were heavily in debt to positivist philosophy of science. Not only was human behaviour thought of in causal terms, but the causality was Humean. Establishing a regularity among types of events stood in for proof of a causal relation. Furthermore a positivist theory of meaning was also involved. What people did was identified through concepts whose meaning was established ostensively, by reference to its observable properties. Hypotheses about the intentions of the actors played no part in picking out kinds of behaviour. What anyone said about what they were doing was neither recorded nor seemed to spark the slightest interest in the investigators. Positivistic theory of science was also involved, and supported this odd view of people. Theory was discounted, and the scientific method was reduced to the experimental testing of Humean-style hypotheses as to what conditions of treatment would prompt what 'behaviour'. Perhaps most striking of all was the individualist metaphysics within which the whole project of the study of social behaviour was set. There was no *social* element in this work at all.

By chance I met Paul Secord, deeply troubled by methodological and metaphysical doubts about the then current state of social psychology. Throughout one fall semester in Nevada we discussed these matters, gradually coming to see that though we came at them from very different backgrounds, our conclusions as to what was amiss were remarkably similar. Three problems needed to be addressed. First of all the unexamined presumptions upon which the traditional programme of research had been erected needed to be brought out, and their shortcomings made as clear as possible. It seemed to us that the irony of a research programme, which loudly proclaimed its hostility to 'philosophy' and yet at the same time was in thrall to a very dubious cluster of philosophical theories, needed emphasising. The second task was to try to identify good work, and to see with what models of human action it had successfully tackled some research project. Finally we hoped to recommend a method for the empirical study of co-ordinated human behaviour patterns which would avoid the pitfalls of the 'experimental' method.

Our discussions confirmed our original intuitions that the troublesome presumptions that had been standing in the way of a better psychology could be boiled down to a combination of a simplistic picture of human beings and a simplistic positivistic philosophy of science which had led to the discounting of theory and a neglect of the meaning of social actions. The physical sciences have depended heavily on the use of analogy and metaphor to create new and fruitful concepts both for the analytical description of opaque and puzzling realities and for the construction of theory. Our second task was to propose analogies and metaphors which had already had some successes to their credit. This led us to explore the dramaturgical model, the idea that some of the concepts by which theatrical performances were described and explained could be applied to puzzling social realities. Further refinements of analysis and explanation could be achieved by adding more specific models in the shape of analogies to games and ceremonies. The explanatory apparatus now included the metaphor of rules. We were struck by the way the development of a new methodology in social psychology had converged on the basic principles of linguistic studies, as proposed by Chomsky. This was not the formalism of his transformational grammar but the powerful distinction between the study of competence, the attempt to find out what someone has to know to be able to carry out some activity, and the study of performance, that is the attempt to find out how, moment by moment, that knowledge is put to work in actually doing something. We argued that it is possible to discover the system of rules and beliefs which encapsulate an actor's social knowledge by the study of the accounts that actors give to justify, excuse and repair social activity. The final step, a defence of an alternative metaphysics of persons, demanded a defence of the generally Rylean idea that a psychological description of a person was not to be taken to be a kind of map of some inner theatre, but a catalogue of capacities, powers and skills. Within this framework of concepts and associated methodology there was only a very small place for a traditional naïve experiment. And this was because the conception of human actors which alone made sense of the traditional methodology, that is people as automata, subject to simple pushes and pulls, was almost wholly indefensible. Secord's and my joint work was widely read and a number of interesting research projects brought to fruition in general accordance with the methodology and metaphysics we had proposed.

However, there were some pretty major omissions in the original formulation of the position, both methodological and metaphysical. Shortly after this work was completed I made the acquaintance of two schools of European psychology, neither of which had then much of a foothold in the Anglo-American academic establishment. There were the 'action theorists', mainly German-speaking and many deriving their projects and their theories from the Russians, Leontiev and ultimately Vygotsky. In discussions with Mario von Cranach I realised that there was a way in which the study of performance, the moment by moment use of rules and beliefs to produce action, could be studied. Again both psychological and philosophical considerations had to be brought to bear. If action is the 'result', in some sense to be worked out, of prior cognitive processes and systems of belief, what form should these be thought to take? If people do have intentions, how should these be conceived? It became clear that a cognitive science of goal-directed behaviour required that the social beliefs and the conventions and rules of different cultures be thought of as organised hierarchically. Philosophers such as Frankfurter and Taylor had proposed this idea but it had not taken root in psychology. But given this philosophical thesis about the cognitive conditions of goal-directed behaviour, how could it be studied in real time? Von Cranach and other action psychologists had hit on a simple but powerful technique. It seems to be a matter of fact that when a routine action sequence is interrupted, whether by increasing the difficulty of the immediate task or by querying the propriety, adequacy and so on of the next step, actors become aware of that fragment of the hierarchical system of rules and beliefs that is involved in the uninterrupted action. By cunningly manipulating the conditions of action von Cranach was able to achieve the impossible (positivistically considered), namely the direct display of the tacit cognitive structures that are involved in the control of orderly action. This is a step beyond the hypothetico-deductive methodology of 'cognitive science'. It is like the discovery of the microscope, by means of which the reality of the hypothetical micro-organisms responsible for disease, could be studied directly.

At about the same time I met J.-P. de Waele, from the Vrij Universitet of Brussels and the Belgian Ministry of Justice. He, too, had been thoroughly disillusioned with 'official' psychological methods. Entrusted with a reform of the methodology for making parole decisions about convicted murderers, he had been drawn towards an even deeper study of the cognitive structures of human minds than had von Cranach. De Waele had devised a method for no less a project than the drawing out of a detailed autobiography for each of the murderers whose release on parole was under consideration. This was to enter into a belief system of greater opacity and much greater complexity than those studied by von Cranach. And again the defence of the technique called for the same kind of combination of philosophical argument, directed against the positivistic conception of scientific knowledge and in favour of scientific realism, and an empirical demonstration of the power of the de Waele method to achieve its practical goals. But more was at stake. If the autobiographical method is to be taken seriously it involves the assumption that in the last analysis what anyone actually does will depend not only upon ways in which that person is similar to others, but in part on idiosyncratic beliefs and memories, interpretations of rules, and so on. So not only does a defence of de Waele's method require a philosophical defence of scientific realism, but also an analysis of the relation between intensive and extensive designs for empirical studies. In the former one begins with a single case taken as typical which is studied in detail, and then creates an extension by collecting all cases sufficiently similar. In the latter one starts by identifying a group and then finding out what the members have in common. While both methods have their part to play, it is the former which opens up the possibility of a detailed investigation of belief systems in all their immense complexity. The intensive design is not the same as the idiographic method (often contrasted with the idea of nomothetic science). In both the intensive design and the idiographic method $N = 1$ but in the latter the individual under investigation is a whole universe and systematic regularities are explored within his or her system of beliefs as they change over time. The very same regularities may be looked for in the intensive design but when found they must be treated as hypotheses about what the next similar case will be like.

With these two advances tied in to the project Secord and I had begun, the detachment of social psychology from its positivistic moorings and its transfer to a realist philosophical climate had begun.

Critics were quick to point out that Secord and I had neglected two dimensions of the explanation of social behaviour, dimensions which were crucial to an adequate explanatory scheme. We had made no effort to locate the models for small scale social processes, such as family reunions, wedding ceremonies, meetings between strangers on airliners and so on, within the larger social environments (to choose a neutral term) within which they must be presumed to occur. Nor had we made any effort to discuss how to relate the systems of rules and beliefs existing at some moment to their historical predecessors and their likely successors. Without these dimensions our pretence to give an account of how one should undertake the explanation of social behaviour, while an enormous advance on the old paradigm, remained hollow. Having the good luck to spend a sabbatical term in a strongly Marxist influenced philosophy department in Denmark I began to reflect on both these problems. The brilliance of Goffman's microsociology forced one to attend to the variety of motives that might exist for putting on this or that social performance. And the display of personal worth, according to the criteria current in one's cultural circles, seemed to me at least as important as the kind of explanatory considerations advanced by Marxists. Yet one can hardly deny that the way the social arrangements for material production are influenced by the logic of the means of that production must play a role. It seemed to me that only when one had formed some clear idea about the social background to the Goffmanian world of institutional and close coupled personal interaction could one tackle the philosophical problem of the nature of the relation between individuals, institutions and larger social formations. And the same considerations applied to hierarchies of processes too. Of equal scope and power to Marx's analysis is the theory of social emulation and expressive displays, offered by Veblen. Suppose one were to think of social life as analytically resolved into 'orders', systems of rights, obligations, duties, assignments of meaning and criteria of worth with the ritual means for their display. Surely Marx describes one order and Veblen another. Their relative importance and direction of mutual influence might be different at different times. But these 'orders' would not be pre-existing, causally potent structures, but rather ways of assigning and displaying motives, in accordance with a bouquet of different rhetorics, through which our social experience could be made sense of. To adopt a Marxist interpretation of some social phenomenon would then not be parallel to proposing an underlying reality which brought about that pattern in events, as one might propose a chemical process in explanation of a physiological phenomenon. Instead it would be a sense-making exercise. Motives would not be little forces in individuals inclining them to this or that action, but the means for public displays of rationality and other socially approved cognitive properties. I found with some excitement that this idea had been proposed by both Kenneth Burke and C. Wright Mills. If there are patterns in the mass behaviour of human beings it will be extraordinarily difficult to find out what they are. And those we can get a handle on, such as migration and voting patterns are likely to be simple and coarse-grained. The rest is rhetoric. Again I found that this idea had been mooted before, and is the main message of the sociological analysis with which Tolstoy rounds off *War and Peace.*

Could the idea of two orders be used to sketch a theory of social change? Secord and I had offered no account of how the existing rule systems came to be and how they might change. Once again it seemed wise to reflect on the existing orthodoxies. Some place should be found for a dialectic process by which something new appears in the social world as a resolution of a tension between two contradictory 'forces'. Equally it seemed to me that Stephen Toulmin's observation that all satisfactory historical explanations should be modelled on the general Darwinian scheme, to avoid implausible assumptions of a positive causal influence from environment to individual, was right. Bringing together these considerations with the idea of the two orders suggested a way in which a schema for the explanation of social change could be built up. For all sorts of reasons people of a certain category could come to feel that the way they were placed in the practical order did not match their location in the expressive order of their society. A change in one or the other could lead to felt disparities. If there were on hand some rhetoric in terms of which the felt disparity could be defined in terms of social practices, the conditions for the invention of new social practices would exist. For instance a political rhetoric was available for the interpretation of the disparity felt by many women between their location in the practical orders of Western societies and their location within the expressive orders of those societies. New practices are proposed in terms of the political rhetoric. But there remains a further process. Only if there are no features of the social and physical environment that make the spread of new practices impossible will the proposals of reformers be taken up. Our social practices are not well-adapted to our situation, they are the least ill-adapted of what is on offer.

By these theoretical steps I hoped to remedy the shortcomings of our original attempt to redefine the philosophical basis of social psychology. But in working all this out I was continually bothered by the feeling that the original analysis of the defects in old paradigm social psychology had missed some quite central matter. There was a further metaphysical assumption at work in the old paradigm which needed to be brought out. My old friend Henri Tajfel had campaigned for a European style in psychology, by which he meant a metaphysics and methodology that broke with the individualism of the psychology practised in the United States. But paradoxically his own work reproduced that same individualism. He talked of processes of social comparison, but they occurred in the 'heads' of individual people. Where did the pervasive but subtle influence that could lead so 'European' a psychologist as Tajfel go astray? Surely it came from the methodology of the naïve experiment. To defend his positivistic devotion to the experiment Tajfel had devised the 'mere ...' psychology. Any way of setting people apart into groups, however arbitrary, would lead them to evaluate the members of their own set more highly than the others. To the obvious objections that nobody comes to the laboratory as a mere human being and that arbitrary groups have none of the social structure within which human beings actually act, Tajfel had no reply, other than a rhetorical claim to be 'doing science'. That claim depended on the willingness of his critics to accept the methodology of the experiment, but that was just what was at issue.

Suppose we abandoned the whole individualist set of assumptions. What would happen to the metaphysics of mankind? What would become of 'persons', 'agency', 'consciousness' and so on? The individualist psychology of the experimental tradition had failed to tackle these features of human kind. Was it just because they were tied in either with moral philosophy or with subjectivity or both? A more subtle explanation is that these apparently most individual features of human psychology are actually the most strongly 'socially constructed'. If Secord and I had failed to take account of the social and historical dimensions of human life, we had equally failed to incorporate human individuality. By that I do not mean those differences between the attributes of human beings that distinguish them from one another qualitatively, but the fact of their numerical difference. Each person is a unique centre of consciousness, and is, in some measure capable of actions that are neither caused nor predetermined by external forces. In the terminology of common sense, each person is a self. Traditionally it has been thought that to be a self a person is somehow inhabited by an extra and hidden entity that is the ultimate location of awareness and that exercises the final control over action. Kant called this the 'noumenal self', an entity which is not given to us in experience. Furthermore psychologists, if they have tried to deal with the phenomenon of the self at all, have tended to treat it as the product of some process of maturation, requiring only a triggering from the social and material environment.

The individualism of the experimental tradition is very much tied up with the embodiment of persons as things in physical (and Newtonian) space and time. Like all things human beings interact causally, and the job of the human scientist is taken to be the investigation of these causal processes. Conversation is at best a secondary reality, one among many modes of interaction. But to put the question 'How do human beings acquire their minds?' in the right context it might be advisable to try the thought experiment of making the conversation the basic reality and the thinghood of people something of lesser importance. That is, the exercise would involve taking people as speakers and hearers first, and as things only secondarily (say thinking of embodiment as a necessary but not a sufficient condition for the ability to converse). One might imagine an array of people as a discrete space, each person being a location at which speech-acts can occur. Public displays of intention and uptake could bind the speech-acts into a world, a conversation. How much of human psychology could be understood within the framework of this thought experiment? We could certainly go some way to establishing the concept of a person in the rights, duties and obligations of speakers and hearers in this simplified world. A location is a person-point when certain rights and duties as a speaker and hearer are accorded in relation to other people-points. At least one of the root-ideas in ascriptions of rationality to persons could be explicated in terms of rights to demand reasons of a speaker and the duty of that speaker to provide them. Indexical expressions such as 'here', 'now', 'this', 'I' and so on would tie speech-acts to those who spoke them. Physical places would be identified only by their proximity to speakers and hearers. In the conversations of this model first person statements would be avowals, manifestations of psychological states and processes, and there could be no problem of whether there had been any subjective accompaniments of these manifestations. Commentary upon such avowals would have to come from others, and the only complex expressions involving pronouns would be of the form 'I think he (she) is feeling sick.'

Suppose now that the person-points learn to conduct conversations *sotto voce*, taking several parts or voices. Social constructionists of the Vygotskyan persuasion would want to claim that the organisation of the private world (subjectivity) could be no other than the privatised organisation of the public world, expressed most subtly and powerfully in the forms of talk. The singularity of the person as a locus of public conversation must necessarily be mirrored in a singularity of self-hood in the privatised conversation. But whereas in the public conversation the indexical force of pronouns tied speakings to places in that conversational place, namely persons, the privatising of complex expressions makes room for the illusion of self-hood. In commenting on my own avowals by the use of forms such as 'I think I am going to be sick', I give myself the status of another person, and adopt the standpoint to myself that another would take to me. This is to give the self theory of G.H. Mead a linguistic turn. To have a mind is to have learned to keep part of the conversation to oneself. By this thought-experiment I would hope to have given a grounding for the thesis that the unities of human individuality, in the numerical sense, are grounded in a social order. I put the matter this way to allow for the possibility of there being more than one kind of human conversation, because there are many ways in which conversational and other rights are assigned to persons, and many ways in which moral responsibility is assigned to the members of a society. These dimensions of variation open up the possibility that just as there are many variants of the generic person among human societies so there might be expected to be many variants of the generic self among human psychologies. Taking such a theory of personal being seriously has consequences for the design of psychological research programmes, into such diverse matters as developmental processes, emotional repertoires and the possibility of different kinds of moral psychologies.

Yet human beings are embodied and do have a thing-like existence among other things. And though, as Peter Strawson has demonstrated, something like the conditions for the identification and re-identification of persons can be found in a world of sounds, our concept of person seems to be exactly appropriate to the conditions of its genesis, namely among embodied beings. But despite this promising beginning Strawson, like most philosophers, turns to the 'interesting' bit, the fact of mindedness, in his later investigations. The body has been left on the butcher's slab more or less since Descartes credited it only with extension. Bodies, like minds, as Strawson has reminded us are the bodies of persons. Where can we go from here? It seems to me that the concept of body has not been fully explored by philosophers, nor has the role of our bodies in our lives been at the centre of a systematic psychological investigation drawing on the conceptual analyses of philosophers. Is the thing-hood of the human body ground for classifying it as a thing?

The exploration of the human use of the concept of body needs to be controlled by some systematic plan. So far as I can see now there are four contexts within which the human body is located. First it is embedded in various moral orders, the subject of moral evaluations, ascribed rights, for instance to an undisturbed existence. Much work has been done by philosophers in this context, for instance in discussions around problems in medical ethics. But even in an excellent study such as Glover's *What Sort of People Should There Be?* the concept of body is studied only incidentally to the main thrust of the argument. Then the body is embedded in a practical context, that in which we identify different kinds of bodies and come to think of bodies as made up of parts. Anthropologists have much to teach philosophers about the variety of such classificatory schemes. Discussions of the significance of classifications by gender fall into this context. Again a third context in which the concept of body is central is created by the pursuit of perfections of various kinds. Concepts of health and illness are concerned with the functional perfection of the body, while such practices as body-building, cosmetic surgery, fitness-seeking and so on testify to an urge for perfections of form. Finally the body appears in various semiotic contexts, as the source and bearer of meanings. Again a good start on the investigation of this context has been made by Liam Hudson (*Bodies of Knowledge*) but a much wider study needs to be made. It is in the exploration of the role of the concept of body in our management of and thinking about these four contexts that I believe a great source of philosophical interest will lie.

7 ON SOME METHODS AND RESULTS OF PHILOSOPHICAL ANALYSIS

Stephan Körner

The difference and interaction between doing something and reflecting on what one is doing manifest themselves not only in practical pursuits but also in theoretical disciplines. There is, for example, a generally acknowledged difference and interaction between mathematics, which consists in asking and answering mathematical questions by mathematical methods, and metamathematics, which consists in characterising the nature of mathematical questions, answers and methods. The distinction between a discipline and its metadiscipline applies also to philosophy — even though philosophy is sometimes vaguely described as being *the* metadiscipline of all disciplines. The history of philosophy abounds with claims to the effect that the discovery of a new method has led or will lead to new and important solutions of old problems or even to solutions of problems which before the discovery of the new method could not even be formulated. Examples are the Socratic method, the Cartesian method of doubt, the Kantian transcendental method, the Hegelian and Marxist dialectical method, Husserl's phenomenological method and various versions of philosophical analysis, which form the topic of this essay. Its main aim is to draw attention to some obscurities and unclarities in influential recent conceptions of philosophical analysis and to show that, and how, by overcoming these defects, philosophy — as distinguished from metaphilosophy, in particular philosophical methodology — can tackle its tasks more effectively.[1]

The chapter begins by briefly recalling and examining the conceptions of philosophical analysis or clarification, as formulated by Moore, Carnap and the later Wittgenstein (section 1). It then argues for the need to draw some distinctions between various kinds of analysis, the conflation of which is the cause of avoidable mistakes (section 2). In the light of these distinctions a classification of concept-object relations, of concept-governing rules and of necessary propositions is briefly outlined (section 3). The relevance of these classifications to various philosophical problems is then shown by means of examples drawn from the philosophy of mathematics, and of other special disciplines (section 4). The chapter ends by indicating the extent to which the *structure* of the system of a person's beliefs implies his acceptance of a metaphysics and by casting a cursory glance at the similar relationship between the system of a person's practical attitudes and his morality (section 5). In accordance with the aims of the present volume, the essay is largely based on my philosophical writings. What is new in it is the statement of the way in which my methodological and my substantive philosophical interests have interacted.

1. Philosophical Analysis According to Moore, Carnap and the Later Wittgenstein

A starting point of the philosophical movement which regards analysis or clarification as the only legitimate part of philosophy is Hume's *Enquiry Concerning Human Understanding*, which ends with the famous words:

> If we take in our hand any volume of divinity or school metaphysics, for instance; let us ask, *Does it contain any abstract reasoning concerning quantity or number?* No. *Does it contain any experimental reasoning concerning matter of fact and existence?* No. Commit it then to the flames: for it can contain nothing but sophistry and illusion.

If Hume had been asked why in conformity with this precept his own *Enquiry* should not be committed to the flames, he might have replied that even though it did not contain any new mathematical theorems or experimental results, it did contain a clarification of some such theorems or results and of their general nature and thus involved the legitimate activity of philosophical analysis. Some analytical philosophers might be less radical and consider various types of non-analytical philosophy as intellectually respectable, but as being of little interest to them. For our purpose it will be sufficient briefly to recall three notions of philosophical analysis, namely those of G.E. Moore, Rudolf Carnap and the later Wittgenstein. All three hold that their very different ways of philosophical analysis do not increase the content of science or mathematics but are nevertheless autonomous and useful, theoretical pursuits. Unlike Moore, Carnap and Wittgenstein hold in addition that any philosophical activity which is not in their sense analytical or clarificatory can contain nothing but sophistry and illusion.

To give an analysis of one concept, the *analysandum*, by another concept, the *analysans*, is according to Moore to state an analysing relation between them, which is exemplified by the relation between 'x is a brother' and 'x is a male sibling' and must fulfil the following conditions: (1) both concepts must in some sense be the same concept; (2) the expression used for the *analysans* must be a different expression from that used for the *analysandum*; (3) the expression used for the *analysans* must explicitly mention concepts which are not explicitly mentioned by the expression used for the *analysandum*. Moore does not consider these conditions to be sufficient since to make them so would require an explanation of what he means by two concepts being identical. He hints at what he has in mind by telling his readers that he regards the concept 'x is a brother' as being identical with the concept 'x is a male sibling' but that he refuses to regard 'x is a cube with twelve edges' as being identical with 'x is a cube', although he insists that the last two concepts are logically equivalent.[2] There is here no need to supplement Moore's requirements — for example, by distinguishing concepts with logically superfluous components from concepts without such components.

The value of Moore's method of analysis may be seen by considering the so-called paradox of analysis, as formulated by C.H. Langford: '... if the verbal expression representing the *analysandum* has the same meaning as the verbal expression representing the *analysans*, the analysis states a bare identity and is trivial; but if the two verbal expressions do not have the same meaning, the analysis is incorrect'.[3] The paradox is removed if one distinguishes, as one must, between the logical relations of deducibility, equivalence and identity and the psychological fact of their discovery. For if this distinction were incorrect, even the most ingenious proof of a mathematical theorem would be trivial. And what saves the discovery of deducibility, equivalence and identity within mathematics from being condemned as necessarily trivial, also saves the discovery of these relations outside mathematics from the same overall condemnation.

Carnap's conception of analysis is both narrower and wider than Moore's. It is narrower in that it is only analysis of science.

For Carnap holds that a philosophy which is not logical analysis of science consists only of pseudo-statements (*Scheinsätze*) and that 'once philosophy is cleansed of its unscientific components, the logic of science remains as its only residue'. Carnap's conception of analysis is wider than Moore's because it results not only in the analysis of isolated concepts but in the formulation of elaborate logical systems, which are identified with the logic underlying all science or some scientific theories.[4] From the point of view of this chapter it is not necessary to discuss the development of Carnap's views of the nature of logic, which he at first identified with logical syntax and later supplemented by logical semantics. It is sufficient to recall that, while in the spirit of Hume he did not claim to have extended our factual knowledge, he not only contributed to its clarification but also made important contributions to the store of instruments used for this purpose.

According to Wittgenstein philosophy differs fundamentally from science and, one might add, from the logic of science in Carnap's sense. For in doing philosophy, rather than in pursuing various spurious activities which go under its name 'we may not advance any theory ... We must do away with all *explanation* and description alone must take its place.' Philosophical problems are

> not empirical problems; they are solved, rather, by looking into the workings of our language, and that in such a way as to make us recognize these workings: *in despite of* an urge to misunderstand them. The problems are solved, not by giving new information, but by arranging what we have always known ...[5]

Wittgenstein's characterisation of his philosophical activity as looking into the workings of language, is not, and is not meant to be, a definition of this activity. The place of definition is taken by metaphors, for example, Wittgenstein's often-quoted comparison of 'our language' — the common language of all of us, as opposed to the specialist languages of mathematicians, scientists and other specialists — with 'an ancient city'. Such a city is 'a maze of little streets and squares, of old and new houses, and of houses with additions from various periods; and this surrounded by a multitude of new boroughs with straight regular streets and new houses.'[6] The only way of finding one's way about in such a city is to follow an experienced guide or to study a reliable guidebook. A chief merit of Wittgenstein's enquiry into the structure of common language lies in his dissatisfaction with a merely general defence of common sense and its linguistic formulation. His description of language games draws attention to, among other things, contrasts between exact formal systems and natural languages and his development of a suitable terminology well serves the purpose of expressing these contrasts.[7]

It might be doubted whether Wittgenstein's conception of philosophy has enough in common with Moore's or Carnap's conception of philosophy to be called 'philosophical analysis'. Among the reasons for regarding these three metaphilosophical activities as species of the same metaphilosophical genus, whether one calls it 'analysis', 'clarification', 'elucidation' or by some other name are the following: according to all of them the generic activity does not add to the available factual information, does not provide any explanation, but (like grammar) makes implicit rules or assumptions explicit.

2. Some Neglected Distinctions Between Different Types of Analysis

A philosophical analysis which does not in any way modify the analysed concept, scientific theory, language game or other suitable subject-matter is in principle perfectly conceivable. Yet the practice of analytical philosophers goes often — whether deliberately or unintentionally — beyond mere clarification. Such a transgression would always be condemned by Wittgenstein. It would be approved by Carnap, if the modification of the *analysandum* is clearly stated and supported by cogent arguments. An example of a 'philosophical analysis', which involves modification, is Russell's discovery of the antinomy involved in the ordinary (or a certain theoretical) concept of class and its replacement by a concept which does not involve the antinomy. If, as is commonly agreed, Russell's procedure belongs to analytical philosophy, it makes good sense to distinguish between two types of analysis, which I have called 'exhibition-analysis' and 'replacement-analysis', and discussed elsewhere at some length. For the purpose of showing the relevance of the metaphilosophical distinction to substantive philosophical issues a few words about the difference between the two kinds of analysis will suffice.

If we restrict ourselves to the analysis of concepts and assume that the meaning of a concept is governed by rules for applying it to the particulars, if any, which are its instances and for relating it to other concepts with which it is compatible, incompatible or stands in other relations, then the exhibition analysis of a concept consists simply in exhibiting all or some of the rules governing it. (This may also be done indirectly, for example, by pointing out its equivalence to another concept, the rules for whose use are assumed to be known.)

A replacement-analysis of a concept consists in its replacement by another, provided that the following requirements are satisfied. (1) The analytical philosopher and the persons addressed by him agree on a criterion of soundness — for example, freedom from contradiction or consistency with a religious belief — which the *analysandum* does not satisfy, but which is satisfied by the *analysans*. (2) The analytical philosopher and the persons addressed by him agree on an analysing or replacement-relation — for example, Moore's or some weaker relation of equivalence — which must hold between the unsound *analysandum* and the sound *analysans*. Exhibition- and replacement-analysis differ from each other in a number of respects. Thus the exhibition-analysis of a concept has one and only one answer, which (in the case of a self-contradictory concept, for example) includes the statement of its being self-contradictory. A replacement-analysis on the other hand may have no answer because its two requirements cannot be satisfied. And it may have more than one answer because they may be satisfied in more ways than one.

Replacement-analysis gives rise to questions which do not arise in exhibition-analysis, the question, for example, why a certain criterion of soundness should be accepted and, more particularly, why, if the acceptance of a certain concept is inconsistent with the acceptance of a certain criterion of soundness, the concept rather than the criterion should be rejected. By drawing attention not only to the rules governing the analysed concepts but also to the criterion of soundness and to the analysing relation, it extends the scope of exhibition-analysis from the rules governing the *analysandum* to the set of rules which in addition govern the *analysans*, the analysing relation and their place in a wider system of concepts, propositions and rules. Thus, the replacement-analysis of, say, scientific or legal concepts may lead to the exhibition-analysis of scientific theories and legal systems and beyond to an exhibition-analysis of features characteristic of the whole system of concepts accepted by a person or group of persons.

Both a global and a local exhibition-analysis result in empirical statements to the effect that a certain person, group of persons or, presumably, everybody has accepted or rejected a certain concept, proposition or rule. It is important to note that the empirical nature of the statement that somebody has accepted or rejected a proposition (for example, the principle of causality, or the law of excluded middle) does *not* imply that the accepted or rejected proposition is empirical. The wider and the more varied the sets of accepted concepts, propositions and rules which are subjected to exhibition-analysis and the wider and the more varied the class of their acceptors, the more likely it is that common generic as well as specifically different features of human thinking and of systems of thought will be discovered, in particular features which are relevant to the traditional concerns of philosophy.

Among the philosophically relevant tasks which a global or, at least, a wide-ranging exhibition-analysis may reveal and try to achieve are the following: the discovery of differences in the concepts of logical consistency, as well as in the accepted rules, if any, for dealing with acknowledged inconsistencies by ranking some classes of propositions as more worthy of being retained than others; the discovery of differences in the type of relation holding between accepted concepts and the particulars to which they are applicable; and the discovery of differences in the types of rules governing concepts. A further important task for a global exhibition-analysis is to compare systems of beliefs or cognitive systems on the one hand with systems of practical attitudes on the other and to solve, or at least to face the problem of, the nature of morality. Whereas Moore regarded this problem as falling within the scope of analytical philosophy, Carnap regarded it as a philosophical pseudo-problem and Wittgenstein as inaccessible to philosophical analysis.

Before briefly turning to these issues it will be useful to prevent the frequent confusion of philosophical with linguistic analysis by drawing attention to a necessary condition which every correct exhibition- or replacement-analysis must satisfy, but which is not satisfied by any correct linguistic analysis. Consider the following characteristic formulations of an exhibition-analysis, briefly *ex*; of a replacement-analysis, briefly *rep*; and a linguistic analysis, briefly *ling*: *ex* = 'A certain person uses a certain concept, say, P' (assumes a certain proposition, say p; follows a conjunction of certain rules, say r); *rep* = 'If P is the *analysandum*, Q the *analysans*,

S the accepted criterion of soundness and *A* the accepted analysing relation, then *Q*, but not *P* satisfies *S* and stands in the analysing relation to *P*'; *ling* = 'The sentence *s* is linguistically correct'. Assuming that our language contains a negation, then it is a necessary condition of the correctness of *ex* that if in it we replace *Q* by *not-Q* (*p* by *not-p*; *r* by *not-r*) the resulting statement is incorrect. It equally is a necessary condition of the correctness of *rep*, that if in it we replace *Q* by *not-Q* the resulting statement is incorrect. But it is a necessary condition of the correctness of *ling* that if in it we replace *s* by *not-s* the resulting statement is also correct. Thus, if *s* is a linguistically correct statement expressing a correct analysis, the negation of *s* is also a linguistically correct statement which, however, expresses an incorrect analysis.

3. Towards a Classification of Concept-object Relations, of Concept-governing Rules and of Necessary Propositions

The analysis of specific concepts leads naturally to a characterisation of concepts in general, which together with the distinction between concepts and particulars will here be taken for granted. It may lead beyond this to an enquiry into various kinds of relations between concepts and particulars — an enquiry the results of which may prove fruitful in various fields of philosophy, such as the philosophy of mathematics or law. The following brief remarks, which are mainly intended to illustrate the interconnections between philosophical methodology and substantive philosophy, are devoted to three different types of relation which may hold between perceptually given particulars and concepts. One is the relation between perceptually given particulars and concepts which are descriptive of, or abstracted from, such particulars. This relation is exemplified by a perceptually given red rose and the concept of redness. It is treated at length in Locke's theory of abstraction and reformulated by his empiricist successors. The second is the relation between perceptually given particulars and concepts interpreting these particulars as objectively or inter-subjectively given. This relation is exemplified by a merely subjective appearance of a red rose and the concept of being perceivable by everybody — a concept which, though not abstracted from perceptually given particulars, is yet applicable to such. It is treated in Kant's transcendental logic. The third is the relation between perceptually given particulars and idealising concepts, that is, concepts which, though inapplicable to such particulars, can in certain contexts and for certain purposes be identified with descriptive concepts which are applicable to them. This relation is exemplified by a perceptually given triangle and the concept of a Euclidean triangle. It is treated in Plato's theory of Forms and the μέθεξις of perceptually given particulars in them.

A further classification of concepts which becomes fairly clear in the course of philosophical analyses, which are not too narrow in scope, is their distinction into exact and inexact concepts and — based on it — the distinction between two kinds of concept-governing rules, which may respectively be called 'subsumptive' and 'creative'. It is easy to give examples of exact concepts, such as 'prime number' and of inexact concepts such as 'green', 'ill', 'loitering'. What may distract attention from considering the difference and its bearing on important philosophical problems is the tendency of some analytical philosophers to follow Frege in disregarding inexact concepts as pseudo-concepts, which must be replaced by purified exact concepts; and the tendency of other analytical philosophers to follow Wittgenstein in relegating the exact concepts to the suburbs of language, which he considers to be of little interest to the philosopher and as likely to obscure his vision of the philosophically important old town.

A concept is exact if, and only if, the rules governing its use admit *only* positive cases, to which it is correctly applicable and incorrectly refusable; and negative cases, to which it is correctly refusable and incorrectly applicable. A concept is inexact if the rules governing its use admit in addition neutral or border-line cases, to which the concept is both correctly applicable and correctly refusable (though not both correctly applied and refused). A rule or conjunction of rules governing the use of a concept is subsumptive if, and only if, it is not, and is not intended to be, modified in the course of its application. A rule or conjunction of rules is creative if and only if it governs an inexact concept; if it allows the neutral cases of the concept to be turned into positive or negative cases; and if it further allows such a decision to be incorporated into the rule. The incorporation consists in regarding the decision as creating a precedent, that is, as providing an additional example of a positive or negative case. Creating a precedent must thus be distinguished from merely turning a neutral case into a positive or negative case.

The application of concepts — whether exact or inexact — to particulars would be pointless if every concept (and hence the negation of every concept) were correctly applied to every particular. For then every conjunction of propositions would be correct and, consequently, every set of propositions would be consistent. The notion of deducibility, which is definable in terms of the inconsistency of the premiss with the denial of the conclusion, would equally lose any point. That not every proposition is true or, in other words, that not every concept is both correctly applied and refused to every particular, may be regarded as the weakest version of the law of non-contradiction and the minimal core of any logic, for example a logic admitting with Frege only exact concepts or a logic which admits also inexact concepts; a 'classical logic' which acknowledges the law of excluded middle as a logical principle or a 'constructivistic logic' which rejects this principle and its deductive equivalents as, at best, heuristic fictions.

A person's principles of logic, that is, the principles determining his notion of consistency and logical deducibility, are supreme in the sense that any proposition which is inconsistent with them must be rejected as logically impossible. A person or group of persons may also accept non-logical principles — for example, the principle of sufficient reason, the principle of continuity or their negation — as supreme, in the sense that he rejects any proposition which is inconsistent with such a principle as non-logically or materially impossible. Whereas global exhibition-analysis exhibits both supreme logical and material principles, a restricted exhibition- or replacement-analysis may exhibit principles which, though neither logically nor materially supreme, dominate a specific region of thought.

The preceding brief remarks about different kinds of concept-object relations, about exact and inexact concepts, about subsumptive and creative rules and about logically and materially necessary propositions are empirical propositions about the way human beings use concepts. In order to avoid misunderstandings, it may be useful to emphasise the following more or less obvious points. (1) As has been noted earlier, to assert that (almost) all human beings accept a certain proposition, for example the weak law of non-contradiction, or to assert that some human beings accept, while others reject, the law of excluded middle is *not* to assert that the accepted or rejected logical proposition is itself an empirical proposition. (2) To assert that (almost) all human beings accept supreme logical and non-logical principles is *not* to assert that they accept the *same* supreme principles. (3) To assert that different groups of people may accept different supreme principles; different descriptive, interpretative and idealising concepts; different subsumptive and creative rules is *not* to deny one's preference for one's own accepted principles, concepts and rules and one's preparedness to argue in their support. (In a similar way a Catholic anthropologist, such as Evans-Pritchard, may draw attention to features which are common to his religion and, say, the religions of the Zande and the Nuer and to features in which these religions differ, without in any way weakening in his religious convictions.)

4. On the Relevance of the Preceding Distinctions to the Philosophy of Mathematics and Other Disciplines

In order to indicate — rather than to support by detailed arguments — the relevance of the preceding distinctions to the philosophy of mathematics, it seems useful to recall the controversy as to whether perceptual space is described by Euclidean geometry, as is held by Kant, or by non-Euclidean geometry, as is held by some followers of Einstein. A possible answer (which I have elsewhere defended in detail) is that perceptual space is described neither by Euclidean nor by a non-Euclidean geometry, but that these geometries are mutually inconsistent idealisations of perceptual space. They do not describe it because they are — among other things — exact, whereas the perceptual spatial concepts are inexact. The application of each of these geometries to perceptual space consists in identifications of geometrical concepts with perceptual ones. Thus in the case of Newtonian physics the perceptual concepts are identified with Euclidean, in the case of relativity-physics with non-Euclidean exact concepts. This view of the nature and application of geometry resembles Plato's view of the *methexis* of empirical phenomena in the Forms. It differs from Plato's view by admitting not only one realm of Forms or one Platonic heaven, but a plurality of them.

What has been said about geometry and its relation to empirical objects applies also to arithmetic, which constitutes an idealisation of empirical aggregates. The idealisation consists on the one hand in replacing inexact empirical number-concepts by exact ones, on the other hand in defining the latter as being members of infinite series of various kinds. This infinitisation, as the latter kind of idealisation may be called, can take various mutually inconsistent forms. Thus the sequence of integers may be defined as a potential or as an actual infinity and in the latter case as an actual infinity satisfying one of a number of mutually inconsistent axioms. While this is not the place to elaborate or to defend this pluralistic version of Plato's philosophy of mathematics, it may be worth noting that whereas it, among other things, proposes an answer to the question of what is involved in applying mathematics, this question does not even arise in the dominant contemporary accounts of the nature of mathematics. For these regard mathematics either as logic, and therefore as universally applicable, or as describing the structure of all perceptual phenomena, that is, as *ipso facto* applicable to all of them.

That scientific theories can also involve idealisation is particularly obvious in the case of physical theories and others using mathematics. Yet mathematisation is not the only modification of the conceptual apparatus, used to describe common experience in a common language. Thus, to give one example, the world of Newtonian dynamics, which consists of nothing but mass-particles, possessing no other properties than mass and momentum and wholly subject to the three laws of motion, differs radically from the world in which human beings lead their lives. The two worlds are not identical, but for certain purposes and in certain contexts identifiable. This means, among other things, that the usual account of scientific prediction must be revised. This so-called deductive account distinguishes three stages within any scientific prediction; namely, description of an initial state of affairs, proof that this state of affairs together with the laws of an accepted scientific theory logically implies another state of affairs; assertion of the so derived state of affairs.

If, as I am prepared to argue, scientific theories are idealisations of a common-sense world, described in a common language, then the mentioned three stages have to be supplemented by two further stages. The common-sense description must, before it can be used in the scientific inference, be idealised, that is, transposed into the language of the theory. And the conclusion of the inference from the idealised initial proposition and the laws of the theory must be de-idealised, that is, transposed into the common language. To neglect the stages of idealisation and de-idealisation may lead, and has led, to serious errors. Thus the wholly deterministic character of the Newtonian world does not imply — and was not meant by Newton to imply — that the world in which we act in accordance with our morality or in violation of it is equally deterministic.

The distinction between subsumptive and creative concept-governing rules is particularly relevant to the philosophy of law. The common sense of the members of a society and the law of the land which is addressed to them and which, if it is to be obeyed, must be understandable by them, have many concepts in common. Among them are concepts governed by creative rules. Yet, whereas the creative rules governing non-legal concepts in general merely *permit* that a neutral case be turned into a positive or negative case and be turned into a precedent, the creative rules governing legal concepts *require* the conversion of neutral into definite cases and, at least, strongly suggest that these cases be treated as precedents. Legal thinking, like mathematical thinking, involves an exactification of concepts. But whereas mathematical exactification is global in that it affects all concepts, legal exactification is local.

Among the main instruments of legal exactification is the creation of rebuttable presumptions (for example, the assumption of Roman law that the husband of a woman is the father of her child), of non-rebuttable presumptions (for example, the assumption of English law that a child which is less than eight years old is incapable of criminal intent) and of legal fictions (for example, the rule of English law that the adopter of a child be treated as if the child were born to the adopter in lawful wedlock). Drawing attention to legal presumptions and fictions is not to imply that similar presumptions and fictions are not part of common-sense thinking, but merely that they may not always coincide. Indeed, because the law is addressed to all the members of a community, it is not surprising that the structure of legal and the structure of common-sense thinking resemble each other very closely. That this is so is confirmed by the interesting fact that the key-concepts and results of Wittgenstein's description of language games have been anticipated by the roman jurists.[8]

5. Philosophical Analysis, Metaphysics and Morality

Some highly meritorious philosophers have employed their versions of philosophical analysis in attempts at proving that metaphysics is avoidable nonsense. Yet, properly understood and practised, philosophical analysis — more particularly, global exhibition-analysis — can be used to show that metaphysics is for almost all human beings unavoidable and makes good sense. Thus everybody accepts principles of a kind which traditionally have been regarded as metaphysical, if apart from the principles of his logic he accepts as supreme also non-logical principles governing the use of (interpretative) concepts the application of which to subjectively given phenomena confers objectivity or at least inter-subjective accessibility upon them. Examples of such supreme objectivity-principles are the principle that if whatever is given subjectively exists also objectively, it must be a substance or feature of a substance in some sense of the term; the principle that it must be a member of a causal chain; the principle that if it exists objectively and is subject to change, the change must be continuous. The history of philosophy and of the sciences contains many examples of different supreme objectivity-principles, accepted by different communities at the same time or by the same community at different times.

A person's objectivity-principles, with which his judgements about the inter-subjectively given world must be consistent, if they are to be acceptable to him, constitute what is often called his 'immanent metaphysics'. It must be distinguished from his transcendent metaphysics, if any, which contains his beliefs about the world as it exists independently of his or any other human experience of it. Examples of transcendent metaphysical beliefs are the doctrine that the world in itself is wholly unknowable, as well as the realist doctrine that it wholly or partly coincides with the world of objective experience. It must, I think, be admitted that agnosticism about transcendent metaphysics is feasible, even if its achievement involves overcoming strong inclinations towards the acceptance of religious beliefs on the one hand and of some version of realism on the other. Yet even a Sextus Empiricus will not be able to avoid an immanent metaphysics — at least not in those situations in which, following recommended sceptical practice, he 'adheres to appearances' and lives 'in accordance with the normal values of life, in an undogmatic manner'.[9]

The preceding brief vindication of immanent metaphysics as unavoidable and as making sense, raises the issue of another doctrine which has been held by some analytical philosophers — especially the philosophers of the Vienna circle and their Anglo-American followers. This is the doctrine that not only metaphysics but also ethics is meaningless. Within the limits of this essay only the following brief remarks can be made, which would be dogmatic, if they were not backed up by arguments put forward in another context.[10] Their main point is that while practical, including moral, attitudes differ from beliefs and cannot, therefore, be meaningful in the same sense, a person's practical attitudes do not form an unstructured heap, but are organised in a way which bears considerable resemblance to the manner in which a person's beliefs are organised. It is this structural similarity which justifies a version of the traditional use of the term 'meaning' by ascribing *cognitive* meaning to beliefs, for example a certain person's belief that an as yet unrealised situation is realisable by his action; and by ascribing *practical* meaning to practical attitudes, for example the person's desire to realise the situation by his action. By characterising practical meaning one prevents, among other things, the mistaken identification of all cognitive meaninglessness with the kind of nonsense expressed by the sentence that virtue is green.

Just as one may believe, disbelieve or suspend judgement about a proposition to the effect that something is the case, so one may have a practical pro-, anti- or indifferent attitude towards (what one believes to be) a practicability. And just as one's beliefs — in the wider sense, including disbeliefs and suspended judgements — can be logically inconsistent, so practical attitudes can be 'practically inconsistent' with each other. Before considering practical inconsistency, it is important to emphasise, as has been noted in different ways by Aristotle, Kant and other philosophers, that practical attitudes may be stratified, that is, directed towards practical attitudes — the former being one level higher than the latter. Thus it is a familiar fact that people, by having a practical attitude towards one of their practical attitudes, for example by having a practical anti-attitude towards their pro-attitude to smoking, may manifest the willingness of their spirit and the weakness of their flesh. (The smoker may show the practical nature of the lower attitude by accepting the offer of cigarettes and of the higher attitude by undergoing an aversion treatment against smoking.)

Three kinds of practical inconsistency may be distinguished: 'practical opposition', which holds between two practical attitudes of the same level which are separately, but not jointly, realisable; 'practical discordance', which holds between two practical attitudes of which one is a practical anti-attitude and the other a practical pro-, anti- or indifferent attitude, towards which the former attitude is directed; and 'practical incongruity', which holds between two practical attitudes if, and only if, each of them is either a pro-attitude directed to two opposed attitudes or else if each of them is an anti-attitude directed to two complementary attitudes (that is, two opposed attitudes of which one will be necessarily realised).

The stratification of a person's practical attitudes is a precondition of his having universal practical attitudes, which are analogous to inter-subjectivity judgements; and of his having universal and supreme practical attitudes, which are analogous to supreme objectivity — or inter-subjectivity principles. A person's practical attitude is universal if, and only if, it is directed towards everybody's (himself included) having a certain practical attitude towards a practicability (for example, my practical pro-attitude towards everybody's having a practical anti-attitude towards smoking). A universal practical attitude is supreme if, and only if, it is not the object of any higher practical attitude.

Just as within a person's system of beliefs his supreme inter-subjectivity principles (which govern the use of his inter-subjectivity- or objectivity-concepts) constitute his immanent metaphysics, so within his system of practical attitudes his supreme and universal practical attitudes constitute his morality. Further analysis, which cannot be undertaken here, exhibits differences between various species of morality — axiological, deontic, concrete and mixed — all of which have different subspecies. To make these distinctions within the *genus* morality and to make similar distinctions within the *genus* metaphysics, is to be no more relativistic or absolutistic than a biologist who distinguishes between biological *genera, species* and varieties.

What has been said about the interaction between a conception of philosophical analysis and substantive philosophical theses clearly suggests that both the tasks of global and the tasks of local analysis are by no means exhausted. As regards the former, it is likely that important generic features of systems of beliefs and practical attitudes have been overlooked and that future changes in these systems will call for revisions and new approaches. A global task which has, I think, to be tackled anew is a philosophical analysis of aesthetic judgements and their relation to beliefs and practical evaluations, including metaphysics and morality. Among the more restricted analytical tasks, which seem to call for further endeavour, are the problem of the relation between history and anthropology and the problem of the role of science and morality in medical thinking.[11]

Notes

1. An outline of my metaphilosophical views, as well as detailed criticisms of exaggerated claims made for some philosophical methods are contained in Ch. 2 of *Fundamental Questions of Philosophy* (Brighton, 1969) and in Ch. 15 of *Metaphysics: Its Structure and Function* (Cambridge, 1984).
2. See *The Philosophy of G.E. Moore* in the *Library of Living Philosophers*, ed. Arthur Schilpp (Evanston and Chicago, 1942), pp. 666f.
3. Ibid., p. 323.
4. See *Logische Syntax der Sprache* (Vienna, 1934), pp. 203-7.
5. *Philosophical Investigations* (trsl. by G.E.M. Anscombe) (Oxford, 1953), section 109).
6. Ibid., section 18.
7. See section 4.
8. See my 'Über Sprachspiele und rechtliche Institutionen' in *Proceedings of the 5th Wittgenstein Symposium* (Vienna, 1981), pp. 481-91.
9. See *Outlines of Pyrrhonism*, Ch. 11.
10. See *Experience and Conduct* (Cambridge, 1976).
11. I might add that my own interest in philosophy was most strongly aroused when, as a law student, I tried to clarify certain legal concepts and when I reflected on the nature of such clarification.

8 LOGIC, ONTOLOGY AND METAPHYSICS

Czeslaw Lejewski

1 What is philosophy? Many different answers have been given to this question in antiquity and in modern times but none has earned general acceptance, and I do not propose to try and improve on any of them. All I want to say is that in my judgement, which I emphatically admit is purely subjective, no body of theories and problems deserves to be called philosophy unless some of these theories and problems fall within the province of metaphysics. But what is metaphysics? This question, like the previous one, has been answered in many different ways, and no doubt new answers will be forthcoming. My own subjective view is that no body of theories and problems deserves the name of metaphysics unless some of these theories and problems add up to constitute ontology. And what is ontology? The answer to this question is to be found in the writings of Aristotle.

2 Book Γ of Aristotle's *Metaphysics* begins with the following passage:

> There is a science which investigates being as being and the attributes which belong to this in virtue of its own nature. Now this is not the same as any of the so called special sciences; for none of these others treats universally of being as being. They cut off a part of being and investigate the attributes of this part; this is what mathematical sciences for instance do. (1003^a21-1003^a26).[1]

Aristotle has no special name for this science of his. He sometimes seems to refer to it very generally as *wisdom* (σοφία) or simply as *philosophy* (φιλοσοφία), and on a few occasions he calls it *first philosophy* (πρώτη φιλοσοφία). Centuries later the science of being as being acquired the name of ontology and came to be regarded by some philosophers as the most important part of metaphysics.

3 The principal characteristic of ontology is, in accordance with Aristotle's conception of the science of being, its universality. The interest of a special science, Aristotle tells us, is limited to certain objects whereas the science of being studies all objects that there are, and does so generally, concerning itself with particular objects only in special cases. Extending Aristotle's idea a little further one can stipulate that if there are kinds of entity other than objects then the science of being should study these kinds of entity as well.

Another characteristic feature of the science of being, according to Aristotle, is this: the science of being lends itself to a very precise treatment and can be presented with the degree of exactitude unattainable in other disciplines. Does this mean that ontology, as conceived by Aristotle but elaborated up to the standards of exactitude established long after his time, can eventually be given the form of a deductive system or that of a body of deductive systems? I shall return to this problem at a later stage of my investigations.

4 In Book B of *Metaphysics* there is a list of 14 problems which, in Aristotle's view, concern the science of being. Among them we find the following:

(i) should the science of being also study *the principles of demonstration* (αἱ ἀρχαὶ ἐξ ὧν δεικνυουσι παντες)?
(ii) whose business is to study *same* (ταὐτό) and *other* (ἕτερον)?[2]

Aristotle's answer to the first question is in the affirmative, and he is quite definite in claiming that the study of *same* and *other* is within the scope of his proposed new science.

The notions of identity and that of difference, that is the notion of non-identity, are logical notions, and to logic belong the principles of demonstration mentioned by Aristotle. For among them he counts the principle of excluded middle and the principle of non-contradiction. Thus, it does not seem to be entirely contrary to the Aristotelian conception of the science of being to hold that at least some ontological theses have also logical connotation.

5 More than 2,000 years after the death of the author of *Metaphysics*, G.E. Moore wrote that the first and the most important problem of philosophy was to give a general description of the whole universe. According to him a description of this sort should provide the answer to the fundamental question: what kind of things are there?[3] By 'things' Moore did not understand 'material things'. Whatever existed, was a thing for Moore. Echoing the words of Aristotle he insisted that no other science was concerned to establish that such and such kinds of entity were the only kinds of entity that there were.

Giving expression to a similar train of thought W.V. Quine begins one of his widely-read essays with the following remark:

> A curious thing about the ontological problem is its simplicity. It can be put in three Anglo-Saxon monosyllables: 'What is there?' It can be answered, moreover, in a word — 'Everything' — and everyone will accept this answer as true. However, this is merely to say that there is what there is. There remains room for disagreement over cases ...[4]

6 I do not propose to explore the problems lurking behind Quine's one-word answer. Instead, I wish to direct my attention to the 'disagreement over cases', and, to begin with, I propose to consider all possible points of view concerning the truth or falsity of the following two propositions:

(1) there exists at least one material object
(2) there exists at least one abstract object

The first point of view entails regarding both propositions as true. I will refer to it as *Platonism* on account of its endorsement of proposition (2).

In accordance with the second point of view, proposition (1) is true but proposition (2) is false. This is in harmony with the principal tenet of *reism* that only things, that is to say material objects, exist.[5]

The third point of view is likely to be supported by the adherents to *idealism* in one of its versions. They believe that whatever exists is a product of our mind or of mind in general. Thus they would deny proposition (1), and would not hesitate to assert proposition (2).

The fourth and the final possible point of view entails the denial of both propositions. It may be attractive to someone who espouses the *nihilism* of Gorgias, the sophist.

Since nihilism and idealism are no concern of mine in the present essay, I will proceed to elaborate a little the first two ontological points of view, Platonism and reism.

7 The truth of proposition (1), recognised by both the Platonist and the reist, can hardly be doubted. We perceive some of the material objects through our senses, directly without any aids or indirectly with the aid of spectacles, microscopes, telescopes hearing aids or other technical devices. In asserting the existence of certain material objects we rely on the witness of other people, and as regards the existence of material objects too distant from us in space or time, or too small or too short-lived to affect us through our senses even indirectly, we have to be satisfied with framing considered hypotheses.

Proposition (2) is denied by the reist but the Platonist can point out that it is embedded in what is loosely called common knowledge, and that it is implied by various pronouncements of the overwhelming majority of philosophers and scientists. Platonic ideas, medieval universals, mathematical objects such as numbers, points, lines, planes and solids, classes postulated by some logicians, the set-theoretician's sets, objects supposedly designated by various theoretical terms of scientists, minds and mental entities, are examples of abstract objects, that over centuries have attracted attention of many students of ontology. Admittedly abstract objects do not affect us through our senses but the assumption of their existence recommends itself to many because of its explanatory power. However, even those who recognise the existence of abstract objects, are not in agreement on the notion of existence embedded, for instance, in the functor 'there exists at least one' when it is used in concatenation with an argument which is supposed to refer to an abstract object.

8 Let us consider again proposition (1) in the context of the following two propositions:

(3) there exists at least one class
(4) there exists at least one number

The notion of existence embedded in the functor 'there exists at least one' is related to the notion of the copula 'is $\binom{a}{an}$' as can be learnt from the proposition which says that

(5) for all *a*, there exists at least one *a* if and only if for some *b*, *b* is an *a*

Now, propositions (5), (1), (3) and (4), between them, imply that

(6) for some *a*, *a* is a material object
(7) for some *a*, *a* is a class
(8) for some *a*, *a* is a number

From each of these last three propositions the following one appears to be inferable:

(9) for some *a*, *a* is a material object or *a* is a class or *a* is a number

Some Platonists will say that proposition (9) is true. In the opinion of other Platonists (9) is a meaningless expression. The disagreement appears to be traceable back to an important though not immediately obvious difference between the ontologies espoused by the parties to the controversy.

The two, tacitly presupposed ontologies will be referred to, generally, as *unicategorial* ontology on the one side and *multicategorial* ontology on the other. On occasions the more specific terms 'unicategorial Platonism' and 'multicategorial Platonism' will also be used.

9 A unicategorial Platonist who recognises the truth of propositions (6)-(9), holds that all material objects are objects, all classes are objects, and all numbers are objects, and that, speaking generally, everything that exists, is an object. For whatever is an object is something and whatever is something is an object. To put it more precisely:

(10) for all *a*, *a* is an object if and only if for some *b*, *a* is a *b*

Our unicategorial Platonist's answer to the fundamental ontological question of G.E. Moore would be this:

(11) there are objects only

Now, proposition (11) contains two assertions. The one simply says that

(12) there are objects,

which means no more and no less than that

(13) there exists at least one object.

The presence of a second, latent, assertion is revealed, not without a measure of ambiguity, by the word 'only'. In the context of (11) the word 'only' may imply that there is nothing else except objects, that is to say, it may imply that

(14) for all a, if there exists at least one a then all as are objects.

which within the framework of a system of logic is equivalent to

(15) for all a, if all objects are as then all as are objects

In the light of these explanations proposition (11) amounts to maintaining that objects form an ontological category, or an ontological universe of discourse. On the other hand the word 'only' as used in (11) may signify that proposition (11) as a whole implies not only that objects form an ontological category but also that there is no other category formed by entities differing in kind from objects.

Among philosophers and logicians whose ontology appears to be unicategorial, the most notable are: Frege, who at the time of completing his famous *Grundgesetze* referred to classes and numbers as objects, Quine, who countenances physical, that is, material objects and classes only, and Kotarbinski, according to whom every object is a material object.

10 The multicategorial ontologist agrees that there are material objects, but he rejects the unicategorial ontologist's assertion that there is only one ontological category of entities. His answer to G.E. Moore's ontological question is: there are objects and, in addition, there are kinds of entity other than the ontological category of objects. Among those other kinds of entity he may count the ontological category of classes, for instance, or the ontological category of numbers. For him there are classes but their mode of existence differs from that of objects and also from that of numbers. Objects constitute an ontological universe of discourse but classes constitute a different ontological universe, and so do numbers. These three different ontological universes, or categories — and there may be more than three — are not sub-universes of a comprehensive ontological universe. Multicategorial ontology does not envisage such an all-embracing universe.

The idea of there being several ontological categories of what there is, is not new. It can be traced back to Aristotle's *Categories* and to his conception of substances, properties and relations, and even more appropriately to his notions of species and genus, to which he refers as secondary substances. For centuries philosophers have maintained, implicitly if not explicitly, that such entities as properties or relations have a being that is different from that of objects.

11 The difference between the ontology of the unicategorial Platonist and that of his multicategorial opponent is reflected in the way they interpret the grammar of ordinary language. Consider, for instance, the following propositions:

(16) the sun is a material object
(17) the class of lions is a species
(18) the number two is an even number

Some unicategorial Platonists will regard propositions (16)-(18) as true and some multicategorial ontologists will concur. This, however, does not mean that they interpret the grammar of these propositions in the same way. In order to clarify their respective interpretations invite them to comment on the following expressions:

(19) the sun is a species
(20) the sun is an even number
(21) the class of lions is an even number

Are these expressions propositions, that is, declarative sentences?

The unicategorial Platonist, who regards the noun expressions occurring in propositions (16)-(18) as belonging to one and the same semantical category, will say that expressions (19)-(21) are well constructed propositions. Semantical categories, he will point out, are substitution classes of the linguist, and this means that the expressions belonging to the same semantical category can be replaced by one another in any meaningful context without destroying the syntactical cohesion of the context. Expressions (19)-(21) are the result of replacing one noun expression by another noun expression in the meaningful context of propositions (16)-(18). Hence they remain syntactically cohesive and must be counted as well formed propositions. Admittedly, they appear to be unusual and odd, but this is so, simply because they are obviously false.

According to the multicategorial ontologist expressions (19)-(21) are not propositions. They lack syntactical cohesion and are more like meaningless sequences of meaningful words. In his view noun expressions of ordinary language do not form a single semantical category. The expression 'material object' is an object expression. The expression 'species' is a class expression, and the expression 'even number' is a number expression. Each of these three expressions belongs to a different semantical category, and this is why replacing 'material object' in (16) by the expression 'species' destroys the syntactical cohesion of (16) as is evident from (19). In a similar way the lack of syntactical cohesion in (20) and (21) can be attributed, in the multicategorial ontologist's opinion, to the disregarding of the categorial differences between the expressions involved in the transforming of propositions (16)-(18) into (19)-(21).

12 Within the semantical category of object expressions the term 'object' is the most general term. The term 'class' is, according to the multicategorial ontologist, the most general term within the semantical category of class expressions, and the term 'number' within that of numbers. Since these three semantical categories differ from one another, the expression 'there exists at least one' in propositions (13), (3) and (4) is syntactically ambiguous. In (13) it is a proposition-forming functor for one argument which is an object expression whereas in proposition (3) it is a proposition-forming functor for one argument which is a class expression, and in (4) — a proposition-forming functor for one argument which is a number expression. A multicategorial ontologist, who does not count species or numbers among objects, will maintain that the copula 'is $(^a_{an})$' in propositions (16)-(18) is affected by a similar ambiguity. In an artificial language of the multicategorial ontologist the differences between the various semantical categories would have to be indicated by the style of the constant terms and also by the style of the respective variables. Thus proposition (9) would have to be replaced by a proposition like the following one:

(22) (for some a, a is a material object) or (for some α, α is a class) or (for some x, x is a number)

And a warning would have to be given that in this language small letters from the beginning of the Latin alphabet are used as variables of the same semantical category as that of object expressions whereas small letters from the beginning of the Greek alphabet stand for class expressions, and small letters from the end of the Latin alphabet for number expressions.

13 The multicategorial ontologist is, of course, a Platonist but, as we have seen, his ontology differs from that of the unicategorial Platonist. The latter envisages various abstract objects, the former — various abstract ontological categories, instead of abstract objects or over and above them. Thus, even among Platonists, the room for disagreement over cases is ample.

According to the reist every object is a material object. His, then, is a very austere ontology, and austere is, relatively, the language he uses to present the positive side of his theory. However, if the reist wants to deny some of the assertions of the unicategorial Platonist, he will have to expand his reistic language by adding to it the vocabulary his opponent uses to refer to abstract objects. And for the purpose of denying some of the assertions of the multicategorial Platonist the reist will have to use the language that is adequate to multicategorial ontology. By doing so the reist does not compromise his reistic standpoint, provided the languages he uses, are, as they should be, ontologically neutral, that is, have no ontological commitment implicitly built into their grammar.

14 In the opening sections I broadly indicated that, in my view, there was a connection between ontology conceived as the science of being and metaphysics. Clearly, not every ontological thesis is a metaphysical thesis, but there are some ontological theses with unmistakable metaphysical connotation. With a view to identifying the latter let us consider the following propositions:

(23) for some a, a is a material object
(24) for all a, it is not the case that a is a material object
(25) for some a, a is an abstract object
(26) for all a, it is not the case that a is an abstract object

The truth of proposition (23) can hardly be doubted. It is supported by empirical evidence. If a proposition is supported by empirical evidence then the same empirical evidence refutes the contradictory of the proposition in question. Thus, proposition (24), which is the contradictory of proposition (23), can be said to be refuted in the light of empirical evidence.

Unlike proposition (23), proposition (25) is not supported by empirical evidence. Abstract objects cannot be seen or touched or apprehended through senses other than the sense of sight or that of touch. And the contradictory of (25), that is to say proposition (26), is not refutable by empirical evidence, which is irrelevant in either case. However, propositions (25) and (26) are ontological propositions since either of them, though not both, can be included in a description of reality. Moreover, since they are independent of empirical evidence, they can be regarded as ontological propositions with metaphysical connotation or simply — as metaphysical propositions.

The noun expression 'material object' can be used, and has been used, in propositions supported by empirical evidence. It can, therefore, be called an *empirical term* and its designata — *empirical objects*. They affect us through our senses and thus get apprehended.

On the other hand, the noun expression 'abstract object' is a *theoretical term*. Existential propositions in which it occurs, and their contradictories, are independent of empirical evidence, and its designata, if there are any, can only be regarded as *theoretical objects* as they do not affect us through our senses either directly or indirectly.

15 Besides empirical noun expressions and theoretical ones there are expressions which belong to semantical categories other than the category of noun expressions, and which, like noun expressions, divide into empirical terms and theoretical terms. Examples of such expressions occur in the following propositions:

(27) for some a and b, a is a part of b
(28) for some a and b, a is earlier than b
(29) for some a and b, a is a set, b is a set, and a is an element of b

It will easily be conceded that (27) is supported by empirical evidence as it means simply that there are objects that have parts. Consequently, the functor 'part of' can be regarded as an empirical term. And the same can be said of the functor 'earlier than' which occurs in (28). For a proposition of the form 'a is earlier than b' means that an object a precedes an object b in time.

Proposition (29), on the other hand, can hardly claim support from empirical evidence. It is a metaphysical proposition. In it the functor 'is an element of', which stands for the set-theoretical 'ε', is a theoretical term, and so is, of course, the noun expression 'set'. A theory which counts (29) among its theses, is an ontology with metaphysical connotation, or, simply, — a metaphysical theory.

16 Another theoretical term is used in the proposition which says that

(30) for some a, a is a momentary object

Momentary objects, if there are any, are theoretical objects. They do not last long enough to affect us through our senses. They are, in fact, not supposed to last at all. However, the theoretical term 'momentary object' differs from the term 'set' in a significant way. It can be defined with the aid of empirical terms. Here is an equivalence which could serve as the required definition:

(31) for all a, a is a momentary object if and only if both (i) a is an object and (ii) for all b and c, if b is a part of a and c is a part of a then it is not the case that b is earlier than c

In proposition (31) all constant terms, except the noun expression 'momentary object', are logical or empirical terms. No proposition which satisfies similar conditions, and which could serve as the definition of the term 'set' or as the definition of the functor 'is an element of', has yet been found.

17 For the purpose of the present essay a definition in which the *definiens* contains, apart from logical terms, only empirical terms or terms definable with the aid of empirical terms, will be called a *realist definition* irrespective of whether the term to be defined, which occurs in the *definiendum*, turns out to be an empirical term or a theoretical term. A term defined by a realist definition will be called a *realist term*. Accordingly, by *realist metaphysics* I will understand a metaphysics whose theses that are independent of empirical evience, contain, apart from logical terms, realist terms only.

A theoretical term not definable with the aid of realist terms will be called an *idealist term*, and by *idealist metaphysic* I will understand a theory that makes use of idealist terms.

This brings to an end the compiling of my meta-ontological and meta-metaphysical terminology on which I intend to draw when it comes to outlining the kind of ontology which in my not unerring opinion does contain a few grains of truth.

18 The ontology of my choice is a version of expanded reism.

Having declared my standpoint I propose, in the first place, to try and make it clearer by producing a list of what, in my view, are the most characteristic theses of reistic ontology at the present stage in its development. I will then explore the possibility of presenting the doctrine as a body of deductive systems.

In my version of reism the following theses obtain:

T1. *There is only one ontological category, namely the category of objects.*

T1 is the reist's answer to G.E. Moore's ontological question. It does not differ from the unicategorial Platonist's answer discussed in section 9, and like the latter it contains two assertions. The one, to the effect that there are objects, can be given the form of proposition (13), which, in view of the following equivalence:

(32) for all a, there exists at least one a if and only if for some b, b is an a,

implies and is implied by

(33) for some *a*, *a* is an object.

In accordance with the other, implicit, assertion there are no entities differing in kind from objects, that is to say there are no other ontological categories over and above the category of objects. This amounts to the rejection of the multicategorial ontology. Such a comprehensive rejection cannot be expressed in terms of a language that complies with the scheme of semantical categories. What one can do is to deny, separately, the existence of the entities which supposedly constitute an ontological category other than the category of objects. In a discussion with a multicategorial ontologist who recognises the ontological category of classes and that of numbers, the reist can state his position by adding to proposition (33) the following two propositions:

(34) for all α, it is not the case that α is a class
(35) for all *x*, it is not the case that *x* is a number

In propositions (33), (34) and (35) the variables '*a*', 'α', and '*x*' belong to different semantical categories, and so do the expressions 'object', 'class', and 'number'. The semantical category of the copula 'is $\binom{a}{an}$' is also different in each of the three propositions.

Neither (34) or (35) nor their contradictories are either supported or refutable by empirical evidence, which takes T1 into the realm of metaphysics. Moreover, since the notion of the copula in propositions referring to entities of any ontological category other than the category of objects is not definable in realist terms, the metaphysical connotation of T1 must be idealist in nature.

T2. *Every object is a material object, that is, a thing.*

An assertion to the effect that whatever is an object is a material object, is embedded in T2. It contradicts the unicategorial Platonist's belief that there are abstract objects, the meaning of the expression 'abstract object' being determined with the aid of the following equivalence:

(36) for all *a*, *a* is an abstract object if and only if both (i) *a* is

an object and (ii) it is not the case that *a* is a material object

Empirical evidence neither supports nor can refute this belief. Consequently, the assertion that there are abstract objects, and T2, which implies that there are no abstract objects, are metaphysical propositions; but it is worth noting that the statement of T2 involves logical and realist terms only.

T3. *We know from experience that there are many things in the world; there is no evidence that the number of things is finite, nor is there any evidence that the number of things is not finite; however, it is assumed by way of hypothesis that there are infinitely many things in the world.*

Obviously, T3 is a piece of metaphysics, but it is a piece of realist metaphysics since the notion of numerical infinity embedded in T3 is a logical notion, and the proposition 'there are infinitely many things' involves no use of idealist terms.

T4. *Many things known to us from experience have parts; no empirical evidence can be brought to support the view that there are objects without parts; its contradictory, namely the view that everything that exists has parts, is assumed as a hypothesis.*

The term 'atom', which is supposed to designate objects that have no parts, is a theoretical term, but its definition is a realist definition. It reads as follows:

(37) for all a, a is an atom if and only if both (i) a is an object and (ii) for all b, it is not the case that b is a part of a

Thus the proposition which denies the existence of atoms, is a metaphysical proposition of the realist kind.

T5. *Every thing known to us from experience lasts, or, to put it in other words, is extended in time; we have no experience of momentary objects; it is assumed, by way of hypothesis, that there are no momentary objects at all; that is to say, it is assumed that every object lasts.*

The expression 'momentary object' is a theoretical term, but proposition (31), which defines it, is a realist definition. It is, therefore, clear that T5 is a metaphysical statement with realist connotation.

T6. *Every thing known to us from experience is bulky; in other words, it is extended in space; no objects that could be described as geometrical points, are given in experience; the reistic hypothesis is that every object is bulky.*

T6 is, like T5, a thesis of the realist metaphysics since the terms 'bulky', that is, 'extended in space', and 'not bulky', that is, 'not extended in space', are empirical and realist respectively.

T7. *The duration of things is a sufficient condition of their having parts; and so is the bulkiness of things; no other sufficient condition of things having parts is given in experience, and in accordance with the reistic hypothesis duration and bulk are not only sufficient conditions of things having parts; they are also necessary conditions, thus it is assumed that while every thing is extended in time and in space, there is no other way in which things are extended.*

The notion of an object extended in a third way, or rather the expression 'object extended in a third way' can be defined with the aid of the following equivalence:

(38) for all a, a is an object extended in a third way if and only if (i) a is an object, (ii) for some b, b is a part of a, (iii) it is not the case that a lasts and (iv) it is not the case that a is bulky

Obviously, the term 'object extended in a third way' is a theoretical term, but its definition is realist. The reist denies the existence of objects extended in a third way, and, consequently asserts that

(39) for all a and b, if b is a part of a then (a lasts or a is bulky)

In fact, the content of T7 can be expressed, in greater detail, as follows:

(40) for all a (for some b, b is a part of a), if and only if (a lasts or a is bulky)

As a metaphysical thesis proposition (40) and T7 belong to realist metaphysics.

T8. *Of the infinitely many things that there are, one thing seems to deserve special consideration; it is the totality of all things, in the collective sense of the term 'totality'; in other words, it is the world or the cosmologist's universe; no one can claim any experiential knowledge of its beginning or of its end; nor does experience give us any clue as to the limits of its bulk; it is assumed, by way of hypothesis, that the universe has no beginning and no end, and that there is no limit to its bulk.*

The world is only one of the infinitely many things, but whatever there is, is a part of it or is identical with it, and to say something about the world is to say something, indirectly, about the totality of what there is, in the distributive sense of the term 'totality'. To put it in other words and with no emphasis on precision, if the world has no beginning and no end, and if there is no limit to its bulk, then one can say that things are always and everywhere.

The term 'object with no beginning and no end' is a theoretical term but a clue to its realist definition will be given in section 24 below.

However, I am unable to offer a realist definition of the term 'limitless as regards bulk'. Consequently, I can only say that T8 is a piece of metaphysics. The question of whether T8, in its entirety, is realist or idealist, will have to be left unanswered.

T9. *Propositions which appear to be true, yet imply the existence of abstract entities of one kind or another, are likely to have a metaphorical meaning and can, as a rule, be rephrased, without any loss of relevant content, so as to have no existential implications, or so as to imply the existence of things only.*

T10. *Propositions which imply the existence of abstract entities of one kind or another, but which in the view of those who propound them, must be taken literally as they are, without any paraphrasing, are to be rejected as false.*

My informal outline of reistic metaphysics ends with T8. Note that only T1, which denies certain existential claims put forward by multicategorial Platonists, has idealist connotation. The remaining seven theses, with some qualification attaching to T8, are of a realist kind. T9 and T10 hint at the method of dealing with what some Platonists regard as counter-examples to reistic ontology.

19 At this juncture I propose to return to the question raised in section 3. Can ontology, as conceived by Aristotle, be given the form of a deductive system or that of a body of deductive systems?

Any general description of reality is likely to consist of several theories, and the description just outlined above is no exception. The interesting point is that the theories which are constituent parts of the reistic description of reality, are not unrelated. Some of them are presupposed by others. A theory **A** is said to be presupposed by a theory **B** just in case the vocabulary exhibited in the theses of **A** has to be used in the theses of **B** together with the vocabulary characteristic of **B** whereas the latter vocabulary is not exhibited in the theses of **A** at all.

It is evident from T5, T7 and T8 of the outline that one of the constituent theories of the reistic ontology is a theory of time relations between things. It will be called *Chronology*. One of its theses is proposition (31). The expressions 'momentary object' and 'earlier than', which occur in (31), belong to the vocabulary peculiar to *Chronology*. The remaining terms that occur in (31) belong to the vocabulary of the theory of part-whole relations, that is, they belong to the vocabulary of *Mereology*. Thus *Mereology* can be said to be presupposed by *Chronology*.

Now, consider proposition (37), which is a mereological thesis. The expressions 'atom' and 'part of', which occur in (37), belong to the vocabulary characteristic of *Mereology*. The remaining vocabulary exhibited in (37) will be regarded by many as part of the vocabulary of logic, and if this view is accepted then one can say, generally, that *Mereology* presupposes logic.

Within the framework of the logic presupposed by *Mereology* two further theories can be distinguished. Propositions (5), (10), (14) and (15) belong to one of them as theses, and the copula 'is

$(^a_{an})$', the general name 'object', and the functors 'there exists at least one' and 'all...are', that occur in them, constitute a small fragment of the vocabulary characteristic of the theory. Judging from its subject matter as reflected in the four theses just enumerated the theory could be called a theory of objects, or a theory of existence, or a theory of what there is, or *Ontology*, admittedly, in a somewhat narrower sense than the sense in which the name 'ontology' is being used throughout the chapter.

The remaining vocabulary as exhibited, for instance, in (5) and in (14) includes the functors 'if and only if' and 'if...then', and the quantifiers 'for all ...' and 'for some ...' together with their respective variables. It also includes the functors 'it is not the case that', 'and', and 'or', the latter two being propositional connectives. This sort of vocabulary will be readily recognised as the vocabulary of the logic of propositions, and it is the logic of propositions that is presupposed by *Ontology*. It constitutes as it were the first chapter of a systematic presentation of the science of being. It presupposes no other theory, and on this account can be described as the most general theory of all. Every theory of lesser generality presupposes the logic of propositions and uses its vocabulary however limited this use may turn out to be.

Now, what kind of logic of propositions — and there are several kinds of logic of propositions — is the most appropriate theory, from the reistic point of view, to serve as the fundamental presupposition of any description of reality? As a philosopher interested in ontology I have no hesitation in suggesting that Leśniewski's *Protothetic* is such a theory.[6]

20 The standard systems of *Protothetic* are based on the functor 'if and only if' and on the universal quantifier 'for all...', with its respective variables, as the only primitive notions, but the first system of *Protothetic* constructed by Leśniewski had the functor 'if...then' instead of 'if and only if' as the only undefined functor. Several standard systems of *Protothetic* have been constructed on the basis of a single axiom each, but these axioms are likely to appear to be unintuitive to many philosophers, so in order to indicate the deductive power and the scope of *Protothetic* it may prove to be helpful to say that a full system of the theory is inferentially equivalent to a full system of the classical two-valued logic strengthened (i) by one of the following two propositions:

(41) for all p, q, and δ, if $((p$ if and only if $q)$ and $\delta(p))$ then $\delta(q)$
(42) for all p, q, and δ, if $\delta(p)$ then if δ (it is not the case that p) then $\delta(q)$

to serve as an additional axiom, and (ii) by the following additional directives: (a) an inference rule allowing for the classical operations involving the universal quantifier; (b) a generalised rule for introducing definitions into the system; and (c) the rule of extensionality for the semantical categories of functors available in *Protothetic*.

Proposition (41) is the law, or principle, of extensionality for propositions, and proposition (42) is the principle of bivalence. Within the framework of *Protothetic* the two principles can be shown to be inferentially equivalent but either of them is controversial on its own merits.

Some logicians and philosophers accept (41) as universally true. Others have no hesitation in rejecting it as palpably false on the strength of numerous counter-examples drawn from common knowledge as expressed in terms of ordinary language. The reist is on the side of the former, indeed he regards as true the principle of extensionality for expressions of any semantical category, and as for apparent counter-examples, he believes that they can be rendered inconclusive by appropriate paraphrasing.

Proposition (42), that is to say the principle of bivalence, reminds us that *every proposition is either true or false*. In a full system of the bivalent, that is, two-valued, logic there are only two non-synonymous constant terms either of which belongs to the semantical category of propositions. They are, of course, definable in the system but are not to be found in ordinary language. In logical symbolism they are usually given the form 'T' and 'F', or '1' and '0', respectively.

Toward the end of the second decade of this century Łukasiewicz discovered an alternative to the classical two-valued logic. Inspired by the way Aristotle and some medieval logicians treated the notions of necessity, possibility, impossibility and contingency, and anxious to free himself from what he regarded as deterministic constraints of the two-valued logic, he constructed a system of three-valued logic. If one extends it into a full system, then one can define in it not only the constants 'T' and 'F' but also a third constant term which belongs to the semantical category of propositions but is not equivalent to either of the first two terms.

A few years later a similar discovery was made by E. Post, who, unlike Łukasiewicz, was motivated by interest in uninterpreted formal structures rather than by any philosophical considerations. Systems of various many-valued logics, including infinitely-many-valued logics, began to appear in the literature. Since any system of the logic of propositions which among its constants has terms that are not synonymous with terms available in a full system of the classical two-valued logic, is, in fact, a system of a many-valued logic, it is not improper to regard as many-valued logics such theories as modal logics, deontic logics and tense logics, to mention only the ones that are most familiar.

My opting for *Protothetic* as the ultimate presupposition of the science of being means that in my opinion neither the arguments against two-valued logic nor the arguments for alternative logics distinguish themselves with much persuasiveness. For one thing, I do not concur with the view that the principle of bivalence implies determinism, in some sense of implying, or is, in some sense, a consequence of it. As regards modalities, I expect them to be eventually accommodated, together with the notion of truth and that of falsehood, in a deductive system of semantics based on two-valued propositional logic as one of its presuppositions. Judging from what can be regarded as its characteristic vocabulary, deontic logic is not in business to make a contribution to ontology, and the aspects of reality which tense logics claim to illuminate, fall within the subject matter of *Chronology*.

The discovery of many-valued logics has helped us to realise that even at the highest level of generality there is scope for alternatives, and that in choosing between them we run the risk of making a wrong guess. It is in bringing about this realisation that the philosophical significance of the discovery lies.

21 In starting my reistic description of reality with *Protothetic* I follow Leśniewski, and I continue to do so by proposing *Ontology*, Leśniewski's *Ontology*, as the second chapter of the description.[7] *Ontology* results from (a) subjoining an *ontological* axiom to a system of *Protothetic*, (b) adapting the directives of *Protothetic* to the new axiom, and (c) prescribing another rule of definition and another rule of extensionality in addition to the adapted directives. The standard system of *Ontology* can be based on a single axiom in which the functor of singular inclusion, that is, the functor 'is

$\binom{a}{an}$' is used as the only primitive term. Several propositions that could serve as single axioms of *Ontology* are known, but the most informative, though not the shortest, is Leśniewski's original axiom established in 1920. It reads as follows:

(43) for all *a* and *b*, *a* is a *b* if and only if (i) for some *c*, *c* is an *a*, (ii) for all *c* and *d*, if *c* is an *a* and *d* is an *a* then *c* is a *d*, and (iii) for all *c*, if *c* is an *a* then *c* is a *b*

As regards the contents of *Ontology*, suffice it to say that within its framework one can derive correlates of the theorems derivable within the framework of Whitehead and Russell's *Principia*. Just as *Principia* is an improvement on Frege's *Grundgesetze* so Leśniewski's *Ontology* is an improvement on *Principia*. The improvements that distinguish *Ontology*, concern the grammar of its language, definitions, and, generally, the directives, which are the rules specifying the conditions under which a new thesis is allowed to be added to the system. If analogous improvements were to be incorporated into *Principia* then the difference between the two systems of logic could be reduced to the difference between the types of logical language used, respectively, by the authors of *Principia* and by Leśniewski. The meaningful expressions of the language of *Principia* can be made to form a hierarchy founded on the semantical category of propositions and on that of singular referential names whereas the hierarchy of the meaningful expressions in *Ontology* rests on the semantical category of propositions and on that of general names, or common nouns. In consequence of names that do not designate anything at all being accommodated within the framework of the theory, the quantifiers binding name-variables have no existential import in the language of *Ontology*, and, in this respect, differ from the quantifiers in the language of *Principia*. From the presuppositions of the system of logic in *Principia* one can infer that there exists at least one object. No such inference can be made in *Ontology*, which is free from defects in 'logical purity'. Thus the reistic hypothesis that the number of different things in the world is not finite, extends *Ontology* as a system of logic into a system of metaphysics, realist metaphysics to be sure, since the notion of numerical infinity is definable within the framework of *Ontology*.

22 As a system of logic *Ontology* is presupposed by *Mereology*, for which the reist is again indebted to Leśniewski.[8] *Mereology* makes a third chapter of the reistic description of reality. It results from subjoining a mereological axiom to a system of *Ontology*. Several propositions that could be used as single mereological axioms have been discovered in the last 45 years, but they are not as intuitive, and not as informative, as the axiomatic foundations on which Leśniewski based the original system of his theory. In that system the functor 'part of' serves as the only undefined mereological term, and the following propositions, some of which are definitions, play the role of axiomatic foundations:

(44) for all a and b, if a is a part of b then both b is an object and it is not the case that b is a part of a

(45) for all a, b, and c, if a is a part of b and b is a part of c then a is a part of c

(46) for all a and b, a is an ingredient of b if and only if both a is an object and (a is a part of b or a is the same object as b)[9]

(47) for all a and b, a is a complete collection of bs if and only if (i) a is an object, (ii) for all c, if c is a b then c is an ingredient of a, and (iii) for all c, if c is an ingredient of a then for some d and e, d is a b, e is an ingredient of c, and e is an ingredient of d

(48) for all a, b, and c, if a is a complete collection of cs and b is a complete collection of cs then a is the same object as b

(49) for all a and b, if a is a b then for some c, c is a complete collection of bs

No existential consequences are deducible within the framework of *Mereology*, which, in this respect, is as logically pure as *Ontology*. However, *Mereology* becomes a metaphysical theory of the realist kind if its axiomatic foundations are strengthened by the addition of definition (37) and by the reistic denial of the existence of mereological atoms.

23 If an object has parts then, in accordance with reism, it is necessary that it should be extended in time or in space. Thus, in the proposed systematic presentation of the science of being *Mereology* is to be presupposed by a general theory of objects as ordered and extended in time or by a general theory of objects as distributed and extended in space. The former theory, which is

Chronology, is simpler from the formal point of view than the latter, to which I will refer as *Stereology*. This is why in the reistic description of objects *Chronology* takes the place of a fourth chapter.

The notion of the temporal order of events or of objects, has been studied by a number of logicians and philosophers. Suffice it to mention the name of Russell and that of Woodger, and of Tarski.[10] Another important notion that falls within the province of a general theory of time, is the notion which relates the duration of one object to the duration of another object. Neither notion seems to be reducible to the other with the aid of appropriate definitions. Thus the system of *Chronology* whose axiomatic foundations will be proposed below, makes an attempt at accommodating both.[11] It requires two primitive terms: 'object wholly earlier than', which is a name-forming functor for one nominal argument and occurs in propositions of the form 'a is an object wholly earlier than b', and 'object whose duration is shorter than that of', which belongs to the same semantical category as the other primitive term, and which occurs in propositions of the form 'a is an object whose duration is shorter than that of b'. The axioms, and the definitions which precede some of the axioms, are to be subjoined to a system of *Mereology*. They are as follows:

(50) for all a and b, if a is an object wholly earlier than b then both b is an object and it is not the case that b is an object wholly earlier than a

(51) for all a, b, c, and d, if ((i) a is an object wholly earlier than b, (ii) c is an ingredient of a, and (iii) d is an ingredient of b) then c is an object wholly earlier than d

(52) for all a, b, and c, if both a is an object wholly earlier than b and c is an object then (a is an object wholly earlier than c or for some d, both d is an ingredient of c and d is an object wholly earlier than b)

(53) for all a and b, if ((i) a is an object, (ii) b is an object and (iii) for all c and d, if both c is an ingredient of a and d is an ingredient of b then for some e and f, (i) e is an ingredient of c, (ii) f is an ingredient of d and (iii) e is an object wholly earlier than f) then a is an object wholly earlier than b

(54) for all a and b, if a is an object whose duration is shorter than that of b then both b is an object and it is not the case

that b is an object whose duration is shorter than that of a

(55) for all a and b, if a is an object whose duration is shorter than that of b then it is not the case that b is an ingredient of a

(56) for all a, b, and c, if both a is an object whose duration is shorter than that of b and c is an object then (a is an object whose duration is shorter than that of c or c is an object whose duration is shorter than that of b)

(57) for all a and b, if a is an object whose duration is shorter than that of b then for some c, both c is an ingredient of b and it is not the case that a is an object whose duration is shorter than that of c

(58) for all a and b, a is an object separated by a time gap from b if and only if both a is an object and (a is an object wholly earlier than b or b is an object wholly earlier than a)

(59) for all a and b, if a is an object separated by a time gap from b then for some c, both c is an ingredient of a and c is an object whose duration is shorter than that of the complete collection of objects each of which is either c or b

(60) for all a and b, if a is an object whose duration is shorter than that of b then for some c and d, (i) c is an ingredient of b, (ii) d is an ingredient of b, and (iii) for all e and f, if both e is an ingredient of c and f is an ingredient of d then (i) e is an object separated by a time gap from f, (ii) a is an object separated by a time gap from e or a is an object separated by a time gap from f, and (iii) a is an object whose duration is shorter than that of the complete collection of objects each of which is either e or f

(61) for all a, b, c, d, e, and f, if (i) a is an object whose duration is shorter than that of b, (ii) c is an ingredient of d, (iii) e is an ingredient of d, (iv) d is the complete collection of objects each of which is either a or f, and (v) (c is an object wholly earlier than e and a is an object wholly earlier than f) or (e is an object wholly earlier than c and f is an object wholly earlier than a) then c is an object whose duration is shorter than that of d

Propositions (50)-(61) represent the first stage in the process of axiomatising *Chronology*. Among the problems still to be examined is the problem of the mutual independence of the proposed axioms. An attempt at solving this problem may result in discovering that some of the axioms are redundant. Another problem concerns the number of the primitive terms on which a system of *Chronology* could be based: could it be reduced to one? Then one has to look for chronological propositions that are independent of the proposed axioms yet appear to be sound on intuitive grounds. They could be used for the purpose of strengthening the axiomatic foundations of the theory provided this would not diminish the degree of its logical purity.

Chronology becomes a metaphysical theory of the realist kind if its axiomatic basis is expanded by the addition of proposition (31), as the definition of 'momentary object', to be followed by the reistic hypothesis to the effect that there are no momentary objects at all.

24 Now, suppose that there are three objects, *a*, *b*, and *c* such that

(i) *a* is the complete collection of objects each of which is a *b* or *c*, and
(ii) *b* is an object wholly earlier than *c*

Clearly, these two assumptions imply the alternation of the following four alternants:

(iii) *b* is an object whose duration is shorter than that of *a* and *c* is an object whose duration is shorter than that of *a*, or
(iv) it is not the case that *b* is an object whose duration is shorter than that of *a* but *c* is an object whose duration is shorter than that of *a*, or
(v) *b* is an object whose duration is shorter than that of *a* and it is not the case that *c* is an object whose duration is shorter than that of *a*, or
(vi) (it is not the case that *b* is an object whose duration is shorter than that of *a*) and (it is not the case that *c* is an object whose duration is shorter than that of *a*)

Conditions (i), (ii) and (iii) seem to be sufficient for *a* to be an object that lasts but is finite in time.

Conditions (i), (ii) and (iv) seem to be sufficient for *a* to be an object that has no beginning but has an end.

Conditions (i), (ii) and (v) seem to be sufficient for a to be an object that has a beginning but has no end.

Conditions (i), (ii) and (vi) seem to be sufficient for a to be an object that has no beginning and no end.

We know from experience that there are objects satisfying conditions (i), (ii) and (iii), but are there objects satisfying conditions (i), (ii) and (vi)? In accordance with T8 of my version of reism the totality of what there is, is such an object. A hypothesis to this effect extends a system of *Chronology* in the direction of realist metaphysics.

25 The union of his three theories, of *Protothetic*, *Ontology* and *Mereology* was regarded by Leśniewski as sufficiently strong to serve as a basis of the whole structure of mathematics. It is also sufficiently strong, as I have been trying to show above, to provide a basis of a deductive presentation of the science of being either in the form that preserves logical purity or in the form that allows for metaphysical ramifications. Admittedly, subjoining propositions (50)-(61) to a system of *Mereology* in order to lay axiomatic foundations for *Chronology* amounts to no more than a first draft of the introduction to the fourth chapter of the general description of reality. A great deal more work will have to be done before a fair copy of the introduction can be attempted.

26 The fifth chapter of the reist's systematic presentation of the science of being is entitled: *Stereology*. It is intended to contain the theory of objects as distributed and extended in space. The theory has a name but it has not even been born yet. 'Is not "Stereology" just another name for what we have come to know as geometry?' — some may ask — 'and if not then what is the difference between geometry and this new theory envisaged by the reist?' The primitive terms of the Euclidean axiomatisation of geometry — and the same is true of the axiomatisations proposed by David Hilbert, by Oswald Veblen, and by E.V. Huntingdon — are all theoretical terms. Thus, in this respect, geometry is like set-theory. Existential propositions involving terms such as 'point', 'line', 'plane', or 'sphere', for instance, cannot be said to have empirical support. Consequently, they are regarded by the reist as metaphysical propositions of an idealist kind.

27 For the reist idealist metaphysics is not acceptable as a final description of reality. He limits his own occasional idealist pronouncements to the denials of the idealist metaphysician's assertions which imply the existence of abstract entities. The reistic version of the science of being is not yet completed. In fact it will never be completed, but at least it seems to have a sound beginning in the form of the union of *Protothetic, Ontology, Mereology* and *Chronology*. As regards *Stereology*, the reist hopes that one day an acceptable way will be found of reducing the traditional terms of geometry to empirical terms. It is on the basis of the latter that the axiomatic foundations of *Stereology* will eventually be built making possible the process of systematising the science of being to be resumed and continued.

Notes

1. *The Works of Aristotle*, vol. VIII, *Metaphysica* (Oxford, 1966).
2. Ibid., 995^{b}6 *sq.* and 995^{b}18 *sq.*
3. G.E. Moore, *Some Main Problems of Philosophy* (London, 1953), p. 1.
4. W.V.O. Quine, *From a Logical Point of View* (Cambridge, Mass., 1953), p. 1.
5. T. Kotarbinski, 'The Fundamental Ideas of Pansomatism', *Mind*, 64 (1955), pp. 488-500.
6. Concerning *Protothetic*, see S. Leśniewski, 'Grundzüge eines neuen Systems der Grundlagen der Mathematik', *Fundamenta Mathematicae*, 14 (1929), pp. 1-81 and his 'Introductory Remarks to the Continuation of my Article: "Grundzüge eines neuen Systems der Grundlagen der Mathematik"', translated from German by W. Teichmann and S. McCall in *Polish Logic 1920-1939*, ed. Storrs McCall (Oxford, 1967), pp. 116-69.
7. See S. Leśniewski, 'Über die Grundlagen er Ontologie', *Comptes rendus des séances de la Société des Sciences et des Lettres de Varsovie*, Classe III, XXIII Anńe (Warszawa, 1939), pp. 111-32.
8. For an exposition of *Mereology*, see S. Leśniwski, 'O podstawach matematyki' ('On the Foundations of Mathematics'), *Przeglad Filozoficzny*, 30 (1927), pp. 164-206; 31 (1928), pp. 261-91; 32 (1929), pp. 60-101; 33 (1930), pp. 77-105, 142-70. For a concise introduction to *Mereology*, see B. Sobociński 'Studies in Leśniewski's Mereology', *Polish Society of Arts and Sciences Abroad*, Yearbook for 1954-5 (London, 1955) pp. 34-43.
9. Within the framework of *Ontology* the following equivalence defines the notion of singular identity:

for all a and b, a is the same object as b if and only if both a is a b and b is an a

10. B. Russell, 'On Order in Time' in B. Russell, *Logic and Knowledge, Essays 1901-1950*, ed. R.C. Marsh (London, 1956), pp. 347-63; J.H. Woodger, *The Axiomatic Method in Biology* (Cambridge, 1937); J.H. Woodger, *The Technique of Theory Construction* (Chicago and London, 1939); A. Tarski, 'Appendix E' in J.H. Woodger, *The Axiomatic Method in Biology*, (Cambridge, 1937), pp. 161-72.
11. See C. Lejewski, 'Ontology: What Next?' in *Sprache und Ontologie/ Language and Ontology*, Proceedings of the 6th International Wittgenstein Symposium (Wien, 1982), pp. 173-85.

9 HOW I SEE PHILOSOPHY*

Karl R. Popper

I

A famous and spirited paper by my late friend Friedrich Waismann bears the title *How I See Philosophy*.[1] There is much in this paper that I admire; and there are a number of points in it with which I can agree, even though my approach is totally different from his.

Fritz Waismann and many of his colleagues take it for granted that philosophers are a special kind of people, and that philosophy can be looked upon as their peculiar activity. And what he tries to do in his paper is to show, with the help of examples, what constitutes the distinctive character of a philosopher, and the distinctive character of philosophy, if compared with other academic subjects such as mathematics or physics. Thus he tries, especially, to give a description of the interests and activities of contemporary academic philosophers, and of the sense in which they can be said to carry on what philosophers did in the past.

Not only is all this very interesting, but Waismann's paper exhibits a considerable degree of personal engagement in these academic activities, and even of excitement. Clearly, he himself is a philosopher, body and soul, in the sense of this special group of philosophers, and clearly, he wishes to convey to us something of the excitement which is shared by the members of this somewhat exclusive community.

II

The way I see philosophy is totally different. I think that all men and all women are philosophers, though some are more so than others. I agree of course that there is such a thing as a distinctive and exclusive group of people, the academic philosophers, but I am far from sharing Waismann's enthusiasm for their activities and for their approach. On the contrary, I feel that there is much to be said for those (they are, in my view, philosophers of a kind) who mistrust academic philosophy. At any rate, I am strongly opposed to an idea (a philosophical idea) whose influence, unexamined and never mentioned, pervades Waismann's brilliant essay: I mean the idea of an intellectual and philosophical élite.[2]

I admit, of course, that there have been a few truly great philosophers, and also a small number of philosophers who, though admirable in many ways, just missed being great. But although what they have produced ought to be of major importance for any academic philosopher, philosophy does not depend on them in the sense in which painting depends upon the great painters or music upon the great composers. Besides, great philosophy — for example, that of the pre-Socratics — antedates all academic and professional philosophy.

III

In my own view, professional philosophy has not done too well. It is in urgent need of an *apologia pro vita sua* — of a defence of its existence.

I even feel that the fact that I am a professional philosopher myself establishes a serious case against me: I feel it as an accusation. I must plead guilty, and offer, like Socrates, my apology.

I refer to Plato's *Apology* because of all works on philosophy ever written I like it best. I conjecture that it is historically true — that it tells us, by and large, what Socrates said before the Athenian Court. I like it because here speaks a man, modest and fearless. And his apology is very simple: he insists that he is aware of his limitations, not wise, except possibly in his awareness of the fact that he is not wise; and that he is a critic, especially of all high-sounding jargon, yet a friend of his fellow men, and a good citizen.

This is not only the apology of Socrates, but in my view it is an impressive apology for philosophy.

IV

But let us look at the case for the prosecution against philosophy. Many philosophers, and among them some of the greatest, have not done too well. I will refer to four of the greatest — Plato,

Hume, Spinoza, and Kant.

Plato, the greatest, profoundest, and most gifted of all philosophers, had an outlook on human life which I find repulsive and indeed horrifying. Yet he was not only a great philosopher and the founder of the greatest professional school of philosophy, but a great and inspired poet; and he wrote, among other beautiful works, *The Apology of Socrates.*

What ailed him, and so many professional philosophers after him, was that, in stark contrast to Socrates, he believed in the élite: in the Kingdom of Philosophy. While Socrates demanded that the statesman should be wise, that is, aware of how little he knows, Plato demanded that the wise, the learned philosophers should be absolute rulers. (Ever since Plato, megalomania has been the philosophers' most widespread occupational disease.) Moreover, in the tenth book of *The Laws* Plato invented an institution that inspired the Inquisition, and he came close to recommending concentration camps for the cure of the souls of dissenters.

David Hume, who was not a professional philosopher, and who was, next to Socrates, perhaps the most candid and well-balanced of all the great philosophers and a thoroughly modest, rational, and reasonably dispassionate man, was led, by an unfortunate and mistaken psychological theory (and by a theory of knowledge which taught him to distrust his own very remarkable powers of reason) to the horrifying doctrine, 'Reason is, and ought only to be, the slave of the passions, and can never pretend to any other office than to serve and obey them.'[3] I am ready to admit that nothing great has ever been achieved without passion, but I believe in the very opposite of Hume's statement. The taming of our passions by that limited reasonableness of which we may be capable is, in my view, the only hope for mankind.

Spinoza, the saint among the great philosophers and like Socrates and like Hume not a philosopher by profession, taught almost exactly the opposite to Hume, but in a way which I, for one, hold to be not only mistaken but also ethically unacceptable. He was a determinist (as was Hume), and human freedom consisted for him solely in having a clear, distinct, and adequate understanding of the true compelling causes of our actions: 'An affect, which is a passion, ceases to be a passion as soon as we form a clear and distinct idea of it.'[4] As long as it is a passion, we are in its clutches and unfree; once we have a clear and distinct idea of it, we are still determined by it, but we have transformed it into part of our reason. And this alone is freedom, Spinoza teaches.

I regard this teaching as an untenable and dangerous form of rationalism, even though I am a rationalist of sorts myself. First of all, I do not believe in determinism, and I do not think that Spinoza or anybody else has produced strong arguments in its support, or in support of a reconciliation of determinism with human freedom (and thus with common sense). It seems to me that Spinoza's determinism is a typical philosopher's mistake, even though it is of course true that much of what we are doing (*but not all*) is determined and even predictable. Secondly, though it may be true in some sense that an excess of what Spinoza means by 'passion' makes us unfree, his formula which I have quoted would make us not responsible for our actions whenever we cannot form a clear, distinct, and adequate rational idea of the motives of our actions. But, I assert, we never can do that; and although to be reasonable in our actions and in our dealings with our fellow creatures is, I think, a most important aim (and Spinoza certainly thought so too), I do not think it an aim which we can ever say that we have reached.

Kant, one of the few admirable and highly original thinkers among professional philosophers, tried to solve Hume's problem of the rejection of reason, and Spinoza's problem of determinism; yet he failed in both attempts.

These are some of the greatest philosophers, philosophers whom I admire much. You will understand why I feel apologetic about philosophy.

V

I never was a member of the Vienna Circle of logical positivists, like my friends Fritz Waismann, Herbert Feigl, and Victor Kraft; in fact, Otto Neurath called me 'the official opposition'. I was never invited to any of the meetings of the Circle, perhaps owing to my well-known opposition to positivism. (I would have been delighted to accept an invitation, for not only were some of the members of the Circle personal friends of mine, but I also had the greatest admiration for some of the other members.) Under the influence of Ludwig Wittgenstein's *Tractatus Logico-Philosophicus*, the Circle had become not only anti-metaphysical, but anti-philosophical. Schlick, the leader of the Circle,[5] formulated this by way of the prophecy that philosophy, 'which never talks sense but utters only meaningless words', will soon disappear, because philosophers will find that 'their audience', tired of empty tirades, have gone away.

Waismann agreed with Wittgenstein and Schlick for many years. I think I can detect in his enthusiasm for philosophy the enthusiasm of the convert.

I always defended philosophy and even metaphysics against the Circle, even though I had to admit that philosophers had not been doing too well. For I believed that many people, and I among them, had genuine philosophical problems of various degrees of seriousness and difficulty, and that these problems were not all insoluble.

Indeed the existence of urgent and serious philosophical problems and the need to discuss them critically is, in my view, the only apology for what may be called professional or academic philosophy.

Wittgenstein and the Vienna Circle denied the existence of serious philosophical problems.

According to the end of the *Tractatus*, the apparent problems of philosophy (including those of the *Tractatus* itself) are pseudo-problems which arise from speaking without having given meaning to all one's words. This theory may be regarded as inspired by Russell's solution of the logical paradoxes as pseudo-propositions which are neither true nor false but meaningless. This led to the modern philosophical technique of branding all sorts of inconvenient propositions or problems as 'meaningless'. The later Wittgenstein used to speak of 'puzzles', caused by the philosophical misuse of language. I can only say that if I had no serious philosophical problems and no hope of solving them, I should have no excuse for being a philosopher: to my mind, there would be no apology for philosophy.

VI

In this section I will list certain views of philosophy and certain activities that are often taken to be characteristic of philosophy which I, for one, find unsatisfactory. The section could be entitled 'How I Do Not See Philosophy'.

1. I do not see philosophy as the solving of linguistic puzzles;

although the elimination of misunderstandings is sometimes a necessary preliminary task.

2. I do not see philosophy as a series of works of art, as striking and original pictures of the world, or as clever and unusual ways of describing the world. I think that if we look upon philosophy in this way, we do a real injustice to the great philosophers. The great philosophers were not engaged in an aesthetic endeavour. They did not try to be architects of clever systems; but like the great scientists they were, first of all, seekers after truth — after true solutions of genuine problems. No, I see the history of philosophy essentially as part of the history of the search for truth, and I reject the *purely* aesthetic view of it, even though beauty is important in philosophy as well as in science.

I am all for intellectual boldness. We cannot be intellectual cowards and seekers for truth at the same time. A seeker for truth must dare to be wise — he must dare to be a revolutionary in the field of thought.

3. I do not see the long history of philosophical systems as one of intellectual edifices in which all possible ideas are tried out, and in which truth may perhaps come to light as a by-product. I believe that we are doing an injustice to the truly great philosophers of the past if we doubt for a moment that every one of them would have discarded his system (as he should have done) had he become convinced that, although perhaps brilliant, it was not a step on the way to truth. (This, incidentally, is the reason why I do not regard Fichte or Hegel as real philosophers: I mistrust their devotion to truth.)

4. I do not see philosophy as an attempt either to clarify or to analyse or to 'explicate' concepts, or words, or languages.

Concepts or words are mere tools for formulating propositions, conjectures, and theories. Concepts or words cannot be true in themselves; they merely serve human descriptive and argumentative language. Our aim should not be to analyse *meanings*, but to seek for interesting and important *truths*; that is, for true *theories*.

5. I do not see philosophy as a way of being clever.

6. I do not see philosophy as a kind of intellectual therapy (Wittgenstein), an activity of helping people out of philosophical perplexities. To my mind, Wittgenstein (in his later work) did not show the fly the way out of the bottle. Rather, I see in the fly, unable to escape from the bottle, a striking self-portrait of

Wittgenstein. (Wittgenstein was a Wittgensteinian case — just as Freud was a Freudian case.)

7. I do not see philosophy as a study of how to express things more precisely or exactly. Precision and exactness are not intellectual values in themselves, and we should never try to be more precise or exact than is demanded by the problem in hand.

8. Accordingly, I do not see philosophy as an attempt to provide the foundations or the conceptual framework for solving problems which may turn up in the nearer or the more distant future. John Locke did so; he wanted to write an essay on ethics, and considered it necessary first to provide the conceptual preliminaries.

His *Essay* consists of these preliminaries, and British philosophy has ever since (with very few exceptions such as some of the political essays of Hume) remained bogged down in these preliminaries.

9. Nor do I see philosophy as an expression of the spirit of the time. This is a Hegelian idea which does not stand up to criticism. Fashions there are in philosophy, as there are in science. But a genuine searcher for truth will not follow fashion; he will distrust fashions and even fight them.

VII

All men and all women are philosophers. If they are not conscious of having philosophical problems, they have, at any rate, philosophical prejudices. Most of these are theories which they take for granted: they have absorbed them from their intellectual environment or from tradition.

Since few of these theories are consciously held, they are prejudices in the sense that they are held without critical examination, even though they may be of great importance for the practical actions of people, and for their whole life.

It is an apology for the existence of professional philosophy that men are needed to *examine critically* these widespread and influential theories.

Theories like these are the insecure starting point of all science and of all philosophy. All philosophy must start from the dubious and often pernicious views of uncritical common sense. Its aim is to reach enlightened, critical, common sense: to reach a view nearer to the truth, and with a less pernicious influence on human life.

VIII

Let me present some examples of widespread philosophical prejudices.

There is a very influential philosophical view of life to the effect that whenever something happens in this world that is really bad (or that we greatly dislike), then there must be somebody responsible for it: there must be somebody who has done it, intentionally. This view is very old. In Homer the envy and the anger of the gods were responsible for most of the terrible things that happened in the field before Troy, and to Troy itself; and it was Poseidon who was responsible for the misadvantures of Odysseus. In later Christian thought it is the Devil who is responsible for evil; in vulgar Marxism it is the conspiracy of the greedy capitalists that prevents the coming of socialism and the establishment of heaven on earth.

The theory which sees war, poverty, and unemployment as the result of some evil intention, of some sinister design, is part of common sense, but it is uncritical. I have called this uncritical common-sense theory the conspiracy theory of society. (One might even call it the conspiracy theory of the world: think of Zeus's bolt of lightening.) It is widely held and, in the form of a search for scapegoats, it has inspired much political strife and has created the most frightful suffering.

One aspect of the conspiracy theory of society is that it encourages real conspiracies. But a critical investigation shows that conspiracies hardly ever attain their aims. Lenin, who held the conspiracy theory, was a conspirator, and so were Mussolini and Hitler. But Lenin's aims were not realised in Russia; nor were Mussolini's or Hitler's aims realised in Italy or in Germany.

All these conspirators become conspirators because they uncritically believed in a conspiracy theory of society.

It may perhaps be a modest but not quite insignificant contribution to philosophy to draw attention to the mistakes of the conspiracy theory of society. Moreover this contribution leads to further contributions such as to the discovery of the significance for society of the *unintended consequences* of human actions, and to the suggestion that we regard it as the aim of the theoretical social sciences to discover those social relations which produce the unintended consequences of our actions.

Take the problem of war. Even a critical philosopher of the status of Bertrand Russell believed that we have to explain wars by psychological motives — by human aggressiveness. I do not deny the existence of aggressiveness, but I am surprised that Russell did not see that most wars in modern times have been inspired by fear of aggression rather than by personal aggressiveness. They have been either ideological wars inspired by the fear of the power of some conspiracy, or wars which nobody wanted but which came about as the result of fear inspired by some objective situation. One example is the mutual fear of aggression which leads to an armaments race and thence to war; perhaps to a preventive war such as even Russell, who was an enemy of war and of aggression, recommended for a time, fearing (rightly) that Russia would soon have the hydrogen bomb. (Nobody wanted the bomb; it was the fear that Hitler would monopolise it which led to its construction.)

Or take a different example of a philosophical prejudice. There is the prejudice that a man's opinions are always determined by his self-interest. This doctrine (which may be described as a degenerate form of Hume's doctrine that reason is, and ought to be, the slave of the passions) is not as a rule applied to oneself (this was done by Hume, who taught modesty and scepticism with respect to our powers of reason, his own included); but it is as a rule only applied to the other fellow — whose opinion differs from our own. It prevents us from listening patiently to opinions which are opposed to our own, and from taking them seriously, because we can explain them by the other fellow's 'interests'. But this makes rational discussion impossible. It leads to a deterioration of our natural curiosity, of our interest in finding out the truth about things. In the place of the important question 'What is the truth about this matter?' it puts another question, less important by far: 'What is your self-interest, what are your hidden motives?' It prevents us from learning from people whose opinions differ from our own, and it leads to a dissolution of the unity of mankind, a unity that is based on our common rationality.

A similar philosophical prejudice is the thesis, at present immensely influential, that rational discussion is possible only between people who agree on fundamentals. This pernicious doctrine implies that rational or critical discussion about fundamentals is impossible, and it leads to consequences as undesirable as those of the doctrines discussed before.[6]

These doctrines are held by many people, but they belong to a field of philosophy which has been one of the main concerns of many professional philosophers: *the theory of knowledge.*

IX

As I see it, the problems of the theory of knowledge form the very heart of philosophy, both of uncritical or popular common-sense philosophy and of academic philosophy. They are even decisive for the theory of ethics (as Jacques Monod has recently reminded us).[7]

Put in a simple way, the main problem here as in other regions of philosophy is the conflict between 'epistemological optimism' and 'epistemological pessimism'. Can we have knowledge? How much can we know? While the epistemological optimist believes in the possibility of human knowledge, the pessimist believes that genuine knowledge is beyond the power of man.

I am an admirer of common sense, though not of all of it; I hold that common sense is our only possible starting point. But we should not attempt to erect an edifice of secure knowledge upon it, but rather criticise it and improve upon it. Thus I am a common-sense realist; I believe in the reality of matter (which I think is the very paradigm of what the word 'real' is meant to denote); and for this reason I should call myself a 'materialist', were it not for the fact that this term also denotes a creed that (a) takes matter as essentially irreducible, and (b) denies the reality of immaterial fields of forces and, of course, also of mind, or consciousness; and of anything else but matter.

I follow common sense in holding that there exists both matter ('world 1') and mind ('world 2'), and I suggest that there exist also other things, especially the products of the human mind, which include our scientific conjectures, theories, and problems ('world 3'). In other words, I am a common-sense pluralist. I am very ready to have this position criticised and replaced by a sounder one, *but all the critical arguments against it which are known to me are, in my opinion, invalid.*[8] (Incidentally, I regard the pluralism here described as needed for ethics.)

All the arguments that have been advanced against a pluralistic realism are based, in the last instance, upon an *uncritical acceptance of the common-sense theory of knowledge* which I regard as the weakest part of common sense.

The common-sense theory of knowledge is highly optimistic in so far as it equates *knowledge* with *certain knowledge*; everything conjectural is, so it holds, not really 'knowledge'. I dismiss this argument as merely verbal. I readily admit that the term 'knowledge' carries in all languages known to me the connotation of certainty. But science consists of hypotheses. And the common-sense programme of starting from what appears to be the most certain or basic knowledge available (observational knowledge), in order to erect on these foundations an edifice of secure knowledge, does not stand up to criticism.

It leads, incidentally, to two non-commonsensical views of reality, which stand in direct contradiction to each other.

1. Immaterialism (Berkeley, Hume, Mach)
2. Behaviourist materialism (Watson, Skinner)

The first of these denies the reality of matter, because the only certain and secure basis of our knowledge consists of our own *perceptual experiences*; and these remain, forever, immaterial.

The second denies the existence of mind (and, incidentally, of human freedom), because all we can really *observe* is human behaviour which is in every way like animal behaviour (except that it incorporates a wide and important field, 'linguistic behaviour').

Both these theories are based upon the invalid common-sense theory of knowledge which leads to the traditional but invalid criticism of the common-sense theory of reality. Both these theories are not ethically neutral, but pernicious: if I wish to comfort a weeping child, I do not wish to stop some irritating perceptions (of mine or of yours); nor do I wish to change the child's behaviour; or to stop drops of water from running down its cheeks. No, my motives are different — undemonstrable, underivable, but *human.*

Immaterialism (which owes its origin to the insistence of Descartes — who was of course no immaterialist — that we must start from an indubitable basis such as the knowledge of our own existence) reached its culmination at the turn of the century with Ernst Mach, but has now lost most of its influence. It is no longer fashionable.

Behaviourism — the denial of the existence of mind — is very fashionable at present. Although it extols observation, it not only flies in the face of all human experience, but it also tries to derive from its theories an ethically horrible theory — the theory of conditioning;[9] although no ethical theory is, in fact, derivable from human nature. (Jacques Monod has rightly emphasised this point;[10] see also my *Open Society and Its Enemies*.[11]) It is to be hoped that this fashion, based upon an uncritical acceptance of the common-sense theory of knowledge whose untenability I have tried to show,[12] will one day lose its influence.

X

As I see philosophy, it never ought to be, and indeed it never can be, divorced from the sciences. Historically, all Western science is an offspring of Greek philosophical speculation about the cosmos, the world order. The common ancestors of all scientists and all philosophers are Homer, Hesiod, and the Presocratics. Central for them is the enquiry into the structure of the universe, and our place in this universe, including the problem of our knowledge of the universe (a problem which, as I see it, remains decisive for all philosophy). And it is the critical enquiry into the sciences, their findings, and their methods which remains a characteristic of philosophical enquiry, even after the sciences have broken away from it. Newton's *Mathematical Principles of Natural Philosophy* marks, in my opinion, the greatest event, the greatest intellectual revolution, in the whole history of mankind. It marks the fulfilment of a dream that was over 2,000 years old; it marks the maturation of science, and its break away from philosophy. But Newton himself, like all great scientists, remained a philosopher; and he remained a critical thinker, a searcher, and sceptical of his own theories. Thus he wrote in his letter to Bentley (25 February 1693) of his own theory which involves action at a distance (italics mine):

> That gravity should be innate, inherent, and essential to matter, *so that one body may act upon another at a distance* . . . is to me so great an absurdity that I believe no man who has in philosophical matters a competent faculty of thinking can ever fall into it.

It was his own theory of action at a distance which led him to both scepticism and mysticism. He reasoned that if all the vastly distant regions of space can interact instantaneously with each other, then this must be due to the omnipresence at the same time of one and the same being in all regions — to the omnipresence of God. It was thus the attempt to solve this problem of action at a distance which led Newton to his mystical theory according to which space is the sensorium of God; a theory in which he transcended science and which combined critical and speculative philosophy and speculative religion. We know that Einstein was similarly motivated.

XI

I admit that there are some very subtle yet most important problems in philosophy which have their natural and indeed their only place in academic philosophy; for example, the problems of mathematical logic and, more generally, the philosophy of mathematics. I am greatly impressed by the astounding progress made in these fields in our century.

But as far as academic philosophy in general is concerned, I am worried by the influence of what Berkeley used to call the 'minute philosophers'. Criticism is the lifeblood of philosophy, to be sure. Yet we should avoid hairsplitting. A minute criticism of minute points without an understanding of the great problems of cosmology, of human knowledge, of ethics, and of political philosophy, and without a serious and devoted attempt to solve them, appears to me fatal. It almost looks as if every printed passage which might with some effort be misunderstood or misinterpreted is good enough to justify the writing of another critical philosophical paper. Scholasticism, in the worst sense of the term, abounds; all the great ideas are buried in a flood of words. At the same time, a certain arrogance and rudeness — once a rarity in philosophical literature — seems to be accepted, by the editors of many of the journals, as a proof of boldness of thought and originality.

I believe it is the duty of every intellectual to be aware of the privileged position he is in. He has a duty to write as simply and clearly as he can, and in as civilised a manner as he can; and never to forget either the great problems which beset mankind and which demand new and bold but patient thought, or the Socratic modesty of the man who knows how little he knows. As against the minute philosophers with their minute problems, I think that the main task of philosophy is to speculate critically about the universe and about our place in the universe, including our powers of knowing and our powers for good and evil.

XIX

I might perhaps end with a bit of decidedly non-academic philosophy.

One of the astronauts involved in the first visit to the moon is credited with a simple and wise remark which he made on his return (I am quoting from memory): 'I have seen some planets in my day, but give me the earth every time.' I think this is not only wisdom, but philosophical wisdom. We do not know how it is that we are alive on this wonderful little planet — or why there should be something like life, to make our planet so beautiful. But here we are, and we have every reason to wonder at it, and to feel grateful for it. It comes close to being a miracle. For all that science can tell us, the universe is almost empty of matter; and where there is matter, the matter is almost everywhere in a chaotic, turbulent state, and uninhabitable. There may be many other planets with life on them. Yet if we pick out at random a place in the universe, then the probability (calculated on the basis of our dubious current cosmology) of finding a life-carrying body at that place will be zero, or almost zero. So life has at any rate the value of something rare; it is precious. We are inclined to forget this, and treat life cheaply, perhaps out of thoughtlessness; or perhaps because this beautiful earth of ours is, no doubt, a bit overcrowded.

All men are philosophers, because in one way or other all take up an attitude towards life and death. There are those who think that life is valueless because it comes to an end. They fail to see that the opposite argument might also be proposed: that if there were no end to life, life would have no value; that it is, in part, the ever-present danger of losing it which helps to bring home to us the value of life.

Notes

*Revised version of a paper first published in *The Owl of Minerva*, ed. by C.J. Bontempo and S.J. Odell (McGraw Hill, New York, 1975), pp. 41-55.

1. F. Waismann in H.D. Lewis (ed.), *Contemporary British Philosophy*, Third Series, 2nds edn. (George Allen & Unwin Ltd, London, 1961), pp. 447-90.

2. This idea comes to the fore in such remarks of Waismann's as 'Indeed, a philosopher is a man who senses as it were hidden crevices in the build of our concepts where others only see the smooth path of commonplaceness before them.' Ibid., p. 448. (See, by contrast my remarks on concepts in *Conjectures and Refutations: The Growth of Scientific Knowledge* (Routledge & Kegan Paul, London, 1963), 4th edn. revised 1972; 8th impression 1984).

3. David Hume, *A Treatise of Human Nature* (1739-1740; ed. Selby-Bigge, Clarendon Press, Oxford, 1888 (and many later reprints), book II, part III, sec. III, p. 415).

4. Benedictus de Spinoza, *Ethics*, book V, proposition III.

5. The Vienna Circle was, in fact, Schlick's private seminar, and members were personally invited by Schlick. (The quoted words are from the concluding paragraphs pp. 10f., of Moritz Schlick, 'Die Wende der Philosophie', *Erkenntnis*, 1, pp. 4-11.)

6. See also my paper 'The Myth of the Framework' in the Schilpp Festschrift, *The Abdication of Philosophy*, E. Freemann (ed.) (Open Court, La Salle, Illinois, 1976).

7. Jacques Monod, *Chance and Necessity* (Alfred Knopf Inc., New York, 1971).

8. See, for example, K.R. Popper, *Objective Knowledge: An Evolutionary Approach* (Clarendon Press, Oxford, 1972; 7th impression, 1985, especially Ch. 2).

9. The conditioner's dream of omnipotence may be found in J.B. Watson's *Behaviourism* and also in the work of B.F. Skinner, for example, *Walden Two* (Macmillan, New York, 1948) or *Beyond Freedom and Dignity* (Alfred Knopf, New York, 1971). I may quote from Watson: 'Give me a dozen healthy infants ... and I'll guarantee to take any one at random and train him to become any type of specialist I might select — doctor, lawyer, artist ... [or] thief' (J.B. Watson, *Behaviourism*, 2nd edn, Routledge, London, 1931, p. 104). Thus everything will depend on the morals of the omnipotent conditioner. (Yet according to the conditioners, these morals are nothing but the product of conditioning.)

10. See note 7.

11. K.R. Popper, *The Open Society and Its Enemies*, 2 vols. (Routledge & Kegan Paul, London, 1945; 5th edn, 1969; 14th impression 1984; Princeton University Press, Princeton, NJ, 1950; and Princeton paperback, 1971).

12. See *Objective Knowledge: An Evolutionary Approach*, Ch. 2.

10 COMPUTER VISION OR MECHANIST MYOPIA?[1]

S.G. Shanker

1. The Recognition of Patterns

There is a story told of how, shortly after having become newly acquainted with the joys of Wordsworth's poetry, John Stuart Mill suffered a serious depression when taken to hear a symphony by Mozart. For it occurred to him in the midst of the rapture which he experienced that, since there are only a finite number of notes, the possibilities of compositional innovation must ultimately — and perhaps in the not too distant future — be exhausted; and in a world without new music man must soon become bored with the familiar. Whether or not the story is apocryphal hardly matters, for the worry behind it is genuine enough. The question of how we are able to generate the infinite from the finite has long troubled philosophers. Even more to the point, however, is the anxiety over how the profession will survive when its store of problems has been exhausted.

Does every passing success which we enjoy take our philosophical heirs one step nearer to unemployment; or worse fate still, to becoming historians of our ideas? The confusions buried here are profound, despite the occasional light relief which they may afford. For they affect our very conception of the nature of philosophy and its role *vis-à-vis* the sciences. If Russell's conception of philosophy is accurate, then we cannot hope to escape Mill's dilemma. On the contrary, we should welcome it, for if the success of a philosophical theory is marked by its transformation into a new science, then our duty must be to do everything in our power to hasten the demise of our discipline at the hands of scientific progress.

Seizing on this point, Wittgenstein responded that we are continually preoccupied with archetypal philosophical problems simply because 'language has remained the same and always introduces us to the same questions' (CV 15). But the fact that philosophy, like history, may be condemned to repeat itself, will hardly result in the 'trivialisation' which Russell so strongly feared would be the result of Wittgenstein's later conception of philosophy. Obviously the significance of a philosophical investigation can only be measured by the importance of the issues which it clarifies. But if we frequently find ourselves dealing with new and possibly more subtle versions of classical themes, this actually augments — it in no way detracts from — their interest; as any admirer of Rachmaninov's 'Rhapsody on a Theme by Paganini', or Milton's *Lycidas* will attest.

Such a bare assertion will not, of course, convince on its own, but how can we augment it? Yet another statement on 'the nature of philosophy', no matter how eloquent, is unlikely to carry any more weight than Wittgenstein's own sparkling remarks on the subject. Nor is it an exercise which Wittgenstein would have approved of if, like so much else in modern philosophy, it is taken to excess. There can be few today in the philosophical community who are not familiar with the rudiments of Wittgenstein's conception of philosophy;[2] or with the plaintive Wittgensteinian refrain that the scientific conception of philosophy remains predominant despite the power of Wittgenstein's insights. Rather than preaching endlessly to the unconverted, the Wittgensteinian must now adopt a different attitude. The merits of Wittgenstein's conception of philosophy will only be established through application, not description; for the proof of the approach will lie in its results, not in its premises. And rarely has philosophy enjoyed a richer surfeit of problems to investigate. It is surely time that we devote our efforts to these, and leave the 'state of philosophy' to speak for itself.

The philosopher need be in no more fear than the mathematician that the enormous growth of his profession threatens his supply of problems. It is worth pondering on the significance of this point, for unlikely as it might seem, Mill's concern over the future state of music has found its counterpart in the alarm which some mathematicians have expressed over the dwindling number of unsolved problems from Hilbert's 'honours class'. To be sure, philosophy should be wary of emulating mathematics too closely here, for the latter is able to insure its own never-ending fund of problems, whereas 'professional' philosophical problems — that is, those that are of sole conceivable interest to philosophers themselves — have a distinctly hollow ring to them; they seem detached from reality (namely, relevance), and thus, idle conundrums for fettered intellects. Like any strictly internal quarrel, they soon become both tedious and dissipating. Admittedly, all genuine philosophical issues threaten to end up in this graveyard of abstract elephants if they suffer from overly-prolonged analysis. But philosophy is saved from this fate by the larger duty which it has to society — to the understanding of new trends and technologies — which is incompatible with the twin evils of intellectual narcissism and occupational incest. Thus, it is to other disciplines that we must look if we are to avoid the slow decay incurred by excessive introversion. And as Wittgenstein pointed out in the 'Bouwsma Notes', it is science above all else which stands ready at hand to replenish the coffers of twentieth-century philosophy.

There is a plentiful supply of new domains awaiting our investigations here, if only our spirits are willing and our skills have been honed. But to accomplish the latter, and perhaps the former as well, philosophy demands very much the same sort of discipline as the study of composition. One need not completely master the problems of the past in order to confront the enigmas of the future, any more than Beethoven needed to master the finer details of counterpoint in order to compose the *Joseph* Cantata. But one must be familiar with these problems, and the frameworks in which they resided, for it is only with this background in place that we will be able to recognise and appreciate the significance of the continuity in the new versions of inherited confusions. There is one area in particular in contemporary thought where such stasis in the midst of change has rendered the science in question a forerunner in the need for philosophical clarification: the burgeoning field of Artificial Intelligence (AI). Given the mechanist ambitions which have flourished in western philosophy from ancient times onwards,[3] it was no doubt inevitable that computer science should have become the receptacle for the store of confusions about the nature of thought and understanding or the relation between mind and body that have accumulated. Thus it is hardly surprising that we should constantly find ourselves confronted in the key areas of AI-research with distinctly familiar philosophical problems, albeit in strikingly new surroundings. No better example of such recurrent leitmotifs can be found than in the current upsurge of interest in 'Pattern Recognition'. Perception has long been at the head of the list of perennial issues in the philosophy of mind; with the obvious importance of the computer revolution, the problem has taken on a new dynamic, and some humanists would say, a sudden urgency.

Pattern Recognition has quickly established itself as one of the foremost issues in AI, despite the relatively meagre success-rate which it has hitherto enjoyed as far as the Mechanist Thesis is concerned. Recently, Alan Kay (who invented the term 'personal computer') has complained that AI has taken 'a wrong turning, and lost sight of its goals'.[4] According to Kay, the problem lies in the increasing demands for immediate, practical results from AI research, as typified in the popular cry today for serviceable Expert Systems. But as Kay sees it, Expert Systems are 'the "designer jeans of computer science". The English language makes them sound like they can do a lot more than they actually can.'[5] If not for the more 'modest' demands which Kay places on 'artificial intelligence', one could almost credit him here with a sound Wittgensteinian insight. For what Kay 'would like to see AI people trying to build is "not superhumans or humans, but mammals", contrivances that can "explore and learn but do not have to use language or learn differential calculus"'. Ultimately, he asserts, '"the basic end of AI research is an appreciation of our own make-up"'.[6] I have tried to deal with the former point about Expert Systems elsewhere;[7] in the present chapter it is this last theme which I would like to take up. For herein lies the key to the explanation of why Pattern Recognition should have attracted so much attention, despite the putatively disappointing results which have so far been obtained.

This last issue takes us somewhat outside the bounds of philosophy proper, into the sociology of AI and the history of mechanist ideas. But these are areas worth our consideration, for on the surface it is difficult to see why 'computer vision' should have become so important to the advocates of the Mechanist Thesis. After all, as far as the latter is concerned, the five senses would seem to be a rather peripheral issue *vis-à-vis* the main problem of 'artificial intelligence'; our ability to build a 'thinking machine' could hardly be dependent on the subsidiary matter of whether such a creature will turn out to be blind and/or mute. Of course, there are, as Kay suggests, strong commercial interests at stake. Much of the impetus behind the phenomenal explosion of AI stems from the considerable backing which scientists have received from private and public sources who often share little of the pure intellectual curiosity which drives the scientist. For them a *seeing* machine is of even more importance than a *thinking* one, given the minimal cognitive abilities required to position a rivet correctly. Yet commercial factors alone do not account for the AI-scientist's growing interest in Pattern Recognition.

Vision seems to hold a special place among the five senses in the creation of life. Our language is suffused with visual metaphors for inspiration and understanding. To the Romantics, vision played a particularly significant role in the mind's confrontation with 'external' reality. In the moving autobiographical account which it sends to its pseudo-Promethean creator, Dr Frankenstein's creature begins:

> It is with considerable difficulty that I remember the original era of my being: all the events of that period appear confused and indistinct. A strange multiplicity of sensations seized me, and I saw, felt, heard, and smelt at the same time; and it was, indeed, a long time before I learned to distinguish between the operations of my various senses. By degrees, I remember, a stronger light pressed upon my nerves, so that I was obliged to shut my eyes. Darkness then came over me and troubled me, but hardly had I felt this when, by opening my eyes, as I now suppose, the light poured in upon me again. I walked and, I believe, descended, but I presently found a great alteration in my sensations. Before, dark and opaque bodies had surrounded me, impervious to my touch or sight; but I now found that I could wander on at liberty, with no obstacles which I could not either surmount or avoid.[8]

We shall consider some of the implications of this picture of perception in the following section; for the moment, it suffices to note the use which has been made of perception in terms of the creation of an artificial form of intelligence. A machine that can *see* is rather like a baby opening and, more importantly, focusing its eyes for the first time. For the image of sight is deeply pregnant of the birth of intelligence: the confrontation between the mind and the world. But even here we have not delved deeply enough to account for the spreading influence of Pattern Recognition research.

The greatest challenge facing a new science is simply: to be recognised as such. The fate of a fledgeling science rests above all else on its ability to project itself as a serious contender for scientific status: to gain credibility and stimulate interest from its scientific peers. But scientists are not immune to the petty jealousies and rivalries which afflict the rest of mankind. Thus, the putative new science must offer some tangible reward for the professional recognition which it so badly needs. And it is precisely here where we can begin to see why Pattern Recognition has already acquired so much importance for the evolution of AI. Pattern Recognition stands at the crossroads of established and *nouveau* science: it both ends off and reinforces a powerful tradition in contemporary psychological thought. From this privileged position it is able to contribute to the consolidation of the Mechanist Thesis and at the same time confirm what is perhaps the predominant theory in cognitive studies in perception. By thus contributing to the entrenchment of each, it is able to join the two parties under that strongest of all bonds: common interest.

In his postscript to the latest edition of *Eye and Brain* Richard Gregory reports that during the past decade 'Several biologists working on perception of animals and men (including the author) changed their affiliations, to design Robots. This became a new science: Artificial Intelligence (AI) or, as it is sometimes called, Machine Intelligence.'[9] AI has benefited enormously from the endorsement of these leading scientists. Yet the relationship is by no means one-sided. Indeed, Gregory is perhaps the perfect example of this two-way traffic. Gregory is famous for his thesis that there are only two feasible contenders for an explanation of perception: the 'passive (Kantian) theory' which regards the perception of reality as direct and immediate, and the 'inferential theory' that perception 'is probably the most sophisticated of all the brain's activities: calling upon its stores of memory data; requiring subtle classifications, comparisons and logical decisions for sensory data to become perception'.[10] Gregory, of course, is one of the most influential spokesmen for the latter theory. In his numerous writings on the subject he has constantly returned to the same theme, the inability of the 'passive theory' to account for the phenomenon of illusory perceptions: a problem which is not only explained by, but which in some ways constitutes the mainspring of the Inferential theory. Yet the Inferential theory is itself dogged by the persistent doubt whether the brain is capable of performing the complex perceptual inferences demanded by the theory *unconsciously*, for we are certainly not aware of such processes.

It is no wonder, given the service which AI is supposed to have performed for the notion of 'mechanical inference', that Gregory should have turned to Pattern Recognition with such alacrity:

> Until recently the notion of unconscious inference seemed to many psychologists to be self-contradictory — as it used to be assumed that consciousness is necessary for inference to be possible. Perhaps again through the influence of computers ... this objection no longer has force. To hold that 'unconscious inference' is a self-contradictory notion now appears as mere semantic inertia.[11]

It is this last statement which is particularly troubling, for it implies that the obstacles confronting the notion of 'unconscious inference' are strictly contingent, and thus that the immediate benefit of Pattern Recognition research has been to overcome those reactionary instincts which resisted the notion of 'unconscious inference' on purely empirical grounds. Indeed, as far as the advocates of the Mechanist Thesis are concerned, their battle has been directed as much against the prejudices created by vulgar belief as the glaring lacunae in neurophysiological knowledge. 'The everyday assumption of a sharp dichotomy between seeing and thinking implicitly denies any possible contribution of the latter to the former', simply because one is usually 'introspectively unaware of the underlying inferential processes that are essential to vision, and unable consciously to call them into play'.[12] Pattern Recognition has thus emerged as something of a *deus ex machina* for the Inferential theory: it has vindicated the postulation of 'unconscious inferences' performed by the brain on the raw data provided by the eyes, and even more importantly, it promises 'to highlight the background assumptions, conceptual schemes, and stimulus cues that determine one's more normal visual experience'.[13]

The question whether these crucial services were only made necessary by and relevant to the demands of their approach is not an area in which mechanists care to delve. Indeed, it is a possibility which, given the basic premisses of their theory of perception, *could not* have occurred to them. Gregory resorts to a highly significant metaphor at the beginning of *Eye and Brain*: 'Like a computer,' he explains, 'the brain accepts information, and makes decisions according to the available information.'[14] But perversely, 'no machine comes anywhere near the human perceptual system in range or speed', and 'It is partly for this reason that detailed study of human perception is important. Finding out what we can of human perception is important not only for our understanding ourselves: it may also suggest ways in which perception can be achieved by machines.'[15] There are clearly a host of assumptions about the nature of perception buried in the very premiss that computer simulations of the recognition of patterns could enable us to further our understanding of perception *per se*; and that a deeper understanding of the latter would facilitate our ability to develop more powerful computer simulations of the former. Given the prior themes that 'Eye and brain combine to give detailed knowledge of objects beyond the range of probing touch',[16] and that the functions performed by the brain mirror those of a computer, the process set off by studies in Pattern Recognition in both the computer and the psychology/neurophysiology laboratories is symbiotic: a development which, so the scientists involved believe, marks a striking advance in our understanding of perception and the credibility of AI.

That something was seriously amiss soon became evident, however, if only because the scientists' early optimism was not vindicated. Even Gregory (who remains a firm convert for reasons which we shall go into more fully below) is the first to admit that 'performance does not justify the claim that Machine Perception matches even the modest biological perception given by simple brains. This,' he concedes, 'is embarrassing.'[17] So much so that, as Gregory sadly reports, 'Some of the biological renegade emigrés into "intelligence technology" (including the author) returned to mice and men.'[18] Some have even 'attacked Artificial Intelligence as being not only difficult but impossible'.[19] But Gregory does not share their pessimism; after all, he pleads, 'Given that eyes and brains work, why should it be *impossible* to make artificial intelligence? Is there something intrinsically unique about brains?'[20] To be sure, 'It has turned out that the fastest (single channel) digital computers are too slow to go through the steps of their programs to reproduce the speed of biological perception. This may suggest that the brain adopts different strategies: that it works by analogue means, or has rich parallel processing facilities so that many processing problems can be solved simultaneously.'[21] But Gregory can see no *a priori* reason why computer scientists should not be able to simulate such complex neural processes, and he thus remains unmoved by what he regards as the formidable technological challenge confronting Pattern Recognition. Hence he concludes that 'perceiving the world involves a series of computer-like tricks, which we should be able to duplicate, but some of the tricks remain to be discovered and, until they are, we cannot build a machine that will see or fully understand our own eyes and brains'.[22]

Gregory's appraisal of the *mechanical* obstacles thwarting the development of computer vision has become the common theme among apologists for Pattern Recognition. In reassuringly prosaic tones Donald Michie explains that

> In robot vision we have to bear in mind that there are two ends to a robot: a front end where the action is, and a back end which ruminates on what the front end and its instructors tell it. Rumination is to a large and unavoidable extent a sequential process. Although expensive, the information traffic is slow, or should be. Hence the overall cost of, say, matching visual descriptions extracted from the camera with stored descriptions, or planning what pictures to take next, need not be unduly high. The main burden, then, of cost-cutting is thrown on the low-level processes going on in the front end, where every possible trick of special hardware and parallel computing should be pressed into service.[23]

Apart from a muted reference to the Mechanist Thesis this all sounds perfectly straightforward, albeit technically daunting. Michie is thus particularly effective in generating enthusiasm for the hope that 'The new array processors, like Dr Michael Duff's CLIP developed at University College, London [which] operate on the parallel principle' might yield the secrets of Machine Perception.[24] We shall examine more closely in section 3 the actual reasons why advocates of the Mechanist Thesis believe that parallel processing might hold the key to computer vision. But before we examine the nature and scope of CLIP, we must first consider whether it is even *conceivable* that advanced hardware and programming techniques will overcome the obstacles which have thwarted the mechanist vision. For the purposes of this introductory section, however, let us merely assess the implications of the possibility that the problem with the Mechanical Perception Thesis might not be technological: that the obstacles here are *logical*, rather than *empirical*. If this proved to be the case then it would mean that at least some of the problems plaguing machine vision will only be resolved by conceptual clarification, not hard- or software modification. In which case we would be forced to consider what implications this would have, not only for research in Pattern Recognition, but even more importantly, for our approach to modern science, and the role which philosophy has to play in its evolution.

One can well appreciate why scientists might be loathe to countenance such philosophical interference. Philosophers have a worrying tendency to suppose that, if they have identified some conceptual muddle in the prose of a theory, then the subject itself stands exposed as a fraud. But rarely do scientific fields expire as the result of a *philosophical* critique. However, when — as frequently occurs — the prose interpretation of a scientific result collapses, the most serious casualty seems to be the pride which many scientists take in what they regard as their solution of some long-standing philosophical issue; for the interpretation in question is invariably one which misreads conceptual confusion for empirical mystery. And it is precisely this hubris which leads scientists into areas that demand our assistance.

A typical example can be found in the confident remarks with which Alan K. Mackworth prefaces his survey of what has so far been achieved in Pattern Recognition:

> In one of its many roles artificial intelligence is cast as the vanguard of an army of psychologists who seek a new paradigm for cognitive and perceptual processes. Despite several clarion calls to this effect, artificial intelligence may well be a vanguard without an army. This paper attempts to show that a small part of the scouted territory is ripe for capture.[25]

One should always be wary of any mention of a 'vanguard', no matter what the context. Apart from this preface, however, Mackworth's paper contains a sober and valuable survey of recent developments in Pattern Recognition. Despite his passing mention to the Inferential theory of perception, it is clear that his real interest is in the development of scene-analysis programs, which he pursues in explicitly mathematical, not psychological terms. And this is a feature which surfaces time and again in the scientific papers on Pattern Recognition.

One cannot help but notice the difference between the confident tones exuded by the computer scientists who are active in

Pattern Recognition versus the defensive attitudes of the psychologists who have a vested interest in their results. Why is it that the former do not share the qualms of the latter? To be sure, their results may have proved embarrassing for the Inferential theory of perception, but have they been at all discreditable as far as the development of computer science is concerned? Here, perhaps, is a case where commercial interests have proved to be a more reliable guide than accepted mechanist wisdom. For modern industry seldom subsidises an obvious failure; certainly, it never *increases* the venture-capital it is prepared to risk unless there are sound grounds to proceed with the research. Perhaps the only failure we have to deal with here is that which has been dealt to the Mechanist Thesis? Perhaps Pattern Recognition is indeed a sign of the great promises contained in the 'creative computer', albeit in terms shorn of the Inferential theory? And what is the greatest heresy of all, perhaps we should avoid tying Pattern Recognition too closely to the apron-strings of the Mechanist Thesis? To be sure, the original influence of the latter is manifest in the very name of the discipline, in much the same way as is true of 'Artificial Intelligence' itself. But Pattern Recognition is an amorphous field; in the words of the British Pattern Recognition Association, it 'includes theory, technique and instrumentation for retrieval, processing and classification of optical, acoustic and other patterns. Some examples of patterns are satellite images, medical and industrial radiographs, optical and electron micrographs, spoken utterances, written characters, physical waveforms and seismic signals.'[26] No mention here, however, of the Inferential theory of perception: is the foregoing what remains once the mechanist confusions have been removed from the prose encompassing the theory? But we anticipate ourselves. As is so often the case with *philosophical* issues, it all depends on how we approach the problem. And as is generally the case, the most promising place to start is with the premisses underpinning the theory.

2. Perceptions as Hypotheses

The first step in the evolution of any theory is to persuade us that there really is a problem to be solved. Despite their natural scepticism, this proves a relatively straightforward task when dealing with fellow scientists; after all, fresh problems are the lifeblood of their profession. But the general public often remains surprisingly unreceptive to the new questions on which progress rests. And, as far as the scientist is concerned, the responsibility for this obstinacy all too often lies with philosophers. To the scientist, philosophers frequently seem dogmatically intent on encouraging the layman to adhere to those 'vulgar beliefs' which the science in question is struggling to transcend. Thus, like some presidential demagogue who seeks to circumvent the checks and balances of representational government with personal addresses to the electorate, scientists frequently begin their popular writings with a deceptively simple account of the issue which, vested with all the authority of the science, is designed to undercut philosophical objections from the outset. In both cases, however, it is impossible — and undesirable — to avoid the constitutional powers that be for long.

In keeping with this custom, Gregory begins *Eye and Brain* with what may look like a commonplace introduction to the state of the art, but which in fact contains a carefully scripted attempt to convince us that there is indeed a serious problem to be solved in perception:

> We are so familiar with seeing, that it takes a leap of imagination to realise that there are problems to be solved. But consider it. We are given tiny distorted upside-down images in the eyes, and we see separate solid objects in surrounding space. From the patterns of stimulation on the retinas we perceive the world of objects, and this is nothing short of a miracle.[27]

So too, in 'The Confounded Eye' he begins: 'Eye and brain combine to give detailed knowledge of objects beyond the range of probing touch. Just how this is achieved remains in many ways mysterious; but we know now that specific features of objects are selected and combined to give an internal account of the object world.'[28] Whatever we might feel about the notion of an 'internal account of the object world', there is nothing surprising in this attitude; if one statement could be said to epitomise the scientific spirit of the twentieth century, it must be Einstein's declaration in *What I Believe* that 'The most beautiful thing we can experience is the mysterious. It is the source of all true art and science.' Most striking of all, however, is the manner in which the traditional roles have been reversed, with scientists becoming the guardians of the arcane, and (so-called 'anti-scientific') philosophers their most implacable opponents.

At the beginning of *The Human Mystery* Sir John Eccles describes how 'Sherrington's magnificent attempt to face up unflinchingly to the mystery involved in the full range of human experience was subjected to a great barrage of criticism ... There have been effective replies. For example, Gilbert Ryle's (1949) *The Concept of Mind* was answered by Beloff's (1962) *The Existence of Mind.*'[29] One senses that Eccles sees himself as facing up 'unflinchingly' to the 'central problem' in 'the human mystery': the function of the brain in thought and perception. And although he remains perfectly receptive to any legitimate scientific critique of his account, he has little patience for what he regards as uninformed philosophical objections. But it is not from any perverse inclination on our part to deny the wonders of the universe or the secrets of the brain that we find ourselves compelled to question the logical cogency of his account of perception. For it is not mystery *per se* which disturbs us, but to be precise, Eccles's conception of the 'quite mysterious way [in which] the retinal picture appears in conscious perception'.[30]

What sort of *mystery* is this? Interestingly, the philosophical overtones of such a question are not, despite their protestations, anathema to the scientists involved. Gregory describes how 'Experimental psychology has grown up from philosophy, and the smoke and the ashes of ancient controversy cling to it still.'[31] Admittedly, the implication here is that naïve philosophical speculation has been displaced by rigorous scientific analysis. Yet Gregory quite rightly points out that 'It is this relation between perceptions and objects which is the classical philosophical problem, and it cannot be ignored when we consider perception as a territory for scientific investigation.'[32] Moreover, it is for this reason that Gregory does not hesitate to treat the 'passive, intuitive view of perception' — and so one assumes, by parity of reasoning, the Inferential theory — as a 'philosophy'.[33] But no Wittgensteinian would be prepared to describe either the Gestalt or the Inferential accounts of perception as *philosophical theories*, even though they may rest on misguided assumptions which can only be removed by philosophical clarification. Nor is any Wittgensteinian philosopher likely to subscribe to Gregory's admonition that 'To philosophers the question is: Can we know before we have perceived? To the psychologist the question is also: Can we perceive before we have learned how to perceive?'[34]

Clearly the crux of this issue is the very notion which Gregory has of a philosophical solution to the problem he has outlined. Such a point is crucial to how we approach his own proposed solution, for given that we are all agreed that we are indeed dealing with a *philosophical problem* here, the issue must obviously devolve onto our understanding of the nature of a *philosophical solution*. In Gregory's eyes, philosophy is seen as anchored to the original, somewhat primitive disputes that have long been superseded by modern scientific discoveries: 'The data that most philosophers consider are limited to sensory experience. This is not so for physics, which accepts data from instruments capable of monitoring characteristics of the world quite unknown before instruments were invented.'[35] Had 'the eighteenth-century empiricists' been familiar with such experiments as those that have been performed on the illusions created by the Ames Room, 'philosophy might have taken a very different course'.[36] Philosophy is thus *qualitatively*, not *categorially* distinct from science; the real difference would appear to lie in the crude tools which the former — armchair science — employs.

Most significant of all, Wittgenstein is also included in this empiricist *post mortem*. In *Mind and Science* Gregory singles out Wittgenstein's brief comments on aspect-seeing in the *Investigations* for mild approval, but with the sharp rebuke that Wittgenstein's emphasis on the unique *philosophical* character of his remarks is completely unwarranted: 'Wittgenstein describes his discussion of ambiguity as a conceptual investigation, but it is possible to investigate these matters experimentally. Indeed, ambiguous figures are extremely useful tools for perceptual research ...'[37] On this reading Wittgenstein is credited with a partial insight into the Inferential theory which, as such, is of little use when compared with the advanced work that has since been done in the psychology laboratories. At least it signifies, however, philosophy's belated attempt to rid itself of its empiricist shackles. But what if the empiricist shoe really fits on the opposite foot: what if Wittgenstein was right and his discussion of ambiguity genuinely is a *conceptual*, not an *experimental* investigation? The very basis of his problem — as he himself describes it — forbids Gregory from refusing to address such a possibility, much as it may run contrary to what he regards as the spirit of philosophy.

In the account of its first moments of consciousness which Dr Frankenstein's creature sends to him (quoted on p. 217 above), we are given a glimpse of a mind lost in a welter of confused sensations. It is surely noteworthy that Shelley seizes on perceptual learning as the creature's first step towards coherent thought; in Gregory's terms, we would say that its brain had learned how to cross the great divide between stimulation and perception, and with that, how to think. Just how it has learned to distinguish the features of objects in order 'to give an internal account of the object world' remains a mystery in Shelley's primitive Lockean terms, but we are left with the impression that here was a spontaneous natural act accomplished by the brain, independent of social influences and *prior to* the acquisition of language. No less a modern Prometheus himself, Gregory has set out to disclose the mechanisms at work here, utilising all the tools which modern science has to offer. What is most striking is that only the latter has changed; the picture itself has remained remarkably constant. Particularly interesting is the role which the notion of unconscious perceptual learning has retained *vis-à-vis* the creation of artificial intelligence.

Perceptual learning as thus conceived constitutes what is perhaps the central premiss underlying the Inferential theory of perception:

> The past cannot be perceived directly; but if stored information, from past experience, is vital for present perception — if the present is read in terms of the past — then we are driven away from an Intuitional or Gestalt position, towards a theory much closer to Helmholtz's notion of perceptions given by inference from sensory and stored data.[38]

It is hardly a coincidence that learning has been defined here[39] in tacitly mechanist terms. As we shall see below, this facilitates the shift to speaking of Mechanical Perception by building in the framework for the latter from the start. But it is not the notion of 'machine learning', nor even of 'brain learning', which concerns Gregory, but rather, the consequences which he draws from this picture.

On the above conception, learning amounts to the brain's storage of information in such a way that it is readily accessible for instant retrieval.[40] Gregory does not undertake to explain *how* the brain accomplishes these feats; such, one is given to understand, is a task for neurophysiologists (aided, perhaps, by AI-scientists). His real purpose is only to confirm that such processes must be present in perception, and in so doing, to join together the disparate forces of physiology, experimental psychology, machine intelligence, and lastly philosophy, under the common banner of 'a general paradigm for perception'.[41] And this, according to Gregory, is provided by the theory that perceptions are inferences. Thus, 'To understand perception, the signal codes and the stored knowledge or assumptions used for deriving perceptual hypotheses must be discovered.'[42] For 'If perceptions are inferences, based on signalled data from the senses and stored in memory, then we should ask: what are these inferences like? Are they like other kinds of inferences? Do they depend upon assumptions? What happens if the assumptions are wrong?'[43] But how do we set about this enquiry when scientists cannot even agree among themselves under whose jurisdiction it falls?

It is here where experimental psychology is called upon to provide the lead for this still juvenile science, given that 'Systematic perceptual errors are important clues for appreciating signal channel limitations, and for discovering hypothesis-generating procedures.'[44] It is not just that perceptual illusions provide a means of identifying some of the various unconscious assumptions applied by the brain in perception; even more important is the crucial rationale which it provides for the whole theory. For 'From our eyes' errors we can look behind the eyes and see something of the most extraordinary and the most complicated functioning system on Earth, to discover at least in outline how it solves problems far too difficult for any computer so far conceived, every time we see an object — or a picture.'[45] Thus, it may require 'a conceptual somersault to accept illusions as the major facts of a science! But this we must do; and once this decision is taken, we can hardly expect physics (or physiology) to provide the paradigm for perception.'[46] But how exactly do the findings of experimental psychologists investigating perceptual illusions validate the Inferential theory of perception? Gregory's answer is immediately forthcoming: if illusions are 'due to misplaced assumptions', then veridical perceptions must obviously be based on legitimate reasoning. In both cases, therefore, perceptions are hypotheses, some of which may be false; and it is from the manifestation of the former that we can infer the existence of the latter:

Perceptions of objects are given by inference, from data given by the senses and stored in memory. On this view, any perception may be false, just as any argument may be false. It may be false because its assumptions are incorrect, or because the form of the argument is fallacious. On this view of perception, illusions take on the same importance that paradoxes and ambiguities have for philosophers concerned with the nature of argument; or how data can be used to discover a truth, or a fact. Illusions then become symptoms of fallacies and unwarranted assumptions about the world of objects.[47]

Gregory is fully aware that with this argument he has altered the meaning of 'illusion', but far from apologising for any irregularity, he urges us to accept that 'It is important to extend our concepts, and our terminology, beyond biology if we are to understand illusion.'[48] Certainly science — as opposed to philosophy — must be free to take any liberties it chooses with the formulation of its *technical* concepts. But the whole force of Gregory's argument derives from the premiss that we are dealing here with our familiar notions: we are not subverting, only modifying them. One is none the less led to query in what way we are still dealing with a phenomenon that can be meaningfully identified as an *illusion*. So too have 'learning', 'assumption', 'hypothesis', 'inference', and most important of all, 'perception', been 'extended'; indeed, the latter itself has received the same treatment. With such sweeping conceptual realignment at work, it becomes exceedingly difficult to identify any of the familiar features which we have hitherto associated with this cluster of concepts. Nor can this complaint be brusquely swept aside; for if the only way that science can resolve the 'mystery of perception' is by conceptual alteration, it can hardly fault philosophy for scrutinising the coherence of the changes proposed.

It is highly illuminating that in the above passage Gregory compares his 'extended' concept to paradoxes, for these too have received extensive 'modification' in recent years at the hands of philosophers of mathematics. Where once paradoxes were regarded by philosophers as self-contradictory statements to be avoided at all costs in an argument, in the modern meta-logical climate they have been compared ('extended') to *koans*: keys to the higher cognitive worlds which are *ineffable* if viewed from too low a conceptual level. In this sense a paradox is nothing of the sort; rather, it is a manifestation of undisclosed depth (comparable to an empirical anomaly). Hence it is really only an apparent paradox (as far as the term is normally understood): 'apparent' because it implicitly expresses what, from a higher point of view, will be revealed as an intelligible truth.[49] On this interpretation the way is then open to treating illusions themselves as a species of paradox, and they can become the proof for Gregory of the brain's higher inferential functions, ineffable to ordinary introspection, but discernible by the tools of science.

It is thus fascinating to compare the way in which Gregory and Douglas Hofstadter approach the same painting from their different perspectives. To Hofstadter, Maurits Escher's *Waterfall* is a 'strange loop' whose inconsistency forces us to ascend through various levels leading from the finite to the infinite, thereby conveying an insight into the hierarchy of 'realities' which can only be disclosed 'meta-theoretically'.[50] To Gregory, Escher's *Waterfall* is proof of the confusions which result when the brain does not possess the correct visual hypothesis to interpret the shape which it has received from the retina.[51] To both, therefore, Escher's illusion is a 'visual paradox' which as such provides an important key to further knowledge. Neither can see any *logical* obstacle to describing a painting as a species of 'paradox': all that is involved here is an 'extension' to the concept of illusion, and through that, a more profound alteration to our understanding of perception. Thus Gregory insists that:

> We begin, surely, to see that the use of the word 'paradox' for pictures is no idle pun based on its more usual use for arguments and scientific enquiry. Perceiving is a kind of thinking. We have examples of ambiguities, paradoxes, distortions and uncertainties in perception as in all other thinking. They bedevil the intelligent eye as they are the causes and the symptoms of error in the most concrete and the most abstract thought.[52]

There is a disturbing hint of circularity running through this argument, however: illusions can only be described as paradoxes on the grounds that perception is inferential, but our justification for the latter claim rests on the prior assumption that we cannot account for the phenomenon of illusions without postulating an Inferential theory of perception.[53] This tension manifests itself in the tenuous account which Gregory must give for the brain's curious inability to modify its store of assumptions despite its awareness of the factors generating an illusion. Throughout his writings Gregory returns to the theme that the fact that 'intellectual knowledge' of the causes of an illusion 'does not always correct perceptual errors' only serves to *confirm* that 'perceptual hypothesis-making is not under intellectual control'.[54] One might be pardoned for thinking that such examples establish the exact opposite: that they *deflate* the Inferential theory, in as much as they demonstrate that how something looks may have nothing to do with what we know about the object. But because he is *already* committed to the premiss that perceptions are hypotheses, Gregory can shift effortlessly to the conclusion that 'Evidently the perceptual hypothesis-generator does not have elaborate check procedures; so we are stuck with this paradox.'[55]

Such a manoeuvre only brings its own store of problems in its wake, however, for now we are suddenly confronted with the disturbing dilemma of determining how we can ever be certain that 'intellectual knowledge' and 'hypothesis generator' are working in harmony. Gregory resigns himself to the inevitable. In familiar empiricist fashion he begins with the problem of other minds: 'just as for the imaginary robot we do not know what, if anything, they experience', so too we must 'regard perception in other people (or in animals) as a more-or-less reasonable postulate. We do not know how to prove it, and perhaps we each argue by a kind of analogy from ourselves.'[56] But never mind this recurrent empiricist leitmotif: we immediately find ourselves thrust back into the arms of Descartes's demon: 'It is possible that I am wrong that the wet-looking blue patch, apparently over there, is the sea; or even that this which I see and touch is indeed my desk. I might possibly be dreaming or drugged. This may be unlikely but it is possible; so my perceptions are not *certain.*'[57] If this is the necessary consequence of the Inferential theory, then something must indeed be conceptually amiss; for the emergence of any such sceptical dilemma provides us with the categorical proof that we are dealing ultimately with what is *au fond* a *philosophical* confusion.[58]

The source for all these troubles can be located in the physicalist shift which has been prefaced to the argument. The psychologist finds himself in an extremely awkward position, straddling as he does the disparate interests of the neurophysiologist and the philosopher. As we have already seen, Gregory regards his primary task as that of uniting these divided parties under a common 'paradigm'. But what he is really trying to bridge is a conceptual, not a professional gulf. It is not that philosophers idle away their time with 'sensory experience' while neurophysiologists study the processes of the brain: the demarcation here is between *perception* and *physiology*! And it is precisely this conceptual divorce which Gregory proposes to conjoin with his Inferential theory of perception. The vehicle for this logically impossible feat is, accordingly, the brain; the source of the mystery, it is the only viable candidate to perform the miraculous. Thus, 'A central problem of visual perception is how the brain interprets the patterns of the eye in terms of external objects.'[59] But this is an argument which forces us *nolens volens* into the Homunculus Fallacy, no matter how respectable our intentions.

Such a criticism threatens to collapse as a blatant *argumentum ad baculum*, however, if it is presented as an adequate objection in its own right. For Gregory is profoundly aware of the dangers of the Homunculus Fallacy, warning his reader that 'we must be clear that there is no "little man inside" doing the arguing, for this leads to intolerable philosophical difficulties'.[60] And as a token of his commitment to this point he is especially careful to enclose the various inferential operations performed by the brain in perception in inverted commas.[61] To charge Gregory with the very fallacy which he has taken such pains to forswear, or to insist that the quotation marks are only a symptom of his logical discomfort and then leave the matter at that, can only appear as churlish. If we are to present a convincing picture of why, despite the caution that has been exercised, the argument is none the less guilty of the Homunculus Fallacy, we must show how the theory is doomed to failure, and why this is due to the conceptual confusions on which it rests, rather than to any empirical shortcomings.

There are two strands to such a critique: first, we must identify the various violations of logical grammar that have been committed, and then clarify the nature of the problems into which these force us. Foremost among the former is undoubtedly the notion of an 'unconscious inference', which we shall consider below. We have already touched on the manner in which both 'illusion' and 'paradox' have been altered, but what about the key term in all this: *perception* itself? The irony of the Inferential theory is that, if it is successful, 'perception' threatens to disappear altogether, leaving us with only the neurophysiological study of the transmission of sensations and the 'storage' of 'patterns', and the putative psychological study of the brain's store of assumptions and inferential-matching techniques. For 'seeing' can be entirely dispensed with if all we are really concerned with are the complex operations performed by the eye/transducer and the brain. Indeed, it *must* be dispensed with if Gregory is to sustain his claim that the Homunculus Fallacy has been avoided. Thus Gregory scrupulously avoids stating that the brain can be said to *see*: rather, *seeing* is defined as the neural interaction between eye and brain.[62] 'What the eyes do is to feed the brain with information coded into neural activity — chains of electrical impulses — which by their code and the patterns of brain activity, represent objects.'[63] Hence, the solution to the mystery of perception would seem to lie in the tacit elimination of the latter from the theory; the gulf is not, after all, between sensation and perception, but rather, between eye and brain.

The matter is by no means so straightforward, however, for the essential drawback of physicalist solutions to philosophical issues is that they seek to abandon the problematic terms involved while remaining faithful to the original framework. In the above quotation we are told that the brain 'decodes' the 'neural information' which it is fed. 'These are combined in the newly discovered cortical "columns". This is — logically — something like being combined to form words: the selected features are evidently basic units of the perceptual "language" of the brain.'[64] The inverted commas are, of course, intended to signify that no literal ascription of a brain-language has actually been suggested,[65] but Gregory does not appreciate just how damaging the picture remains. For he is now committed to the premiss that the brain operates as a *normative agent*, following the various rules (such as 'scaling') which he has postulated.[66] The claim to having avoided the Homunculus Fallacy thus becomes hopelessly strained; for the price of protecting the brain from an 'inner eye' is that the 'perceptions are built up by following rules from assumptions',[67] and no amount of scare quotes can save the argument from this normative foundation. It is precisely here where much of the attraction of the Mechanist Thesis resides, for the real problem with attributing inferences to the brain — whether conscious or otherwise — lies in the logical barrier preventing us from describing the brain as a *rule-following organ*. Most perplexing of all is our utter failure to identify anything even remotely resembling a 'neural rule' for the brain to follow. But if computers can be described as rule-following mechanisms — that is, if a first step towards mapping the nature of these rules can be taken — then the way seems open to ascribing the same functions (albeit in a different structure) to the brain.

If this were not enough, matters soon get much worse. Gregory explains that 'When we look at something, the pattern of neural activity represents the object and to the brain *is* the object.'[68] In other words, 'objects' must go the same way as 'perception'. But, as Gregory himself insists, 'what we perceive is far more than patterns — we perceive *objects* as existing in their space and time'.[69] Yet if perception has been reduced to these neurophysiological terms, and if all the brain deals with are patterns, then how can we retrieve objects? Perhaps future physiologists will simply dismiss objects as 'logical fictions' which were originally invented for popular consumption, and can now be happily discarded in a rigorous science? But the solution to the mystery of perception can hardly be that we do not, strictly speaking, see anything (in so far as the brain is solely engaged in the synthesis of patterns). Certainly, this is not at all where we started; on the contrary, it was emphasised that what we are dealing with just is the familiar act of seeing objects in space. But how is such a conclusion to be avoided?

Gregory explains that 'Objects are far more than patterns of stimulation: objects have pasts and futures: when we know its past or can guess its future, an object transcends experience and becomes an embodiment of knowledge and expectation without which life beyond the simplest is not possible.'[70] The latter are, of course, the cognitive perceptual processes which constitute the backbone of Gregory's theory. But where does the end result of these operations take place? Not in the brain, for if that were the case we would find ourselves lumbered once again with the Homunculus Fallacy that it is the brain which sees the objects whose presence it infers. Gregory himself insists that while 'We do have "mental pictures" ... this should not suggest that there are corresponding electrical pictures in the brain.' For 'The notion of brain pictures is conceptually dangerous. It is apt to suggest that these supposed pictures are themselves seen with a kind of inner eye involving another picture, and another eye ... and so on.'[71] Rather, 'This picture is perceived,' according to Eccles, 'in the mind. It is a mistake to think that it can therefore be discovered in the brain, where instead there is only the coded information in countless neuronal discharges.'[72] But if it is the mind which sees objects, then the problem has merely been shifted back a level, for now we must discover how the brain communicates its decisions to the mind. Thus we are left with 'that most mysterious of all phenomena — the interaction of mental events ... with brain events'.[73]

Here, then, is the final dilemma with which we are confronted: if we adopt a mind-brain identity thesis, we are soon landed with either the Homunculus Fallacy or the disappearance of perception; if we adopt a dualist thesis, we are immediately thrust back to the initial mystery with which all this started, albeit in somewhat transformed terms. But perhaps that in itself marks an advance? When he first states his thesis that perceptions depend on assumptions — about the nature of which we still know nothing — Gregory hastens to add that 'We may not as yet know the physiology behind all this; but at least we can ask, and hope to answer, this kind of question.'[74] But as we can see from the foregoing, the real problem with the Inferential theory is that it forces us to ask what is ultimately the wrong kind of question! For it is a question which seeks to transgress the *logical* demarcation between perception and brain-states. The reductionist impulse sees these as contingently independent strata which a successful theory will synthesise. In other words, they represent different processes in the same phenomenon, as they occur on different cognitive levels. But in order to generate this thesis, the argument must adopt the following methodology: it begins by defining the operations of the brain in terms of perception, but then reverses the picture by defining perception in terms of the brain's operations. Then, given the brain/CPU identity thesis touched on above, the exact same procedure can be replicated in the Mechanical Perception thesis: it begins by defining the steps of a scene-analysis program in terms of the brain's perceptual/inferential operations, and then shapes our understanding of the mysterious processes which occur in 'hypercolumnar analysis' in terms of the algorithms used in such programs. To grasp the full implications of this latter shift, however, we must descend with the argument to yet a lower level, in order to grapple with the (neuro-)physicalist assumptions underlying both the Inferential theory and the Mechanical Perception Thesis.

3. Perception versus Information-processing

If we approach the Mechanical Perception Thesis by way of Gregory, we immediately find ourselves on familiar ground. Indeed, so much so that one might be forgiven for wondering whether Gregory is defining 'machine vision' in terms of the eye, or the reverse. In fact, we must be scrupulous about according psychology its due precedence here; for it was only with the Inferential framework already in place that it seemed intelligible to describe the operations of a Pattern Recognition system in perceptual terms. But one might easily conclude upon first encounter with the scientific writings in Pattern Recognition that this genetic account is the exact reverse of what actually occurred: that the Inferential theory of (biological) perception was extrapolated from AI paradigms. For the tone of the theory has now become unreservedly mechanist; 'Biological information processing,' Gregory tells us, 'is almost incredibly efficient ... An important reason for the speed and efficiency of the visual system is its very large number of parallel channels — at least 10^6 for the human eye.'[75] But this move raises a whole host of new problems for the psychological study of perception.

Where, in the previous section, our primary danger was that of attributing the psychologist's findings to the brain, the hazard has suddenly become that of attributing some complex 'matching' or 'labelling' algorithm to the visual cortex. Clearly the symbiotic nature of the two disciplines renders the Mechanical Perception Thesis as dangerous to psychology as the Inferential theory is to AI. But if this shift has not yet become seriously debilitating, it is only because it immediately lands us with an obvious anomaly: 'Sequential processing is inevitably slow (which handicaps the ear) but the eye, though limited by the limited band-width of its channels, is faster than any man-made computer.'[76] That is, in purely mechanical terms, the processing capabilities of advanced VLSI technology seems vastly more powerful than the biological system, and yet the eye and brain easily outperform even the most sophisticated fourth-generation computer. How are we to explain this apparent paradox?

Once again, 'illusions' are pressed into service. The 'biological visual system' makes up for its comparative lack of processing speed with 'various "strategy" short cuts'.[77] As we saw in the preceding section, illusions are supposed to demonstrate the existence of the former, in so far as they are the result of 'short-cuts' which, because of some peculiarity in the object/scene perceived, lead us into error. By the same token, this points to the explanation for the otherwise puzzling failure of 'mechanical visual systems' to match the performance levels of the eye: AI-scientists have clearly not yet developed 'strategy short-cuts' to rival the brain's superior store of assumptions. And it is at this point that the Inferential theory raises an intriguing possibility for the development of Pattern Recognition. The standard explanation for the brain's advantage over the machine is that the former employs some (as yet undisclosed) form of parallel processing, whereas the latter has hitherto been confined to sequential processing. Hence the secret to Mechanical Perception would seem to lie in the development of parallel techniques, at both preprocessing and processing levels. But Gregory's approach opens up a further dimension to the argument: given that we shall one day learn about the inferential processes underpinning human perception, should it not then be possible to apply the information thus obtained, not only as a means of understanding, but also of improving machine perception? And as a first step towards that distant prospect, if we could manufacture a system which experienced similar illusions to ourselves, would that not suggest that we were narrowing the gap between 'biological' and 'mechanical' 'strategy short-cuts', and hence between human and machine perception? In which case illusions would appear to have not just an important, but perhaps a crucial practical role to play in the evolution of Pattern Recognition.[78]

On this approach human (that is, 'biological') and machine perception are merely two species of the same general phenomenon: they are technically, but not categorially distinct. Hence it is logically possible — although, perhaps, empirically undesirable — to simulate the operations of 'biological' perception mechanically. What is of greatest scientific importance for the development of machine vision is simply the question of how our understanding of the biological species of perception should influence our development of the mechanical; particularly if Pattern Recognition is to make the transition from static to dynamic image-processing. And given the predominance of the Inferential theory, it is hardly surprising that the first advances in Pattern Recognition were originally regarded and are now carefully presented in Inferential terms. Thus, Mackworth describes how L.G. Roberts' primitive

Pattern Recognition 'program created a scene-analysis paradigm that remains dominant. As a working theory, for that is what an artificial-intelligence program is, it firmly established an active model of perception as a cycle of four processes: discovering cues, activating a hypothesis, testing the hypothesis, and inferring the consequences.'[79] It is no coincidence that, as Mackworth immediately explains, this paradigm 'echoes Helmholtz's approach';[80] for the latter is what really establishes the parameters for the subsequent mechanist application. A seemingly crude question which we might ask at the outset, therefore, is: what actually remains in a 'scene-analysis' program when this framework is removed?

One's instinctive response to the Mechanical Perception Thesis is that what we really have here are cybernetic mechanisms employing self-modifying algorithms for co-ordinating photographic patterns with semantic trees in order to identify and perhaps manipulate certain aspects of the system's environment. The trouble is that 'co-ordinating' is such a loaded term. For, as far as the advocate of the Mechanist Thesis is concerned, it conveys the *interpretation* of the data that has been recorded/transmitted: 'The most important question to be faced' by the pioneers in machine vision 'was how to write programs that coordinate the use of these separate, but interrelated, knowledge systems to achieve sensible picture interpretations'.[81] The problem with the above criticism, from a mechanist point of view, is simply that it ignores the significance of stored information in these processes. Herein lies the essential element which, in the eyes of the partisans, transforms the exercise from a subdiscipline of engineering into a foray into the upper reaches of Artificial Intelligence.

Admittedly, when you first read about the level of scene-analysis that has now been achieved in Pattern Recognition systems, you may experience a slight twinge of disappointment. This is what the scientists themselves refer to as a 'toy world' of simple objects which seems light-years from our ordinary world of perception. What could be so exciting about a program that is able to identify blocks and cubes from a narrowly circumscribed frame? The answer to this is: from the apparent inferential steps, however crude, that the program demonstrates in its ability to synthesise previous patterns and apply these to new cases. And knowing what we do about perception, we can hypothesise that we have at least taken the first steps, however tentative, towards Machine Perception, just as the prosimian brain must have evolved from equally primitive origins.

In an earlier work I examined the use and abuse of the concept of *learning* which prefigures in the mechanist interpretation of such scene-analysis programs.[82] In essence I tried to show that the assumption that we can describe self-modifying recursive algorithms as 'learning programs' chiefly derives from the tendency to interpret the various operations of these systems in terms of concept-acquisition rather than concept-construction. What these putative 'learning programs' really amount to are the implementation of formal methods for constructing and adapting complex semantic trees which can be mapped onto an expanding range of configurations. It is not this aspect of the argument which I wish to pursue here, however, but rather, the significance which this picture of the two related species of perception — biological and mechanical — has had for the evolution, not only of Pattern Recognition, but for AI itself. We can best appreciate the importance of this point by examining the planning papers in which AI-scientists give free rein to their imagination and their ambitions; for it is here that we most clearly encounter the full heuristic pictures underpinning the various aspects of the Mechanist Thesis. Moreover, it is here where we can best appreciate the reason why Pattern Recognition has assumed such importance to AI.

In 'A Cognitive Architecture for Computer Vision' B.H. McCormick, E. Kent and C.R. Dyer explain that 'the design of a machine visual system paralleling known biological visual system architecture affords the best opportunity to initiate the inevitable evolution of cognitive machines'.[83] In other words, the very fact that we are simulating biological processes will by its very nature accelerate the pace of AI, since the former must themselves operate on mechanist principles, and Machine Perception promises us what is perhaps the most direct point of entry into the simulation of the brain's higher cognitive functions.[84] Most striking of all is the authors' enthusiastic declaration that 'Much of our sense of excitement about the proposed project stems from this biological paradigm.'[85] The great danger posed by such a picture, however, is whether the prose of the theory has created a seriously distorted conception of both the problem and the methods whereby it is being slowly resolved, and has thus encouraged some AI-scientists to focus on an inappropriate approach *only because* of this picture, when what is needed is some form of lateral thinking which, by definition, is freed from preconceived expectations and assumptions. Would their sense of excitement diminish in any way if some alternative and less glamorous — for example, applied mathematical — framework was substituted for this Promethean vision? And more to the point, would their interest flag, or would their results improve?

It all depends on the force of the heuristic model, which in turn depends on the cogency of the neurophysiological theory on which it rests. For McCormick *et al.* long to develop 'an "inferotemporal cortex machine" which examines the low-level world model with an attention-driven spotlight or window', and even though 'at this time, neither the physiological nor the image processing fields are sufficiently developed for higher-level analysis', nevertheless the model suggests an approach which will 'determine their probable input requirements', since these can be patterned on the much better known preprocessing operations of biological visual systems.[86] But does the brain contain an 'infero-temporal cortex' in the higher stages of the visual system, as yet undetected but almost certain to be there if the picture is to be trusted? And without this premiss, what becomes of the justification for basing our initial research on the 'better known preprocessing operations' of the retina?

The fallacy on which this argument rests is one of the direct results of the Inferential theory of perception. The fact that we are only able to see because of the electrical signals which are passed along the nerve fibres from the retina to the visual cortex in no way entails that these logically distinct *conceptual* levels can in any way be conflated, as is typically done by referring to these signals as the 'information' or 'data' which the brain 'interprets' or 'decodes'. Thus, even a putatively harmless question such as 'How does the brain recognise that the object is a table from the fragmentary information it has received?' seduces us into pursuing the confused reductionist route which leads ultimately into the Inferential fallacy. For, of course, the brain *recognises* nothing; it is *we* who recognise that the object is a table, even though we can only glimpse a corner of it. If asked why we have assumed that it is a table, we would no doubt refer to our experience of what tables look like; but the question itself is seriously askew, for while we may say that it just looks like a table, or that that is what 'table' means, it makes little sense to speak of *assuming* that it is a table in an environment outside of the psychology laboratories. The fact that our perceptual judgements can always be falsified does not entail that perception is irrevocably uncertain: only that perceptual judgements — short of the bedrock judgements of perception (for example, in normal lighting, etc.) — are defeasible. To express a doubt in relation to the latter, however, is not to question the validity of the 'unconscious inferences on which the perception is based', but rather, to demonstrate one's failure to grasp the meaning of the terms employed.

Likewise, if asked why the figures in the Ames room appear to have such different sizes, our answer must proceed by describing the peculiar structure of the room. That is, question and answer must operate on the same conceptual level. The obvious objection to this, however, is that it fails to account for the phenomenon of psychological conditioning which Gregory explores. For if we pursue the above line of argument, we shall be forced to conclude that the reason why Zulus do not share our illusion is simply because the figures look the same size to them: that life in a 'circular culture' apparently renders one immune to 'rectangular' illusions. But, of course, the problem which interests the psychologist is precisely *why* the Ames room should look so different to the two cultures. The difficult point to grasp here is that while our answer to this latter question must have nothing to do with any putative 'tacit assumptions' which are 'stored in their brains', this is not to deny that there may not be some significant neurological difference between ourselves and the Zulus, or that there might even be a discernible causal link between the Zulus' conditioning and the structure of their visual cortex. Only that, even if such causal factors were discovered, this would still not license the logical violation of the conceptual demarcation between neurophysiology and perception, and thus, still not explain why the figures 'look the same size' to them. A coherent explanation of the relation between conditioning and visual experience is one that must, like an aesthetic explanation of our enjoyment of a painting, proceed *on the relevant conceptual level*: in this case, one which is confined solely to the level of their perceptions.

In similar fashion, Colin Blakemore raises the intriguing question in 'The Baffled Brain' of how we are able to recognise, with little or no hesitation, such a vast number of different faces. Even a sympathetic reader of the present argument may still want to press home the question, 'How, in strictly causal terms, is such an extraordinary feat accomplished?' But to search in the brain for a store of 'memory-pictures', suitably 'decoded' into 'neural patterns', is to fall victim to the confusions outlined above.[87] Rather, the short answer to Blakemore's problem is simply — in his own terms — that the axons of geniculate cells are passed along the optical nerves into the primary visual cortex and somehow from there into other cortical areas on the sides of the brain and to the superior colliculus. The composition of the neural networks whereby this process is accomplished may be 'fantastically complicated', but it is a mystery which science is slowly penetrating. Blakemore feels, however, that the mystery here is how 'the visual system [is] able to discriminate and recognize the featural differences'.[88] Yet it is the subject — and not his visual cortex! — who discriminates and recognises featural differences. As Blakemore explains, 'Human perception depends ultimately on activity within the nerve cells of the brain.'[89] But the causal conditions of perception are not themselves the perceptions. Penfield's stimulation experiments on the cerebral cortex made his patients see flashing, coloured shapes in their visual field: not in their occipital lobes. For, as Blakemore himself points out in regard to the sensation of seeing stars when struck on the skull: 'The cause of these stars is in the brain but the stars themselves are just as much part of the perceptual world as real stars are.'[90] But Blakemore prefaces his survey of recent developments in neurophysiology with the Inferential premiss that perceptions are hypotheses, and it is this which leads him to assign such cognitive abilities to the brain as the discrimination of visual features.

The ultimate fallacy here, therefore, is that of assigning the neurophysiologist's inferences to the brain itself. This hardly means that there is no mystery to be solved in the mechanics of vision: only that we must be careful not to violate the logical barrier between perception and physiology when formulating it. The problem is: how do we describe these processes without introducing concepts from the cognitive level of perception which set us off on the irrevocably fruitless search for pseudo-inferential neurological operations? Despite the great advances that have been made over the past few decades in our understanding of how the initial stimuli in the primary sensory areas trigger off an electrochemical change in the receptors, and how these impulses are passed along the nerve fibres and across synapses into the appropriate primary cortical area where they evoke a sharp potential change, we still seem, on the above picture, no further advanced as far as our understanding of the vital issue is concerned: how is all this translated into 'conscious perception'? This is the glaring lacuna in our knowledge with which we began the preceding section: the 'mysterious way [in which] the retinal picture appears in conscious perception'. But the purpose of the foregoing critique is to bring us to the point where we can see that the gulf that yawns here is conceptual, not empirical: a result of the confused attempt to reduce perception to its causes.

Such a *logically* impossible undertaking results in the conclusion that, somehow, 'the reconstitution of the perceived image is due to the self-conscious mind that scans and reads out from the appropriate feature-recognition modules of the visual areas'.[91] The feeling is that something must be *seen*, and something must do the *seeing* at the physical level. For the only way to make sense of the mystery created by transgressing the logical boundary between perception and neurophysiology seems to be by first postulating some form of 'reconstituted image' in the brain, and then an appropriate faculty to 'scan and read' these 'pictures'. To achieve this, the impulses must be treated as coded pieces of information, and the neural routes become 'vertically organised information channels'.[92] Reconstituted images must then be made up of these tiny bits of information, but the question remains, where exactly are they reassembled? Our failure to discover any traces of these neural phenomena is perforce interpreted as an indication of the brain's complexity, rather than a symptom of our conceptual confusion. For without this picture of the brain's unfathomable higher cognitive functions to guide us, there is little reason to proceed on the assumption that at the more tractable 'preprocesser level, existing physiological models offer sufficient detail for substantial guidance'.[93] Were the slowness of sequential processing the sole rationale for constructing cellular logic arrays, some might well begin to question the wisdom of investing more resources in a potentially quixotic enterprise. But parallel processing is supposed to simulate, not just the 'strategy short-cuts', but the entire neocortical columnar processing mechanisms of biological visual systems. The two sides of this *circulus in probando* are thus mutually reinforcing: the Inferential hypothesis justifies the premiss that biological visual preprocessing can be simulated mechanically, and the claimed feasibility of the latter research provides further justification for the Inferential hypothesis.

It is important that we are clear about the nature of the philosophical objection which is being raised here. If you consider the number of cells into which an ordinary television frame tessellates, it seems clear that some sort of parallel processing will be needed to avoid the type of problems which would undermine any attempt to develop an advanced computer chess program using a straightforward 'brute force' searching technique.[94] Yet there is a serious tension between the cost of using sophisticated microprocessors in each cell versus the poor speed afforded by low-power arrays. Whether or not the type of visual analyser (consisting of a stack of array and interconnection elements) envisaged by McCormick *et al.*, or the CLIP 4 ('cellular logic image processor') large-scale integrated circuit array developed by Michael Duff offers a more suitable type of image-processing technology on which to construct Pattern Recognition systems is an obviously legitimate and important empirical matter which will only be settled by the rigours of laboratory testing and the demands of commercial feasibility.[95] What cannot be allowed, however, is the misguided attempt to prejudice the issue by bolstering the visual analyser in the manner tacitly adopted by McCormick *et al.* with the claim that it will satisfy the dictates of biological simulation. And yet, in their defence, it could justly be claimed that this is nothing more than the logical consequence of the Inferential theory. Once again, then, we are forced to scrutinise the cogency of the framework: this time, at what is clearly its bedrock premiss.

The McCormick proposal is the result of working backwards from the initial assumption that the higher cognitive functions of the visual system are inferential to the fundamental assumption that, even before we consider the stages of preprocessing and feature extraction, we must develop a prosthetic apparatus which will supply the program's induction algorithm with the appropriate data. In other words, the Mechanical Perception Thesis demands a device which will translate images into information in such a way that this can be suitably encoded and subsequently decoded. We arrive, therefore, at the significance of describing electronic signals as *bits of information*, in both the ordinary and the specialised computer senses of the term? Such a theme is apparently licensed by Lettvin, Maturana, McCulloch and Pitts's influential theory that the frog's retina must analyse the images it has received before it transmits this abstracted information to the visual centres, since the enormous number of receptors (approximately one million) involved makes it highly unlikely that the frog's brain could handle so much information in its raw state.⁹⁶ How, the mechanist wonders, could there be any philosophical objection to the supposition that we can simulate, if not the frog's, at any rate the lamprey's 'preprocessing' system?

This seemingly innocuous question conceals, however, a serious conceptual transgression. For what we have now been asked to accept — under the bewitching influence of information theory — is that a *cognitive ability* can be assigned to a ganglion! What Lettvin *et al.* did establish is that they could distinguish five anatomically distinct types of ganglion cells in the frog's retina, each of which responds to a specific range of light changes or moving contours. But they merely *assumed* that these receptors receive and transmit *information* in the ordinary sense of the term, and thus that each group of ganglion cells must perform some quasi-cognitive function (which they sought to identify by registering the reaction of a specific set of cells to observed objects and light changes). Without this premiss they would only have been entitled to conclude that these receptors are a form of signal switch which are only activated by a narrow band of impulses: they no more *analyse* these electrical impulses than a plant's chlorophyll analyses the photons which activate its photosynthetic processes. To be sure, we say that the frog, unlike a Venus' flytrap, sees its prey; but the frog sees the fly *because* the changing contrast detectors respond to sudden movements, and not as a result of the detectors' hypothetical 'analysis' of these movements as the probable traces of a fly. The temptation to construe the mechanics of the frog's retina in these 'pre-inferential' terms only arises from — indeed, must arise from — the prior assumption that the frog's 'infero-temporal cortex', no less than our own, lies ever ready to receive information on which to exercise its higher cognitive functions. Remove this picture and what you are left with is a neurological theory about the causal links which occur in the frog's visual system: a theory which, when confined to the physical level at which it operates, is solely concerned with mapping the electrical reactions of the various groups of cells onto changes in the frog's visual field and/or its motor reactions.

The case is not quite so straightforward, however, when we turn to the mechanist version of this argument. For here we have to deal not only with the considerable authority which the argument enjoys from its neurophysiological precedent, but even more importantly, with the obvious fact that the great utility of computers lies in our ability to store and manipulate information in them electronically. This in turn reflects back on the neurophysicalist theory, lending vital support to the thesis that the retina is actively engaged in the abstraction of relevant information from the multitude of sensations with which it is bombarded. To the mechanist this whole issue will thus appear a relatively trivial matter: in the tessellation of an image we first transform the picture into a number of small cells which, for the sake of illustration, can all be treated as either black or white, and then assign a binary coding of 0 or 1 to each of these cells. Even if this does not constitute an adequate simulation of how the frog's eye transmits information to the frog's brain, such a process nevertheless represents a clear-cut example of the manner in which a photographic image can be decomposed into strings of information which can be easily manipulated by computers. From there the way is directly open to the far more challenging task of extracting a recognisable set of features from this store of information: the real hurdle at which most Pattern Recognition systems fail.

The fact remains, however, that we are still being asked to accept — on the basis of the neuro-physicalist picture — that a *cognitive ability* can be assigned, this time not to a ganglion, but rather, to a 'visual analyser'.[97] We need not enter here into the finer complexities of 'image preprocessing', but it is important that we acquire some feel for the type of operation which occurs at this stage of the system. In practice, most commercial devices employ a straightforward thresholding technique, in which the signal from every single pixel is examined to see if it is above or below an established threshold, and assigned a binary code accordingly. But obviously such a system must be severely restricted, and thus of comparatively little interest to the AI-scientist.[98] For, disregarding the complications introduced by colour, the fact remains that not even a monochrome system exhibits a stark black-and-white pattern. But the shift to a system which distinguishes between shades of grey involves a formidable combinatorial explosion. An ordinary picture of 256 × 256 pixels, for example, will on average have approximately 256 grey-levels, yielding 16 million signals for every picture. Moreover, one of the first problems which arises in Pattern Recognition is that the images under observation are rarely pristine, with the result that a method must be devised to extract distinct edges from the commonly fuzzy data transmitted. To accomplish this, some kind of computation which will highlight the contours of 'noisy' edges is clearly demanded. By working from the existing brightness signals, we attempt to generalise and idealise brightness contrasts in order to identify independent edges. (This might be provided by a 'point-spread function' which calculates average brightness arrays from the image in order to sharpen the contrast between subtle or irregular alterations in light intensity.)

The important point for our purposes is that, whatever the type of 'filtering' function employed, we need some form of computational method to intensify brightness changes from the disarray of signals transmitted. The Mechanical Perception Thesis trades, however, on the crucial shift that, from the premiss that we can refine and store images using the above algebraic method, we can draw the much stronger conclusion that it is the stack of array and interconnection elements which analyses and transmits the information-bits to the system's (hypercolumnar) induction algorithm (the sum total of which constitutes machine vision). With just this cognitive chink to begin with, we can then swiftly return to the full Mechanist Thesis, for the one thing which a 'pre-inferential' inception most obviously calls for is a higher inferential completion. But in a crucial sense the information thus stored lies forever beyond the reach of a computer's 'comprehension', for the very reason that to attribute such capacities to a computer would indeed be to credit it with cognitive abilities! Herein lies the start to the slippery slope which will ultimately result in the removal of the scare quotes from 'computer's "comprehension"'. We can no more attribute *our ability* to encode the signal from a pixel to a computer, however, than we can interpret the program's self-modifying induction algorithm as a set of 'mechanical rules' which the computer 'follows'. For in each case we would be compelled to violate the logical demarcation which exists between the concepts of *normative action* versus *mechanical operation.*[99]

Not surprisingly, the mechanist cannot see the force of this objection, little appreciating that to violate the logical grammar of 'analyse' in the manner proposed is to present the core of the Mechanist Thesis in such a way that all the subsequent arguments function as corollaries rather than proofs. To be sure, this may seem to render the theory impregnable to philosophical scrutiny, but it is the protection afforded by circularity rather than hypothetico-deductive rigour. Rather than assuming the very point of contention from the outset, a sound argument is one that bases its conclusions on the evidence provided rather than the dictates of *a priori* consistency. But the power of metaphors is such that this distinction is all too easy to misconstrue. Still, the mechanist might insist that this criticism is vitiated by the very point on which it turns: namely that we can only appreciate the cognitive nature of the system's 'preprocessing' stages in light of the program's higher 'inferential' operations. The criticism presented here might thus apply to the type of crude photo-electric sensors that are used in automatic doors, but it ignores the role of the inferences based on the program's stored 'world model' which provides the essence of machine vision. The only way to terminate this dispute, therefore, will be by examining the algorithms themselves: the putative 'hypotheses' on which all the hopes of the Inferential theory and the Mechanical Perception Thesis must ride.

4. The Dispossession of the Mechanist Monopoly

Undoubtedly one of the most suitable candidates for our case study is the work by L.G. Roberts which was touched on in the preceding section. Roberts's program suffers from several notable defects, not the least of which are the crudity of the models which it can handle (namely, cubes, rectangular wedges, and hexagonal prisms) and the artificiality of the highlighted illumination on which it depends. Yet for our purposes these are assets, given that they simplify the salient technical points that must be covered. Its chief importance to Pattern Recognition — and thus to this paper — however, lies in the 'paradigm' which it established for the Mechanical Perception Thesis: the so-called 'model of perception as a cycle of four processes: discovering cues, activating a hypothesis, testing the hypothesis, and inferring the consequences' which Mackworth describes (cf. section 3). Furthermore, it has the special significance for us that, as Mackworth points out, it established this paradigm in a manner which is highly reminiscent of the Helmholtz/Gregory theory of perception. Indeed, in a crucial sense, Roberts's program marks the emergence of the Inferential theory as the *primum mobile* of the Mechanical Perception Thesis. For on the accepted interpretation, Roberts's program successfully performed three vital inferential steps: it made assumptions, tested hypotheses, and drew conclusions on the basis of these results. But before we embrace this version of the Mechanist Thesis, let us first consider each of the program operations which underlie these putative cognitive abilities in turn.

Although he makes no explicit mention of Gregory's theory, Roberts certainly takes great pains at the outset of 'Machine Perception of Three-Dimensional Solids' to present his own interpretation of the significance of his program within an Inferential framework. Thus he argues that, from the 'large volume of psychophysical research on human depth perception and shape recognition' that has been performed, we know that 'the perception of depth in a monocular picture is based completely upon the assumptions of the observer. Some of the assumptions are about the nature of the real world and some are based on the observer's familiarity with the objects.'[100] Admittedly, he does not formally commit himself to the premiss that these 'assumptions' occur in the brain, nor does he actually state that the assumptions which the program adopts constitute simulations of these neurophysiological hypotheses, but in the account which follows both of these themes are tacitly understood. This is particularly clear in the brief remarks on the reasoning underlying his theory with which he prefaces his paper: 'The perception of solid objects', he maintains, 'is a process which can be based on the properties of three-dimensional transformations and the laws of nature.' Hence, 'By carefully utilizing these properties, a procedure has been developed which not only identifies objects, but also determines their orientation and position in space.'[101] Even more importantly, it is precisely this theme which Roberts returns to when he concludes at the end of his paper that, whatever significance his program might have for Pattern Recognition, 'The biggest benefit of this investigation ... is an increased understanding of the possible processes of visual perception.'[102]

Roberts begins his report of the two stages in his program (there are, in fact, two distinct programs) with an account of the various 'perceptual assumptions' which the program employs. The first is that the pictures scanned by the computer are photographs of the real world, and thus, that the images are perspective transformations of three-dimensional fields. It is next assumed that these images consist of solid objects, and that these well-defined objects are either a transformation of a preconceived model or are composed of such parts. Finally, the first program employs a 'support theorem' which assumes that every object is supported by another object or by a ground plane. The point of these 'assumptions' is plain enough: they are intended to enable the system to compute which model and transformation will best represent a given object in an image. That is, the program attempts to map models onto figures by transforming model points into picture points; if a model and transformation can be found that are isomorphic with the picture lines and points, the program will register those lines and points as a picture of the figure which is given by the transformation of the model, thereby identifying the object.

It is worth pausing on the significance of this argument before we proceed to examine the mechanics of the programs themselves, however, for the problem is that, to speak of 'assumptions' in this vague way leaves it unclear who should properly be accredited with their possession. Roberts tells us that 'Without these assumptions [a] picture is just another two-dimensional image, whereas with them the human is rarely confused about the depth relationships represented in the picture.'[103] But, disregarding the cogency of the conception of perception presented here, are we meant to attribute the same ability to the computer? Boden leaves us in no doubt in her summary of Roberts's work about who should be acknowledged as the bearer of these assumptions: 'Roberts' program', she explains, 'assumes that the world (the target domain) is made up of three classes of object, occurring either singly or merged to form compound objects.'[104] It is on the basis of these assumptions that Roberts's program 'could recognize partially occluded objects even though they were largely hidden by others lying in front of them'.[105] The mechanist picture operating here, therefore, is that, unless the computer first assumes that the image it is scanning is a simple or compound object (whether partially hidden or otherwise), it will not be able to grasp which particular object it is which it sees.

The naïve reaction to this argument is, of course, that a *program* can no more 'assume' that an image being scanned is a cube than the frog's retina 'assumes' that the sudden movement in its visual field is a fly. In each case, however, there must be some powerful inducement which has led its advocates to overlook the many complications which such a theme entails, and it is our duty to clarify and, if possible, undermine the fallacy on which this picture rests. We can begin to understand some of the factors which have prompted this presupposition in Roberts's claim that

> When an object is so well hidden that a dimension cannot be determined, this dimension must be estimated. An example of

this case would be when only the top of a building is visible over another. The first assumption we make is that the object is supported by the ground plane. But a second assumption is needed to place the object, and the program assumes that the hidden object just touches the object in front. This is not a very good assumption, but there are no good assumptions.[106]

No better example could be found of the manner in which the Inferential theory and the Mechanical Perception Thesis feed off one another. We have already seen, however, that there are strong grounds to question this way of describing our perception of a partially concealed object; not surprisingly, therefore, the situation is no less strained in the case of the program.

What Roberts really means here is that the program runs through the various models stored in its knowledge base until (if) it arrives at a set of points which can account for the visible properties of the object. In the case of highly occluded figures there may be no alternative to a simple 'brute force' approach, and thus it would appear that it is because of the element of uncertainty in this relatively random approach that the searching technique is down-graded to the status of 'assumption'. But whatever the cause, it seems clear from the wording of the above passage that, far from being the program, it was Roberts himself who assumed that if a partially occluded line descends in the same direction it will reach either another object or else the ground plane (in order to calculate, using a set of encoded 'heuristic rules',[107] the three-dimensional length of edges and the angles between conjoined lines; these rules might be of the form, 'If line α proceeds in direction x to the ground plane it will meet line β and the angle between them will be ø', or 'If figure α is a cube supporting a rectangular wedge β then the base edges of β must lie in the plane of the upper surface of α'). We shall consider the mathematical nature of the operations carried out in more detail below; the point to see here is merely how misleading it can be to speak of 'assumptions' at all in this context.

So too, to speak of the program's 'assuming' (or as Mackworth puts it, 'believing'[108]) 'that the world consists of cubes, wedges, and prisms' seems a distinctly peculiar — and obviously loaded — way to describe the fact that the program's matching algorithm only ranges over a domain consisting of three distinct models. Even to speak of these as 'models' of objects betrays a significant mechanist tension. Boden explains how the program's 'concept or schematic "model" of a cuboid is stored in the data structure in the form of an abstract geometrical definition, which describes all the surfaces, edges, and corners of a cuboid without committing itself to any particular size or shape'.[109] But disregarding the covert assumption that the program 'possesses concepts', or that the program is capable of 'withholding judgement' on matters pertaining to size and shape, we should focus on the further assumption that the 'abstract geometrical definition' constitutes a 'model' of a cube. But how can a *model* 'describe' anything? Boden is forced into this position by the fact that, as we shall see below, all the knowledge base really contains are lists of co-ordinates of end-points from which the lines of the various figures can be mapped. To transform this into a model the mechanist has no choice but to treat these matrices as 'descriptions' of the parts of an object. This move has the virtue that it meshes with the Inferential theme that 'although the world cannot be paradoxical (or ambiguous) perception can be — showing that it is a kind of description',[110] but it leaves us with an extremely unusual type of model: one which no one familiar with cubes, wedges, and prisms would be able to recognise; apart, of course, from the system!

What the matrices actually provide us with, however — together with the equations for plotting them — are rules for the construction of a set of figures which are isomorphic with cubes, wedges and prisms. They are certainly not algebraic 'descriptions' of the latter geometrical concepts, nor strictly speaking, do these rules provide us with *models of cubes*, as these might be geometrically defined. The confusion operating here is similar to that which treats the equations of co-ordinate geometry as descriptions of classical geometrical configurations, when what they really constitute are the construction of a new set of concepts which thus extend the family of related concepts in geometry (itself a family-resemblance term). The 'cubes' constructed by these algebraic matrices may share many important features with cubes as ordinarily understood (for example, they yield figures with six congruent square faces, eight vertices, and twelve edges), but the meaning of the term 'cube' can only be understood in terms of the rules of the system in which it is defined. Hence, in much the same way as originally occurred with the inception of analytic geometry the family-resemblance concept 'cube' has been extended with these algebraic matrices.[111] But the mechanist cannot accept this

Computer Vision or Mechanist Myopia? 253

point if he is to satisfy the demands of the archetypal picture of perception as a mapping between 'external object' and 'internal representation': in this case, between picture and model (cf. section 2).

This mounting perplexity must soon lead one to suspect that it is not the program making the various assumptions outlined above, but rather, the Mechanist Thesis itself; for unless *we assume* that the computer recognises these images as objects, we shall not then be able to make sense of the subsequent claim that the program recognises cubes, wedges and prisms. In essence, the mechanist argument is that it is only because the program assumes that the image it is confronted with is one of the three objects stored in its 'world knowledge' that it is able to identify, by trial and error, which particular object is being scanned. And since the program is able to pick out any of the three objects from a wide assortment of photographs with considerable accuracy, Roberts's method offers a promising start for the Mechanical Perception Thesis, if not for Pattern Recognition proper. To be sure, the program's cognitive foundation may be extremely limited, but these are none the less *bona fide* inferences based on recognisable assumptions. The philosophical issue which this raises, however, is whether this is not an implicit vicious circle; for the success of the program can only be defined in Inferential terms if the premiss that the program makes assumptions has already been accepted. Certainly there can be no suggestion here of the system's *seeing* an image and then testing whether it corresponds to its model of a cube if such an argument is intended to be read as an objective report on the opening stages of the system, from which the proposed mechanist conclusions are supposed to follow ineluctably. But without this framework firmly in place, all that we find when we look at the nature of the 'assumptions' we are supposed to be dealing with are mappings between the program's 'models' and line drawings of the original photograph, which are processed by a differential operator and then tested against a set of lines and end-points drawn from the knowledge base to see how well they correlate with the differential picture. Does this in any way constitute, as the mechanist contends, the essence of (mechanical) inference based on the program's various 'interpretations'?

Significantly, when Roberts describes the opening phase of his program he makes no reference to any of these 'assumptions', nor is there any mention of the program's putative 'discovery of cues' or the 'activation and testing of hypotheses'. Yet it is hardly surprising that Roberts should have abandoned the beguiling themes of mechanist prose as soon as he switches to explaining the mechanics of his system; for these could only serve to obscure the true mathematical nature of the operations whereby the program proceeds. According to Boden, on the other hand, the first stage in Roberts's system

> requires an analysis or structural description of the picture in terms that are relevant to the particular representational system, or theory of mapping, involved. That is, the 'parts' of the picture must be *cues* that relate to the target domain in ways defined by the inner conceptual scheme. It follows that 'parts' (like 'cues') is a subjective, or intentional, notion and is not equivalent to purely physical features of the picture.[112]

This must be the case because, according to the Inferential theory, colours and shapes 'are "data" or "cues" used for inferring depth and form by active brain processes'.[113] No less significant, however, is the fact that Boden fails to provide a concrete guide as to how this occurs, relying instead on the reiterated Inferential assumption that 'From a strictly objective point of view, a picture just *is* marks on paper — and wholly uninformative to boot. From a subjective (interpretative) point of view, it may or may not contain lines, or colored regions, or angles of various sorts.'[114] Thus, it is not the first part of Roberts's program, but rather the first part of the mechanist interpretation which makes this demand. All that the first program itself reveals on closer inspection is a complex filtering process in which there is no semblance of the cognitive 'analysis' of the 'subjective, or intentional' 'cues' which the Mechanist Thesis demands.

The immediate problem which Roberts faced was twofold: first, to transform the photograph (with a photomultiplier and converter) into a digitised matrix which could be stored in the computer (requiring approximately half a million bits for one raster), and then the much more difficult task of establishing the essential edges, lines and junctions in the computer display of the photograph. The mechanist-inspired rationale for this approach is that biological perception depends to an inordinate extent on the recognition of boundaries; the real reason why this seemed a sensible point at which to begin was simply that the boundaries of objects manifest a sharp discontinuity in brightness intensity. To compute the edges from this Roberts used a differential operator to produce a tentative line-drawing of the stored image. (This applies two separate functions which compute the intensity values of the picture and then enhance any intensity differences — much in the manner described in the preceding section — in order to sharpen edges and reduce background noise.) The next step is to select a suitable set of picture lines to co-ordinate with the stored matrix. By a multistep process which calculates whether points lie on a given line, a set of feature points together with the direction of the lines which pass through them is built up. Then, using a simple threshold technique, neighbouring points that lie on the same line can be connected and stray points eliminated, thereby filtering out much of the background noise.

The result of this process is a preliminary line drawing in which large gaps or multiple interconnections may appear. To tidy this up the unwanted lines are removed by a technique which leaves the overall topology of the drawing intact, providing us with a structural outline which can be filled out by joining up the various line-fragments using a sequential least-mean-square error-fitting routine. (The solution, in essence, is to calculate the best coefficients for the line equation $ax + by = c$ by working backwards whenever the error threshold is reached in order to decrease the angle between the computed line and the existing line segments.) Small line-segments can thus be joined to longer line-segments, extraneous short line-segments can be merged or removed, and the co-ordinates of end-points can be calculated and revised. The process is still not complete, however, for it remains to join the still unconnected line-segments that lie on the same plane, remove those which fall below a threshold value, and eliminate any superfluous junctions. Ideally, the final result will be a perspective projection of the surface boundaries of a three dimensional object with visible width and no two-dimensional markings; in practice, a large proportion of the finished line-drawings fail to meet the second program's brightness intensity threshold. 'The entire picture-to-line-drawing process', Roberts confesses, 'is not optimal but works for simple pictures. It has several useful parts; the differentiation, the feature point extraction, and the mean-square line fitting are the best parts.'[115] Its main import is that it marks the discovery of how small line-segments and junctions can be exploited by recursive algorithms which use the data provided by filtered pixels to calculate the length and direction of discontinuous or partially occluded lines in a three-dimensional drawing.

There is no more room in this preliminary mathematical reduction for the 'cognitive analysis of structural cues', therefore, than there would be had we examined the mechanics of the CAT-scan. But perhaps the hopes for the Mechanical Perception Thesis can be revived at the next stage of the program: 'the *picture interpreter*' which, as Boden describes it, 'interprets the line representation in 3D terms'.[116] As Boden conceives it, 'the picture interpreter ... starts off with a (description representing a) pattern of lines, and has to find the approved polygons in it'.[117] That is, the program searches for a transformed model which, together with the transform, completely accounts for the group of connected lines in the object. Stated in these terms it should be clear, however, that the program will immediately come up against a serious obstacle: to calculate every possible transform and projection using a blind search technique would create a completely unmanageable combinatorial explosion. To compensate for this some sort of search strategy must clearly be implemented. In the first stage of the three-dimensional display program which Roberts developed to deal with this problem he produced what he refers to as 'a three-dimensional description' of the objects projected in the line drawing. But 'description' as we have just seen really means a list of end-point co-ordinates, one pair for each line. From this data are produced (by matching end-point pairs with line-block and point-block lists) a set of polygons whose boundaries and area are traced by calculating the sum of their exterior angles at each vertex. This also serves to establish how many sides the polygon has and whether it is convex or concave (in Roberts's program provision was only made for convex polygons with 3, 4, or 6 sides).

The next step is to match these polygon structures with those matrices stored in the knowledge base that have a topologically equivalent set of points. On the mechanist interpretation this is translated as the application and testing to hypotheses: 'once a model has been addressed by cues', Boden explains, 'it can then actively construct hypotheses that lead the program to look for further, confirmatory, cues'. For example, 'The cuboid model provisionally matches the approved polygon in the cue with one of the abstractly defined cuboid faces, and predicts a series of topologically equivalent pairs of points between model and picture.'[118] The premiss operating here is that 'Ultimately, matching "establishes an interpretation" of input data, where an interpretation is the correspondence between models represented in a computer and the external world of phenomena and objects.'[119] This, of course, uses 'interpretation' in the model-theoretic sense; but even if you permit the covert attempt to blur the lines between interpretation as ordinarily understood in perceptual contexts and this technical notion of 'interpretation', you still cannot confuse our ability to program the computer to process a sequence of matrices with some intentional decision performed by the computer.[120] But if you remove the anthropomorphic overtones from this picture all that you are left with is a relatively straightforward bottom-up/top-down matching operation which is used, not to test hypotheses or draw 'unconscious' inferences, but less prosaically, to compute the results of a sequence of cross-mappings.[121] Once again a mean-square error technique is pressed into service: this time to calculate the optimal transformation matrix onto which the points can be mapped.[122] Those matrices which may match the picture topologically but cannot fit exactly without deformation are eliminated. Once a matrix has been found that falls within the threshold it is checked against the picture to see whether the remainder of the matrix fits the external boundaries of the object in the picture. Any matrix which produces points outside these boundaries is immediately discarded; those retained can be used to represent all or part of the object.

There are still several operations to be performed (namely, the matrix can be duplicated, stored, displayed, and modified), but since these do not impinge in quite the same manner on the Mechanist Thesis, we can bypass these latter stages. The one remaining aspect of the program which we cannot afford to ignore, however, is the case where the transform and model are used to represent only part of an object. For from this Roberts developed a method for mapping what he and those following him refer to as 'compound objects', which has given rise to a compositional theory of biological/mechanical perception. Once again we can see the unexpected conceptual strains which the Mechanist Thesis imposes on our ordinary concepts. To speak of, for example, a table as a 'compound object' is really only the surface of a bold new theory of perception, tailored to meet the peculiar type of recursive perceptual operations performed by the system. Interestingly (and perhaps significantly), it bears a striking resemblance to the compositional theory of meaning and the generative theory of understanding which have recently become so popular in linguistics and the philosophy of language. Reverting to the problem raised by Blakemore which we examined in section 3, we might just as easily ask, how is it possible to 'recognise' an infinite number of objects when the brain can only store a finite number of models? The answer to this conundrum could only be provided by a compositional theory of perception, and fortunately, the Mechanical Perception Thesis now lies ready at hand to provide an insight into how this might be accomplished.

'Compound objects' are formed by joining together two or more simple objects in such a way that adjacent models share a common front plane. (For example, A parallelepiped can be decomposed into a prism abutting rectangular wedges.) In this manner complex unapproved polygons can be broken down into a set of simple polygons, each of which can be mapped onto a model and transform. The external boundary polygon must obviously be left intact, since it provides the framework for any subsequent decompositional analysis. Internal lines, however, can be deleted, introduced, or merged according to the set of construction rules which are used to plot the simple polygons. When all of the internal lines have been connected and there are no superfluous lines left over in the matrix the simple polygon is registered. When the entire process has been completed the matrix can be rotated, allowing us to view the 3D object from any angle (with the appropriate 'hidden lines' deleted). Thus the hope was born that, with a suitable set of matrices to begin with, future programs could be developed which would be able to recognise far more sophisticated scenes. The Mechanist Thesis also received a fillip, for the prospect of building complex scene analysis programs seems to promise the eventual fulfilment of its evolutionary conception of mechanical perception. Only the neurophysiologist was left to suffer for these fancies, for along with his other charges, he had now been left with the hopeless task of searching for the brain's store of basic models (suitably encoded, of course) and the bottom-up/top-down neurological operations from which all complex perception is built up.

It would be unfair to hold Roberts responsible for these developments; if anything, he himself was merely the victim of the confusion so central to the Mechanist Thesis that what begins as a simulation can end up as a prototype. From the mechanist point of view expressed by M.B. Clowes the paradigm established by Roberts's program 'integrates varieties of inference evocative of problem solving with a view of perception as based upon cues'.[123] Yet immediately after this Clowes quite rightly points out that 'Without doubt the metaphors that are invoked by "reasoning", "inference", "cues", may be displaced by others, or more likely, may come to be underpinned by computational forms more able to do them justice.'[124] I find myself in complete agreement with the first part of this sentiment, but I doubt that Clowes appreciates its full significance (or the serious tension which it creates in his review). For, as far as the mechanist is concerned, these are not *metaphors*!

Clowes's attitude is plainly reminiscent of the pragmatic outlook so often demonstrated by scientists and mathematicians: the value of metaphors is entirely heuristic, and thus expendable. The diehard mechanist, on the other hand, is a rather more dogmatic creature; he has an equally profound interest in the success of the venture, but primarily in so far as this can be seized on as a vindication of his 'philosophical' thesis. It is this obduracy, however, which will ultimately lead to the demise of his theory. Hitherto, the persistence of the Mechanist Thesis has depended above all else on the endorsement which it has received from AI-scientists. Sensing the interest in their work stimulated by the Thesis, and intrigued by the possibility of resolving classical philosophical disputes in their laboratories, they were more than willing to embrace the Mechanist Metaphor as a working hypothesis: but only on approval. For the march of AI is far too rapid to remain fettered to an outmoded metaphor, and especially if that metaphor that should begin to distort, and thence obstruct, the development of the science. Unfortunately, the crux of the Mechanist Thesis is that it *cannot* embrace these trends; rather, it is forced, in the manner of any preconceived world-view, to adapt any new developments so that they fit into its framework. Without the sanction afforded by the scientists, however, the Mechanist Thesis will quickly witness the erosion of its appeal. And Clowes's aside — which is so worrying for the mechanist precisely because it is so casual — clearly marks the sounding of the Mechanist Metaphor's death knell.

5. Machine Visions

There are really two sides to this critique; which is to say, the removal of conceptual confusions may be a sufficient reward in itself, but it can also have valuable practical consequences. This is not just a case of prising scientists away from the forlorn quest for a misleading metaphor; in this case there are important commercial interests at stake as well. It is always difficult to anticipate what off-shoots will sprout from a new scientific enterprise, but for the time being the primary importance of machine vision lies in its industrial applications. Machine vision is already widely used in various engineering, pharmaceutical, and high-risk industries. These systems are now widely employed for routine inspection checks, and thus for product quality control. Flexible automation has also reached the point where it can play a useful — if limited — role in assembly operations, by monitoring conveyors in order to fix the orientation of parts for robot grippers to manipulate. With the promising commercial possibilities that are swiftly emerging, it is obviously as crucial for companies to understand how the new technology can serve them as how it cannot. Those looking for a surrogate plant manager who will combine creativity with round-the-clock vigilance will be sadly disappointed. On the other hand, those who have become resigned to intransigent problems in areas such as inspection or guidance may be pleasantly surprised.

The most exciting prospect opened up by machine vision clearly lies in the implementation of Pattern Recognition programs that are linked to CAD and Expert Systems in the development of Robotics. Forgoing any mention of the distant vistas which knowledge engineers find so captivating, we can safely say that, for the immediate future, the problem will be to design a flexible automation system which can pick out parts that have been randomly scattered in a bin or objects in an uncontrolled scene. Unfortunately, the very term 'robot' seems to bring out the worst of the latent mechanist tendencies which Western culture has for so long harboured. Capek may have intended to attack the mechanisation of society by naming his automatons after the Czech word *robota* (meaning 'compulsory service'), but the satire has misfired: by resorting to anthropomorphism in order to underline his anxiety, Capek fell victim to and in the process further consolidated the very danger he was trying to avert. For although the word 'robot' may be of recent invention, the picture on which it rests is of ancient lineage. According to the *OED* the word 'android' can be traced back to the early eighteenth century; 'automaton' to the early seventeenth (with obvious roots in the Greek αὐτόματον). But this is not intended as a lesson in etymology; the point is that, from Archytas of Tarentum's legendary mechanical flying pigeon through Vaucanson's mechanical duck (that could simulate eating, drinking, and excreting) to Kempelen's mechanical chess-player (with which Napoleon once played), Western society has been fascinated by the Promethean vision of creating a mechanism capable of spontaneous thought and action. Machine vision thus owes its very name to this age-old conceit.

The trouble is that, as soon as one tries to eradicate the confusions on which the Mechanist Thesis breeds, the cry of 'Luddite' immediately goes up; even when there was never any intention of disparaging the importance of the ongoing research in AI. But the aim of this chapter has been to clarify — not to impugn — the development of Pattern Recognition systems. Some of the pretensions which AI currently boasts may be lost in the process, but none of the excitement need be sacrificed. As Ralph Cornes recently warned:

> You might get the impression from what you read that the world of computing is a world of constant innovation populated largely by technical whizz-kids. The reality is rather different. It is a world of practitioners who are trying to solve problems that range from the squalid, through the mundane, to the exotic, but rarely correspond to the technical breakthroughs that you read about.[125]

It is the reality of Pattern Recognition that we need to disclose. Certainly a sober estimation of the significance of scene-analysis programs need not alter the glamour which machine vision currently enjoys; if anything the exact opposite should occur, as the ingenious principles on which these systems operate is better understood. It is thus to computer scientists that philosophers must look for any support. But although the omens may be improving, they could yet not be described as fully auspicious. For it is still the norm to come across such comments as Earl C. Joseph's admonition that 'Robots should not be confused with automation. The technology exists, so that a prototype new industrial microprocessor-based robot could see, think, talk, learn and respond to voice commands — but it does not look like a human being. Rather, industrial robots are automated arms.'[126] Here what is at fault is only the popular image which androids have acquired, but not the reasoning which underpins their mechanist stature.

The goal of this chapter has been to remove the mechanist foundation which supports this confusion, but only so as to step back and better admire the imposing scientific edifice which remains standing. Taken together, the Inferential and the Mechanical Perception Theories serve one another as the antecedent and consequent of a sweeping *circulus in probando*, all the more powerful because they operate on such a grand scale. We begin with a framework in search of the evidence which it needs for verification, and then move to a wealth of information which only needs a framework to give it a focus. Thus, the advocates of the Inferential theory can postulate any number of neurological 'assumptions', but for all their exertions they remain postulations. In Pattern Recognition, on the other hand, the mechanics of the system are open to plain view, but without the Inferential theory to give them a unique purpose, they look suspiciously like a branch of physics and optics. Ballard and Brown explain at the beginning of *Computer Vision* that computers provide 'a congenial tool for research into visual perception': they are 'versatile and forgiving experimental subjects', and yet 'demanding critics'. Most important of all, 'Computers offer new metaphors for perceptual psychology (also neurology, linguistics, and philosophy); they provide powerful and influential conceptual tools for thinking about perception and cognition.'[127] But it was psychology (benefiting from the bygone services of the philosophy of mind) which provided the metaphor in the first place, only to be returned by AI, neatly embellished with a host of technical notions to lend substance to the languishing psychological theory. They would both do well to heed Valéry's warning to beware 'The folly of mistaking a paradox for a discovery, a metaphor for a proof.'

Notes

1. I am deeply indebted to Peter Hacker's unpublished writings on perception; in particular, to the first draft of his paper, 'Experimental Methods and Conceptual Confusion: An Investigation into R.L. Gregory's Theory of Perception'. Hacker's work marks, I believe, a landmark in the philosophy of perception. Pattern Recognition is but one example of the many important areas where his insights must be carefully applied.

2. If such an exception still exists, he is advised to read forthwith G.P. Baker and P.M.S. Hacker's *Wittgenstein: Understanding and Meaning. Volume 1 of An Analytical Commentary of the Philosophical Investigations* (Basil Blackwell,

Oxford 1980), and *Wittgenstein: Rules, Grammar and Necessity. Volume 2 of An Analytical Commentary on the Philosophical Investigations* (Basil Blackwell, Oxford, 1985).
3. Cf. Keith Gunderson, *Mentality and Machines: A Survey of the Artificial Intelligence Debate* (Croom Helm, London, 1985), Ch. 1.
4. Cf. *Computer Guardian*, 10 October 1985.
5. Ibid.
6. Ibid.
7. Cf. S.G. Shanker, 'The Decline and Fall of the Mechanist Metaphor' in *Artificial Intelligence: The Case Against*, Rainer Born (ed.) (Croom Helm, London, 1986).
8. Mary Shelley, *Frankenstein, or the Modern Prometheus* (Penguin Books, Harmondsworth, 1985), p. 144.
9. R.L. Gregory, *Eye and Brain: The Psychology of Seeing*, 3rd edn. (Weidenfeld and Nicholson, London, 1979), p. 226.
10. R.L. Gregory, 'The Confounded Eye' in *Illusion in Nature and Art*, R.L. Gregory and E.H. Gombrich (eds.) (Duckworth, London, 1973), p. 50.
11. Ibid., p. 51.
12. Margaret Boden, *Artificial Intelligence and Natural Man* (Harvester Press, Brighton, 1977), p. 179.
13. Ibid.
14. *Eye and Brain*, p. 42.
15. Ibid.
16. 'The Confounded Eye', p. 50.
17. *Eye and Brain*, p. 236.
18. Ibid.
19. Ibid.
20. Ibid.
21. Ibid., p. 235.
22. Ibid., p. 226.
23. Donald Michie, *Machine Intelligence* (Gordon and Breach Science Publishers, London, 1982), p. 176.
24. Ibid., p. 177.
25. Alan K. Mackworth, 'Model-driven Interpretation in Intelligent Vision Systems', *Perception*, vol. 5 (1976), p. 349.
26. From a 'Prospectus' issued by the British Pattern Recognition Association.
27. *Eye and Brain*, p. 9.
28. 'The Confounded Eye', p. 50.
29. John C. Eccles, *The Human Mystery* (Routledge & Kegan Paul, London, 1984), p. 4.
30. Ibid., p. 166.
31. *Eye and Brain*, p. 190.
32. R.L. Gregory, 'A Look at Biological and Machine Perception' in D. Michie (ed.), *Machine Intelligence*, 7, Edinburgh, 1973, p. 377.
33. Cf. 'The Confounded Eye', p. 51.
34. Ibid.
35. R.L. Gregory, *The Intelligent Eye* (Weidenfeld & Nicolson, London, 1970), p. 15; cf. *Eye and Brain*, p. 15.
36. Ibid., pp. 27-8.
37. R.L. Gregory, *Mind in Science: A History of Explanation in Psychology and Physics* (Penguin Books, Harmondsworth, 1984), p. 391.
38. 'The Confounded Eye', pp. 53-4; cf. *The Intelligent Eye*, pp. 20, 22.
39. Or rather, *redefined*; cf. section 6 on 'Learning Systems' in my 'The

Decline and Fall of the Mechanist Metaphor'.
   40. Cf. R.L. Gregory, 'Will Seeing Machines Have Illusions?', *Machine Intelligence*, vol. I, Collins, N.L. and Michie, D. (eds) (Edinburgh and London, 1967), p. 170:

   Biological seeing machines handle spatial patterns which must be classified, stored and compared. Some kind of filing system with ready access is required, and in human perception the perceptual 'filing cards' contain a wealth of information going far beyond purely sensory characteristics.

   41. 'A Look at Biological and Machine Perception', p. 377.
   42. 'Perceptions as Hypotheses', *Phil Trans R Soc Lond*, B 290 (1980), p. 181.
   43. 'The Confounded Eye', p. 55.
   44. 'Perceptions as hypotheses', p. 181.
   45. *The Intelligent Eye*, p. 60.
   46. 'A Look at Biological and Machine Perception', p. 377.
   47. 'The Confounded Eye', p. 51.
   48. Ibid.
   49. Cf. my *The Significance of Gödel's Theorem*, forthcoming.
   50. Cf. Douglas R. Hofstadter, *Gödel, Escher, Bach: An Eternal Golden Braid* (Penguin Books, Harmondsworth, 1981), pp. 10-15.
   51. Cf. *The Intelligent Eye*, pp. 50-60.
   52. Ibid., p. 59.
   53. Cp. 'The Confounded Eye', p. 55.
   54. 'The Confounded Eye', p. 85.
   55. Ibid., p. 88.
   56. Ibid., p. 61.
   57. Ibid.
   58. I shall not rehearse here the reasons why I believe that philosophical sceptical dilemmas are invariably the result of conceptual confusions. The substance of my argument can be found in *Wittgenstein and the Turning Point in the Philosophy of Mathematics* (London, Croom Helm, 1987).
   59. *The Intelligent Eye*, p. 15.
   60. Ibid., p. 30.
   61. For example, cf. *Eye and Brain*, pp. 60, 90.
   62. Others are not nearly so careful. In *The Mind* (Hodder and Stoughton, London, 1984), pp. 180-1, Anthony Smith explains that 'The eye may be the visual organ, but it is the brain that sees ... The brain sees, and also chooses what it wants to see ... Vision, in short, used to be what the eye did. It has now shifted and is what the brain does with the facts that come its way via the optic nerves.'
   63. *Eye and Brain*, p. 9.
   64. *The Intelligent Eye*, p. 24.
   65. Even though he is far less circumspect elsewhere; for example, cf. *Eye and Brain*, p. 60.
   66. For example, cf. 'The Confounded Eye', p. 67; *The Intelligent Eye*, p. 25.
   67. Gregory continues: 'Figures and objects of this kind [namely, the Penrose 'impossible triangle'] present useful opportunities for discovering perceptual assumptions and rules by which perceptual hypotheses that may conflict with high level knowledge are generated "upwards" from assumptions by rule-following.' 'Perceptions as Hypotheses', pp. 191-2.
   68. Ibid.
   69. *The Intelligent Eye*, p. 15.
   70. *Eye and Brain*, p. 10.
   71. Ibid., p. 48.

72. *The Human Mystery*, p. 174.
73. Ibid., p. 210.
74. 'The Confounded Eye', p. 55.
75. 'Will Seeing Machines Have Illusions?', p. 169.
76. Ibid.
77. Ibid., p. 170.
78. For a glimpse of this argument in action, cf. 'Model-driven Interpretation in Intelligent Vision Systems', p. 357; *Mind in Science*, p. 379.
79. 'Model-driven Interpretation in Intelligent Vision Systems', p. 351.
80. Ibid.
81. Ibid., p. 350.
82. Cf. 'The Decline and Fall of the Mechanist Metaphor', section 6.
83. Bruce H. McCormick, Ernest Kent, and Charles R. Dyer, 'A Cognitive Architecture for Computer Vision' in *Fifth Generation Computer Systems*, Moto-Oka, T. (ed.) (North-Holland Publishing Company, Amsterdam, 1982), p. 245.
84. Thus they argue that

If we can model columnar processing adequately and can mimic its methods for communicating with neighboring and remote columns, then it may prove to be the case that our architectural work is in some fundamental sense accomplished — that this class of machine has the full potential to emulate high levels of cognition. (Ibid., p. 246.)

85. Ibid.
86. Ibid., pp. 252-3.
87. According to Gregory, 'We may guess that there is an intimate connection [in object-perception] with memory stores, but at the present time how memory is stored is not known. It is not even known whether single cells store units of memory, or whether memories are stored as patterns involving very many cells.' *The Intelligent Eye*, pp. 24-5.
88. 'The Baffled Brain' in *Illusion in Nature and Art*, p. 9.
89. Ibid., p. 19.
90. Ibid., p. 17.
91. *The Human Mystery*, p. 174.
92. 'A Cognitive Architecture for Computer Vision', p. 250.
93. Ibid., p. 248.
94. Cf. 'The Decline and Fall of the Mechanist Metaphor', section 5.
95. Cf. M.J.B. Duff, 'Seeing Machines' in *Intelligent Systems: The Unprecedented Opportunity*, Hayes, J.E. and Michie, D. (eds.) (Ellis Horwood Ltd, Chichester, 1984).
96. Cf. 'What the Frog's Eye Tells the Frog's Brain', *Proc Inst Radio Engrs NY* vol. 47 (1959).
97. Although some have argued that the retina might literally employ some version of the type of 'convolution' functions that have been developed; cf P.H. Winston, *Artificial Intelligence*, 2nd edn (Addison-Wesley Publishing Company, Reading, Mass., 1984), pp. 346ff.
98. They are chiefly confined to inspection systems which use photodiode arrays to compare stored and present pictures of a limited number of objects.
99. Cf. 'The Decline and Fall of the Mechanist Metaphor', section 4.
100. L.G. Roberts, 'Machine Perception of Three-Dimensional Solids' in *Optical and Electro-optical Information Processing*, Tippett, J.T., Berkowitz, D.A., Clapp, L.C., Koester, C.J. and Vanderburgh, A. (eds.) (MIT Press, Cambridge, Mass., 1965), p. 162.
101. Ibid., p. 159.

102. Ibid., p. 194; cf. Gregory's conclusion that 'we must wait upon developments in the science of machine Intelligence (or 'Artificial' Intelligence) to gain deeper insight into the logic (valid and fallacious) of brain function. If so, machines will teach us humanity.' 'The Confounded Eye', p. 82.
103. Ibid., p. 162.
104. Boden, *Artificial Intelligence*, p. 182.
105. Ibid., p. 181.
106. Ibid., p. 181.
107. Itself a misnomer; cf. 'The Decline and Fall of the Mechanist Metaphor'.
108. 'Model-driven Interpretation in Intelligent Vision Systems', p. 350.
109. Boden, *Artificial Intelligence*, p. 182.
110. 'The Confounded Eye', p. 66.
111. I hope to deal with these issues in a forthcoming work on 'The Significance of Gödel's Theorem'.
112. Boden, *Artificial Intelligence*, p. 183.
113. *Eye and Brain*, p. 181.
114. Ibid.
115. Roberts, 'Machine Perception of Three-dimensional Solids', p. 174.
116. Boden, *Artificial Intelligence*, p. 187.
117. Ibid.
118. Ibid.
119. Dana H. Ballard and Christopher M. Brown, *Computer Vision* (Prentice Hall, Inc., Englewood Cliffs, 1982), p. 352.
120. This is a familiar manoeuvre in the mechanist strategy, first articulated by Turing in his interpretation of computer chess; cf. 'The Decline and Fall of the Mechanist Metaphor', section 5.
121. The simple way to account for this anomaly, however, is redefine the psychological concepts of perception in terms of these computer operations. Thus Gregory quite happily accepts that 'The object-recognizing and object-creating rules are applied *upwards* to filter and structure the input. (It is, however, interesting to note that they may have been *developed* downwards, by generalized experience of what are, through the development of perception, taken as objects.)' 'Perceptions as Hypotheses', p. 188.
122. In mathematical terms, the topological problem is to find the model-to-picture transform H such that the matrix A of n points (x,y,z,w) from the model can be mapped onto the matrix B of n points (y,z,w) in the picture (AH $\cong$ B). In order to introduce an equality sign we need a diagonal scale matrix D which allows the w_i points in A and B to differ (AH = DB). Using the minimum square error technique to solve the 3_n equations thus created we set out to calculate the value of D. Once D has been obtained H can be found, and we can then map the points of the model matrix A onto the picture matrix B using the equation B = HA^{-1}. Thus, the model A and transform H identify the type and location of the object in the picture. (Further details of the equations used in this calculation can be found in Appendix B of 'Machine Perception of Three-Dimensional Solids'.)
123. M.B. Clowes, 'Scene Analysis and Picture Grammars' in *Graphic Languages*, Nake, F. and Rosenfeld, A. (eds.) (North-Holland, Amsterdam, 1972), p. 81.
124. Ibid.
125. Ralph Cornes, 'How to Match the Genius to the Job', *Computer Guardian*, 28 November 1985, p. 15.
126. E.C. Joseph, 'Robots of the Future' in *Intelligent Systems*, p. 130.
127. *Computer Vision*, pp. 9,12.

11 THEORIES OF MEANING AND SPEAKERS' KNOWLEDGE

Crispin Wright

This chapter is concerned with recent — 1970s — trends and emphases in British philosophy of language, particularly as practised in Oxford. The question, what form should be assumed by a satisfactory theory of meaning for a natural language, quite suddenly came to seem absolutely fundamental, with the most comprehensive philosophical insights at stake. My concern here, however, is not to survey that issue, or to comment on the general significance it was (and still is) widely believed to have, but to explore certain assumptions which those who led opposite sides in the debate — principally Professors Davidson and Dummett — seem to have had in common: assumptions whose correctness is arguably not just essential for the philosophical significance — even a fairly local philosophical significance — of a 'theory of meaning' but is tacitly presupposed by the greater part of all philosophical semantic endeavour.

I

Davidson's proposal[1] that a theory of meaning for a natural language should take the form of a recursive truth definition in the style which Tarski devised for certain formal languages is opposed, or qualified, by Dummett in three principal respects. First, such a theory could be at best the core of a fully fledged theory of meaning; it would need to be embedded within a theory of *force*, a theory concerned with the differences between assertion, command, question, wish, and other modes of illocution, and which made plain how these different types of speech act were signalled in the language under study.[2] Second, whereas Davidson seems content, in the case where the language in which the theory is formulated includes as a proper part of the language theorised about, that the theory should be *homophonic* — that is, that the form taken by its meaning-delivering theorems should involve *use* of the very sentences whose meaning is being characterised — Dummett requires that the theory should be *full-blooded*, that it should, where possible, analyse and illuminate meanings.³ Third, Dummett has disputed Davidson's choice of truth as the central notion in terms of which an account of meaning should be given: if what the theory says about any particular sentence aspires to be what anyone familiar with the meaning of that sentence knows, there are 'anti-realist' arguments, made familiar by Dummett, why it cannot in general suffice for the theory to assign truth-conditions to sentences.⁴

These are substantial differences. But they all concern what Dummett sees as deficiencies in the *output* of a theory of the projected kind — the first two being deficiencies of omission, while the third, though absolutely fundamental at the level of interpretation, may require no substantial alteration of the form of a Davidsonian theory. Dummett's criticism does not express any antagonism to Davidson's overall project; indeed, the points of agreement seem more striking than the disagreements. Davidson intends that a theory of truth is acceptable as a theory of meaning only if (i) it is finitely axiomatisable and (ii) it delivers a T-theorem for each declarative sentence of the object language in a manner that reflects the semantic structure discerned in that sentence.⁵ Why should the theory be finitely axiomatisable? Different passages in Davidson's writings suggest slightly different answers. Sometimes the thought is that understanding a language involves the capacity to make sense of no end of distinct expressions, and that this (potential) infinity contrasts sharply with the finitude of our capacities in general (most relevantly, presumably, the finitude of our capacities for information storage). A finitely based theory of meaning of the sort he is recommending will, Davidson believes, give us an insight into '... how an infinite aptitude can be encompassed by finite accomplishments'.⁶ A neighbouring but distinct point is that if a language admits of characterisation by a finitely based Davidsonian theory, then we have an insight into how the language can be learnable.⁷ The point is distinct because creatures with infinite capacities for information storage but no other infinitary abilities could only learn finitely much in a finite time. Finally, not quite the same thought as either of these is the idea that

> ... Speakers of a language can effectively determine the meaning or meanings of an arbitrary expression (if it has a meaning)

and ... it is the central task of a theory of meaning to show how this is possible.[8]

The theory of meaning is thus to contribute towards the explanation of how speakers can understand sentences which are novel to them. This thought is different because the question would arise — if it is a good question at all — for infinite creatures too, and for finite languages which, while semantically structured, possess no indefinitely iterable devices of the sort which generate a potential infinity of meaningful sentences.

However, the marginal distinctions among the questions, How can finite minds have infinite abilities?, How can languages be learnable?, How can speakers determine the meanings of novel utterances?, are not important. What is important is that the capacity of Davidsonian theory to assist in the provision of answers to any of them requires that it be admissible to think of actual speakers as equipped with the information codified in the axioms of a successful Davidsonian theory, and as prone to deploy that information in ways reflected by the derivations of meaning-delivering theorems afforded by the theory. Whether the theory aspires to cast light on *our* ability, finite as we are, to master a potentially infinite language, or *our* ability to complete the learning of the language, or on *our* ability to understand novel utterances, or on all three, success must depend, it seems, on its being permissible to suppose that it encodes information which *we* actually possess.

If Davidson is somewhat inexplicit about this, Dummett is not. A very definite commitment to the idea that the explanatory ambitions of a theory of meaning depend upon recourse to some idea of speakers' *implicit knowledge* of its axiomatic contents is evinced in his writings on the topic. For instance:

> A theory of meaning will, then, represent the practical ability possessed by a speaker as consisting in his grasp of a set of propositions; since the speaker derives his understanding of a sentence from the meanings of its component words, these propositions will most naturally form a deductively connected system. The knowledge of these propositions that is attributed to a speaker can only be an implicit knowledge. In general, it cannot be demanded of someone who has any given practical ability that he have more than an implicit knowledge of those

propositions by means of which we give a theoretical representation of that ability.[9]

In an earlier paper, Dummett refers to

> ... our intuitive conviction that a speaker derives his understanding of a sentence from his understanding of the words composing it and the way they are put together.[10]

and relates Davidsonian theory to this intuitive conviction by the remark that

> What plays the role, within a theory of meaning of Davidson's kind, of a grasp of the meanings of the words is a knowledge of the axioms governing these words.[11]

Further

> It is one of the merits of a theory of meaning which represents mastery of a language as the knowledge not of isolated, but of deductively interconnected propositions, that it makes due acknowledgement of the undoubted fact that a process of derivation of some kind is involved in the understanding of a sentence.[12]

For Dummett, the explanatory ambitions of a theory of meaning would seem to be entirely dependent upon the permissibility of thinking of speakers of its object language as knowing the propositions which its axioms codify and of their deriving their understanding of (novel) sentences in a manner mirrored by the derivation, in the theory, of the appropriate theorems.

There is accordingly a case for saying that, whatever their differences, Dummett and Davidson are in broad agreement about the interest of the project of a theory of meaning of this sort, and about the manner in which such a theory needs to be interpreted if it is to sustain that interest; and that they share a broad, underlying assumption about the nature of linguistic competence, namely, that it is fruitfully to be compared — at least in its basics — to any open-ended computational ability which — like, say, the ability to do simple arithmetical multiplications — deploys finite information in rule-prescribed ways. The difference is just that the knowledge which constitutes understanding of a language is gained, for the most part, not from an explicit statement — in contrast, for example, with the multiplication tables, or the rules of chess — but by immersion in the practice of speaking the language in question.

That we understand novel utterances because we understand the words in them and significance of the way in which they are put together is apt to strike one as a platitude. But it is no platitude that the sort of project which Dummett, explicitly, and Davidson, implicitly, seem to have in view makes philosophical sense. If the gap is not immediately apparent, it ought to suffice to reflect that the platitude need only be regarded as describing a feature of the 'grammar' of *misunderstanding*: nobody may properly be described as misunderstanding a sentence unless guilty of some more specific misunderstanding, either of words deployed within it or of its syntax. Contraposing, we have the incontestable claim that if someone understands the vocabulary and syntax of a significant sentence, then they understand the (type) sentence. Platitude is left behind when the antecedent of this conditional is taken to describe an ulterior state of information which *enables* a subject to understand the sentence.

This chapter is concerned with a number of inter-connected questions. Let us say that a theory is *compositional* just in case it meets the two Davidsonian constraints, (i) and (ii), noted above. Section II is concerned with the question whether there can be any good motive for insisting on compositionality in theories of meaning which *avoids* recourse to the idea of actual speakers' implicit knowledge. Baker and Hacker[13] have recently described Davidson's comparative inexplicitness on the topic as 'artful' — their thought being, I imagine, that, for the sort of reason outlined above, the questions on which Davidson hopes for illumination cannot be answered by Davidsonian theorising unless implicit knowledge is invoked, but that Davidson has preferred not to elaborate on the issue, perceiving it for the Pandora's Box which they believe it to be. However that may be, it is important to be clear whether, besides the three mentioned, there is any different question, not directly concerned with the capacities of actual speakers, which devising a compositional theory of meaning might help to answer. Only if there is not, will we be committed, should it emerge that there is absolutely nothing to be made of the notion of implicit knowledge, to regarding Davidson's project as a waste of time. Section III then takes up the question, what, if any, defensible conception of implicit knowledge may be attained? Is there cause for confidence that a notion can be made good which is apt to allow a compositional theory to be explanatory of actual speakers' capacities?

If no suitable notion of implicit knowledge can be extricated, it naturally occurs to one to wonder how that leaves matters with the realism/anti-realism dispute in the theory of meaning. For the essence of the most influential anti-realist critique of classical semantics is exactly that it cannot be a theory of speakers' understanding: that it places impossible demands on the range of what speakers may reasonably be regarded as (implicitly) knowing. The anti-realist charge is that if 'truth' is understood as the realist intends, there is, in an important class of cases, no such thing as knowing the truth-conditions of a sentence. If this is to be a criticism of realist semantics it is essential that understanding may be regarded as a species of knowledge. And it is obvious that if it may, it cannot *everywhere* consist in *explicit* knowledge. The ability to paraphrase a sentence is a (defeasible) ground for crediting somebody with understanding it, but it is not an ability which we have for a large class of sentences which we think we understand (and our language might, in any case, have been such as to contain the resources for no such paraphrase). Accordingly, if understanding is knowledge at all, the kind of knowledge it *essentially* is must, it seems, be implicit. An important argument running through Dummett's writings[14] is exactly that only an anti-realist theory of meaning can sustain the demands made on the notion of implicit knowledge which, as we have seen, he believes that the theory of meaning must make. Section IV will contend that the anti-realist critique is not undermined by the worries about the notion of implicit knowledge whose well-foundedness there is most cause to suspect.

II

Doubts about the notion of implicit knowledge have surfaced frequently in the literature, even in the writings of those sympathetic to the spirit of the Davidsonian project. John Foster, for instance, writes:

> ... having seen the generality of the theory required, we may

wonder whether we should ascribe it to the speaker at all. The knowledge we would have to attribute to him is not, typically, what he would attribute to himself. His mastery of English equips him to interpret its expressions, but not to state the general principles to which these interpretations conform. Is it not unnatural, even incoherent, to ascribe states of knowledge to which the subject himself has no conscious access?[15]

But Foster believes that the issue can be side-stepped:

> ... we can capture all that matters to the philosophy of meaning by putting the original project the other way around. Rather than ask for a statement of the knowledge implicit in linguistic competence, let us ask for a statement of a theory whose knowledge would suffice for such competence. Instead of demanding a statement of those metalinguistic facts which the mastery of a language implicitly recognises, let us demand a statement of those facts explicit recognition of which gives mastery. What we are then demanding is still a theory of meaning, but without the questionable assumption that one who has mastered the language has, at some deep level, absorbed the information which it supplies. The theory reveals the semantic machinery which competence works, but leaves undetermined the psychological form in which competence exists.[16]

There are two thoughts here. First, there is the idea that the quest for a theory of meaning does not need to be motivated by the desire to understand the capacities of actual speakers of a given language. It is enough, in Foster's view, that we seek to describe knowledge which *would* generate those capacities, whether or not it is the source of actual speakers' possession of them. If it is wondered why we should seek to do that, Foster's answer seems to be, second, that what the theorist of meaning is interested in is primarily *the way the language works*. While we should not, perhaps despair of the possibility that the theory might illuminate the 'psychological form' of actual speakers' linguistic competence, the primary object is to describe the 'semantic machinery' which drives the language.

The trouble with this is that the demands which Foster is making of the notion of meaning — the demands implicit in the image of 'semantic machinery' — threaten no less conceptual strain than the demands on the notion of knowledge — those generated by its qualification as 'implicit' — which he is trying to avoid. The intuitive response to Foster's proposal would be that it generates an intolerable divide between the concepts of meaning and understanding: truths about meaning have to be, ultimately, constituted by facts about understanding, so to aspire to a theory which aims to describe 'semantic machinery' independently of any assumption about what speakers of the language know is to aspire to a theory with no proper subject matter.[17]

This response may involve over-simplification — depending on how 'ultimately' is understood — but it has great force, it seems to me, at the level of semantic primitives: expressions whose meanings are independent of the meanings of all other expressions of the language except those of which they are constituents, and to which a Davidsonian theory would devote its proper axioms. I do not think we can attach any content to the supposition that such an expression has a meaning except in so far as meaning is thought of as constituted, at least in part, by *convention*; and I do not think we can attain an account of the distinction between a convention and a corresponding regularity except by invoking the idea of practitioners' *intention*, qualified in various ways, to uphold that regularity. If both these, admittedly very vague, thoughts are correct, then the proper standing of the axioms of a theory of meaning must, it would seem, be grounded in speakers' intentions; and Foster's apparent belief that the theory can have an autonomous subject matter is of doubtful coherence.

There is another objection, perhaps less fundamental but more immediately clinically fatal. The fact is that there seems to be no necessary connection between Foster's recommendation that the theory should describe information which *would* suffice for mastery of a given, typical natural language and the constraint of compositionality. Or better: there seems to be no such connection in the case on which Davidsonians typically concentrate — the homophonic case. If one is aiming at construction of a heterophonic theory — whether because the object-language is quite different from that in which the theory is to be couched, or because one is aiming at a high degree of *full-bloodedness* in Dummett's sense — it may very well be that there is no way of completing Foster's task unless one aims for compositionality; that no other approach can effectively provide meaning-delivering theorems for every declarative sentence in the object language. In the homophonic case matters stand differently. Provided we have a recursive specification of the syntax of the (declarative part of the) language, and provided we are content with the disquotational form of meaning-delivering theorem for which theories of truth are famous, Foster's project is well enough served by a semantic 'theory' which merely stipulates as an axiom every instance of the schema:

A is T if and only if P,

where 'P' may be replaced by any declarative sentence of the object language and 'A' by the quotational name of that sentence. This theory is not finitely axiomatised, but it is finitely *stated* and, in conjunction with the appropriate recursive syntax, it does yield the means for effectively arriving at a meaning-delivering theorem — assuming we have no independent reservations about truth theories on that score — for each declarative sentence in the object-language. It thus fits Foster's bill: it describes information whose possession would suffice for mastery of the (declarative part of the) object-language. At least, it does so provided a compositional Davidsonian theory whose T-theorematic output coincided with the axioms of this theory would do so. It is true, of course, that the non-compositional theory could not be used to *impart* this information to someone who did not already have it — but then no homophonic theory, whether compositional or not, fares better in that regard. The moral is simple: the ambition to describe information which would suffice for mastery of a particular language may impose certain constraints on the form taken by the theorems of a theory of meaning, but it imposes no interesting constraint on the mechanics of the theory.

We are looking for a project whose execution would call for a compositional theory of meaning but which would not demand that actual speakers be deemed to know the full contents of that theory. Foster's thought, in effect, was to idealise the language with a view to a theory of how *it*, autonomously, works. A quite different thought would aim to see compositionality as called for by the ambition to describe not some body of knowledge which speakers putatively have but what they are typically able *to do*. Suppose we essay to regard each of the T-theorems of a Davidsonian theory as descriptive of a sub-competence which someone who fully understands the object language has: a sub-competence constituted by sensitivity, in using the relevant sentence, to the constraint which the appropriate T-theorem captures. Have we completely described the general competence in which mastery of the (declarative part of the) relevant language consists when we have a theory which correctly describes all these sub-competences? There is a prima facie persuasive reason why we should ask for more. No matter what ability we are concerned to describe, and however complete our characterisation of its ingredient abilities, the description is incomplete if the ingredients have certain causal interrelations about which it keeps silence. Someone who has a strong tennis game may have a good drive, a good lob, and a good slice on his backhand wing; but a *full* description of his skills would not restrict itself to the statement that each of these strokes is dependable if, let us suppose, the lob and the drive — when, unusually, either is fragile — tend to break down together, although the slice tends to remain a strong shot even when the rest of his game is off-colour. So with the theory of meaning: a full description of the competence possessed by speakers should not merely characterise its ingredients but ought also to reflect their (causal) interrelations. This may inspire what Martin Davies[18] calls the *Mirror Constraint*. Suppose it is true of speakers (*a*) that once they know what $S_1, \ldots, S_n$ mean, they are able to know what the distinct sentence, S, means without any further exposure to the use of the language; and (*b*) that if induced to revise their belief about what S means, they would need no further inducement to revise their beliefs about what some of $S_1, \ldots, S_n$ mean. Then the Mirror Constraint says simply that if, and only if, speakers' sub-competences with S, $S_1, \ldots, S_n$ are so interrelated, an adequate theory of meaning for their language should ensure that those of its resources which suffice for the derivation of meaning-delivering theorems for each of $S_1, \ldots, S_n$ should also suffice for the derivation of such a theorem for S.[19] A theory which satisfies the Mirror Constraint will thus be one whose deductive structure reflects the (causal) interrelations among speakers' sub-competences. When speakers are able to move to understanding of a novel utterance without special explanation, the theory will mirror their ability by supplying the means for deriving an appropriate theorem utilising only axioms adequate for the specification of the meanings of sentences which they previously understood; and when speakers change their beliefs about the meaning of some sentence, appropriate modifications to the meaning-delivering theorem for that sentence will enjoin revisions in its axiomatic parentage which in turn entail shifts of meaning in exactly those sentences of which they consequentially change their understanding. Davies himself raises various objections to the Mirror Constraint.[20] But he does not raise what I think is the most serious: that it provides no real reason for putting structure into a *semantic* theory. Let it be granted that the interrelations of competence whose reflection the Mirror Constraint seeks to ensure are worth describing. Still, why not describe them directly — why run the dogleg of having them 'reflected' in the deductive articulation of a theory of meaning? There is nothing to prevent a critic of the Mirror Constraint from taking over the syntax, and catalogue of semantic primitives, incorporated in a theory of meaning which satisfies it. He may then advance a theory of meaning of the infinitary sort canvassed above, adding only a rider to the effect that speakers are generally able to understand novel sentences, provided they involve only familiar semantic primitives, and that changes in their semantic beliefs about a sentence tend to be associated with changes in their semantic beliefs about *all* sentences — or at least all about which they have any such belief — containing some one or more of the semantic primitives figuring in that sentence. Admittedly, such a rider would not be a detailed, or axiomatic, description of the interrelations which the Mirror Constraint would have a theory of meaning reflect. But there is every reason to think that the recursive *syntax* which the theorist adjoins to his infinitary semantic theory would supply the materials for the more specific description task. He needs only to ensure that the syntax itself meets the Mirror Constraint: that when, and only when, speakers' understanding of $S_1, \ldots, S_n$ and S are interrelated as described, those ingredients in the axiomatic basis and set of recursions for the syntax which suffice to characterise each of $S_1, \ldots, S_n$ as well-formed suffice so to characterise S.

There is a different line of thought in Davies's discussion which seems more promising. It depends upon our being willing to entertain the idea that there is an admixture of rational inductive and deductive inference which can take a subject from knowledge of the meanings of a finite set of sentences to knowledge of the meaning of a sentence which is not in that set and is novel to him. It is, Davies writes,

... the possibility of self-conscious, reflective projection of meanings which encourages the attempt to provide a theory of meaning which not only delivers the correct meaning specifications but also reveals how the meanings of sentences depend upon the recurrence of particular syntactic constituents...[21]

Davies proceeds to propose what he calls the *Structural Constraint*: in effect, that if, but only if, it would be possible for someone who knew what $S_1,\ldots,S_n$ each means to proceed, by rational inductive and deductive methods and without further empirical investigation, to knowledge of what S means, the smallest set of axiomatic resources which suffice, in a theory of meaning for the language in question, to furnish meaning-delivering theorems for each of $S_1,\ldots,S_n$ should also yield a meaning-delivering theorem for S. The effect of this constraint is that compositionality in a theory of meaning is demanded not by characteristics of actual speakers *qua* actual speakers but by the nature of an idealised epistemology of understanding. Whatever actual speakers do or do not know, it seems highly plausible that there is such a thing, in certain cases, as rational inference from knowledge of the meanings of the sentences in a particular set to knowledge of the meaning of a sentence outside that set: the cases in question are precisely those where, intuitively, the semantically contributive vocabulary and syntax of the new sentence are all variously on display among the sentences in the set. The effect of the Structural Constraint is that a satisfactory theory of meaning should mirror not the propensities for meaning-projection and revision of actual speakers but those of an ideal speaker, whose every semantic belief is informed by self-conscious rational inductive and deductive inference.

In fact it seems reasonable to demand more. A satisfactory theory of meaning should not merely 'reflect' the path that will be taken by the ideal speaker, by discerning structure whenever he discerns structure, but should represent the inferences which he would — or could, *qua* rational — actually draw. Thus whenever he is able to advance to knowledge of the meaning of S from knowledge of the meanings of $S_1,\ldots,S_n$, the latter knowledge should constitute good evidence for the truth of those axioms in the theory needed to derive the meaning-delivering theorem for S; and the movement up, as it were, to the axioms and then down to that theorem ought to be the very movement which knowledge of the meanings of $S_1,\ldots,S_n$ is deemed to put a rational speaker in position to make. It is not completely clear whether Davies has this stronger interpretation of the Structural Constraint in mind. But it seems to be more satisfactory. The weaker interpretation is apt to make the constraint seem somewhat arbitrary: what question, exactly, would the theory of meaning have to be addressed to in order for it to be necessary that it discerns semantic structure in a group of sentences when and only when the ideal speaker would 'project' among them but not necessary that it represent inferential moves which he could, *qua* ideal, actually make? Under the stronger interpretation, however, the overriding question is clear. It is: granted that it is possible for a speaker to know, or at least to form rational beliefs, about the meanings of utterances whose use he has never witnessed, how in detail might this be possible?

This has to be a good question unless we are utterly sceptical about whether there is ever any *rational* route to an understanding of novel utterances. The project of trying to answer it has the interest that attaches to any programme of reconstructive analytic epistemology. Such projects have been a major current in the history of English-speaking philosophy: whether motivated by sceptical challenges or not, philosophers have repeatedly been drawn to the task of trying to explain how statements of some particular sort — about God, or the material world, or other minds, for instance — *could* be susceptible to rational cognition (even if our practice is to rely upon criteria of acceptability which fall far short of it). Admittedly, the sceptic about meaning is a somewhat recent entry on the philosophical scene; the project of constructing theories of meaning of the sort we are interested in did not originate as a response to sceptical pressure, and the various forms of scepticism about meaning which have comparatively recently come into prominence in any case concern more basic matters than knowledge of the meaning of novel utterances. Still, the possibility of such knowledge provides the material for a perfectly familiar species of analytical enquiry.

That is the principal recommendation of this section. There *is* a recognisably *philosophical* project — at least it ought to be recognisable to anyone educated in the twentieth-century Anglo-American philosophical tradition — to which constructing a formal theory of meaning would be a contribution. This project has no immediate connection with the quest to explain the capacities of actual speakers of natural languages; the task to which a completed, adequate theory of meaning would contribute would rather be that of explaining how a complete knowledge of a particular natural language could be a rational achievement. We have no conception of how that might be so unless the rational subject is permitted to discern sub-sentential semantic structure. It follows that such a theory would have to comply with the second ingredient condition of compositionality, as the notion was introduced above, that the meaning-delivering theorems for sentences be derived within the theory in a manner which reflects the semantic contribution made by those sentences' constituents. The need for the first ingredient, that the axiomatic basis be finite, is less immediate: it is not evident that a rational being could not be in possession of infinitely many logically independent items of information. But it may be anticipated that if we are concerned with the powers of an ideally rational *human* speaker — so that the finitude of our capacities remains a constraint on the form which the theory should take — the *learnability* of the language — the possibility of a finite but rational creature coming to know the meaning of any particular sentence of it by way of exposure to and projection from the use of finitely many other sentences — will require that only a finitely axiomatised theory will fit the bill.[22]

Whatever we conclude, then, about the capacity of a formal theory of meaning to be yoked to the task of explaining actual speakers' abilities, there is an interpretation of the Davidson/Dummett project which promises to allow it to stand independently as legitimate *a priori* philosophy. This interpretation may or may not accord with part of the intentions of the leading protagonists in the field. But it does contrive to supply, after all, some sense for Foster's notion that a natural language might have the sort of autonomy which would allow its theoretical description not to be directly a theory about actual speakers' semantic knowledge; and it suggests, in consequence, how the disinfection of the concept of implicit knowledge need not be a precondition for the philosophical health of the project of constructing theories of meaning.[23]

III

In order for a theory of meaning to be explanatory of the linguistic capacities of actual speakers, there has to be, it seems, a sense in which its axioms are true of them; or, at least, there have to be properties of the speakers for whose description the axioms are needed. It would be an error to suppose that the notion that speakers *implicitly know* the content of such a set of axioms is the only way of meeting this condition. It is evidently a tempting and natural suggestion — witness the widespread use of such ideas in the writings of theoretical linguists. But it is exceedingly difficult to be clear whether it is ultimately coherent.

The most immediate objection is based on the thought that the axioms of a theory of meaning ought to correspond to semantic *rules*. To amplify: such an axiom is supposed to describe the semantically relevant features of an expression; how could it do that if it failed to embody a condition on the correct use of that expression? For the meaning of an expression is essentially something normative; it is, crudely, only because expressions have meaning that there is such a thing as correct, or incorrect, use of them. This normativity does not *per se* conflict with the capacity of the theory to contribute towards the explanation of speakers' linguistic 'creativity' — their capacity to understand novel utterances; the proposal will be that the feature of a speaker which such an axiom will reflect is precisely his knowledge of it. If we are given, for instance, a statement of the powers of the pieces in chess, there is no tension about supposing that it may serve both to articulate the norms determining what is and is not a legal move and to contribute towards the explanation of players' capacity to recognise the legality/illegality of moves which they have not previously encountered. The double function is secured by the bridging assumption that the players recognise exactly the rules which the statement describes. The salient point is therefore the need for a bridging assumption which hypothesises practitioners' recognition of the set of norms which the axioms codify.

Now, if something like a Davidsonian theory is indeed possible for English, it is a mighty iceberg about whose overall shape we have very little idea. We know that it would be a theory of great complexity which would impose a good deal of regimentation on the surface grammar of our language. The handling of tense, adverbs, predicate modifiers, modality, intentionality, and even quantifiers are all controversial topics. The tendency, understandably, among researchers in the field has been to stay close to the Tarskian prototype and to the syntax of predicate calculus. But while interesting work has been done, even the most committed would have to allow that progress towards realisation of the grand design has not been spectacular. Accordingly, someone who believes that English, or at least a good deal of it, does indeed admit of complete semantic description by means of a compositional formal theory would at present be hard pressed to justify a high degree of confidence that work has proceeded along the right sort of lines, or has been inspired by the most fruitful paradigms. In other words, apart from knowing that it will be difficult to design, complex of articulation, and is likely to contain at present unforeseen devices, we have *very little* idea what a formal theory of meaning for a natural language of expressive power comparable to that of English would be like. Yet it is the axioms of such a theory which the implicit knowledge proposal would have us regard as normative with respect to our linguistic practice. Are there not manifest philosophical difficulties with the idea that our linguistic behaviour should be regarded as informed by our recognition of principles which we cannot state, which played no explicit part in our linguistic training, which will probably involve concepts of great sophistication and technicality, and which we might not recognise even if presented with a formulation? How can a principle function as a rule if those who engage in the practice which it is supposed to regulate have no consciousness of it?

Dummett writes:

> What plays the role, within a theory of meaning of Davidson's kind, of a grasp of the meanings of the words is a knowledge of the axioms governing those words: in our example [that of 'the earth moves'] these may be stated as '"the earth" denotes the earth' and 'it is true to say of something "it moves" if and only if that thing moves'. (This latter formulation of the axiom governing 'moves' is stated without appeal to the technical device of satisfaction by an infinite sequence, and is only an approximate indication of what is wanted: but, if we are intending a serious representation of what is known by anyone able to speak English, we cannot literally credit him with an understanding of that technical device.)[24]

We can sympathise with Dummett's reservations: it is a plausible enough constraint upon the significant attribution of belief, *a fortiori* of knowledge, that a subject possesses the concepts which figure in the content of the belief attributed to him, and it is utterly implausible that ordinary speakers of English should be credited with an understanding, at any level, of concepts like satisfaction, infinite sequence, and the star functor. But Dummett's thought here is vulnerable to a simple dilemma. If this sort of technical apparatus is necessary for the development of a theory of meaning for a typical natural language, then speakers may not, on his own admission, be credited with a full implicit knowledge of that theory but only, perhaps, of a part of it; and the claims of the theory to provide a model of how speakers actually achieve an understanding of novel utterances must therefore be severely qualified. If, on the other hand, the technical apparatus is merely a convenience, an explanation is owing of how it may be dispensed with and the axiomatic and recursive basis of the theory developed purely in terms of concepts whose attribution to speakers is altogether more plausible. The promise of a theory of meaning to illuminate actual speakers' linguistic 'creativity' will then depend entirely on the success of this explanation — an explanation which we have, so far, not the slightest idea how to construct.

It will be apparent that there are two special and separate difficulties here which a general vindication of the notion of implicit knowledge would not necessarily resolve. There is the problem of explaining how a *rule* can be implicitly known; how, that is, it can function as a rule — exert a regulative influence — if practitioners are unaware of it. And there is the problem of how contents, putatively implicitly known, may involve concepts for their possessing which there is no direct evidence in practitioners' performance and which may, indeed, be sufficiently abstruse to be beyond their powers — at least their *apparent* powers — of comprehension. However, I do not think that either problem is immediately fatal. It is true, of course, that a rule as a possible object of consultation has to be a possible object of consciousness. But it is perfectly obvious that the axioms of a homophonic theory of meaning are not meant to be rules in this sense since — because they use the expressions which they mention — only someone who already understood those expressions, and hence had no need to consult such 'rules', would be capable of consulting them. It does not follow that the axioms cannot be regarded as statements of rule at all, however. It would indeed be fatal to their claim to contain a theory of *meaning* if they could not. But the simple fact is that the characterisation of a convention does not have to proceed in terms which could be used to explain the convention to someone previously ignorant of it. It is a convention of English that 'red' in its most basic, literal sense, is correctly predicated only of things which are red. Speakers of English who are credited with an understanding of 'red' in its most basic and literal sense are thereby credited, *inter alia*, with the intention to uphold this pattern of predication as a matter of convention. There is no better statement of the convention than the one I have given. And it is, at the same time, perfectly useless as an explanation of what the convention is to someone who doesn't already know it. The dilemma is therefore a false one: the axioms of a theory of meaning do not have to be explanatory, or 'objects of consultation', on pain of failing to concern meaning. It suffices that they describe linguistic conventions. And the question of speakers' implicit knowledge of them is thus, in effect, the question whether speakers may be regarded as implicitly recognising the conventions which they state.

The proper analysis of the notion of convention is a subtle business.[25] It may be that the idea of a convention which is merely implicitly recognised would turn out to put the notion under great strain. But prima facie there seems no reason to expect so.[26] Whatever the details of a correct analysis, convention is going to turn out to supervene upon peoples' intentions, fundamentally the intention to uphold the regularity which the convention prescribes. The crucial question is therefore whether — whether or not they are, or can be brought to be, aware of it — the axioms and recursions of a theory of meaning might succeed in describing a set of linguistic constraints which competent speakers of English may be regarded as intending to uphold. If the answer is negative, the attempt to interpret the relation between speakers and an appropriate theory of meaning for their language as that of implicit knowledge must fail; but if affirmative, that interpretation has a chance of success. In any event it is to assail a man of straw to insist that the implicit knowledge theorist should explain how a principle can be actively regulative of a practice when none of the participants can profess to know it.[27] The issue rather concerns constraints on the ascription of intention. Does it make sense to ascribe intentions to people which they cannot articulate? Or intentions a correct description of which they cannot recognise when given it?

It is important to recognise that what is at issue here is not the propriety of *extending* the notion of intention so as to accommodate the implicit knowledge theorist's needs. If ordinary practice is to be the guide, it is clear that we *already* use intention, and cognate notions, in ways that can make his position seem quite natural. The attribution of intention is entailed whenever we credit a subject with agency; and we implicitly credit a subject with agency — the capacity for action, in the proper sense of the word — whenever we deem it appropriate to offer *rationalistic* explanations of their performance, explanations which proceed by the ascription of a system of beliefs and desires. Now the fact is — philosophically suspect, or not, as the practice may be — that we go in for simple rationalistic explanations of the behaviour of more intelligent animals. If a dog sets off from his home at roughly the same time each day, no one would think it outrageous to be offered the explanation that he expects his master to be returning home at about that time and wants to see him. Some philosophers (ironically enough, Davidson[28]) would argue that any rationalistic explanation of the behaviour of a languageless creature is misconceived. My point is only the descriptive one that such explanations are *commonplace*: in the above example, the dog is implicitly credited with the intention to intercept his master — an intention of which it can neither give nor recognise an adequate description.

Consider this case. It does not happen, but might, that small children could learn to play chess long before they could learn to understand speech — or at least to attain the level of understanding necessary to give or follow explicit descriptions of the rules of chess, or of points in the theory of the game, etc. They learn the moves, let us suppose, by just the sort of patient mixture of drill, demonstration and (inadvertent) reward by which any ordinary child learns the names for colours, or farmyard animals. And then, remarkably, some of them acquire the ability to play not merely legally but well, responding with subtlety and inventiveness to board configurations which they have never encountered before. It would be overwhelmingly natural to credit such children not merely with knowledge of the rules of chess but with the sort of insight into the potentialities of a situation which any good chess player possesses. It is, however, difficult to understand how such insight should be supposed to function if it is not essentially a faculty of *inference*: inference which goes to work on premisses including, *inter alia*, the rules determining the powers of movement and capture of the various types of piece. It seems to me undeniable that, pre-philosophically as it were, we should be quite content to explain such childrens' performance by ascribing to them the knowledge and intentions constitutive of an understanding of, and the practice of playing by, the rules of chess; we would regard them as able to apprehend the implications of those rules for the potentialities of a particular state of play and thereby to inform their selection of moves with the aim of winning, or at least avoiding defeat.

The parallel with the demands made by the implicit-knowledge interpretations of the theory of meaning, the speakers being credited with knowledge of the axioms and with the capacity to apprehend their more or less remote consequences, is obvious. Indeed, the analogy may seem close enough to call the validity of what I have suggested would be our natural response to the hypothetical children into question. But to stress: my point is only that, whether or not the implicit knowledge interpretation of the theory of meaning is ultimately coherent, the objection to it — for all we have so far seen, at least — ought not to be that it puts an impossible strain on our *ordinary* understanding of notions like knowledge, belief, intention, inference, etc. On the contrary, it is aspects of our ordinary understanding of those notions which make the implicit knowledge interpretation seem natural. If it is to be rejected, the prospect is thus not of excision of an unwarranted extension of our ordinary understanding but of revision of it.

The example of the dog is suggestive in a different way. Since Brentano, it has been the more or less received wisdom in the philosophy of mind that the truth-conditions of ascriptions of propositional attitude are indifferent to reference failure in the proposition in question, but sensitive to the inter-substitution of co-referential expressions. Whether or not these are genuinely semantic (contrast, pragmatic) phenomena, it is open to question whether either is a feature of the sorts of context in which we ascribe beliefs to, for example, a dog. As far as indifference to existence is concerned, we go in for the ascription of propositional attitudes to animals only with a view to rationalising, after a fashion, their modes of interaction with items which figure in their experience; since no non-existent items so figure, there is simply no explanatory role to be played by the ascription to them of attitudes to propositions which we can express only by recourse to empty singular terms.[29] Inter-substitutivity is less straightforward. It is natural to report that the dog expects to see his master in the road, unnatural to report that he expects to see Joe Smith, or the high street newsagent. But the latter descriptions strike us as unacceptable only because we are unwilling to impute to the dog any conception of a personal proper name or the institution of newspaper selling. And the fact is that matters stand no better with the relevant concept *master*. A dog's master is, *inter alia*, ultimately responsible for its welfare and ultimately liable for its good conduct. He has the right to move it around (within, for example, restrictions imposed by quarantine laws), and even to dispose of it. Does the dog know all that? There is a temptation to reply that the dog has, as it were, a *thinner* conception of his master — one shorn of institutional trappings and based entirely on the history of interaction between them. I advise anyone who feels this temptation to attempt to specify this alleged conception, bearing in mind that the terms used must in no way exceed the concepts which may plausibly be attributed to the dog. I do not anticipate success. The truth, I suggest, is that we have no definite idea what concept we are attributing to a dog in describing its behaviour in this sort of way; and that the (unsurprising) explanation of this unclarity is that we are not seriously attributing *a concept* at all. 'His master' is a term which we use for the convenience of ourselves or our audience; there is no constraint of fidelity to a mode of conceiving employed by the dog. If the man in question was known to most of those present as the high street newsagent, whose arrival was keenly awaited, and if the relation of the dog to this man was of no importance in context, it would not be unnatural to report that the dog had rushed off in the expectation of meeting the newsagent on the road.[30]

It is, of course, uncontentious that it is not *always* a paramount constraint on the satisfactory reportage of propositional attitudes that the content-specifying part involve only concepts attributable to the subject. So much has long been recognised. What I am now suggesting is something stronger: it is our practice, in certain cases, to ascribe propositional attitudes in such a way that not only do we not intend the form of words which we use to reflect the modes of conceiving pursued by the subject but, more, there *is* no form of words which, if it were important to us, would suit that purpose. One response would be that this, if true, displays a serious indeterminacy in the beliefs, etc., attributed and so calls into doubt the propriety of the attribution. But a different response is possible: that it may be perfectly proper to ascribe certain propositional attitudes to a subject even though there is no, as it were, *canonical* specification of the content of those attitudes, no specification of their content which exactly captures their content-for-the-subject. Despite the recent concentration of effort on 'folk psychology' and the intentional, I think we are some distance from the insights to motivate either response. But if the second is tenable, the likely abstruseness of the concepts necessary for the formulation of a full-blown theory of meaning need no longer constitute an objection to the implicit knowledge conception. Crudely: if a dog may have beliefs of which there is no formulation save by the use of concepts some of which should not be attributed to the dog, then perhaps speakers of a natural language may have intentions of which there is, again, no satisfactory account save by recourse to technicalities of which they have no concept. I do not know what it is right to think about this. I would urge only that those who would treat the objection from technicality as decisive against the implicit knowledge conception should recognise what they are doing: it is not so much a matter of siding with common sense as taking (to the best of my knowledge) an unargued stance on fundamental questions in the philosophy of mind concerning what are the proper limits of explanation by the postulation of intentional states and what are proper constraints on the reportage of the content of such states.

There are, however, more subtle objections to the implicit knowledge conception. Let it be accepted that the prodigious children could properly be described as implicitly knowing the rules of chess and as possessing an appropriate range of intentions, and a measure of insight, which that knowledge served to inform. Still, the situation is not perfectly parallel to what is required in the case of a theory of meaning. The difference is that the axioms and recursions of a theory of meaning do not relate to correct linguistic practice as the 'axioms' of a theory of chess — that is, the rules of the game — relate to correct play. Someone who intentionally and in good faith moves his Queen in the manner of a Knight shows that he doesn't know the rules prescribing the powers of movement of the Queen. There is no comparably simple and direct way of showing that you do not know the axiom governing the use, in English, of 'red' or 'elephant'. That is because only a use of a *sentence* makes, as Wittgenstein put it, a move in the language game. Thus an illicit move cannot violate a single axiom; rather, it has to violate a meaning-delivering theorem, and thereby all the axioms and recursive clauses involved in its derivation. Which among these you should then be deemed to be in ignorance of is a matter to be settled by reference to your use of other sentences in the derivation of whose meaning-delivering theorems those same clauses are involved, in the light of holistic constraints.

So much is obvious enough. Why does it constitute a problem? What it shows is that, even if the chess example is deemed to be entirely persuasive of the propriety *in general* of the ideas of implicit knowledge of rules, and of implicit inference, it cannot commit us to more, in the case of the theory of meaning, than the propriety of the notion that speakers implicitly know the meaning-delivering *theorems*, and can carry out (implicit) inferences from them. Whereas, of course, what needs to be legitimated is implicit knowledge of the axioms; and implicit inferences *to* the theorems (which, in any case, speakers are likely to know explicitly). The attraction of attributing implicit knowledge of the rules of chess to the fictional children is based on two things: first, their behaviour has all the trappings of intelligence, insight and purpose which would make it virtually impossible for us to regard it as anything but intentional; second, since they behave exactly as if they knew the rules of chess, the kind of rationalistic explanation which viewing their behaviour as intentional demands can hardly do better than ascribe such knowledge to them. The strength of the analogy is that both points apply to linguistic competence too: it manifestly has the richness which invites rationalistic explanation, and — if a theory of meaning is possible at all — the behaviour which would display knowledge of it would be exactly the behaviour constitutive of linguistic competence. But the weakness of the analogy is that behaving, in all respects short of explicit statement, as if one knew a theory of meaning cannot be distinguished from behaving as if one knew its meaning-delivering theorems; whereas there is no proper subset of the theorems of the 'theory' of chess whose knowledge would constitute the ability to play. The suggestion that speakers implicitly know a full theory of meaning for their language makes demands on the notion of implicit knowledge which have no counterpart in the chess example.

The additional demands, of course, are precisely what have to be made if the implicit knowledge conception is to provide an explanation of speakers' capacity to understand novel utterances. But is it not a welcome and foreseen effect of the attribution of implicit knowledge of the rules of chess to the children that we thereby secure the means to explain their recognition of the legality, or otherwise, of moves that they have never considered before? Surely. The difference is that the case for attributing implicit knowledge of the rules of chess to the children does not entirely consist in this phenomenon, but can be stated independently of it. The rules of chess comprise the *smallest* theory — of this particular subject matter; we shall, of course, need to attribute a lot of other information to them, of different sorts — which we need in order to give the envisaged sort of rationalistic explanation of their behaviour. Moreover, each item of knowledge which we thereby attribute to them has its own distinctive kind of behavioural display. If we seek a theory of meaning with these same two features, in contrast, we shall wind up with the sort of infinitary axiom schema which figured in the discussion of Foster above. The explanation of the children's ability to judge novel moves in point of legality may thus be viewed as a welcome by-product of an independently motivated attribution of implicit knowledge to them. That is not at all the situation with the implicit knowledge conception of the theory of meaning; linguistic 'creativity' here provides the entire *raison d'être*.

The response will be that it cannot be satisfactory just to credit speakers with knowledge of what is stated by perhaps indefinitely many meaning-delivering theorems, some of which concern sentences which they have never encountered, and leave it at that. The question must arise: what is the basis of this knowledge? My point, however, is not that we should discount this question but that the kind of play made with implicit knowledge in the fictional chess case — which was meant to epitomise the strength of the intuitions that underlie the implicit knowledge conception — provides no precedent for the supposition that this question should have a *psychological* answer. There has to be a perfectly respectable scientific question about the sources of our possession of the knowledge which the meaning-delivering theorems of a satisfactory theory of meaning would describe. But there is no *a priori* reason why the answer to this question should have to proceed via the postulation of further cognitive states. The sought-for finite basis may be better described in non-psychological terms.

There is an argument in Gareth Evans's discussion[31] which suggests that extending the notion of speakers' implicit knowledge to encompass the axioms and derivations within a theory of meaning would be a definite error. A rat may acquire the disposition to avoid a kind of foodstuff which is poisonous and has caused it sickness in the past. And we might casually ascribe its unwillingness to eat this material — or one that looked/smelt similar — to the belief that it was poisonous. But we should not, Evans urges, let casual language induce casual thought. Beliefs are essentially things which interact with desires and intentions in the production of behaviour. They are also essentially involved in the production of other beliefs. To ascribe a belief is significant only as part of the ascription of a *system* of beliefs. And what behaviour is expressive of a certain belief depends, in general, upon the other ingredients in this system and in the system of the subject's intentions and desires. Thus my belief that a certain substance is poisonous may manifest itself in a literally indefinite variety of ways. I may, like the rat, avoid the substance. But I may also take steps to ensure my family avoid it, or take steps to ensure they don't! I may take small but daily increasing quantities of the stuff in the belief that I can thereby inure myself against its effects and that background circumstances are such that it may stand to my advantage to have done so. I may take a large quantity if I wish to commit suicide; and a smaller one if I wish to malinger my way out of some obligation. My belief that the substance is poisonous is thus, as Evans puts it, at the service of indefinitely many potential projects corresponding to indefinitely many transformations in my other beliefs and desires. With the rat, in contrast, concepts like the desire for suicide, or malign intent, can get no grip. The 'desires' which we are prepared to attribute to it are restricted, in the described context, to avoidance of distress; and its 'belief' that the substance is poisonous has consequently no other expression than in shunning it.

Evans's point, well made by this example, is that rationalistic explanations of behaviour are so much idle patter unless we are willing to credit the subject with the sophistication of a manifold system of interacting and evolving beliefs and desires, of a degree of organisation sufficient to obstruct straightforward dispositional reductions of any particular belief ascription. There is no such obstruction in the case of the rat. Describing it as believing that the substance is poisonous adds nothing to the claim that it has suffered from it in the past and is now disposed to avoid it. If the rat were, for example, to shift some of the substance to the habitual feeding place of an aggressor, to prevent her children from taking it, and to introduce some of it into the tea cup of the experimenter, on the other hand, we might begin to feel an incentive for serious rationalistic theorising.

The force of this train of thought becomes apparent as soon as we ask how a defender of the implicit knowledge conception can distinguish those putatively intentional states, whose content he specifies using the axioms of a theory of meaning, which he wishes to attribute to speakers from the sort of dispositions whose behavioural expression is so inflexibly related to them as to disqualify them from the role of components in serious rationalistic theorising. One of the chess-playing children will standardly manifest his knowledge of the rule governing the powers of movement and capture of the Queen by conforming to it. But other manifestations are possible: he may attempt to correct an opponent who breaks the rule, refuse to play with someone who makes a habit of doing so, or even deliberately break the rule himself as a somewhat unconventional mode of resignation, or by way of a pretended incompetence in the hope of short-circuiting a game he would rather not play. Likewise, someone who is credited with implicit knowledge of a meaning-delivering theorem may express his knowledge in an indefinite variety of ways, including, in appropriate contexts, lying, assent, and silence. But the (implicit) knowledge of a meaning theoretic *axiom* would seem to be harnessed to the single project of forming beliefs about the content of sentences which contain the expression, or exemplify the mode of construction, which it concerns. Certainly, the precise beliefs which are formed will vary as a function of the content of the other relevant axioms of which a subject is also being supposed to have implicit knowledge. But what is supposed to be the role of *desire*? What is the (implicit?) desire which explains why the subject puts his semantic axiomatic beliefs to just this use, and what are the different uses to which they might be put if his desires were different?

The question draws a complete blank. The case is, in fact, worse than with the rat. We can begin to tell some sort of story — I did so above — of what sort of enrichment and complication of rodent behaviour might enable us to regard the belief that a substance was poisonous as manifested, via a particular kind of behaviour, along with something other than the desire to avoid discomfort. But what is the desire which, in conjuction with the knowledge represented by the meaning-theoretic axioms, is manifested in the formation of beliefs about the meanings of sentences? And what other manifestation might that knowledge have if this desire was different?[32] The truth is that the content of ascribing implicit knowledge of a meaning-theoretic axiom would appear to be no more than the ascription of a disposition to form beliefs about the meanings of sentences featuring the expression, or mode of construction, which

Theories of Meaning and Speakers' Knowledge 293

it concerns: the disposition, precisely, to form beliefs which are appropriately constrained by the content of the axiom. Although Evans allows his discussion to proceed in terms of what he calls 'tacit knowledge', his own response to this train of thought is to abjure any form of intentionalistic construal of the relation between speakers and the axiomatic content of a theory of meaning. Rather, the axioms should indeed be seen precisely as describing certain dispositions which competent speakers have.[33]

The reader must form his own judgement about whether the point really is fatal to the prospects of any sort of intentionalistic construal of the relation between speakers and axioms. Let me, though, attempt to ensure that he does so in awareness of some limitations of Evans's own positive proposals. I shall pursue Evans's example of a simple language containing just ten singular terms, a, b, c,..., and ten one-place predicates, F, G, H,..., together with the single sentence-forming operation of singular term-predicate concatenation. The language thus has 100 possible sentences, and allows of a finite but non-compositional truth-theoretic axiomatisation consisting of 100 corresponding instances of the T-schema. Call this axiomatisation T_1; and contrast it with the compositional axiomatisation, T_2 which has 21 axioms: ten assigning denotations to the singular terms; ten stipulating satisfaction-conditions for the predicates; and a compositional axiom to the effect that a sentence coupling a name with a predicate is true if and only if the object denoted by the name satisfies the predicate. Evans's negative proposal is that T_2 should not be seen as describing the contents of any sort of intentional states of speakers of the object language. His positive proposal is that it should be seen as describing dispositions which they have; and, crucially, that even when so interpreted, it may be preferable to T_1.

The immediate question is: *what* dispositions, exactly, does T_2 describe? Evans's own account proceeds in terms of a notion of 'tacit knowledge' — by way of deference, no doubt, to the free-wheeling use made of intentional terminology by so many psychologists and psycholinguists — which, in contrast with what the considerations above might prompt us to regard as *genuinely* intentional states, does admit of an apparently straightforward dispositional account. His suggestion is that a speaker U tacitly knows that, for instance, the denotation of a is John if and only if he has a disposition such that:

(Πϕ) (Π ψ) [if U tacitly knows that an object satisfies ϕ if and only if it is ψ; and U hears an utterance having the form ϕa; then U will judge that: the utterance is true if and only if John is ψ]

Likewise a speaker U tacitly knows that, for instance, an object satisfies *F* if and only if it is bald, if and only if he has a disposition such that:

(Πx) (Πα) [if U tacitly knows that the denotation of α is x, and U hears an utterance having the form *F*α ; then U will judge that: the utterance is true if and only if x is bald][34]

These proposals seem more or less inevitable. 'Tacit knowledge' ought to be a disposition which constitutes understanding; and what is it to understand a subsentential expression of Evans's simple language except to be disposed to make the right judgements about the truth conditions of sentences containing it provided one understands the accompanying name or predicate? But there are a number of difficulties.

The first is, once again, that it is not clear how this interpretation of the relation between speakers and the axioms can provide a reason for preferring T_2 to T_1. The dispositions which T_2 assigns to speakers are dispositions of judgement concerning whole sentences; so why not simply describe them directly by using T_1? Evans's answer is that he intends the notion of disposition to which he is appealing to be understood in a 'full-blooded sense': the ascription of a disposition is to be interpreted as the ascription of an underlying state from which the relevant patterns of behaviour, described in the conditional which articulates what the disposition is a disposition to do (causally), flow. Thus the difference between T_1 and T_2 is that the former ascribes 100 distinct such states to competent speakers of the object language whereas

tacit knowledge of T_2 requires that there should be 20 such states of the subject — one corresponding to each expression of the language which the theory treats separately — such that the causal explanation of why the subject reacts in the way that he does to any sentence of the language involves two of these states, and any one of these states is involved in the explanation of the way he reacts to 10 sentences containing a common element.[35]

In Evans's view the claims of T_1 and T_2 to describe speakers' competence may thus, under favourable circumstances, be empirically adjudicated. A satisfactory neurophysiological account of competence would be decisive;[35a] but even in advance of attaining that, strong evidence for the superiority of T_2 would be afforded by the empirical findings (a) that speakers acquire the capacity to understand so far unencountered specimens from among the 100 possible sentences on the basis of exposure to utterances which contain the relevant constituents; and (b) that when speakers *lose* competence with any of the sentences — owing to forgetfulness, or disease, or damage — they tend simultaneously to lose competence with all the sentences which feature one, or both of its constituents.

Now, although I think Evans's deference to neurophysiology is mistaken — since it is evidence of types (a) and (b) which would determine our conception of what kind of neurophysiological theory to settle for — and although it is not clear exactly what account of identity and distinctness among (neurophysiological) *states* should provide the backcloth to his suggestions, the kind of data which he envisages would obviously be highly significant. But the question, of course, is why such data would properly motivate the adoption of T_2, rather than T_1 supplemented with some appropriate hypotheses, of a non-semantical sort, about the presumed causal substructure of the dispositions which T_1 describes. This is essentially the objection which featured in the discussion of the 'Mirror Constraint' earlier, and Evans's discussion contains, so far as I can see, no answer to it. The requirement that a theory of meaning should both describe the dispositions which the competent display in their handling of whole sentences and reflect the underlying causal structure of those dispositions — as witnessed by the details of their acquisition and loss and, perhaps, by their neurophysiology — provides absolutely no basis for preferring a theory of meaning to a description, or list, of the meaning-delivering theorems, supplemented by claims like

> Some single neurophysiological state is involved in the causal explanation of a speaker's competence with any sentence which features the expression *a*.

Why adopt T_2, or any theory whose axioms have a *semantical* subject matter, if the task is to reflect the *causal* structure of the dispositions which correspond to the meaning-delivering theorems?

There is a connection between this point and a peculiarity in Evans's exposition which the alert reader will already have noticed. Why does Evans speak of tacit knowledge of T_2 as involving *twenty* states of the subject when the axioms of T_2 are *twenty-one*? The answer is obvious enough. The account which Evans offers of the dispositions which constitute tacit knowledge of the denotations of singular terms and the satisfaction conditions of predicates have the effect that a speaker who possesses them is thereby disposed to attach the proper significance to name-predicate coupling — since he is thereby disposed to attach the proper significance to sentences formed by coupling names and predicates. But this leaves Evans's proposal open to a simple objection. T_2 would be crippled without the compositional axiom, but if the brief of its axioms were *merely* the description of the dispositions which, on Evans's account, constitute tacit knowledge of them, the compositional axiom ought to be redundant. However, there is in view no plausible modification of Evans's proposals concerning the dispositions relevant to singular terms and predicates which would need to be supplemented by a separate dispositional account concerning the compositional axiom. So the conclusion has to be that Evans's proposals misdescribe the content of the axioms of T_2. The conclusion of the preceding argument is therefore reinforced. We can grant that Evans has provided reason why a theory which concerned itself with a description of the dispositions which constituted a speaker's competence might wish to construe some of these dispositions as concerned with subsentential expressions. But since any compositional theory of meaning for a typical natural language will incorporate something like T_2, and since T_2 will not sustain that interpretation of its brief, Evans has provided no reason why we should seek a compositional theory of meaning.

Evans's proposal is apt to seem dissatisfying in a further respect. His account of what tacit knowledge of the denotation of a singular term disposes a subject to do appeals to a prior understanding of what it is to have tacit knowledge of the satisfaction conditions of a predicate; and vice versa. The two sets of dispositions are thus, as Evans acknowledges, 'interdefined'. Why is that not a recipe for vicious circularity? No one can follow Evans's characterisation of what it is for U tacitly to know that the denotation of *a* is John unless he already understands what it is for U to have tacit knowledge of the satisfaction conditions of predicates in the language in question. If he doesn't understand that, Evans's account will plainly be of no avail to him, since it demands a prior understanding of what it is for U tacitly to know — of some arbitrarily selected singular term, which might be *a* — that its denotation is so-and-so. This circularity may seem harmless for two reasons. First, it reflects an undoubted feature of our intuitive conception of what it is to understand subsentential expressions: to understand a name *is* to have the capacity to understand utterances in which it figures, provided one understands the remaining constituents and the mode of construction; and to understand the remaining constituents and the mode of construction *is* to have the capacity to understand utterances in which they feature provided one understands the rest of the sentence, which, in the basic case, takes us back to proper names. Second, circularity of this sort need in any case be no objection if the task is not to provide an *introductory* explanation of the concepts in question but to offer some measure of characterisation of them.

Both these points are fair. But the worry is not that the 'interdefinability' of Evans's axiomatic dispositions reflects no feature of our intuitive conception of what it is to understand the constituents of a sentence, but that, naïvely, perhaps, one wants something better in the characterisation of a *disposition*. To characterise a disposition ought to be to characterise both what it is a disposition to do and the circumstances under which it will be manifest. Often we settle for very imperfectly precise characterisations of both. But the complaint here is not of imprecision. If, for instance, I characterise the ductility of a metal by reference to certain observable phenomena which occur under background circumstances *including* the possession by the substance of certain further dispositions; and if it then turns out that a characterisation of the distinctive manifestations of some of these further dispositions is possible only by reference to background circumstances in which the substances are assumed to be ductile — if that is the best that can be done, the reproach does not seem foolish that I have so far simply *failed to say* what ductility is. Evans's proposals would seem to leave the dispositions which they aim to characterise in this uncomfortable-seeming position. However, I offer the point more as something which someone who wished to advance Evans's account should say something about than as an objection. Perhaps a more sophisticated account of the notion of a disposition would remove the worry; my own suggestion would be that Evans's proposal should have proceeded by reference to states of a different sort — his real interest, after all, is in the underlying 'categorical' bases. But I anticipate.

One final point about Evans's proposals is worth emphasis. He writes:

> ... it is implicit in what has gone before that the notion of tacit knowledge of a [compositional] theory of meaning, explained as I have explained it, cannot be used to explain the capacity to understand new sentences.[36]

This is because the dispositions which, on Evans's account, constitute tacit knowledge of the axioms of T_2, for example, precisely *are* the dispositions to judge correctly the truth-conditions of novel sentences in the language in question. Evans's claim on behalf of a compositional theory of meaning is that it is likely to give the empirically best attested description of what these dispositions are. I think he is right that, even if there is no force whatever in the foregoing objections, this is the most that, on his account of the matter, could be claimed. Accordingly, an *explanation* of speakers' 'creativity' would have to consist, for Evans, in an account of how it is that speakers are prone to acquire just these dispositions on the basis of the incomplete and imperfect sampling in which a typical training in the use of a natural language consists.

This still leaves a theorist of meaning with a contribution to make to the explanatory project. Before an account can be given of the aetiology of the relevant dispositions, we need to know what they are. The ability of a learner to understand a novel utterance can, presumably, be made to seem non-miraculous only if the sample of uses which induced in him the dispositions which he thereby exercises themselves involved exercise of corresponding dispositions on the part of those whose speech he witnessed.

> Consequently, when a capacity to understand novel sentences is observed, the theorist of meaning has an indispensable role to play in its explanation, since he must exhibit the regularity between the old and the new.[37]

What is striking about this suggestion is the width of the gulf which it opens between what, on Evans's account, the theorist of meaning should be about and what in practice those philosophers who have taken an interest — none more than Evans — in the project of a theory of meaning have been content to do. One clear implication of Evans's account, for instance, is that the construction of a useful theory of meaning does demand elevation from the armchair. Data are needed about trainees' learning patterns — about just what 'projections' they tend to be able to make on the basis of exposure to just what class of sample — and about patterns of loss, before we can so much as form a best guess at the syntactic categories in terms of which Evans's basic dispositions should be described. This is not what has happened. The relevant syntactic categories have been persistently supposed to be, more or less, those which Frege invented; 'regimentation' of the surface grammar of natural language is acknowledged to be inevitable in the construction of a theory of the sought-for kind. I submit that if Evans's account of the project is the right one, this *a priori* indifference to the *overt form* of many of the utterances which the novice speaker is able 'creatively' to understand is rather strange methodology. Not that the surface/depth grammar distinction may not be amenable to excellent empirical motivation. My point is that philosophical theorists of meaning seem to have assumed its propriety without reliance on the kind of data which, if Evans's account of their project were correct, it ought to depend on.

I do not mean to suggest that those philosophers who have set about the Davidsonian project with respect to (fragments of) English have relied on no data which could properly be viewed as empirical. They have relied, of course, on a rich set of intuitions about particular meanings, and the significance of particular constructions, which competent speakers of English tend to share. The point is rather that they have, by and large, relied on no data concerning language acquisition and loss. Admittedly, this may be taken as showing not that Evans's account of how we should conceive the relation between actual speakers and the target theory is altogether misconceived but only that the right account has not greatly impinged upon the consciousness of workers in the field. So it is worth noting, to conclude this section, that there is a proposal, similar in spirit to Evans's but different in detail, which harmonises rather better with the relatively a prioristic approach that theorists have followed.

As is familiar, certain species of bird display what appears to be a remarkable ability to find their way home from distant and unfamiliar locations. The ability appears remarkable because unless we were allowed to rely on special equipment and knowledge — compasses, charts, the disposition of the stars, and so on — we could not emulate it. How do they do it? There are, of course, a number of differences between this problem and that of linguistic creativity. For one thing, there is no analogue of compositionality; no platitudinous answer, like 'By understanding the words and the way in which they are put together', is in the offing to constrain a satisfactory answer. For another, part of what has to be resolved is the range of sensory cues to which the birds should be thought of as responding — whereas it is taken to be a *datum* that speakers respond to the overt visible or audible structure of a sentence. But what is importantly parallel is that we do not know how to approach the question about, in particular, pigeons unless we are allowed to construct a theory which, like a theory of meaning, serves to articulate possible modes of information processing. We would seek, that is to say, a theory which, if conjoined with supplementary information about features of its novel location which would, according to our best account of a pigeon's sensory apparatus, be discernible by the bird, would serve to issue in theorems whose content would be an instruction about what (sensed object) to fly towards. Of course, the suggestion that actual birds might *know* the content of such a theory would be vulnerable to the principal objection raised above. But it is in any case a suggestion to which we are not tempted; we do not, in setting about devising such a theory, regard ourselves as committed to viewing pigeons as intentional agents. On the contrary: the idea is to make them intelligible as a sophisticated sort of *mechanism.*

In a way, it is incidental that there are any such creatures. Even if there were not, the question could be posed whether a device could be designed which would 'home' in the way that pigeons actually do. A positive answer to the question would require a demonstration how a mechanism sensitive to certain features of its environment could process the data thereby accumulated so as to be disposed to relocate itself in the appropriate way. At the first stage, this is *entirely* an information-processing problem: it calls, in effect, for the devising of an appropriate computer program. At the second stage, the problem would be that of explaining how this program, plus the relevant capacities of sensitivity and movement, might be incorporated into a physically possible device. The sort of understanding of the actual capacities of pigeons which is called for would be achieved exactly when enough was known about them to enable us to understand how in detail they embody such a device. And, of course, there can be no such understanding before we have formed the appropriate theoretical conception of the powers which the device must have. Doing that requires writing the computer program.

Three points are notable. First, devising such a program is not an *empirical* problem. What is sought is an axiomatic theory which, fed with (successive) appropriately formulated descriptions of environments distinct from 'home', will generate (successive) theorems encoding a successful homing strategy. This is a kind of problem which, when sufficiently precisely formulated, can be cracked in the armchair. The corresponding armchair problem for the theorist of meaning is to devise a theory which will take us from a description of relevant features of an arbitrary utterance to a theorem which characterises its meaning. Second, the theorist will not best serve the next stage of the explanatory project — that of making good the claim that actual human beings embody, as it were, the relevant program — if he produces a theory with an infinitary axiom base. We do not understand what it would be to build a computer which incorporated infinitely many logically independent items of information in its program but no finite axiomatisation of them. Simply to postulate that biological evolution can do what we cannot would be to reformulate rather than solve the original problem. And it is in any case unclear what could constitute a neurophysiological reason for thinking that a pigeon, or human being, was the living embodiment of such a theory. A finiteness constraint at least thus appears to flow naturally from consideration of the overall character of the explanation which we are seeking. Finally, the connection between the axioms of the theory and speakers' (or pigeons') dispositions is less direct than on Evans's account. A completed explanation along the lines envisaged will of course involve the identification of (presumably neurophysiological) states which embody the various items of information corresponding to the axioms of the program. But these states need not be individuated, so far as I can see, as (categorical bases for) distinct dispositions; nor, in general, does there appear to be any *a priori* reason why the correspondence between the axioms and their neurophysiological realisations should be one-to-one.

I claim for this approach only that it may indicate the shape of a better account of the relevance of a theory of meaning to explaining the capacities of actual speakers than can be provided by play with the notion of 'implicit' intentional states, or by Evans's dispositionalist account. No doubt it will encounter problems of its own. It is obvious, above all, that clarification is needed of what it is for a system to 'embody' information — clarification which only a philosopher who is unusually well-informed in computational, psychological, and neurophysiological science is likely to be able to achieve — and that there has to be, at least initially, a legitimate doubt in any case about the extension of this sort of notion to natural systems. I have wanted to indicate only that the horizon is not empty of all prospect of satisfactorily yoking together the philosophical project of a theory of meaning and the explanation of actual speakers' linguistic 'creativity'.

IV

It remains to draw some conclusions about how our discussion bears on the realism/anti-realism debate, when it is conceived in Dummett's way. The answer, it should now be clear, is: not at all. The anti-realist claim is that nobody may reasonably be credited with knowledge of the truth-conditions of any of a very substantial class of statements. (Precisely what class will depend upon the degree of anti-realism espoused.) The conclusion is then drawn that truth may not play the central role in a comprehensive theory of (statement) meaning — at least not when understood *à la mode réalistique*. The justification for this conclusion is that the theory is supposed to represent the knowledge in which understanding of the sentences of a language consists, which it must be failing to do if it cannot do better than articulate that knowledge in terms of concepts which they cannot have. Now if the discussion of implicit knowledge above had yielded the result that a theory of meaning simply cannot be concerned with the description of speakers' knowledge at all, then the anti-realist critique of (realist) truth-conditional semantics could not take exactly this form. But two points need emphasis. First, what emerged as problematic was the idea of speakers' implicit knowledge of the content of the *axioms* of a theory of meaning — no reason emerged to doubt the propriety of crediting them with implicit knowledge of the content of the meaning-delivering *theorems*; and I anticipate that no such reason could be produced which did not demand rejection of the idea of implicit knowledge altogether. Second, if the more radical anti-realist claims about the dubiety of a conception of verification-transcendent truth are correct, we — the theorists — have no business involving that 'notion' in any sort of theory, whether conceived as descriptive of the content of object-language speakers' understanding or not. There has been some curious muddle about this simple point in recent realist commentary.[38] So perhaps it is worth emphasising the obvious: whether or not the theory of meaning is conceived — as Dummett always urges it must be — as a theory of speakers' understanding, the project is, trivially, constrained by the demand that the concepts which it uses be in good order. Criticism of that particular ingredient in Dummett's philosophy of language, or highlighting of the non-sequitur involved in the transition from the claims (1) that the meaning of a sentence is what someone who understands it knows, and (2) that the meaning of a sentence is determined by its truth-conditions, to (3) one who understands a sentence knows its truth-conditions,[39] is therefore entirely futile if what one is trying to do is to protect realist semantics from anti-realist attack. Indeed the anti-realist case has no less bearing on the desirable form for a theory of meaning to take if the project is conceived as having nothing directly to do with the concepts of actual speakers but is concerned entirely with the idealised epistemology of language acquisition, after the fashion of the proposal extracted earlier from Davies's discussion.[40]

Notes

1. The locus classicus is his 'Truth and Meaning', *Synthese*, 17 (1967), pp. 304-23. The paper is reprinted as Essay 2 in D. Davidson, *Inquiries into Truth and Interpretation* (Oxford University Press, 1984). This whole volume, and especially the section consisting of the first five essays, is pervaded by the proposal.
2. See, for example, M. Dummett, 'What Is a Theory of Meaning? (II)', in G. Evans and J. McDowell (eds.), *Truth and Meaning* (Oxford University Press, 1975). pp. 72-6 and *passim*.
3. See M. Dummett, 'What Is a Theory of Meaning?' in S. Guttenplan (ed.), *Mind and Language* (Oxford University Press, 1974), pp. 102-6 and *passim*.
4. These arguments are widespread in Dummett's writings. See especially 'What Is a Theory of Meaning? (II)' and Essays 1, 10, 11, 14 and 21 in his *Truth and Other Enigmas* (Duckworth, 1978). Note, however, page xxii of the latter's Preface where Dummett expresses dissatisfaction with the idea that the anti-realist arguments call in question the propriety of truth-conditional theories of meaning, suggesting

instead that their bearing is on the proper interpretation of *truth.*
   5. See the indexed references under *finiteness requirement* in *Inquiries into Truth and Interpretation,* and pp. 56-7 (of Essay 4, 'Semantics for Natural Languages') which the indexer missed. For those quite innocent of these matters, the 'T-theorems' take the form illustrated by

'Snow is white', is true if and only if snow is white,

whereby the quoted sentence is used to characterise its own truth-conditions and hence — controversially — its own meaning.
   6. *Inquiries into Truth and Interpretation,* Essay 1 ('Theories of Meaning and Learnable Languages'), p. 8.
   7. See, for example, 'Truth and Meaning', opening paragraph.
   8. *Inquiries into Truth and Interpretation,* Essay 2 ('Truth and Meaning'), p. 35.
   9. 'What Is a Theory of Meaning? (II)', p. 70.
   10. Ibid., p. 109.
   11. Ibid.
   12. Ibid., p. 112.
   13. G.P. Baker and P.M.S. Hacker, *Language, Sense and Nonsense* (Blackwell, 1984).
   14. See note 4.
   15. From his 'Meaning and Truth Theory' in Evans and McDowell (eds.), pp. 1-2.
   16. Foster, ibid., p. 2.
   17. Compare the 'metaphysical perspective' of Elizabeth Fricker's, 'Semantic Structure and Speakers' Understanding', *Aristotelian Society Proceedings,* LXXXIII (1982-3), section I.
   18. Martin Davies, *Meaning, Quantification, Necessity* (Routledge and Kegan Paul, 1981), Ch. III, p. 53 and following.
   19. This does not coincide exactly with Davies's formulation, but differs, I believe, in no important respect.
   20. For instance, that the constraint provides no guidance to the semantic theorist if the studied language has no actual speakers; and leaves no space for the idea that speakers might fail to know the meanings of sentences which were nevertheless determinate, fixed by syntactic constructions and semantic features familiar to them.
   21. Davies, ibid., p. 56.
   22. Davies shows, in fact, that on natural assumptions about what is requisite for the learnability of a language, the Structural Constraint enjoins that a theory satisfying it will indeed be finitely axiomatised. See *Meaning, Quantification, Necessity,* Ch. III, section 2.
   23. One important reservation about the proposal would concern whether knowledge of the meanings of an appropriate $S_1,\ldots,S_n$ could be enjoyed *independently* of knowledge of the meaning of an S to which, according to the sought-for theory, a rational projection from an understanding of $S_1,\ldots,S_n$ would be possible. The opposing thought, urged on me in discussion by Elizabeth Fricker and suggested by some of her argumentation in the paper cited in n.17 above (see in particular section IV), would be, in effect, that understanding any such S is a *criterion* for knowing the meanings of $S_1,\ldots,S_n$. Whereas the project of describing a basis for a rational inference to the meaning of S has content only if it is possible to be apprised of the basis and yet fail so to exploit it.
   Clearly there is no objection of this kind where we are concerned with a *second* language: of course it is possible for an English speaker to know *what* each of finitely

many French sentences means without having any idea *why*. The question is whether that distinction, between knowing what a sentence means and why it means it, has content for a first language — can there be such a thing as understanding a sentence of one's only language without understanding its semantic structure? It seems we would have to deny that there can if an explanation is to be possible of why — supposing it is so — sentence understanding has the sort of holistic character claimed by the objection. But notice, in that case, that we should then have a quite different form of response to the problem of motivating compositionality. A homophonic theory consisting of a recursive syntax plus an infinitary semantic axiom schema, or — for a finite language — a 'listiform' theory consisting simply of specifications of the meanings of all its sentences, would no longer have a claim to characterise what someone who understood the object-language thereby knew. At least, it would not do so with sufficient explicitness: a fully explicit account would have to contain the resources for describing, for each object-language sentence, not merely what it means but why it meant it.

A fully satisfactory treatment of our topic would have to investigate this through to a conclusion. But I have felt justified in not attempting this here, because of the prospect that the objection, if sustained, would still conserve an *a priori* motive for compositionality.

24. 'What is a Theory of Meaning?', pp. 109-10.

25. The locus classicus is David Lewis's *Convention: A Philosophical Study* (Harvard, 1969).

26. I intend no judgement, by this remark, about whether the very strong epistemic conditions involved in Lewis's original account *would* permit meaning-theoretic axioms of which subjects were unaware to encode conventions. But the crucial question is in any case that about intention to which the text now moves.

27. One cause for complaint about Baker's and Hacker's book (see n. 13 above) is their predilection for such opposition. There are other causes. See my review, 'Understanding Novel Utterances' in the *Times Literary Supplement* for 11 January 1985.

28. See 'Thought and Talk', Essay 11 of *Inquiries into Truth and Interpretation*.

29. Any apparent counter-example to this claim is going to be controversial and marginal at best. One possibility: if humans, who share a magic mushroom, for example, can co-hallucinate — 'Look at that little green man sitting by the window' — there might be circumstances in which a dog would best be described as, for example, barking at such a 'common object' of hallucination. But I can envisage no other circumstances in which we would have cause to use an empty singular term — rather than a quantifier — in ascribing an intentional state to an animal.

30. Indeed, why ascribe to a dog so much as a *sortal concept* of man, a conception of his master as a recurrent *particular*, rather than view it as operating a primitive feature-placing scheme of concepts? Note however that if the main claim of the text — that 'there is no constraint of fidelity to [the subject's] mode of conceiving' in such cases — is correct, it does not follow that co-extensive expressions will be unrestrictedly intersubstitutive in the relevant class of contexts. Whether that is so will depend on what *other* (audience- and reporter-related) constraints are in operation. Any purported counter-example to the main claim will therefore have to be shown not to be the effect of other such constraints.

31. Gareth Evans, 'Semantic Theory and Tacit Knowledge' in C. Leich and S. Holtzman (eds.), *Wittgenstein: to Follow a Rule*. See especially section III. Compare Martin Davies, *Meaning, Quantification, Necessity*, pp. 83-6.

32. Matters stand quite difficultly, of course, once the knowledge becomes *explicit*: lying, assent, silence, sarcastic denial, etc., all provide differing modes of expressing it, *modulo* variable contexts and desires. This, I think, is the correct form

of reply to John Campbell's point about the relative paucity of projects which knowledge, for example, of the plot structure of *Bleak House* might be 'at the service of'. In the relevant sense — that of explaining co-varying behaviour as other beliefs and desires are varied — such knowldge is indeed at the service of many projects.

33. It is notable that Evans's argument is explicitly directed only against the supposition that speakers *believe* what the axioms state. Earlier we had cause to take seriously the suggestion that *intention* might be the best candidate, from the point of view of the implicit knowledge conception, for the psychological bond between speakers and the contents of the axioms. The proposal was, roughly, that speakers should be credited with whatever (implicit) intentions would suffice to confer the status of conventions on the axioms. Might this make a difference? For there does not seem to be the same kind of holistic flexibility in what counts as manifesting a particular intention which obtains in the case of belief. If the belief that a substance is poisonous may be manifested in any number of ways, among which avoiding eating it is only one — though a usual — case, the intention to avoid eating it, for instance, is manifested by doing just that.

The suggestion is difficult to appraise in the absence of a detailed proposal. But there is some cause for pessimism. It is, to begin with, an error to suppose that there is a simple analytic connection between the content of an intention and the behaviour which manifests it. There is such a connection, but it is with whatever behaviour *implements* the intention; whereas the intention may be manifested by unsuccessful efforts to implement it, and indeed by any behaviour which the subject believes may (help to) carry it through. Intention, properly so regarded, will accordingly sustain a similar variety of possible modes of expression to that which characterises belief. Evans's challenge ought therefore still to be good: how is the attribution of implicit intentions to be distinguished from, and justified in preference to, the attribution of dispositions to speak, and interpret the speech of others, in accordance with the meaning-theoretic axioms? Intention is distinguished from a mere disposition by the possibility of misguided attempts at fulfilment and by the subject's adaptability: his capacity to envisage a variety of ways in which it might be fulfilled and to modify his path accordingly. How can these ideas be made to grip in the present case?

In any case, intention cannot be the *whole* story. To be party to a convention is to have both intentions of a certain sort *and* beliefs — beliefs about just what regularities upholding the convention will require to be sustained. In David Lewis's study, for instance, it is necessary, if a regularity is to be conventional, that each of the participants expects the others to sustain it and that everyone prefers to sustain it if the others do (since a solution to a 'co-ordination problem' is thereby achieved). So the challenge is immediate: how is the putative *belief* that everyone else will conform to the axioms of a theory of meaning to be distinguished from the *disposition* to form beliefs, as one successfully encounters novel utterances, that their behaviour will, *ceteris paribus*, conform to the requirements of the meaning-delivering theorems for those utterances?

34. 'Π' is here a universal substitutional quantifier; and the variables, ϕ, α, ψ, and x, have respectively, the substitution classes of names of predicate expressions of the object language, names of names of the object language, predicate expressions of the metalanguage (English) and proper names of the metalanguage (English). Cf. Evans, *Semantic Theory and Tacit Knowledge*, pp. 124-5.

35. Evans, 'Semantic Theory and Tacit Knowledge', p. 125.
35a. Ibid., p. 127.
36. Ibid., p. 134.
37. Ibid., pp. 135-6.
38. An example is Michael Devitt's Chapter 12, 'Dummett's Anti-Realism', of

his *Realism and Truth* (Blackwell, 1984).
  39. Cf. Devitt, *Realism and Truth*, pp. 207-8.
  40. I would like to thank Martin Davies and Elizabeth Fricker for detailed and very helpful comments on an earlier draft, and Mark Johnston and David Lewis for some useful remarks on some of this material presented during my graduate seminar at Princeton in autumn 1985.

CONTRIBUTORS

Gordon Baker grew up in the United States and was educated first at Harvard (AB in mathematics). He then completed his education at Oxford (BA in Literae Humaniores, DPhil in philosophy). Since 1968 he has been Fellow and Tutor in Philosophy at St John's College, Oxford. With Dr P.M.S. Hacker he is co-author of *Wittgenstein: Understanding and Meaning* (1980), *Frege: Logical Excavations* (1984), *Language, Sense & Nonsense* (1984), *Scepticism, Rules and Language* (1984), and *Wittgenstein: Rules, Grammar and Necessity* (1985).

Renford Bambrough has been a Fellow of St John's College, Cambridge since 1950. He was Dean of the College from 1964 to 1979 and President from 1979 to 1983. He is Sidgwick Lecturer in Philosophy in the University of Cambridge and was Stanton Lecturer in Philosophy of Religion from 1962 to 1965. Since 1972 he has been Editor of *Philosophy*, the journal of the Royal Institute of Philosophy. His books include *Reason, Truth and God* (1969) and *Moral Scepticism and Moral Knowledge* (1979). He has held visiting appointments at Cornell University, the University of California, Berkeley, the University of Oregon and the University of Melbourne. In 1983 he was Presidential Fellow of the Carnegie Foundation at Princeton. He is a member of the Council for the Accreditation of Teacher Education.

Antony Flew is Emeritus Professor of Philosophy at the University of Reading, England and Distinguished Research Fellow at the Social Philosophy and Policy Center, Bowling Green, Ohio. He is Vice President of the Rationalist Press Association, sometime Chairman of the Executive Committee of the Voluntary Euthanasia Society and founder member of the Council of the Freedom Association. Among his books are *An Introduction to Western Philosophy* (1971), *A Rational Animal* (1978), *The Politics of Procrustes* (1981), *Darwinian Evolution* (1984), and *Thinking about Social Thinking* (1985).

Ernest Gellner was born in Paris in December 1925. He was educated partly in Prague and partly in England, first at St Alban's County School, and then Balliol College, Oxford (Open Scholar). He was on the staff of the London School of Economics between 1949 and 1984, where he was Professor of Philosophy from 1962. Whilst teaching philosophy he also carried out special anthropological fieldwork in North Africa intermittently during the period 1954-61, and obtained a PhD in Social Anthropology in 1961. Among his books are *Words and Things* (1959), *Thought and Change* (1964), *Saints of the Atlas* (1969), *Legitimation of Belief* (1974), *The Devil in Modern Philosophy* (1974), and *The Psychoanalytic Movement* (1985). Since 1984 he has been William Wyse Professor of Social Anthropology in the University of Cambridge.

Richard Hare was educated at Rugby and Balliol College, Oxford. He was a Fellow and Tutor in philosophy at Balliol College from 1947 until 1966 and White's Professor of Moral Philosophy at Oxford and a Fellow of Corpus Christi College, Oxford between 1966 and 1983. He became a Fellow of the British Academy in 1964 and has been Graduate Research Professor of Philosophy at the University of Florida at Gainesville since 1983. Among his publications are *The Language of Morals* (1952), *Freedom and Reason* (1963), *Essays on Philosophical Method* (1971), *Practical Inferences* (1971), *Applications of Moral Philosophy* (1972), *Moral Thinking* (1981), and *Plato* (1982).

Rom Harré was born in New Zealand in 1927. He obtained a BSc in 1948 (Engineering and Mathematics) and an MA in 1953 (Philosophy and Anthropology) at the University of Auckland, New Zealand. He was a Physics and Mathematics teacher at Kings College, Auckland from 1949 until 1953, Lecturer in Applied Mathematics at the University of the Punjab, Lahore in 1953-4, Research Fellow at the University of Birmingham in 1956-7, Lecturer in Philosophy of Science at the University of Leicester 1957-9, and presently has been University Lecturer in Philosophy of Science, Oxford since 1960, and a Fellow of Linacre College, Oxford since 1963. Among his books are *An Introduction to the Logic of the Sciences* (1960), *Matter and Method* (1964), *The Anticipation of Nature* (1965), *The Principles of Scientific Thinking* (1970), *The Philosophies of Science* (1972), and *Great Experiments* (1981).

Stephan Körner was born in 1913 in Ostrava (Czechoslovakia) and educated at a classical gymnasium, Charles University (Prague), and Trinity Hall (Cambridge). He was engaged in army service from 1936-9 and 1943-6. He was Professor of Philosophy at Bristol University from 1952-79 and Yale University from 1970-83. He has been Honorar Professor at Graz University since 1982. Among his publications are *Conceptual Thinking* (1955), *Kant* (1955), *The Philosophy of Mathematics* (1960), *Experience and Theory* (1966), *What is Philosophy?* (1969), *Categorial Frameworks* (1970), *Experience and Conduct* (1976), and *Metaphysics: Its Structure and Function* (1984).

Czeslaw Lejewski was born in 1913. He graduated at the University of Warsaw with the degree of 'Magister Filozofii' (Classics). After the War he made his home in the UK and completed his postgraduate studies by obtaining a PhD (logic and scientific method) from the University of London in 1955. From October 1956 he lectured in philosophy at the University of Manchester, and in 1966 he was appointed to the chair of philosophy, which he held until retirement in 1980. He was a visiting professor in the University of Notre Dame, Indiana in 1960-1 and a guest professor in the University of Salzburg in the summer semester of 1983-4. Professor Lejewski has published over fifty essays and articles in symbolic logic, history of logic, metaphysics, and philosophy of language.

Karl Popper was born in Vienna in 1902 and studied mathematics, physics, and philosophy at the University of Vienna. He has an MA from the University of New Zealand and a DLit from the University of London. He was Senior Lecturer in Philosophy at the University of New Zealand from 1937-45, Reader in Logic at the University of London from 1945-8, Professor of Logic and Scientific Method at the London School of Economics from 1949-69, and Emeritus Professor there since 1969. He became a Fellow of the British Academy in 1958, a Fellow of the Royal Society in 1976, and was knighted in 1965. Among his publications are *Logik der Forschung* (1953), *The Open Society and Its Enemies* (1945), *The Poverty of Historicism* (1957) and *Conjectures and Refutations: the Growth of Scientific Knowledge* (1963).

Stuart Shanker obtained a BA and MA in English Literature at

Victoria College in the University of Toronto, a BA in Philosophy, Politics, and Economics at Magdalen College, Oxford, and a BPhil and DPhil in philosophy at Christ Church, Oxford. His awards include the Marian Buck Fellowship at Christ Church, an I.O.D.E. Fellowship, Canada Council Doctoral Fellowship, and a Canada Council Postdoctoral Fellowship. Among his publications are *Wittgenstein and the Turning Point in the Philosophy of Mathematics* (1986), he edited the four volumes of *Ludwig Wittgenstein: Critical Assessments* (1986), and with V.A. Shanker compiled *A Wittgenstein Bibliography* (1986).

Crispin Wright has held the Chair of Logic and Metaphysics at the University of St Andrews since 1978. He was a Fellow of All Souls College, Oxford from 1969 to 1978, and has held Visiting Professorships at the University of Pennsylvania and Princeton University. His publications include *Wittgenstein on the Foundations of Mathematics* (1980), *Frege's Conception of Numbers as Objects* (1983) and *Realism, Meaning, and Truth* (1986).

INDEX

Aitchison, Ian 142
Alembert, Jean le Rond d' 137
American society 115-16
Analytic philosophy (*see* Oxford philosophy) 1, 155-63, 167-70
Archytas of Tarentum 261
Aristotle 70, 79-80, 168, 171-3, 177, 187, 189
Arithmetical propositions 42-4, 47-50
Aronson, J. 140
Artificial Intelligence (*see* Pattern Recognition) 215-66 *passim*
Expert systems 217
Atheism 80-1
Augustinian picture of language 5
Austin, John 73, 78-9, 99, 102, 124

Baker, Gordon 1-57, 271
Ballard, Dana H. 266
Bambrough, Renford Preface, 58-71
Bede, Cuthbert Preface
Beethoven, Ludwig von 215
Behaviourism 208-9
Berkeley, George 79, 208, 210
Blakemore, Colin 241-2, 258
Bloch, Sidney 83
Boden, Margaret 250-2, 254, 256
Bodies 152-3
Boscovich, Roger Joseph 137
Brentano, Franz 286
Brown, Christopher M. 262
Burke, Kenneth 148

Campbell, N.R. 136
Carnap, Rudolf 154-60
Causality 137-8
Cavell, Stanley 102
Church, Alonzo 135
Clowes, M.B. 258-9
Collingwood, R.G. 106
Compatibilism 81-2
Concepts 8, 12
    Formal concepts 34-5
Concept script 6, 46
Conventionalism 47, 284
Cornes, Ralph 261
Cranach, Mario von 145-6

Darwin, Charles 90, 92
Davidson, Donald 119, 267-71, 274-5, 280, 281-2, 285
Davies, Martin 276-9, 303
Descartes, Rene Preface, 69, 79, 152, 208
Dilthey, Wilhelm Preface, 110
Dispositions 293-9
Duff, Michael 221, 244
Duhem, Pierre 137
Dummett, Michael 267-72, 272, 280, 282-3, 302-3
Dyer, C.R. 239

Eccles, John 225, 234
Eddington, Arthur 77
Einstein, Albert 164, 210, 224
Engels, Friedrich 90, 110
Epicurus 75
Epistemology 69-70, 207-8
Evans, Gareth 290-9, 301-2
Explanation 18

Faraday, Michael 137
Feigl, Herbert 201
Fichte, Johann Gottlieb 203
Flew, Antony 72-97
Flew, R.N. 72-3
Foster, John 272-5, 280, 290
Freewill versus determinism 81-2
Frege, Gottlob 2-14 *passim*, 32, 33, 34, 36, 41-51 *passim*, 69, 162-3, 176, 191, 299
Freud, Sigmund 204
Function theory 4, 6, 8, 12, 46-7

Gellner, Ernest 98-117
Geometry 31
Gilbert, William 136, 137
Glover, Jonathan 153
God 84-5
Gorgias 173
Grammar 30, 41, 50
Gregory, Richard (*see* Inferential theory of perception) 218-21, 224-37, 241, 248-9
Grice, Paul 78

312

Hacker, P.M.S. 271
Hales, Stephen 136
Hare, R.M. 60, 112, 118-34
Harré. Rom 135-53
Heath, Peter 79
Hegel, G.W.F. 203
Heidegger, Martin 69
Helmholtz, Hermann Ludwig von 238, 248
Hempel, Carl 135, 136, 139
Hermeneutics 108-11
Hesiod 209
Hilbert, David 196, 214
Hobbes, Thomas 105
Hofstadter, Douglas R. 230
Homer 209
Homunculus fallacy 232-3
Hudson, Liam 153
Hume, David 79, 80, 88, 89, 91, 92, 137, 138, 155, 157, 200, 204, 205, 208
Huntingdon, E.V. 196
Huxley, Julian 76

Idealism 109-10
Identity 172
Information-processing 236-48
Intention 284-5

James, William 71
Jeans, James 77
Joad, C.E.M. 76
Johnston, E.I. 63
Joseph, Earl C. 261
Judgement 12
Justice 92-4

Kant, Immanuel 72, 73, 76, 79, 150, 161, 164, 168, 200, 201
Kay, Alan 217
Kempelen, Wolfgang von 261
Kent, E. 239
Knight, D.M. 137
Knox, T.M. 79
Körner, Stephan Preface, 154-70
Kotarbinski, Tadeusz 176
Kraft, Victor 201

Lakatos, Imre 141
Langford, C.H. 156
Language 7, 15-16, 99, 101
Learning 227, 239
Leibniz, Gottfried Wilhelm 105
Lejewski, Czeslaw 171-97

Lenin, V.I. 77, 205
Leśniewski, Stansilaw 188, 190-2, 196
  Protothetic 188-90, 196
Lettvin, J.Y. 244
Locke, John 79, 141-2, 161, 204
Logic 4, 7, 8, 35-6, 172
  Many-valued logics 189-90
  Logical syntax 35
  Logical truth 36
Łukasiewicz, Jan 189, 190

McCormick, B.H. 239-40, 244
McCulloch, W.S. 244
MacIntyre, Alasdair 85, 118-34 *passim*
Mabbott, John 78, 89
Mach, Ernst 208
Mackie, John 87, 118
Mackworth, Alan K. 222, 237-8, 248, 251
Maclaurin's paradox 136
Madden, E.H. 137
Malcolm, Norman Preface
Malthus, T.R. 90, 92
Marx, Karl 90, 110, 148
Mathematical proof 44, 48
Maturana, H.R. 244
Maxwell, James Clerk 136
Mead, G.H. 152
Meaning 9, 25-6, 29-30, 138
  Theory of meaning 23, 267-307
  Force 267
  Realism/anti-realism 268, 272, 302-3
Mereology 187, 191-3, 196
Metaphysics 167-8, 171-97
Michie, Donald 221
Mill, J.S. 213-14
Mills, C. Wright 148
Milton, John 62
Monod, Jacques 207, 209
Moore, G.E. 43, 70, 74, 112, 154-60, 172-3, 175, 176, 182
Moral philosophy 111-13, 118-34, 168-9
  Descriptivism 118-34 *passim*
  Prescriptivism 123-4, 128

Needham, Joseph 77
Neurath, Otto 201
Newton, Isaac 166, 209-10
Norman, Robert 137

Occam's Razor 8, 22, 33

Index

Ontology 9, 138, 171-97
   Abstract objects 174, 180, 183-4
Ostensive definition 37
Oxford philosophy (see Analytic philosophy) 78-80, 99-102

Paradox 229-30
Parapsychology 88-9
Pascal, Blaise 20
Peirce, C.S. 71
Penfield, Wilder 242
Perception 219-62 *passim*
   Illusions 228-31, 237, 241
      Ames room 241
   Inferential theory of perception (see Richard Gregory) 219-62 *passim*
   Pattern Recognition (see Artificial Intelligence) 215-66 *passim*
   Vision 217
Persons 86-8, 150-2
Phillips, D.Z. 87
Philosophical explanations 18-21
Philosophical questions 10, 37, 40, 58-71
Philosophical theories 11-13, 18, 38-40
Philosophy of law 166
Philosophy of mathematics 46-9
   Platonism 165
Philosophy of science 135-53
Philosophy versus science 9-11, 14, 20, 22, 24-5, 32-41, 52-5, 64-5, 157, 209, 213-15
Pitts, W. 244
Plato 60, 61, 70, 79-80, 162, 164, 199, 200
Political philosophy 114-15
Popper, Karl 77, 140-1, 198-211
Post, Emil 190
Propositional attitudes 286-8
Punishment 83

Quantification theory 10-11, 135-6
Quine, W.V.O. 119, 173, 176

Raverat, Gwen 74
Rawls, John 114
Reddaway, Peter 83
Revisionism 7
Roberts, L.G. 237-8, 248-59
Rule-following 26-8, 30, 129-30
Rules 26-30, 35, 37, 43, 164-5, 283-4
Rules of grammar 25-6, 30-2, 35, 37, 40

Russell, Bertrand 2, 22, 24, 33, 34, 86, 135, 158, 191, 193, 202, 205, 213-14
Russell's paradox 11
Ryle, Gilbert 59-60, 77, 78, 79, 99, 102, 130

Scepticism 231
Schiller, F.C.S. 127
Schlick, Moritz 201-2
Science 138-9, 217-18
   Scientific theory 165-6
Secord, Paul 144, 145, 147, 148, 150
Semantic theory 29-30
Sense/Reference distinction 6, 42
Sextus Empiricus 167
Shanker, S.G. 213-66
Shelley, Mary 217, 227
Skinner, B.F. 208
Smart, J.J.C. 74, 82
Smith, Adam 90
Soal, S.G. 88
Social psychology 143-52
Sociology of science 139
Socrates 61, 65, 70, 199, 200
Space 165
Spinoza, Benedict 105, 200-1
Stebbing, Susan 77
Strawson, P.F. 135, 136, 152
Swinburne, Richard 85

Tacit knowledge 269-72, 280-302 *passim*
Tajfel, Henri 149
Tarski, Alfred 193, 267
Taylor, C. 146
Thought 6-7
Tiberius 75
Tolstoy, Leo 148
Toulmin, Stephen 136, 149
Truth 7, 11

Understanding 16-18, 20, 21, 29, 272

Valéry, Paul 262
Vauconson, Jacques de 261
Veblen, Oswald 196
Veblen, Thorsten 148
Verificationism 31
Vienna Circle 201-2

Waele, J.-P. de 146
Waismann, Friedrich 43, 198-9, 201, 202

Watson, John B. 208
Whitehead, A.N. 191
Whyte, L.L. 137
Williams, Pearce 137
Wisdom, John 61, 71, 99
Wittgenstein, Ludwig Preface, 3, 5, 10, 21, 22-32, 24, 32, 41-55 *passim*, 60, 61, 64, 65, 68, 69, 70, 71, 99-108, 110, 129, 130-1, 154-60, 162, 166, 201, 202, 203-4, 213-14, 226, 288
    Continuity thesis 24-5
    his conception of philosophy 32-41
Woodger, J.H. 193
Wordsworth, William 60, 62
Wright, Crispin 267-307